DATE DUE			
REN May '77			
REN May 7 8			

OCCUPATIONS AND THE SOCIAL STRUCTURE

SECOND EDITION

OCCUPATIONS AND THE SOCIAL STRUCTURE

Richard H. Hall

University of Minnesota

PRENTICE-HALL, INC., *Englewood Cliffs, New Jersey*

Library of Congress Cataloging in Publication Data

Hall, Richard H
    Occupations and the social structure.

    (Prentice-Hall sociology series)
    Includes bibliographical references and index.
    1. Occupations. I. Title.
HB2581.H33 1975   301.44'4   74-23243
ISBN 0-13-629345-X

Prentice-Hall Sociology Series
Neil J. Smelser, Editor

Printed in the United States of America

10 9 8 7 6 5 4 3 2 1

Prentice-Hall International, Inc., *London*
Prentice-Hall of Australia, Pty. Ltd., *Sydney*
Prentice-Hall of Canada, Ltd., *Toronto*
Prentice-Hall of India Private Limited, *New Delhi*
Prentice-Hall of Japan, Inc.,*Tokyo*

to Ed and Tom

and

Tom and Julie

CONTENTS

PREFACE *xi*

I

Occupations: The Context and the Individual   *1*

1   **DEFINITIONS AND DISTINCTIONS** *2*

The Definition Problem   Plan of Analysis   Summary and Conclusions

2   **THE CONTEXT OF CONTEMPORARY OCCUPATIONS** *10*

Structural Changes   Value Changes
The Contemporary Occupational Context
The Changing Organizational Environment
A Note on the Relationships Among Occupations, Organizations,
    and the Social Context
A Note on Unemployment   Summary and Conclusions

3   **THE INDIVIDUAL AND OCCUPATIONS** *28*

The Motivation to Work   The Components of Work Motivation
Expectancy Theory   Reactions to Work   Job Satisfactions
Stresses, Tension, and Alienation   The Extent of the Problem
Who is Dissatisfied?   The Factory Worker
Executives and White-Collar Workers   Summary and Conclusions

II

Types of Occupations   *67*

4   THE PROFESSIONS *69*

The Professional Model   The Negative Side of the Professional Model
The Settings of Professional Work   The Individual Practitioner
The Autonomous Professional Organization
The Heteronomous Professional Organization   The Professional Department
An Altered Professional Model?   Knowledge and Knowledge Obsolesence
Women and the Professions and Professional Women
Regulations and the Professions   Professional Self-Regulation   The Client
Unionization   The Minority Professional   Paraprofessionals
Summary and Conclusions

5   MANAGERS, PROPRIETORS, AND OFFICIALS *136*

Executives   Managers   Proprietors   Officials
Women and Minority Group Members   Summary and Conclusions

6   WHITE-COLLAR WORKERS *165*

Background   Changes in White-Collar Work   The Changed Worker
The Nature of White-Collar Work: Multiple Settings
The Organizational Control of White-Collar Work   Summary and Conclusions

7   CRAFTSMEN AND FOREMEN *187*

The Crafts   Foremen   Summary and Conclusions

8   SEMISKILLED AND UNSKILLED WORKERS *213*

The Semiskilled   Reactions to Semiskilled Work   The Unskilled
Summary and Conclusions

Occupations and the Social Structure   *237*

**9   SOCIAL STRATIFICATION, MOBILITY, AND
CAREER PATTERNS** *239*

Occupations and the Stratification System
Explanations of Occupational Status Differences   Mobility and Occupations
Career Patterns   Summary and Conclusions

10   FAMILY AND EDUCATION *281*

The Family   The Housewife   Occupations and Education
Summary and Conclusions

11   TECHNOLOGY *314*

The Nature of Technological Change
The Impact of Technological Change on the Occupational Structure
Technology and the Worker   Alternative Technologies
The Yugoslavian Approach   Limitations on Job Redesign
    Technological Change and Employment Versus Unemployment
Technological Change and the Future of Occupations
Summary and Conclusions

12   OCCUPATIONS AND THE POLITICAL SYSTEM *356*

Occupations and Political Participation
Power and Politics in the Occupational Setting   Summary and Conclusions

INDEX *373*

PREFACE

A friend recently asked me why I was preparing a second edition of *Occupations and the Social Structure*. The answer was at once easy and difficult. The easy part was the fact that, since the writing of the first edition, there has been a good amount of research that is germane to occupational sociology. It simply seemed to be time to update the book.

The more difficult part came in considering the context in which this book has been rewritten. Like all occupations, that of preparing a book takes place in a social context. The early 1970s have seen an upsurge in interest in work and the worker. This culminated in a series of presentations on TV and cover stories in opinion-shaping magazines such as *Time* and *Newsweek*. The U.S. Department of Health, Education and Welfare sponsored the publication of *Work in America*, a book that has raised a great deal of controversy (and little action). In addition, the women's movement has led to new data and new interpretations of old data in regard to the place of women in the occupational setting. The treatment in the first edition of women's roles is now extremely dated. Similarly, the situation in regard to minority group members has also altered since the writing of the first edition. The interpretations of the field of occupational sociology must respond to the changes that have taken place.

There are two other motivations for this edition. The first is the fact that the first edition received constructive criticism from colleagues in reviews of the book and in less formal letters and conversations. These criticisms have been most beneficial. Even more beneficial is the second motivation. I elected to use the first edition in several of my own classes in occupational sociology. In order not to bore the students and myself, I was forced to search for new information and interpretations, with a resultant self-criticism of the original work.

All of these factors led to the decision to prepare the present volume. I would like to thank Eliot Freidson, Carol Kronus, and Helena Znaniecki Lopata for their excellent criticisms of the first draft of this volume. Ed Stanford, Shirley Stone, and Barbara Christenberry of Prentice-Hall have been extemely helpful during the preparation of the book. My secretary, Karen Hageland, while not stuck with the typing job this time, was extremely helpful in running errands, making photocopies of materials, and generally being supportive. As ever, my wife, Sherry, and Tom and Julie were patient with the usual disorientations that authors seem to go through in the preparation of a book.

OCCUPATIONS
AND THE
SOCIAL
STRUCTURE

part I

Occupations: The Context and the Individual

1

DEFINITIONS
AND DISTINCTIONS

The centrality of an individual's occupation to his[1] life is a fact that requires little verification. During the adult years, work is rivaled only by sleep as a routine activity. Much of the time before and after the working period of life is related to work. The preoccupational period is typically spent in acquiring skills that can be used in the occupational world. Postoccupational life, or retirement, is related to work by income received through pension plans or national old-age insurance plans. More important, perhaps, this period is also one in which an individual looks back to his work as a major reference point for his retirement. Thus, regardless of the level of satisfaction or intrinsic interest a person has in his job, work is a central part of life. These remarks apply to work performed inside the home, which can legitimately be called an occupation.

While the relationships described above are perhaps obvious, the same cannot be said for the relationships between occupations and the social structure. Though there is general agreement that occupations and social status are highly associated, there is less agreement as to why this is so. Similarly, employing organizations rely heavily on educational organizations for their human "raw materials," but exactly why this reliance has grown is unclear. Technological change has certain adverse effects on some workers, while for others the effect is positive. Even more subtle are the relationships between an individual's place in the social

[1]"His" in this context has no reference to gender.

2

structure, in terms of his socioeconomic status, education, and work experience, and his motivations and reactions to work.

This book is designed to relate occupations to the broader social structure. It assumes that the relationships are somewhat stable and thus subject to analysis. At the same time, there is no assumption made that the relationships are necessarily harmonious or pleasant for either the individual or the social structure. To be sure, most people work on a regular basis without overt revolt, and most of the basic and learned needs of society are met because goods and services have been provided by the labor force. At the same time, there is clear evidence that a significant proportion of the labor force does not receive equal hiring or promotional opportunities, is underpaid by most criteria, is bored and alienated by the work being performed, and has little or no prospect for advancement. Smaller proportions of the labor force, although still involving large numbers of people, are temporarily or almost permanently unemployed or are engaged in deviant or illegal occupations such as prostitution or selling drugs. The position taken in the book is that this is a result of the linkage between the occupation involved and the social structure rather than a consequence of individual psychological functioning.

The analysis of the relationships between occupations and the social structure assumes that these are changing relationships. The relationship of the family to the occupational world is experiencing rapid change as the women's movement affects both the opportunity structure for women and the types of aspirations and expectations that women hold. Events of the last decade have greatly altered the position of blacks and other minority group members in the occupational world. The most noticeable impact here appears to be an increased polarization, with movement into the middle and upper-middle occupational strata for some minority group members and a slipping even farther behind for others at the bottom of the occupational hierarchy. It is the intent of this book to call attention to patterns of stability and change; where no pattern can be easily seen, the existing confusion will be identified.

THE DEFINITION PROBLEM

The obvious first step in any analysis is to define the subject matter. In the case of occupations, many definitions are available, but Nels Anderson's point, that "definitions of work tell us little about it, and apparently the making of such definitions has never given man much concern,"[2] is probably close to the truth. The reason for the lack of con-

[2] *Dimensions of Work* (New York: David McKay Co., Inc., 1964), p. 1.

cern is undoubtedly the fact that the term "occupation" has a very real meaning for almost all people. Nevertheless, a definition is needed, and it must be inclusive in two ways. It must, first, include the great variety of activities that can legitimately be called occupations and, second, suggest the fact that an occupation has multiple consequences for the individual and society.

The authors of *Work in America: Report of a Special Task Force to the Secretary of Health, Education, and Welfare* have grappled with the definitional problem.[3] They comment:

> We measure that which we can measure, and this often means that a rich and complex phenomenon is reduced to one dimension, which then becomes prominent and eclipses the other dimensions. This is particularly true of "work," which is often defined as "paid employment." The definition conforms with one readily measurable aspect of work but utterly ignores its profound personal and social aspects and often leads to a distorted view of society.
>
> Using housework as an example, we can see the absurdity of defining work as "paid employment." A housewife, according to this definition, does not work. But if a husband must replace her services—with a housekeeper, cook, baby sitter—these replacements become workers, and the husband has added to the Gross National Product the many thousands of dollars the replacements are paid. It is therefore an inconsistency in our definition of work to say that a woman who cares for her own children is not working, but if she takes a job looking after the children of others, she is working.
>
> Viewing work in terms of pay alone has also produced a synonimity of "pay" and "worth," so that higher-paid individuals are thought by many to have greater personal worth than those who are receiving less pay. At the bottom of this scale, a person without pay becomes "worthless." The confusion of pay with worth is a result of historical events and traditions apparently rooted in the distinction between "noble" and "ignoble" tasks. History might have been otherwise and garbage men, for example, in recognition of their contribution to health, might have been accorded monetary rewards similar to those received by physicians. Certainly, it takes little reflection to conclude that, except in crude economic terms, no one is worth nothing, nor is anyone worth a hundred times more than another merely because he is paid a hundred times as much.
>
> We can come closer to a multi-dimensional definition of work if we define it as "an activity that produces something of value for other people." This definition broadens the scope of what we call work and places it within a social context. It also implies that there is a purpose to work. We know that the housewife is *really* working, whether she is paid or not; she is being productive for other people. Substituting the children a woman cares

[3]Prepared under the auspices of the W. E. Upjohn Institute for Employment Research (Cambridge, Mass.: M.I.T. Press, 1973).

for does not change the nature of her work, only the "others" for whom she is productive. And voluntary tasks are certainly work, although they are not remunerated. . . .[4]

Before proceeding with the definitional issue, an important distinction must be made. The discussion from *Work in America* was focused around *work*, while the major concern here is with *occupations*. For the purposes of this analysis, *work* will be considered the activity that is performed in the occupational role. Work and occupation are often used synonymously with little loss in clarity. The term occupation seems preferable when used in a broader context. "What is your occupation?" implies a title that in turn implies the kind of work performed and some social valuation about the role. On the other hand, "What kind of work do you do?" requests information about the specific activity performed in the occupation. While this distinction will be blurred in many instances, it seems useful for the analyses to follow.

Turning now to definitions of occupations per se, we can see the roots of some of the considerations with which the subsequent analyses will deal. Arthur Salz, for example notes that "occupation may be defined as that specific activity with a market value which an individual continually pursues for the purpose of obtaining a steady flow of income. This activity also determines the social position of the individual."[5] While the emphasis on remuneration remains, the inclusion of the additional idea of determining social position suggests the centrality of occupations for both the individual and the social structure. This is especially true when social position is taken to mean more than position in an organizational hierarchy or stratification system. Thus the occupation determines the individual's relationships with and to other individuals in the same and other occupations because the positions themselves are related.

Everett Hughes also sees the meaning of occupation in broad terms; he states that "an occupation, in essence, is not some particular set of activities; it is the part of an individual in any ongoing set of activities. The system may be large or small, simple or complex."[6] Hughes emphasizes the social relationships surrounding an occupation, not in order to minimize the financial side, but to keep it in perspective as part of a more inclusive set of social relationships. Similarly, Anne Roe defines an occupation as "whatever an adult spends most of his time doing . . . the

[4]*Ibid.*, pp. 2–3.

[5]"Occupations: Theory and History," *Encyclopedia of the Social Sciences* (New York: Macmillan Company, 1944), XI, 424.

[6]"The Study of Occupations," in *Sociology Today*, ed. R. K. Merton, L. Broom, and L. S. Cottrell (New York: Harper & Row, 1965), p. 445.

major focus of a person's activities and usually of his thoughts."[7] This definition suggests the importance of an occupation to the individual. It also, therefore, suggests that this major focus is transmitted into the social process and thus means that occupations are a major component of the social structure.

With these considerations in mind, a definition of occupation can be offered that encompasses the variety of activities and outcomes that must be taken into account in the analysis of occupations. *An occupation is the social role performed by adult members of society that directly and/ or indirectly yields social and financial consequences and that constitutes a major focus in the life of an adult.*

The limitation to the adult years in the definition is in recognition of the fact that schooling and occupational experiences prior to this period are essentially preparations for the occupational role of an adult. Delbert Miller and William Form have suggested that the work career can be separated into five parts: the preparatory, initial, trial, stable, and retirement periods.[8] For the purposes of this definition, the preparatory and initial periods are not included in what is being labeled an occupation. The initial period includes summer and part-time jobs that a person may have as he passes through adolescence. While these jobs may be important in developing work habits and attitudes, they are not truly occupations since they are recognized as temporary.

The definition recognizes the multiplicity of outcomes of occupations for the individual and society without minimizing the centrality of financial rewards. Rather obviously, the degree to which the financial aspect of the occupational contribution is important to the individual varies with the individual's own outlook toward his work, as will be discussed later. The inclusion of the idea of indirect consequences is intended to recognize the fact that a number of roles that have the characteristics of occupations do not confer direct financial or social rewards. The housewife, for example, does not receive pay for her work. Her work does, however, have important indirect yields, particularly if part of her husband's career depends upon her success in the housewife's role. By the same token, the role of the graduate- or professional-school student has indirect (future) yields. In terms of this definition, graduate work can legitimately be called an occupation, even though it is usually of limited duration,[9] since graduate or professional students approach their work

---

[7] *The Psychology of Occupations* (New York: John Wiley & Sons, Inc., 1956), p. 3.
[8] *Industrial Sociology* (New York: Harper & Row, 1964), pp. 541–45.
[9] While this particular role is designed to serve as a preparation for a career, it appears to involve more than the preparatory phase discussed by Miller and Form.

in the same way their contemporaries not in the educational system do. The centrality to life on the one hand and the hours spent at "work" on the other suggest that this interpretation is not inappropriate, even though the period is preparatory for another occupation. The role of this type of student is similar to that of a "junior executive" or a new member of a large law firm during the first years of employment in its preparatory and temporary nature, although its financial and social yields lie in the future.

The definition of occupation given above has an advantage over some of the other definitions in that it calls attention to the fact that an individual can react to a social role whether he is playing it or not. An individual can shun the "straight" occupational world and choose an alternative lifestyle. The fact remains that this is an active shunning of a known or fantasized role. The role itself remains meaningful.

PLAN OF ANALYSIS

The rather broadly based definition we have adopted suggests that an occupation has ramifications for both the individual and society. The major focus of this analysis will be on the latter point, the inter-relationships between occupations and the social structure. At the same time, some attention will be given to the impact of occupations on the individual, principally with regard to *why* people work and *what kinds* of satisfactions, rewards, dissatisfactions, and stresses they experience in their work.

The procedure to be followed in this analysis will be first to examine briefly the antecedents of contemporary occupations. The current composition of the labor force will then be examined, with particular emphasis on significant shifts in both the nature and location of occupations. Next will come an analysis of the individual's responses to work, his motivations, his satisfactions, and his dissatisfactions. In order to analyze the relationships between occupations and the social structure, it will be necessary to subdivide the broad range of occupations into reasonably homogeneous categories, since different occupations have widely varied meanings and rewards. While no perfect typology of occupations is available, the categorization developed by the U.S. Bureau of the Census will be roughly followed. Variations within each category will be noted, since it is clear that such broad types as professionals contain wide variations in performance, outlook, training, and reward patterns. These steps will serve as the background for the more intensive analysis of occupations as they are categorized by the census. These categories are:

1. Professionals
2. Managers, proprietors, and officials
3. Clerical and kindred workers
4. Skilled workers and foremen
5. Semiskilled workers
6. Unskilled workers (including farm and nonfarm workers)

While the occupations are categorized in this manner primarily for convenience, it should be evident that this categorization corresponds to a rough approximation of the social-stratification system. It is important to note that the amounts of information available about the work areas outlined above are not equal. Professionals, for example, have been examined much more intensively than any of the other groups, and there is a surprising lack of adequate information about managers, executives, and farm employees. For this reason, the treatment of the different types of occupations will vary both in length and, unfortunately, in substantive knowledge.

The balance of the analysis will be concerned with the relationships between occupations and the wider social structure. Some of these relationships will have been made explicit by this time, especially the ways in which work in organizations has become a major component of the social structure. Here the first area to be analyzed will be the connection between the social-stratification system and occupations, the importance of which is implied in the typology of occupations suggested above. Included in this will be discussions of the interrelated factors of mobility and career patterns. The analysis will then shift to the relationships between occupations and the familial, political, educational, and technological systems and to the effects of technological change. While technology is not an "institution" in the same manner as the other areas discussed, the interactions among the producers of changing technology—essentially the research and development complex in education, industry, and government—appear well enough developed to at least suggest that technology can be treated as one of the institutional areas.

SUMMARY AND CONCLUSIONS

The definition of occupation given in this chapter (the social role performed by adult members of society that directly and/or indirectly yields social and financial consequences and that constitutes a major focus in the life of an adult) will serve as the basis for the analysis in the balance of this book. In the chapters that follow, we will trace the historical roots of contemporary occupations and discuss the individual's orientations toward, and reactions to, his occupation. An analysis of the various types of occupations will then provide an understanding of the heterogeneity of occupations found in the system. The final section of the book will discuss the manner in which occupations are related to the balance of the social system. As will be seen, this relationship is not one of total harmony. Both the integrative and conflictual patterns of interaction between occupations and the social structure will be considered.

2

THE CONTEXT
OF CONTEMPORARY
OCCUPATIONS

The most striking characteristics of contemporary occupations are (1) that occupations are carried out in organizations, and (2) that skill and knowledge, rather than physical force, are their hallmark. These characteristics are striking in that they are so different from the ways in which work has been traditionally pictured. Although there is little in the way of evidence regarding the ideas people carried around with them about occupations even a few years ago, it would seem that the strong farmer behind his plow, the country doctor making his rounds, or the ample housewife and mother preparing dinner for a large and loving family are popular and probably accurate portrayals of the ways in which many people thought about occupations until the very recent past. This imagery, touched with nostalgia, also contained the idea that workers were really happy and were dedicated to "hard work for an honest day's pay." Given the long hours worked, the physical demands of much of the work performed, and unpleasant working conditions, it is naive to think of the worker in the past as living in some sort of occupational good old days. At the same time, it is instructive to look at some of the historical changes that have occurred before turning to a careful examination of the contemporary occupational context.

A BRIEF HISTORY OF OCCUPATIONS AND WORK

Obviously work is different in an urbanized, industrialized society from what it was in the past, but the nature of the differences and the changes that have led to the broad spectrum of contemporary occupations are probably less evident. The purpose of this section is to explore the nature of, and reasons for, these changes, which provide at least a partial basis for the examination of the relationships between occupations and the social structure. While the various changes are an accomplished fact, they can yield insights into the present. These changes are especially important in that some of the current relationships are not ones of equilibrium. That is, strains that exist between certain aspects of contemporary occupations and institutions, such as the family or educational system, are, at least in part, historically based.

We will take two perspectives on the history of work. Besides examining the changes that have occurred in the relations between work and other aspects of society, we will also examine the changed values or meanings that people have applied to their work.[1] One of the lasting intellectual debates has been whether changes in the social structure have led to changes in values or whether value changes must occur before the structure can change.[2] While this is an interesting, if unsettled, issue, it is fruitless to attempt its resolution here. Instead, the assumption will be made that the changes are concurrent, without suggesting a priority. In a rather simple way, it does not matter which came first, since changes in both structure and values have occurred that have had an impact on contemporary occupations. The changes are more important for the present analysis than any causal relationships that happen to exist. With this in mind, structural changes will be considered first, primarily because shifts in the orientation toward work can probably be more easily understood if the shifts in the nature of work are first discussed.

STRUCTURAL CHANGES

Any examination of the history of occupations must begin with two facts about contemporary occupations. The first is that work is something done as a separate activity, apart from the rest of a person's life. The phrase "go to work" exemplifies this characteristic. Work is carried on outside the home. More important, modern occupations involve

---

[1]Such factors as the removal of work from the home and the impact of changing technology on occupations have identifiable historical roots.

[2]The classical development of these structural approaches is Marx's insistence on the priority of economic (structural) factors in social change. See Karl Marx, *Capital*, trans. Samuel Moore and Edward Aveling, ed. Frederick Engels (London: George Allen & Unwin, 1946). Weber, on the other hand, took the position that value changes (religion) precede structural developments. See Max Weber, *The Protestant Ethic and the Spirit of Capitalism*, trans. Talcott Parsons (London: George Allen & Unwin, 1935), pp. 35–78.

activities that are distinctly different from those activities carried on in nonwork, or leisure, time.[3] The skills and social relationships of modern occupations are not just those that are learned as one becomes socialized into adulthood. Instead, they are specific to the occupation, often are not transferable to other occupations and in the case of social relationships, are not transferable if the location of the occupation shifts.

The second major fact of modern occupations is that they are carried out in organizational settings.[4] The movement of work away from individualized settings has accelerated until some 85 percent of the labor force now work as employees. Organizational employment is a characteristic of the total labor force; even occupations that retain the image of individualism, such as the professions, have been considerably affected by this trend. Much of what is called private practice in the professions is carried out in organizations, such as law firms or medical clinics, which, as will be discussed later, are in many ways similar to other kinds of organizations.[5] This movement to organizations amplifies the effects of the separation of work from the rest of life, not only because occupations are physically located in organizations, but also because the organizational arrangements themselves produce requirements and social relationships that are not found when work is carried out by the solo worker or the worker in the small, usually family, grouping.

If these are the dominant characteristics of modern occupations and if they are rather recent in their evolution, then what were the earlier conditions of work?

The change most often noted is the shift from craft production to factory production, a shift that involved a great deal more than just the change in technologies of work. As Anderson points out, "each craft had its place in the community and each worker had his place in some craft."[6] A man's craft thus directly tied him to the social structure, with the crafts having distinctive social rankings. The entire socialization process prepared one for taking his ascribed place in the community. Not only was a man's occupation set but also, apparently, he had no aspiration for other types of work. This period was one of relative social stability, although the stability was clearly short lived. The stereotyped image that we have

[3]See Sigmund Nosow and William H. Form, *Man, Work and Society* (New York: Basic Books, 1962), p. 11, and Nels Anderson, *Dimensions of Work* (New York: David McKay Co., 1964), p. 3.

[4]See Theodore Caplow, *The Sociology of Work* (Minneapolis: University of Minnesota Press, 1954), pp. 20–21, and Robert Presthus, *The Organizational Society* (New York: Alfred A. Knopf, 1962), pp. 59–92.

[5]See Erwin O. Smigel, *The Wall Street Lawyer* (New York: Free Press of Glencoe, Inc., 1964).

[6]*Dimensions of Work*, p. 5.

of the craft era is one of happy workers dedicated to their work without thoughts of, or desires for, different occupations.

This stereotype is probably, like most others, inaccurate, a deduction we can make from the rather simple fact that changes have occurred. Changes occur because of the infusion of different ideas into a social system, and these different ideas come about, at least partially, as a consequence of dissatisfaction with the existing system. Another inaccuracy of the stereotype is that, during this period, crafts were not the dominant occupation. The society was predominantly agrarian.[7] While farming and the crafts share a number of characteristics, such as the total involvement of the individual in his work and the integration of work with the rest of life, the important fact remains that farming as an occupation involves a greater variety of skills and activities and less control of the work environment than do the crafts. But despite the danger of utilizing too simple a picture of the craft era, many of the changes in the occupational world can be analyzed using the crafts as a starting point. Some of the important changes have been examined by Reinhard Bendix, who states:

> In practice, the workers were managed by a reliance upon the traditions of craftmanship and of the master-servant relationship. However important these traditions were for industrialization, they were not always compatible with the requirements of industrial production. Traditionally, skilled work was performed at a leisurely pace or in spurts of great intensity, but always at the discretion of the individual worker. In modern industry work must be performed above all with regular intensity. Traditionally the skilled worker was trained to work accurately on individual designs; in modern industry he must adapt his sense of accuracy to the requirements of standardization. In handicraft production, each individual owned his own tools and was responsible for their care; by and large this is not true in modern industry, so that care of tools and machinery is divorced from the pride of ownership. Traditionally, skills were handed down from generation to generation and, consequently, were subject to individual variations. In industry the effort has been to standardize the steps of work performance as much as possible.[8]

Another view of this transition is offered by Thorstein Veblen, who notes that the initial shift took place in craft industries, such as brewing or tanning, that were rather easily transformed into group work and then into larger industrial complexes. As this occurred, the worker increasingly began to keep pace with the work process, rather than the reverse. Thus

[7]While the occupational distribution of this era cannot be analyzed through census data, it is obvious that agricultural occupations have been numerically dominant until only very recently.

[8]*Work and Authority in Industry* (New York: John Wiley & Sons, 1956), pp. 203–4.

the industrial worker began to be tied inexorably to the machinery of the work process. The requirements for becoming a worker also changed. Veblen suggests that at this point increased training on the part of prospective workers became essential, thus making the schooling demanded for general preparation "unremittingly more exacting."[9]

The paradox of the simpler work in the machine era requiring a greater amount of education than the more exacting craft work is more apparent than real. The worker in the craft era did not need formal education; he simply "grew up" in the craft, learning the skills and behaviors necessary for such a craftsman as part of the normal socialization process in the home. The industrial worker, on the other hand, did not have this type of learning environment. More important, he did not have the family-based ties to the work process or to the authority system of the factory. School provided, as it does today, exposure to training in mental and mechanical skills *and* to the impersonal discipline inherent in the industrial-work setting.

The shift from craft work has been the change most widely noted in occupational literature, since it appears to symbolize other similar shifts. A change of perhaps equal importance, which developed at about the same time, was the movement of work into organizations. Organizations themselves were not, of course, a new phenomenon. Military, religious, and public bureaucracies existed in the majority of developed societies before these developments in Western Europe.[10] The important factor in the industrial revolution was therefore not the emergence of organizations but rather the relationship between the individual and the organization. Workers at all levels in the emerging industrial and later governmental organizations appear to have had a fundamentally different orientation to the employing organization than in the past.

A useful way of viewing this change is to apply, *ex post facto*, Amitai Etzioni's typology of organizations to the changes occurring during this era.[11] Etzioni suggests three major organizational types, each characterized by a distinct power structure and manner of involvement on the part of the lower participants. The first type is the *coercive* organization, which uses coercion as the major means of control over lower participants, who, in turn, feel alienated from the organization. The sec-

---

[9]*The Instinct of Workmanship* (New York: Macmillan Company, 1914), p. 309.

[10]See Max Weber, *The Theory of Social and Economic Organization*, trans. A. M. Henderson and Talcott Parsons (New York: Free Press of Glencoe, 1947), pp. 341–82, for an analysis of the forms and consequences of organizational arrangements in the preindustrial period.

[11]*A Comparative Analysis of Complex Organizations* (New York: Free Press of Glencoe, 1961), pp. 12–40.

ond type is the *normative* organization, in which normative power (be-lief in the goals of the organization) serves as the major source of control over lower participants, who are characterized by high commitment to the organization. The conscription-based military forces of the period and the religious organizations of the era are examples, respectively, of these two types of organizations.

The third type of organization, the *utilitarian*, uses remuneration as the basis for control, with the lower participants of the organization tied to the organization by a calculative orientation. This type of organization undoubtedly existed throughout history in such systems as the Chinese, Egyptian, or Roman public bureaucracies. What is significant is that it became the dominant organizational form during and after the industrial revolution. Workers and management alike came into the organizations because they perceived that they could get something (remuneration) out of it. While family loyalties and/or tradition played, and in some cases continue to play, a role in occupational selection in such a system, the emergent industrial organizations were rather clearly utilitarian.

Anderson provides a somewhat related approach to the same phe-nomena; he notes that the earlier era could be characterized by an *ascription orientation*, in which the worker and his occupation were closely associated.[12] Anderson suggests that in this type of system the person's occupation was often symbolized by his appearance, dress, or other appointments that he maintained off the job. A type of hat or cap, a particular kind of jacket, a particular kind of walk (bowlegs among cowboys) were signs of a person's occupation. Just as important, accord-ing to Anderson, was the fact that the occupation was passed on from father to son in the majority of the cases. The contrasting type of system, characterized by an *achievement orientation*, is based on accomplishment rather than inheritance and on separation of life from work. This system, of course, is highly typical of modern occupations.

Before leaving this discussion of structural shifts, it should be noted that just as the occupational structure of the preindustrial era was not solely the craft system, the movement to the industrial-organizational era was not uniform, intra- or internationally. Agricultural and craft pursuits have remained and have been maintained in all societies and have been remarkably resistant to change. Nevertheless, of course, the majority of occupations have shifted away from such settings. As will be seen later in this chapter, it is a mistake to think that change has stopped with industrialization. The picture of the occupational structure as one based on industrialization is perhaps as incorrect today as assuming that it is

---

[12]*Dimensions of Work*, p. 3.

based on agriculture and crafts. Before turning to this, however, we will examine some of the value changes that have occurred.

VALUE CHANGES

The most comprehensive overview of the meanings attached to work through different historical eras is provided by Adriano Tilgher.[13] In the Greek era, work was viewed as a curse, at least insofar as it involved manual as opposed to intellectual labor. The source of this curse was the gods, who hated man. According to Tilgher, the Romans held a very similar view of work. He notes that Cicero believed that the only worthy occupations for a free man were agriculture and business, if the latter led to a situation of retirement and rural peace. The Hebrew view of work was essentially similar, but with the additional rationale that work was drudgery because it was the way in which man could atone for the original sin. At the same time, work received a slightly higher meaning in that it was a way by which spiritual dignity could be captured.

As might be expected, early Christianity differed little from its Hebrew antecedents. One additional meaning was attached to work in that the fruits of one's labor could legitimately be shared with the less fortunate. The doctrine that idleness was akin to sinfulness also appeared during this era. But, Tilgher points out, despite this new interpretation, work as such had no intrinsic meaning; rather it was a means to other, loftier ends. This interpretation of work was apparently maintained through the Middle Ages, with the idea growing that work was appropriate for all people as a means of spiritual purification. The coming of the Reformation saw little change in this basic attitude, except for a small, but vital, reinterpretation. Luther saw work as a form of serving God. Whatever a person's occupation, if the work was performed to the best of one's ability, it had equal spiritual value with all other forms of work.

A more significant shift in the meaning of work occurred with the advent of Calvinism. Calvin built upon the older traditions of work as the will of God and the need for all men to work. To this he added the idea that the results of work, profits, had only one legitimate use, to finance new ventures for additional profit and thus for additional investment. This concept, of course, is totally compatible with the rise of capitalism, as Weber so forcefully argued. An additional, important aspect of

---

[13]*Work: What It has Meant to Men Through the Ages,* trans. Dorothy C. Fisher (New York: Harcourt, Brace & World, 1930).

Calvinist doctrine was that man had an obligation to God to attempt to achieve the highest possible and most rewarding occupation. Thus striving for upward mobility is morally justified.

The development of socialism gave an additional interpretation to work. It was viewed not as a form of expiation, but rather as something that man wanted to do as the normal way of living. Each was to receive value equal to his work, and drudgery would be reduced by scientific advances, allowing more time for nonwork activities.

Tilgher notes that the "religion of work," so basic to capitalism, may be beginning to falter in the twentieth century as a new orientation toward recreation and leisure develops. Nevertheless, there is strong evidence that work still occupies a central place in the lives of most workers. In a 1955 study, Nancy Morse and R. S. Weiss found that the vast majority of workers in the United States state that they would continue working even if they were given the opportunity to maintain their lifestyle without work.[14] While there may have been some shifts in this orientation in recent years, work remains central for most workers. These data, plus other research findings regarding the *meanings* that people attach to work, suggest that there is no single meaning for all workers. This raises some questions regarding Tilgher's conclusions about the modal values attached to work at different points in history, since it is quite unlikely that all Greeks or early Christians had exactly the same ideas about work. At the same time, of course, the shifts that Tilgher traces do seem reasonable, and we can acknowledge the fact that work has assumed different meanings to people at different times. In the next chapter, we will look in detail at the meanings and reactions that are formed around work at the present time—a time critically affected by the continuing shifts in the context of contemporary occupations.

THE CONTEMPORARY OCCUPATIONAL CONTEXT

The easiest way to understand the dynamic situations that have led to and are part of the contemporary occupational context is to examine some data about employment patterns over the last century. Table 2-1 presents the distribution of members of the labor force in broad economic sectors. These data show two outstanding trends. The first is the well-known shift away from agriculture. As Phillip Hauser points out, "although the data have many limitations, it is clear that the predominant proportion of the work force in the United States, about 72 percent,

[14]"The Function and Meaning of Work and the Job," *American Sociological Review*, XX, 2 (April 1955), 192.

TABLE 2-1. Sector Distribution of Employment by Goods and Services, 1870–1940 (in thousands)

	1870	1900	1920	1940
Total	12,900	29,000	41,600	49,860
Goods-producing total	10,630	19,620	23,600	25,610
Agriculture, forestry, and fishing	7,450	10,900	11,400	9,100
Manufacturing	2,250	6,300	10,800	11,900
Mining	180	760	1,230	1,100
Construction	750	1,660	2,170	3,510
Service-producing total	2,990	9,020	15,490	24,250
Trade, finance, and real estate	830	2,760	4,800	8,700
Transportation and utilities	640	2,100	4,190	4,150
Professional service	230	1,150	2,250	4,000
Domestic and personal service	1,190	2,710	3,330	5,710
Government (Not elsewhere classified)	100	300	920	1,690

Source: Adapted from *Historical Statistics of the United States: 1820–1940*, series D57–71, p. 74.

Note: The totals do not always add up because of small numbers not allocated, and rounding of figures.

(was) farm workers in 1820. By 1900, the proportion of workers engaged in farm occupations had shrunk by almost 50 percent and was at a level of 37 percent. By 1960 only 6.3 percent of the labor force was in agriculture."[15]

This does not, of course, suggest that there has been less agricultural production, but rather that the smaller proportion of workers has been able to produce more through technological and organizational innovations. If current projections are accurate, the decline in agricultural employment will continue until such time as agricultural production falls below the demand level, when a slight upturn in this type of employment could be anticipated.

A careful examination of these data reveals the second and perhaps more important trend. While the shift away from agriculture meant a movement to industry, for the most part, there has been a rapid shift away from industry, with significant increases coming in the services, rather than in goods production. We are now apparently in a services-producing occupational era. Additional light can be cast on this by considering some additional data.

Table 2-2 is an examination of the world's labor force. It can be seen

[15]"Labor Force," in *Handbook of Modern Sociology*, ed. Robert E. L. Faris (Chicago, Ill.: Rand McNally & Company, 1964), p. 182.

that there are huge variations in the proportions of the labor force engaged in all three of the sectors identified—agriculture, industry, and services. These variations are obviously related to the stage of social and economic development of the regions in question. It can be noted that all of the most developed areas share the dominance of the services sector.

TABLE 2-2. Percentage Distribution of the World's Total Labour Force, and Labour Force in Agriculture, Industry and Services, by Region and Continent, 1960

Region	Total labour force	Agriculture	Industry	Services
World	100.0	100.0	100.0	100.0
Africa	8.7	11.6	4.0	5.2
Western Africa	3.1	4.3	1.2	1.7
Eastern Africa	2.3	3.3	0.9	1.0
Middle Africa	1.1	1.6	0.3	0.3
Northern Africa	1.7	2.1	0.9	1.4
Southern Africa	0.5	0.3	0.7	0.7
Northern America	5.9	0.8	12.1	13.6
Latin America	5.5	4.6	5.7	7.6
Middle America (Mainland)	1.1	1.1	1.1	1.3
Caribbean	0.6	0.5	0.6	0.7
Tropical South America	2.8	2.5	2.5	3.8
Temperate South America	0.9	0.4	1.6	1.7
Asia	56.1	68.8	36.0	41.5
East Asia (Mainland)	24.6	32.1	12.7	16.0
Japan	3.4	1.9	5.0	5.8
Other East Asia	1.2	1.3	0.7	1.3
Middle South Asia	18.4	22.6	13.6	12.1
South-East Asia	6.9	9.0	2.9	5.2
South-West Asia	1.6	1.9	1.1	1.2
Europe	14.7	7.2	29.1	21.5
Western Europe	4.6	1.1	10.8	8.2
Northern Europe	2.7	0.5	6.2	5.1
Eastern Europe	3.8	2.9	6.1	3.8
Southern Europe	3.7	2.6	6.0	4.3
Oceania[1]	0.5	0.2	0.8	0.8
Australia and New Zealand	0.4	0.1	0.8	0.8
Melanesia	0.1	0.1	—	—
U.S.S.R.	8.6	6.9	12.3	9.8

[1]Excluding Polynesia and Micronesia.

Source: Samuel Baum, "The World's Labour Force and its Industrial Distribution, 1950 and 1960," *International Labour Review*, 95 (January–February 1967), 102. More recent data are not yet available.

Note: Due to independent rounding the sum of the parts may not add up to group totals.

What are these services? They range from such needs (rights?) as health and welfare services and education to such luxuries as ski or scuba diving instruction. The huge travel and communications industries provide services. The largest single block of services, in terms of employment, is found in the government. Interestingly, as recent data indicate, the highest employment in the government is at the local and state level. Police and fire departments, sanitation and recreation departments, taxation and planning departments, and courts, libraries, and jails are local services. These are typically duplicated at the state or provincial level and again at the federal level. Each of these levels of government has its own unique configuration, but government employment denotes service, even if it does not seem that way. The term "civil service" is, of course, designed to denote the service aspect of government work.

There is another aspect to the changes in the social structure, which is different from those already discussed. This is the fact that *knowledge* has perhaps become as critical as capital in determining an occupation's and an individual's position in the social system. The importance of knowledge can be demonstrated by referral to data shown in Table 2-3. The most striking thing in this projection to 1985 is the increase in the "professional and technical workers" category. These are workers who use knowledge in their work and sell their knowledge on the market place. By the same token, there is also a substantial increase forecast for clerical workers, whose task it is to "handle" information.

In Daniel Bell's opinion, it is knowledge that is the critical component of the "post-industrial" condition in which the United States currently finds itself.[16] It is worthwhile examining some of the characteristics of this postindustrial situation because they are in direct contrast with some popular notions about the world and because they are so critical for the world in which work is performed.

Bell suggests that there are five dimensions or components of the post-industrial era. The *first* is the creation of a service economy. This has been demonstrated already, as has the *second* component—the pre-eminence of the professional and technical class.[17] The numerical growth of this set of occupations can be seen in Table 2-3. Certainly these occupations are crucial and powerful and well rewarded. An important question remains, however, of whether these occupations have become "pre-eminent." It is not difficult to find persuasive arguments that the *control* of society still lies in the hands of those who control the wealth, with the professional and technical personnel essentially doing the bidding of the controlling

[16]Daniel Bell, *The Coming of Post-Industrial Society* (New York: Basic Books, 1973).
[17]*Ibid.*, pp. 14–15.

TABLE 2-3. Percent Distribution of Employment, by Major Occupational Group, 1960 and 1972, and projected 1980 and 1985.

Occupational group	1960[1]	1972	1980	1985
Total	100.0	100.0	100.0	100.0
White-collar workers	43.1	47.8	51.5	52.9
Professional and technical workers	11.0	14.0	15.7	16.8
Managers and administrators	11.2	9.8	10.5	10.3
Sales workers	6.4	6.6	6.6	6.4
Clerical workers	14.5	17.4	18.7	19.4
Blue-collar workers	36.3	35.0	33.1	32.3
Craftsmen and kindred workers	13.3	13.2	12.8	12.8
Operatives[2]	17.3	16.6	15.6	15.1
Nonfarm laborers	5.7	5.2	4.7	4.4
Service workers	12.7	13.4	13.3	13.2
Private household workers	3.0	1.8	1.3	1.1
Other service workers	9.7	11.6	12.0	12.9
Farm workers	7.9	3.8	2.1	1.6

[1]Data for 1960 were adjusted to reflect the occupational classification in the 1970 census to make it comparable to the 1972 and projected 1980 and 1985 data.
[2]Includes the 1970 census classification, operatives, except transport and transport equipment operatives.

Source: Neal H. Rosenthal, "The United States Economy in 1985: Projected Changes in Occupations," *Monthly Labor Review* 96 (November 1973), 19.

class.[18] For the moment, we can say that whoever is pre-eminent—the wealthy or the holders of knowledge—both must be highly trained in the use of people who have knowledge or in the use of the knowledge itself.

Bell's *third* component of the postindustrial society is perhaps the most difficult to understand and appreciate. It involves the "primacy of theoretical knowledge."[19] This is a critical idea in that it gets at the heart of the differences between past industrial development and current and future postindustrial development. Most of the major industries of the past (with some still dominant into the present) have been based around inventions—steel, automobiles, railroads, and even aviation—that were developed on the basis of trial and error approaches. On the other hand, industries such as chemicals, electronics, computers, aerospace, and lasers have emerged from theoretically based developments. The control of wars and of the economy is increasingly based on abstract theoretical

[18]For discussions of this point see C. Wright Mills, *The Power Elite* (New York: Oxford University Press, 1956); Paul M. Sweezy, *The Present as History: Essays and Reviews on Capitalism and Socialism* (New York: Monthly Review Press, 1962); and William Domhoff, *The Higher Circles: The Governing Class in America* (New York: Vintage Books, 1970).

[19]Bell, *Post-Industrial Society*, pp. 18–26.

principles. Predictions are made about what will occur after specific decisions are made or steps are taken. If the outcomes verify the theory, the theory is strengthened; if not, the theory is modified for the next set of predictions.

Discussions of this sort raise the legitimate spectre of societal control in the hands of those who have constructed the theory that has been selected to guide the society. This is a frightening prospect if the theories are wrong or the theoreticians mad. It is also frightening if the theories are one-sided, as would be a theory that just looked at the economic consequences of decisions to be made in the international or domestic spheres and ignored the social and/or political consequences. These considerations are legitimate concerns for postindustrial societies. The problems are intensified when one realizes that an expert in one field is by definition not an expert in other fields. The person must specialize to gain the expertise; the very act of specialization takes one down a knowledge path that is distinct from other knowledge paths.

Since the majority of the population is not composed of persons able to utilize this theoretical knowledge, the idea of the postindustrial society contains the seeds for postdemocratic societies, with control in the hands of the few. The degree to which this is a possibility lies in the extent to which pluralism is permitted to exist. If there is recognition of competing reasonable theories and thus of experts, the danger is lessened. If there is recognition of areas of knowledge and action about which there are not theoretical insights, the danger is also weakened. Nonetheless, problems of social control will assume a very different character in a postindustrial society. The major question will remain—who is controlling, but perhaps added to this will be the question—do we know we are being controlled?[20]

Without attempting to alleviate this pessimistic note, the author must note that a *vast* amount of traditional industrial activity continues. While one could argue about the ultimate source of control of industrial efforts, the fact remains that the more traditional industrial condition is the normal environment for many workers at all levels. Even most services are provided on the basis of a traditional industrial model. A major element of the traditional manner in which work is carried out in the industrial setting is that work is done in organizations, typically large and complex organizations. The consequences of this for the occupational world will be dealt with shortly.

---

[20]This point is stressed by Alain Touraine, *The Post-Industrial Society: Tomorrow's Social History: Classes, Conflicts and Culture in the Programmed Society* (New York: Random House, 1971). First published in 1969 by Editions Denoel, S. A. R. L., Paris.

The *fourth* dimension of the postindustrial society is that technology can be planned.[21] By planning technology, the outcomes of new developments can be predicted, based on the theory behind the development itself. According to Bell, planned technology will enable society to prevent such previously unanticipated consequences as the pollution of air and water by fertilizer runoffs and automobile emissions. These can be predicted with technological planning and assessment.

The *fifth* and final component of the postindustrial society is the development of a new intellectual technology. This involves "the substitution of algorithms (problem-solving rules) for intuitive judgements."[22] In this manner, what appear to be extremely complex issues become simple when the appropriate problem-solving rule is applied. Of course, the question remains open regarding the nature of and the selection of the proper problem-solving rule.

One can certainly argue with Bell's description of the postindustrial society and with the conclusion that the developed nations of the world are already in it. The fact remains that the conditions that Bell describes must certainly be viewed as strong tendencies. These tendencies are a major and perhaps dominant aspect of the contemporary context of occupations.

The tendencies that have been presented are the present and future context of occupations. This context comes to life for all occupations when it becomes part of the actual working environment. *Organizations* contribute to and form this working environment. The contribution of organizations to the working environment is quite subtle. It is through organizations that the ideas and techniques that have been described are developed and promoted. It is in organizations that decisions are made to make further investments in research and development programs. It is in organizations that decisions are made to provide more governmental funds for research programs or to cut back the rate of such funding. While many of these decisions are politically based, both in private industry and in government, the fact remains that the final decisions are reached through deliberations in organizations.

Both private and public investment in the research, education, and knowledge arenas have led to the current importance of knowledge. These investments have been based on the belief of these organizations that the development of such knowledge would be organizationally beneficial. Knowledge created in one organization tends to flow to others, especially given the scientific norm of universality of research results, so that there tends to be a universal character to the developments that

[21]*Ibid.*, p. 26.
[22]*Ibid.*, pp. 27–33.

have been described. The importance of knowledge thus becomes a fact of life in all organizations and part of the immediate work context for all occupations.

THE CHANGING ORGANIZATIONAL ENVIRONMENT

Much of the previous discussion has been semicsoteric. The participants in the creation and dissemination of knowledge are scientists, engineers, and top organizational decision makers. They deal in areas that are truly known only to themselves, since everyone else is by definition a layman. At the same time, the ramifications of the postindustrial system can be felt throughout the entire occupational world. This can be most vividly illustrated when work organizations are examined, with automation in production organizations being a simple example. Automation is simply an application of ideas. The ideas themselves are of a relatively low order when compared with some of the issues with which Bell was dealing. Nevertheless, the workers in a bread factory, for example, have a very different type of job when the bakery is not automated as compared to when it is. Workers in a retail store, who essentially operate a remote computer terminal when ringing up a charge account sale, are also similarly affected by the altered ways of carrying out work.

The organizations in which all of this is occurring are themselves affected by the changing worlds around them. With the growth of services, organizations become more "people-oriented." Much of the work is concerned with face-to-face interactions with customers, clients, and other organizational members. The increase in the number of sales and clerical personnel and of management is indicative of the importance of interpersonal interactions in organizations. The importance of working with ideas is also critical to the modern organization. These organizations are idea processers.

Evidence from organizational research strongly suggests that both of these trends will result in "de-bureaucratization" of organizational structures. One type of evidence is based on the fact that organizations totally or partially composed of personnel engaged in working with ideas or people are in fact less bureaucratic than their more product-oriented counterparts.[23] In organizations that deal in activities oriented toward products, ideas, and people, the latter two are found in departments or

---

[23]For a discussion of the factors involved in this structural differentiation, see Talcott Parsons, *Structure Process in Modern Society* (New York: Free Press of Glencoe, 1960), p. 70, and Eugene Litwak, "Models of Organization Which Permit Conflict," *American Journal of Sociology*, LXVII (September 1961), 177–84.

segments that are less bureaucratized than the more product-oriented balance of the organization.[24]

A second type of evidence derives from analyses of management techniques, which repeatedly suggest that less formalized and routinized supervisory principles are required in the idea and people sectors of the organization. Thus, the organizations in which people work are themselves changing along with the broader social environment.

A NOTE ON THE RELATIONSHIPS AMONG OCCUPATIONS, ORGANIZATIONS, AND THE SOCIAL CONTEXT

Most of the discussion in this chapter has contained a sense of cohesion between the occupational, organizational, and broader social contexts. It has perhaps appeared that a change in the social context is followed smoothly and automatically by the properly related change in organizations, where in turn all of the occupations accept the changes warmly and with good feeling. *This is incorrect.* Organizations resist change. Occupations resist change. Both can also actively seek change in the face of resistance from some other sector. For example, in 1973 the United Automobile Workers sought a program of voluntary overtime in their contract negotiations with the automobile manufacturers in the United States. Here the occupational group was seeking change, with the organizations showing resistance.

As social change occurs, there is conflict and tension with the other sectors. The occupations at the forefront of the postindustrial movement are impatient with and seek changes in the rest of society. These tensions and conflicts are resolved in the short run, but redevelop or emerge in new forms in the longer run. The context of contemporary occupations is thus change and conflict, as it has always been.

A NOTE ON UNEMPLOYMENT

The movement into the industrial era from the agricultural era had an impact above and beyond the changing occupational patterns. The concept of unemployment did not exist until the industrial era, since relatively few workers were employed. That is, the ascription-based work of the earlier era precluded layoffs or depressions as they are known today. While periods of severe economic and social hardship existed, the

[24]Richard H. Hall, "Intra-Organizational Structure Variation: Application of the Basic Model," *Administrative Science Quarterly*, VII (December 1962), 295–308.

person still had a job in the sense that his craft or agricultural work could still be performed. The movement into the organizational-industrial situation established a new relationship that allowed a person to be separated from his job or not to be hired or not to be able to find work in the first place.

Unemployment has both personal and social consequences; as Hauser suggests, "unemployment is probably among the more catastrophic and critical experiences both of the person and family."[25] At the societal level, the fact that unemployment is most likely to be severe among the young, the aged, women, minority groups, and those persons who have been laid off because of technological change is indicative of their lack of integration into the occupational structure and, if the thesis of this volume is correct, into the total social structure. The severe consequences of unemployment provide further support for the analysis of social/occupational change and conflict.

SUMMARY AND CONCLUSIONS

The changes in the occupational system and attitudes toward work, which have been traced in this chapter, are an example of the importance and limitations inherent in a strictly historical analysis. On the positive side, knowledge of the characteristics of the agricultural and industrial eras provides insights into the contemporary occupational structure. Behavior and values are carried over from the past into the present. At the same time, the contemporary occupational system differs from those of the past. Reliance upon old understandings inhibits a full understanding of the present.

The dominant theme in this chapter has been social change as it affects the occupational structure and the distribution of people therein. The current situation of work as a separate, organizationally based activity emerged from the agrarian and craft era. Within the contemporary framework, a change from the industrially based system to one that has been labeled postindustrial appears to be taking place. If this analysis is correct, contemporary occupations will increasingly be concerned with ideas as opposed to objects. Direct interactions with people may become proportionally more important, both in the provision of services and, within the occupational system itself, in an ever wider array of jobs. Despite this movement, the production of agricultural and industrial goods will not diminish in importance but will involve less of the occu-

[25]"Labor Force," p. 185.

pational structure. The changes that have been discussed will probably not be as revolutionary as those that transpired during the industrialization process, when work emerged as a separate activity and when the organizational bases of contemporary occupations were laid. With these changes, however, different work motivations, rewards, and stresses will probably evolve, as the next chapter will indicate.

3

THE INDIVIDUAL
AND OCCUPATIONS

In this chapter we turn from the social context of occupations to the individual and look at how the individual interacts with the occupational world. There are three major related issues to be discussed. The first is the question—why do people work? This seems simple at first consideration but becomes much more complex when considered more fully. The second issue involves the positive satisfactions that people derive from their work, while the third issue turns the coin over and examines the negative aspects of occupations for the individual. Obviously the second and third topics are closely associated with the original motivation to work, but the subjects are important enough in their own right to warrant separate discussions. Before beginning the discussion, it should be noted that the subject matter here is most properly the possession of industrial and occupational psychologists. There is a body of research and writing on this topic alone that is probably greater than all of the material available on occupational sociology. The intent of this chapter is to introduce the major issues and problems in this area.

THE MOTIVATION TO WORK

People have to and want to work. This is the simplest answer to work motivation. While this is a simple answer, it is also rather correct, though not specific enough for utilization in any careful analysis. It is clear that, for the overwhelming majority of the population, work is necessary for subsistence. At the same time, this overwhelming majority also believes in work for its own sake, at least in some way. Occupations thus serve two kinds of needs for the individual. But the "subsistence need" has evolved from the necessity of some kind of work for mere survival to a state wherein the definition of subsistence is highly relative. The line between basic maintenance of life and the pursuit of greater comforts and luxuries in the "subsistence area" (food and shelter) has been crossed for the majority of occupations. Even if the subsistence need at this level of greater affluence is no longer related to survival, the motivation to work and the subsequent kinds of activities are designed to assure the individual the level of comfort he has learned to expect in the subsistence area. A person thus has to work in order to maintain what he considers to be his level of subsistence. This does not imply, of course, that everyone who is employed earns enough to live at this higher level.

There is strong evidence to suggest that among those who are unemployed, for whatever reasons, the desire to work is present. In an analysis of 4,410 working and nonworking poor males and females, Leonard Goodwin found that the poor, in general, have a strong work orientation.[1] He concludes:

> Evidence from this study unambiguously supports the following conclusion: poor people—males and females, blacks and whites, youths and adults—identify their self-esteem with work as strongly as do the nonpoor. They express as much willingness to take job training if unable to earn a living and to work even if they were to have an adequate income. They have, moreover, as high life aspirations as do the nonpoor and want the same things, among them a good education and a nice place to live. The study reveals no differences between poor and nonpoor when it comes to life goals and wanting to work.[2]

There are, however, some important variations in this motivation to work among the unemployed. Goodwin found that the more a person experiences failure in the work world, the lower his desire to work. Thus, for the unemployed, as for everyone else, the desire to work and the strength and content of this desire are learned during the course of one's socialization.

THE COMPONENTS OF WORK MOTIVATION

Victor Vroom provides a useful overview of the various factors that are important as work motivations. He notes, first of all, that wages,

[1]*Do the Poor Want to Work?* (Washington, D. C.: Brookings Institution, 1972).
[2]*Ibid.*, p. 112.

including all of the various sorts of financial remunerations associated with the term fringe benefits, are an "indisputable source of the desire of people to work."[3] Fringe benefits include retirement and insurance programs, as well as miscellaneous inducements such as meals, educational programs, and recreational opportunities. One small college, for example, offers a free membership in the local country club as a faculty recruitment device. As discussed previously, these financial rewards contain connotations for one's social status and general style of life and are more than a means for simple subsistence. Vroom notes that while the salary provided by an occupation is important, it is certainly not the sole source of motivation.

A second motivational basis for work is the expenditure of physical and/or mental energy.[4] Vroom notes that while most theories of behavior are based on the assumption that a person will try to avoid the expenditure of energy or at least select behavior patterns involving a minimum of such expenditure, good evidence suggests that some energy expenditure is satisfying rather than dissatisfying. Obvious examples of this phenomenon are the recreational patterns of people who are desk bound while on the job. Golf courses and tennis courts are generally filled by people who feel the need for exercise after a work week of physical inactivity. Alfred C. Clarke's analysis of the leisure patterns within the various social classes is instructive in this regard.[5] While there are distinct social-class differences in leisure activities, almost all activities involve some form of physical or mental activity.

While one might argue that watching television and spending time in taverns are at best passive activities, except for some slight arm movement, in general these activities involve the use of mental energy. Other forms of leisure rather clearly require both mental and physical energy expenditure. A legitimate question in the area of leisure patterns is the extent to which the person engages in the various activities because he wants to or because he feels that he is expected to do so. However, nonwork or leisure time does take the form of energy usage, regardless of a person's reasons for participating. Human beings thus do not remain inert when not confronted with occupational role requirements. If this form of activity is rewarding to the individual, then it can at least be inferred that energy expenditure on the job also serves as part of the complex of motivations.

[3]Delbert Miller and William Form, *Industrial Sociology*, (New York: Harper & Row, 1964), pp. 433–35.

[4]Victor Vroom, *Work and Motivation*, p. 32. (New York: John Wiley & Sons, 1964), p. 30.

[5]"Leisure and Occupational Prestige," *American Sociological Review*, XXI, 3 (June 1956), 301–7.

Vroom also notes that some recent research has suggested that animals will engage in activity as a consequence of activity deprivation. He proposes that energy expenditure up to some point has positive consequences, but beyond that point such expenditure becomes a negative factor. The analysis of animals focused on physiological needs for activity; when one adds to this the importance of the learned need to work and to be active, the case is further strengthened. Vroom cites Weber's analysis that the Protestant ethic contributed to the kinds of activity that allowed capitalism to develop, since the proposition that it is moral to be active can serve as a powerful work motivation.[6] Gerhard Lenski's recent work also generally affirms the Weberian analysis, in that it shows that those persons who believe in the Protestant ethic (Protestants or not) tend to have stronger advancement aspirations.[7] Thus the need for activity probably has both a physiological and a learned basis, though the interplay between these two factors has not yet been examined systematically. For our purposes, such an examination would be desirable, but is not necessary, since the need for activity serves as at least a partial source of work motivations. As will be suggested below, the importance of energy expenditure itself varies in relationship to the other sources of motivation.

The third motivational basis for work, according to Vroom, is the production of goods and services and involves the intrinsic satisfaction a person derives from successfully manipulating some part of his environment.[8] Vroom cites evidence from experimental and general psychology to demonstrate that tasks are carried on without external rewards, for their own sake. Rather obviously, some occupations allow more satisfaction of this sort than others. An additional aspect of this motivational base is the fact that the performance of the work role can produce a moral satisfaction for the individual. Saving souls, defending the accused, advancing the frontiers of knowledge, and broadening students' intellectual horizons serve the moral commitments of many clergymen, attorneys, scientists, and teachers. Here, again, the importance of this motivational basis varies from occupation to occupation.

A fourth motivational basis is social interaction.[9] Most work roles involve interactions, whether with customers, clients, or members of an identifiable work group, as part of the expected behavior. Components of this motivational base include having influence over others, being liked by others, and being controlled by others. These components, which

[6]*Work and Motivation*, pp. 36–37.
[7]*The Religious Factor* (New York: Doubleday & Co., 1963), pp. 89–92.
[8]*Work and Motivation*, p. 37.
[9]*Ibid.*, p. 39.

vary among themselves in terms of their importance in particular occupations, function as inducements to engage in work. A person can derive his most gratifying social interactions on the job, whatever his basis of gratification might be.

The final basis for work motivations, according to Vroom, is social status.[10] As will be discussed later in detail, occupations are perhaps the best single determinant of social status. For the social scientist or the layman, knowledge of a person's occupation gives an immediate and usually accurate indication of social status. As a motivational force, for most segments of the social structure, social status is gained simply by working. If social status is important to the individual, in the sense that he wishes to hold his own or improve his position, then it will be an important component of his motivational system; and if social status is important to a large segment of the population, then it will be important throughout society.

The five motivational bases have been treated as though they were all equal in importance. This point of view is challenged by several writers, best known of whom is Abraham Maslow.[11] Maslow suggests that work motivations are based around a *hierarchy* of needs. The order of these needs is:

1. Physiological requirements (food, shelter, etc.)
2. Safety and security
3. Love, companionship, and affection
4. Esteem of self and from others
5. Self-actualization (being able to realize one's own potential to the fullest)

The basis of Maslow's approach to motivation is that as one need is satisfied, the next highest need becomes salient to the individual. In a society such as the United States where the majority of people in occupations have the first and usually the second of these needs fulfilled, the "higher order" needs become the primary motivators. These are what people seek in their work. This notion of a hierarchy of needs has a powerful practical implication. If workers at all types of occupations are to be motivated, then the concentration should be on higher and higher levels of motivation, since with lower level needs satisfied, there is a systematic move toward the need for self-actualization.

This approach is increasingly being criticized on both practical and theoretical grounds. A major criticism is that the hierarchy of needs approach reflects what might well be a hierarchy among some people,

[10]*Ibid.*, p. 41.
[11]Abraham Maslow, *Motivation and Personality* (New York: Harper & Row, 1954).

particularly academic types, but may not be accurate for most of the population. More important, there have been some important research findings that indicate major reversals in the order that Maslow posited. Maslow himself recognized the possibilities of reversals in the hierarchy but basically dismissed them as unimportant and abnormal. The research findings seem to indicate otherwise.

There are some interesting reversals in the hierarchy by demographic category. Age, for example, has been shown to have important variations. Miner has shown that for a significant proportion of the labor force, the need for esteem reaches a peak during the twenties and then tapers off as the person gets older.[12] Social interaction needs increase with age. This is probably linked to the negative connotation given to aging (even past thirty) in our society, so that esteem becomes less viable for the individual. It is important to note that the definition given to aging is from the society and is not something within the individual.

There are also sexual differences in regard to these needs. Again, due to sociocultural definitions, females have been more concerned with fulfilling social needs, while achievement and esteem have meant more to men.[13] Anastasi suggests that the greater male aggressiveness stems from both biological and social origins.[14] As the socialization of females changes to reflect an alternative view of the role of females, the social aspect of this would be expected to change. The exact role of biological factors here is still not clearly known. Regardless of origin, of course, there are these sexual differences that throw doubts upon the utility of a hierarchy of needs.

Another line of criticism of the hierarchy of needs approach comes from examinations of workers with different cultural backgrounds. In some cases it is found that the self-actualization need either is not present or is actively rejected.[15] According to Hulin and Blood, this is particularly likely to be the case among blue-collar, urban workers. What is posited to be a universal hierarchy may actually only be operative for part of the population. Even for that part of the population where there is such a hierarchy, the reversals in order noted above throw some serious doubts about the hierarchy's applicability and utility as a work motivation theory.

[12]John B. Miner, *Personnel and Industrial Relationships: A Managerial Approach* (New York: Macmillan Company, 1969).

[13]See, for example, D. C. McClelland *et al., The Achievement Motive* (New York: Appleton-Century-Crofts, 1953).

[14]Anne Anastasi, *Differential Psychology*, 3rd ed. (New York: Macmillan Company, 1958).

[15]Charles L. Hulin and Milton R. Blood, "Job Enlargement, Individual Differences, and Worker Responses," *Psychological Bulletin*, LXIX, 1 (1968), 41–55.

Another major approach to work motivation is the approach taken by Frederick Herzberg and his associates.[16] This is known as the Motivation-Hygiene Theory. While much of this approach is concerned with satisfaction and dissatisfaction, it is also important for the understanding of motivation and will be dealt with here. This is a dual-factor theory of motivation and satisfaction. The theory suggests a first component made up of factors that are related to the intrinsic conditions of the job. These factors are known as the motivators or satisfiers. The other set of factors contains characteristics of the extrinsic aspects of the work and general work conditions and is known as the hygienes or dissatisfiers. The reason for this two-factor theory and the names applied to the factors arose out of Herzberg's early research, in which he found that the things that seemed to lead to satisfaction were of a different order than those that led to dissatisfaction. This lead to the conclusion that there were two dimensions or factors to the work motivation picture.

Robert J. House and Lawrence A. Wigdor summarize the major aspects of the theory in the following way:

> The satisfiers are related to the nature of the work itself and the rewards that flow directly from the performance of that work. The most potent of these are those characteristics that foster the individual's needs for self-actualization and self-realization in his work. These work-related or intrinsic factors are achievement, recognition, work itself, responsibility, and advancement. [Note the similarity to Maslow.—Author]
>
> A sense of performing interesting and important work (work itself), job responsibility, and advancement are the most important factors for a lasting change. Achievement, more so than recognition, was frequently associated with the long-range factors of responsibility and of the work itself. Recognition that produces good feelings about the job does not necessarily have to come from superiors; it might come from peers, customers, or subordinates. Where recognition is based on achievement, it produces the more intense satisfaction.
>
> The dissatisfaction factors are associated with the individual's relationship to the context or environment in which he does his work. The most important of these is company policy and administration that promotes ineffectiveness or inefficiency within the organization. The second most important is incompetent technical supervision—supervision that lacks knowledge of the job or ability to delegate responsibility and teach. Working conditions, interpersonal relations with supervisors, salary, and lack of recognition and achievement can also cause dissatisfaction.[17]

[16]See Frederick Herzberg, *Work and the Nature of Man* (Cleveland, Ohio: World Publishing Company, 1966); Herzberg *et al., Job Attitudes: Review of Research and Opinion* (Pittsburgh, Pa.: Psychological Services of Pittsburgh, 1957); and Herzberg, B. Mausner, and B. Snyderman, *The Motivation to Work*, 2nd ed. (New York: John Wiley & Sons, 1959).

[17]"Herzberg's Dual-factor Theory of Job Satisfaction and Motivation: A Review of the Evidence and a Criticism," *Personnel Psychology* 20 (Winter 1967), 370.

The presence of "non-dissatisfiers" or hygienes, such as good working conditions or good supervision, will not lead to satisfaction, but will prevent dissatisfaction, according to the theory. Similarly, the absence of satisfiers or motivators will not lead to dissatisfaction, but simply the absence of satisfaction. While this makes sense in certain cases, the theory is weakened by the reliance upon the Maslow-like hierarchy. Again, research suggests that the hierarchy or ordering suggested in the theory does not exist when workers at different organizational levels are compared.[18] Also, summaries of research studies done on this theory have indicated that unless an almost identical methodology to that used by Herzberg and his followers is employed, the two factors do not come out as predicted. This in and of itself does not destroy the theory, but certainly raises important questions about its universality.

The dual-factor theory does have the advantage of pointing out that the motivation to work *can* be based on the desire of the individual to seek positive rewards and avoid negative sanctions. The contents of these positive and negative sanctions may be the same or different. For example, a person might want to work to earn more money (positive) and avoid earning less money (negative). Another person might work to achieve self-actualization and avoid dull routines. It is undoubtedly an error to assume that all people have a hierarchy of needs as proposed by Maslow and assumed by Herzberg. It is quite possible that all people have *a* hierarchy, but the contents and order of the hierarchy are subject to wide variation. Thus far, none of the theories of work motivation have been entirely satisfactory. There is not a universally accepted theory presently available. The approach to be discussed next, expectancy theory, avoids some of the pitfalls of the approaches that have been discussed and perhaps is the most generally applicable approach now available.

EXPECTANCY THEORY

Expectancy theory is probably the most universally accepted theory of work motivation at the present time. It makes none of the assumptions of a hierarchy, which are so troublesome in the theories that have been discussed. According to Wahba and House,

> The theory is based on two familiar concepts: expectancy (subjective probability) and valence (anticipated value). The theory proposes, generally, that work-related behavior can be predicted once we know the valences and probabilities people attach to certain outcomes. According to the

[18]*Ibid.*, and H. Roy Kaplan, Curt Tausky, and Bhopinder S. Bolaria, "The Human Relations View of Motivation: Fact or Fantasy," *Organizational Dynamics*, 1 (Autumn 1972), 67–80.

theory, an individual chooses the behaviors he engages in on the basis of the interaction between: (1) the valences he perceives to be associated with the outcomes of the behavior under consideration; and (2) his subjective estimate of the probability that his behavior will indeed result in the outcomes. It is further proposed that the resulting function is a nonlinear monotonically increasing product of expectations and valences.[19]

While Wahba and House criticize the theory because it assumes too much rationality on the part of the individual in assigning weights and choosing among alternative courses of potential action, the theory has the definite advantage of applicability in all occupational settings and does not contain unwarranted assumptions about the content of the individual's expectations and values. There are complex derivations from the basic model in expectancy theory that are not of concern here. For our purposes, the theory can be used in conjunction with Vroom's bases of work motivation. Thus a person will be motivated to work in a situation in which his expectancy of receiving a wage of sufficient valence to him is coupled with the probability of expending his desired amount of energy, with his desired level of intrinsic satisfaction, and so on. Since people have different arrays of motivations in terms of the extent to which they desire these motivational bases, work motivation takes different forms among different people. Not only does the configuration among the motivational bases vary, but the total amount of work motivation also undoubtedly varies. This conclusion about the variance among the motivational bases and the variation in the total amount of work motivation is indicated in Fig. 3-1, in which highly stereotyped images of particular occupational members are depicted.

When the question of why people work is viewed from a more general perspective, a number of conclusions can be drawn. First, the individual brings with him a set of expectations regarding what he should get out of his work. These expectations are a result of his previous socialization, which has also developed within him motivations to work, and both motivations and expectations can vary widely. Experiences in an occupation can strengthen, modify, completely change, or have no impact on the amount of motivation and the kinds of motivations and expectations that a person brings to a job. If his expectations are insufficiently met and he has the opportunity to change jobs, he will do so in an attempt to satisfy these expectations more completely. In many cases, of course, he may be unable to make a change and may work in a state of prolonged dissatisfaction. On the positive side, the occupation

[19]Mahmoud A. Wahba and Robert J. House, "Expectancy Theory in Work and Motivation: Some Logical and Methodological Issues" (Baruch College, The City University of New York, 1971), p. 1.

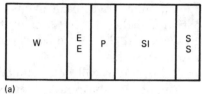

(a)

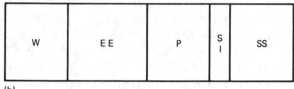

(b)

(c)

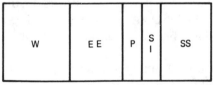

(d)

Figure 3-1. (a) Female Secretary, 22, pretty. (b) Female Lawyer, married, 45, ambitious. (c) Male Auto Worker, married, 25, four children. (d) Male Professional Football Player, single, 23, Quarterback. W = Wages, EE = Energy Expenditures, P = Production of Goods or Services, SI = Social Interaction, SS = Social Status.

and his motivations and expectations may coincide well, leading to a continued state of satisfaction. In any event, the meaning of work to an individual at any point in his life is a cumulative result of his socialization before beginning the occupation and the ongoing socialization that occurs on the job. Motivations to work and the meanings derived from work are thus part of a dynamic process.

In order to illustrate this point, two studies will be examined briefly. The first is an analysis of differing educational-aspiration levels among a sample of working-class high school students. Educational aspirations are related to work motivations in two ways. In a general sense, educational aspirations, like work motivations, are expectations about a significant phase of life. More specifically, educational aspirations contribute to work motivations in that the level of education desired and achieved is a component of the overall socialization process, which itself leads to particular motivational types and levels. In this particular study, by Irving Krauss, the well-known relationship between social-class position and plans for attending college was again documented.[20] Of the middle-class youths in the sample, 64 percent planned to attend college, whereas only 41 percent of the working-class youths had such aspirations. An intensive examination of the working-class youths revealed systematic reasons for the differing aspiration levels. First was the existence of a status discrepancy between the parents of those having higher aspirations (college-attendance plans). The important status discrepancy was in the direction of the mother having higher status than the father in terms of her job and/or her education. Mothers in this position apparently push their children toward higher aspirations. While the exact dynamics of this situation are not examined because data are unavailable from this study, Krauss suggests that the mothers may be aware of, and instill in their children, the idea that there are horizons beyond a working-class life. In some cases, of course, a "don't be like your father" syndrome might operate.

Other factors that contribute to differences among aspiration levels are the presence of other family members and friends who have college experience, participation in extracurricular activities in high school with peers who plan to attend college, and fathers who hold positions in the higher levels of the working class, such as foremen or skilled craftsmen. But for our purposes, the specific nature of the sources of differing aspirational levels is not the central issue; what is important is the fact that the home and school environment, together with later experiences, contribute to distinctly different aspirational (motivational) levels within

[20]"Sources of Educational Aspirations Among Working Class Youth," *American Sociological Review*, 29 (December 1964), 867–79.

the same class and between classes. Aspirational levels are, of course, only a part of the overall set of motivations to work, but the process whereby differing background experiences contribute to work motivations is probably similar in all aspects of the work motivations discussed.

REACTIONS TO WORK

When the focus is changed to an examination of the reactions of individuals to their occupational environment, the work of Robert Presthus is instructive.[21] Presthus examined the manner in which employees react to their life in large organizations and identified three major types of adaptation. The first type is the "upwardly-mobile."[22] A person who adapts in this way, typically an executive, is characterized by high morale, strong identification with the organization, and acceptance of the legitimacy of the organizational demands on the individual. The upwardly mobile individuals internalize the organization's values, stress good interpersonal relations, dislike controversy and those who dissent from the general organizational direction, and are strongly oriented toward action. A major motivating force for a person of this type is the improvement of his status. He will probably become a joiner of organizations that will enhance his opportunities for advancement. The person who adapts in this way is in some senses a captive of the organization, but the question of individual autonomy notwithstanding, the adaptation is useful for both the organization and the individual. It coincides with the expectations and motivations that the person has brought with him to the job and serves to reinforce them. Since the opportunities for advancement in status are limited, real stress may occur for this type of individual if his advancement is temporarily or permanently blocked.[23]

The second type of adaptation to the organization is what Presthus characterizes as the indifferent response.[24] The indifferent worker withdraws from competition for the rewards the organization has to offer. Presthus believes that this response characterizes the majority of the wage and salary earners in large organizations. Their interests are directed toward off-the-job pursuits, with only lip service paid to the goals of the organization. Presthus believes that this response is encouraged by the bureaucratic conditions in large organizations and, although most

[21]*The Organizational Society* (New York: Alfred A. Knopf, 1962).
[22]*Ibid.*, pp. 164–204.
[23]See Dero A. Saunders, "Executive Discontent," *Fortune Magazine*, LIV, 4 (October 1956), 154–56, 244, 245, 250–51 for an analysis of the stress induced when upward mobility is perceived to be blocked.
[24]*The Organizational Society*, pp. 205–56.

characteristic of the blue-collar and lower white-collar workers, can be found among those professionals and executives who become disenchanted with organizational life.

The final adaptive mode, according to Presthus, is the ambivalent.[25] He notes:

> In both personal and organizational terms, the ambivalent's self-system is generally dysfunctional. Creative and anxious, his values conflict with bureaucratic claims for loyalty and adaptability. While the upward mobile finds the organization congenial, and the indifferent refuses to become engaged, the ambivalent can neither reject its promise of success and power, nor can he play the roles required to compete for them.[26]

The ambivalent is likely to be introverted, with limited interpersonal abilities. He is likely to be a specialist with ties to his specialist (professional) colleagues as a reference group. Bureaucratic hierarchical standards, as such, are likely to be an anathema to him, even when they are legitimate. He tends to view the world through glasses ground to his own prescription and thus cannot accept the standards of success with which the organization confronts him; at the same time, he wants success as he himself has defined it. This type of orientation tends to lead to a worsening of interpersonal relations for the ambivalent, since others do not conform to his individual standards. Presthus suggests that this type of response creates a dysfunctional form of anxiety for both the individual and the organization. He does not suggest that this is the modal pattern among specialists or scientists within large organizations, but he does seem to imply that it is likely to occur in this employee group. Though it will be suggested that large bureaucratic organizations need not confront the professional person with a working environment different from the normal professional environment, the antiorganizational response that Presthus describes is undoubtedly common. If the trend toward greater specialization and the increasing emphasis on advanced scientific and technological training within the labor force in general continues, then this response might become still more prevalent, as more of these highly trained types are found in various organizations. On the other hand, the extremely individualized and antiorganizational response may become less prevalent as the socialization of scientists and specialists begins to include formal and informal introductions to the facts of organizational life, with the result that the individual may be better able to balance his personal and organizational demands. Unfortunately, data

[25]*Ibid.*, pp. 257–86.
[26]*Ibid.*, p. 257.

are not available to determine if this antiorganizational response is increasing or decreasing.

This analysis of Presthus' work has been designed to demonstrate that the motivations a person brings to his occupation interact with the conditions of the occupation, leading to a variety of responses to the work situation. Whether the Presthus formulation is inclusive of all such responses is not the major issue. The responses are based on a person's previous socialization and the current situation.

We have been arguing that people respond to their work and are shaped by it. But what of the reverse? Do people shape their work? In a comprehensive study of 3,101 men in the United States, Melvin Kohn and Carmi Schooler found that there is a reciprocal effect.[27] They state: "We believe that the job does play a part in shaping the man, that there is a continuing interplay throughout his career between man affecting job and job affecting man."[28] They further conclude that: "A man's job affects his perceptions, values, and thinking processes primarily because it confronts him with demands he must try to meet. These demands, in turn, are to a great extent determined by the job's location in the larger structures of the economy and the society. It is chiefly by shaping the everyday realities men must face that social structure exerts its psychological impact."[29]

We can thus conclude this section with the observation that the individual brings a set of expectations to the occupation. These expectations are based on previous experience and the individual's social background. The occupation further shapes the individual, as he or she interacts with the work requirements. People respond to their occupations based on their own expectations and their perceptions of the occupational conditions. It is to these responses that we now turn.

JOB SATISFACTIONS

The most evident fact about job satisfaction is that it varies, in terms of the overall amount of satisfaction, directly with a person's position in the occupational hierarchy. Alex Inkeles has demonstrated that this is true across national lines in Western industrialized nations, as

[27]Melvin L. Kohn and Carmi Schooler, "Occupational Experience and Psychological Functioning: An Assessment of Reciprocal Effects," *American Sociological Review* 38 (February 1973), 97–118.
[28]*Ibid.*, p. 116.
[29]*Ibid.*, p. 117.

Table 3-1 indicates.[30] While the international differences are interesting, they cannot be taken as conclusive, given the fact that different questions were asked in each setting, but the major point is the consistency of the hierarchical relationship. Indeed, in light of what was said earlier about motivations to work, we might expect those occupations that have a higher status to be most likely to return positive reinforcements to the individual for his motivations. As might be expected, there are variations in the amount and types of satisfactions at, as well as between, the various hierarchical levels, as will be discussed below. But, again following Inkeles' work, findings from the Soviet Union and the United States are congruent in terms of what workers at varying levels value about their jobs, as Table 3-2 indicates. The importance of pay and security is inversely related to hierarchical level, while interesting work varies directly with the worker's level.

Further insights into these relationships can be attained by examining the components of job satisfaction among two diverse occupations. The first, the automobile-assembly-line worker, was intensively examined in 1955 by Ely Chinoy,[31] who found that the auto worker works in a situation where the work itself is largely meaningless, with little opportunity to gain intrinsic satisfactions. Even the satisfaction of earning money is somewhat blunted by the fact that the pay differentials between jobs are so slight that an increase in pay, while rewarding, cannot set a particular worker apart from his fellows. Instead of being a satisfaction as such, his wages are apparently viewed as a normal expectation from putting in a certain amount of time on the job. This is not to suggest that money and the secondary pleasures that it can bring are unimportant to the auto worker. Rather, the satisfaction derived from the money earned is not from the work itself, but from pleasures that his wages afford in the "real world" for the worker. Thus, as this perhaps overly simplified view of the auto worker suggests, he does not actually derive satisfactions from his wages as part of his job. They are part of life's satisfactions, but not of the job's.

Although auto work is probably not the best example of blue-collar or semiskilled work, the boredom and monotony of it leads to the conclusion that job satisfactions in this type of work must be derived from interpersonal relations or from those rewards available off the job. Chinoy notes that some auto workers spend time dreaming about other kinds of work; they are able to pass the time and utilize their minds, if they so

---

[30]"Industrial Man: The Relation of Status to Experience, Perception, and Value," *American Journal of Sociology,* LXVI (July 1960), 1–31.

[31]*Automobile Workers and the American Dream* (New York: Doubleday & Company, Inc., 1955).

TABLE 3-1. National Comparisons of Job Satisfaction, by Occupation
Percentage Satisfied[1]

U.S.S.R.		U.S.		Germany		Italy		Sweden		Norway	
Administrative, professional	77	Large business	100								
		Small business	91								
Semiprofessional	70	Professional	82	Professional	75			Upper class	84	Upper class	95
White collar	60	White collar	82	Upper white collar	65						
				Civil servants	51						
				Lower white collar	33			Middle class	72	Middle class	88
Skilled worker	62	Skilled manual	84	Skilled worker	47	Skilled worker	68				
Semiskilled	45	Semiskilled	76	Semiskilled	21	Artisan	62	Working class	69	Working class	83
Unskilled	23	Unskilled	72	Unskilled	11	Unskilled	57				
Peasant	12			Farm labor	23	Farm labor	43				

[1]U.S.S.R.—percentage answering "Yes" to: "Did you like the job you held in 1940?" (Soviet-refugee data, Russian Research Center, Harvard University). U.S.—percentage answering "Yes" to: "Are you satisfied or dissatisfied with your present job? (Richard Centers, "Motivational Aspects of Occupational Stratification," *Journal of Social Psychology*, XXVII (1948, 100). Germany—percentage who would choose present occupation in response to: "If you were again 15 years old and could start again, would you choose your present occupation or another one?" (from German poll data, courtesy of S.M. Lipset). Italy—those "satisfied" or "fairly satisfied" with work (*Doxa Bolletineo*). Sweden and Norway—percentage giving "satisfied" in response to question: "Are you satisfied with your present occupation, or do you think that something else would suit you better?" (Hadley W. Cantril, ed., *Public Opinion, 1935–1946* (Princeton, N.J.: Princeton University Press, 1951), p. 535).

Source: Reprinted from Alex Inkeles, "Industrial Man: The Relation of Status to Experience, Perception, and Value," *American Journal of Sociology*, LXVI, 1 (July 1960), 6, by permission of The University of Chicago Press. © 1960 by The University of Chicago.

TABLE 3-2. Quality Most Desired in a Work Situation, in Percentages by Country and Occupations

	Preferences of Sample of Soviet Refugees[1]				
Occupation	Adequate Pay	Interesting Work	Free of Fear	All Others	N
Intelligentsia	8	62	6	24	95
White collar	23	31	13	33	62
Skilled workers	22	27	15	36	33
Ordinary workers	48	20	13	19	56
Peasants	57	9	17	17	35

	Preferences of Sample in United States[2]				
Occupation	High Pay	Interesting Work[3]	Security	Independence	Other
Large business	6	52	2	7	33
Professional	3	50	3	12	32
Small business	6	41	5	22	26
White collar	7	42	12	17	22
Skilled manual	4	36	13	22	25
Semiskilled	6	20	26	24	24
Unskilled	8	19	29	15	29
Farm tenant and laborer	12	21	20	18	29

[1]Based on coding of qualitative personal interviews from the Harvard Project on the Soviet Social System.
[2]Based on R. Centers, "Motivational Aspects of Occupational Stratification," *Journal of Social Psychology*, XXVIII (November 1948), 187–218, Table 11.
[3]Includes: "A very interesting job" and "A job where you could express your feelings, ideas, talent, or skill."

Source: Reprinted from Alex Inkeles, "Industrial Man: The Relation of Status to Experience, Perception, and Value," *American Journal of Sociology*, LXVI, 1 (July 1960), 10, by permission of The University of Chicago Press. © 1960 by The University of Chicago.

desire, in these off-the-job kinds of activities. The direct job satisfactions are at the best quite limited.

In another study of automobile-assembly-line workers, Charles Walker and Robert Guest arrived at essentially the same conclusions as did Chinoy.[32] They note that for the majority of the workers, the pacing and repetitiveness of the work limits the direct satisfactions that

[32]"The Man on the Assembly Line," *Harvard Business Review*, XXX (May–June 1962), 71–88.

can be derived from it. For some workers, however, the assembly line appears to offer a source of competition. The worker does not expect to win the competition but may derive pleasure in at least breaking even. Walker and Guest quote the following comments:

> I do my job well. I get some satisfaction from keeping up with a rapid-fire job. On days when the cars come off slowly, I sometimes get bored.
> I get satisfaction from doing my job right and keeping up with the line. It makes you feel good . . . when the line is going like hell and you step in and catch up with it.[33]

While these are comments of the minority, they do suggest that machine pacing does not provoke rebellion or criticism among all who are confronted with it. By the same token, the repetitiveness of the work also can be linked to satisfactions for a minority of the workers, as these comments suggest:

> I keep doing the same thing all the time, but it doesn't make any difference to me.
> I like doing the same thing all the time. I'd rather stay right where I am. When I come in in the morning, I like to know exactly what I'll be doing.
> I like to repeat the same thing, and every car is different anyway. So my job is interesting enough.[34]

In these cases of positive satisfactions, as well as in those of dissatisfaction, which will be touched on later, the major factor is the mix between the worker's expectations (personality) that he brings to the job and the characteristics of the job. In the case of the men who find assembly-line work both challenging and satisfying, their expectation level is such that a position that appears to be more challenging to an outside observer might create a high level of anxiety and dissatisfaction for them.

In contrast to the auto worker, the executive generally experiences more job satisfaction, however it is measured. This greater satisfaction results from the fact that the job itself offers the individual a wider range of activities of the sort he has learned to expect. This is not to suggest that all executives are happier or better adjusted than all assembly-line or blue-collar workers. The stresses on a particular executive may be more real and more severe than on a particular blue-collar worker, but at the same time the general relationship between hierarchical level and amount of job satisfaction remains a rather systematically documented

---

[33]*Ibid.*, p. 77.
[34]*Ibid.*, pp. 77–78.

phenomenon. One could ask whether or not the executive, having learned to expect more satisfaction, reports a higher level thereof in order to protect his self-image, but this is not our major concern. Similarly, one could question the biases of researchers in the area of job satisfaction since they also are white-collar professionals and might be looking for the aspects of an occupation that are satisfying to themselves. Thus researchers tend to find that executives have the same kinds of satisfactions while blue-collar workers do not. But even if this were the fact, as it might well be, it is not particularly important. The executive perceives himself to be more satisfied with his work than the blue-collar worker, and even if he is fooling himself and the researcher, he still acts on the basis of how he feels about the situation. For him (note the assumption that he is a he) the job satisfies a number of needs.

For examples of the kinds of needs that an executive has and that are generally met by his work, Lyman Porter's article is instructive.[35] Porter asked executives in a number of organizations of varying sizes what their occupational desires were. They responded by noting, first, a desire for security in the sense that their employment would not be terminated. A second type of need was social; they wanted to develop close friends on the job and also help other people. A third type of need was status or esteem in the organization and in the wider community, as well as self-esteem. A fourth need category was autonomy, by which they meant possessing authority, having an opportunity for independent thought, and participating in setting the goals for the organization and the methods and procedures of obtaining them. The final need category was self-actualization, which involves feelings of personal growth and development, of fulfillment through the utilization of skills, and of accomplishment. It is interesting to note that financial desires are not included in this list, except by inference in the security area. This is probably a consequence of having sufficient incomes, so that this issue becomes less crucial; or perhaps it results from a feeling on the part of the researcher or the executives themselves that money is less central than the more socially based needs that were mentioned.

These needs, of course, become the bases for the satisfactions that the executives feel. Porter found that the needs were generally more sufficiently met as the hierarchy was ascended. An interesting exception to this finding was that lower and lower-middle managers in small corporations were happier than those in larger organizations. Thus there are variations in job satisfaction within the executive category, as well as between executives and workers at lower levels in organizations. Porter

[35]"Job Attitudes in Management: Perceived Importance of Need on a Function of Job Level," *Journal of Applied Psychology*, XLVII, 2 (December 1963), 141–48.

also notes that executives in larger organizations have more social needs and that these can probably be met if the work units are kept moderately small.

A more general set of findings in regard to the bases of satisfaction is reported in *Work in America*. The evidence from a sample of 1,533 American workers at all occupational levels indicated that the following factors were most important (among a set of 25 possible factors):

1. Interesting work
2. Enough help and equipment to get the job done
3. Enough information to get the job done
4. Enough authority to get the job done
5. Good pay
6. Opportunity to develop social skills
7. Job security
8. Seeing the results of one's work[36]

Without for the moment worrying about how these factors might configure themselves for specific workers or types of workers, we see that this research supports our basic approach that it is the meeting of expectations that contributes to satisfaction. When these expectations are not met and other conditions and factors enter the picture, we then have conditions of stress, tension, and alienation.

STRESSES, TENSION, AND ALIENATION

We turn now to the negative side of the coin for the individual —the dissatisfactions that are experienced in the occupational setting. This is a topic that has received an increasing amount of attention from diverse sources ranging from the government to industry to labor unions to novelists to social scientists. In all of the discussions of satisfaction, one point is clear, though imperfectly. This is that no category of workers is free of dissatisfaction. From the most exalted occupations to the meanest, dissatisfaction with some phase of work can be found. The plan for the analysis here is to first assess the extent of dissatisfaction, secondly to look at dissatisfaction among general types of occupations and types of workers, and finally to examine particular forms of dissatisfaction in depth.

[36]*Work in America: Report of a Special Task Force to the Secretary of Health, Education, and Welfare,* prepared under the auspices of the W. E. Upjohn Institute for Employment Research (Cambridge, Mass.: M.I.T. Press, 1973), p. 13.

THE EXTENT OF THE PROBLEM

There is no clear-cut answer to the question of the extent of dissatisfaction. The authors of *Work in America* suggest that it is quite high, citing evidence from a variety of sources. In one study, less than one-half of a sample of white, male, blue-collar workers stated that they were satisfied with their work most of the time. Another study cited found that only 43 percent of white-collar workers would again choose the kind of work they were currently doing. This figure drops to 24 percent for blue-collar workers. The general trend in these findings is that the higher the status of the occupation, the less the dissatisfaction expressed.[37] These sorts of data present the dismal picture that most workers are dissatisfied, but there are other answers to the same question about dissatisfaction.

Citing evidence from a number of sources, H. Roy Kaplan finds that:

1. Workers desire more control in their work routines, but still expect management to manage. A major study of 65 organizations found little difference between the amount of control workers wanted and the existing distribution of control in their organizations.

2. Men employed in bureaucratic organizations tend to be more intellectually flexible and more open to new experiences, are more self directed in their values, and have greater self-esteem than men who work in non-bureaucratic organizations.

3. Job complexity has an effect on psychological functioning, but it may be perceived and interpreted differently by workers as being important or unimportant.

4. While there are pockets of dissatisfaction, and perhaps alienation, among segments of the labor force, the majority of workers appear to be satisfied with their jobs.

5. Studies in the United States and abroad on alienation from work, job complexity, and technology indicate that while there may be some negative effects associated with these variables in the workplace, there is little evidence to support the contention that negative work experiences are carried beyond the workplace and are transferred into generalized feelings of alienation and anomie.[38]

The clear contradictions between Kaplan's conclusions and those presented in *Work in America* and elsewhere point up the difficulties in dealing with the rather global concept of dissatisfaction. Certainly everyone who has an occupation experiences dissatisfaction at one time or

[37]*Ibid.*, pp. 15–17.
[38]"How *Do* Workers View Their Work in America?" *Monthly Labor Review* (June 1973), p. 47.

another. Certainly, also, there are particular types of jobs that produce more dissatisfaction than others. The critical point, regardless of the absence of a specific answer to the question of the extent of dissatisfaction, is that dissatisfaction does exist and takes a variety of specific forms in particular settings. The most crucial evidence of this comes in the form of behavioral indicators, such as absenteeism, sabotage, or turnover. Furthermore, even if dissatisfaction is not taken from the job to the world outside of work, to the family or political group, for example, the fact that people are dissatisfied on the job means that a major portion of some people's lives is not providing the extent of pleasure, satisfaction, or tolerability that other people in other occupations experience.

WHAT ARE THE SOURCES OF DISSATISFACTION?

People can be dissatisfied about just any aspect of their work. Table 3-3 indicates the sources of dissatisfaction from a national sample of workers of all types. It is interesting to note that while a generally greater percentage of workers reported a problem area in their work in 1973, a generally smaller percentage regarded these problems as sizeable or great. While the differences are too small to be considered evidence that there are more work problems or that they are less important, these data do suggest there has not been a tremendous upsurge in discontent in recent years.

Sources of dissatisfaction are linked to what is important to the worker. For example, women cite sex discrimination much more than the total sample, and blacks clearly see racial discrimination as a major problem. The critical nature of experience and expectations is most clearly seen in the case of expenses for illness or injury. In 1973, only three percent of the sample was concerned about this issue, whereas 66 percent of those who had experienced illness or injury regarded it as a problem.

While dissatisfaction has many sources, it finds its expression in the experiences of individuals. In the next section we will examine the different kinds of responses that people experience according to the kind of work they do.

WHO IS DISSATISFIED?

The discussion in this section will be taken from *Work in America*, which, while it may overstate the extent of the problem, neatly indicates some of its elements. The most dissatisfied set of workers is the blue-collar employees. Mass production and other forms of routinized

TABLE 3-3. Ranking of Labor Standards Problem Areas, 1969 and 1973
[Percent Distribution]

Problem area	Percentage of workers reporting one problem or more in each area[1]		Percentage of those reporting the problem who regarded it as "sizeable" or "great"	
	1969	1973	1969	1973
Health and safety hazards	38	41	50	43
Transportation to and from work	35	40	39	37
Inadequate fringe benefits	39	39	43	39
Wage and salary workers only	45	44	–	–
Unpleasant physical working conditions	33	39	38	36
Inconvenient or excessive hours	30	39	38	34
Inadequate family income	26	21	62	56
Work-related illness or injury (within past 3 years)	13	14	56	48
Unsteady employment	10	9	37	35
Occupational handicaps	9	9	39	30
Invasion of privacy by employer	8	9	28	26
Wage and salary workers only	9	10	–	–
How democratically one's union is run	6	9	[2]58	54
Union members only	18	29	–	–
Mistreatment by employment agencies (within past 3 years)	7	8	68	72
Those who had dealt with an agency in past 3 years	47	52	–	–
How well one's union is managed	5	6	[2]58	[2]60

Union members only	17	23	–	–
Failure to receive wages or salary due (within past 3 years)	5	6	[2]43	[2]44
Those who at some time in 3 years prior to 1969 had worked for wages or salary				
Those who when interviewed in 1973 were wage and salary workers	6	–	–	–
Sex discrimination	3	5	[2]42	[2]37
Women only	8	13	–	–
Age discrimination	5	4	[2]35	[2]35
Inadequate expense coverage during work-related illness or injury (within past 3 years)				
Those who at some time in past 3 years had been away from work for 2 weeks or more due to a work-related illness or injury	4	3	[2]39	[2]45
Race or national origin discrimination	68	66	–	–
Blacks only	3	3	[2]53	[2]52
Wage garnishment or assignment (within past 3 years)	17	15	[2]72	[2]58
Those who at some time in 3 years prior to 1969 had worked for wages or salary	2	1	–	–
Those who when interviewed in 1973 were wage and salary workers	–	1	–	–

Source: Robert P. Quinn, Thomas W. Mangione, and Martha S. Baldi de Mandilovitch, "Evaluating Working Conditions in America," *Monthly Labor Review*, 96 (November 1973), 35.

[1]Based on the full samples of 1,533 in 1969 and 2,157 in 1973 unless otherwise stated in row description.
[2]The base of this percentage was either less than 100 in the 1969 unweighted sample or less than 140 in the 1973 weighted sample.

work, together with the position of the worker at the bottom of the organizational hierarchy, combine to offer the worker little opportunity for interesting work or advancement. The worker is likely to be faced with

(1) a work situation and hierarchical organization that provides little discretion in pace and schedule, (2) a career that has been blocked and chaotic, and (3) a stage in the life that puts the "squeeze" on the worker (large numbers of dependent children and low amounts of savings).[39]

Added to this is the fact that

the blue-collar worker must punch time clocks, making it difficult for him to arrange his work schedule to manage such personal chores as visiting the doctor, getting his car repaired, and visiting the school to discuss his children's problems. More basically, 27 percent of all workers have no paid vacations, 40 percent no sick leave, and perhaps 70 percent will never receive a private pension check. . . . Virtually all of those workers who are without these benefits are found among the ranks of non-professionals.[40]

White-collar workers and managers do not escape the dissatisfaction syndrome. As will be seen later, white-collar work is becoming more like manual work, particularly with the advent of computerized offices, and many lower level white-collar workers are beginning to realize that there is almost no likelihood of much advancement. For managers, the problems come at middle management, where there can be a great deal of responsibility without the corresponding authority. There is also an age factor here, with managers in their late 30s frequently feeling that they have reached a plateau with little further movement up the organization possible.

Dissatisfaction also appears to vary by age and sex. There are strong indications that younger workers are increasingly disenchanted with work that they define as meaningless. Women represent another category that experiences (and will perhaps increasingly experience) dissatisfaction at work. The women's movement has highlighted some of the problems that women face, but it is probably among those women least active in the women's movement that the occupations with the highest potentials for dissatisfaction are found—the typist, the keypunch operator, the bank clerk, the telephone operator, or the assembly line worker (where women are overrepresented). The problems faced by all workers are undoubtedly exacerbated when the worker is a woman and is aware of the implications of the women's movement.

[39]*Work in America*, p. 31.
[40]*Ibid.*, p. 36. This entire discussion is based on chap. 2 of this book.

We have not exhausted all of the material available about work dissatisfaction and the people it affects. Additional aspects of this topic will be discussed when specific types of occupations are considered. We have also not dealt here with the minority worker. To all of the problems associated with work dissatisfaction that have been discussed—type of work, age, and sex—minority group membership must be added as an additional burden. The motivation to work and the satisfaction and dissatisfaction sources are the same, regardless of whether or not a person is a member of a minority group. Discrimination can only be viewed as an additional source of dissatisfaction.

A more detailed understanding of the dissatisfaction issue can be obtained by looking intensively at two occupational groups—the factory worker and the executive, and it is to this final section in our discussion of dissatisfaction that we now turn.

THE FACTORY WORKER

There is a long-standing tradition that the factory worker is the one who experiences the most stress, dissatisfaction, and alienation. Karl Marx, for example, spoke of the alienation of the working masses.[41] According to Marxian analysis, the worker has no power over the production process and becomes little more than another machine, isolated from the production system even though a part of it. In a later analysis, Simone Weil took a similar view of the worker:

> All or nearly all factory workers, even the most free in their bearing, have an almost imperceptible something about their movements, their look, and especially the set of the lips, which reveals that they have been obliged to consider themselves as nothing.[42]

Georges Friedman suggests that the extreme specialization in factory work is oppressive and leads to dissatisfactions on the part of workers.[43] On the basis of their analysis of the auto worker, Walker and Guest conclude: "It seems to us significant that the average worker appeared to be oppressed by this sense of anonymity *in spite of the fact that he declared himself well satisfied with his rate of pay and the security of*

[41]See Erich Fromm, *Marx's Concept of Man* (New York: Frederick Ungar Publishing. Co., 1961), pp. 44–58.

[42]"Factory Work," in *Politics*, trans. F. Giovaelli, III, 11 (December 1946), 370; reprinted in Nosow and Form, *Man, Work and Society* (New York: Basic Books), p. 453.

[43]*The Anatomy of Work* (New York: Free Press of Glencoe, 1961).

his job."[44] These authors and others tend to view factory workers as a rather homogeneous group, who share common background characteristics and reactions to their jobs.

The view of the factory worker or blue-collar worker as dissatisfied is not uncommon. Whether it is correct or not is a question that can at least be partially answered by an analysis of Robert Blauner's investigation of industrial workers' reactions to their occupational situation.[45] His particular focus is on the amount and kinds of alienation that workers exhibit on the job, Blauner's approach to alienation is similar to the contemporary approach to the concept, which is to analyze its component parts.[46] Unlike some analysts, Blauner uses the concept of alienation as a research device, rather than as a polemically based attack on contemporary or historical conditions.

Four aspects of alienation are considered. First is *powerlessness.*[47] A powerless person is an object controlled and manipulated by others or by an impersonal system, such as technology. He cannot assert himself as an agent of change or modify the conditions of his domination. He reacts rather than acts. The opposite of this condition is freedom and control over one's own life. Blauner points out that the modern worker, at all levels, is separated from ownership, and that the vast majority of all workers, at all levels, are separated from the decision-making process. At the same time, an indirect source of control over the conditions of his employment is available to him through unionization and a growing amount of industrial democracy found in many employment situations. Thus while there are factors that operate to increase the amount of powerlessness a person experiences, counter trends are also evident.

Blauner's main concern, however, is not with these conditions, which are to some extent removed from the worker's immediate situation, important as they may be. The amount of control an individual has over his immediate situation is his dominant concern. Blauner therefore examines a person's freedom of physical movement, his freedom to make choices, his freedom from constraints regarding the pace of his work, his control over the quantity and quality of his work, and his freedom to select his own work techniques and routine. The basic assumption is the more freedom a person has, the less alienation.

[44]"The Man on the Assembly Line," p. 83.

[45]*Alienation and Freedom* (Chicago: University of Chicago Press, 1964).

[46]For an analysis of the various meanings of the concept of alienation and some of the techniques used in their measurement, see Melvin Seeman, "On the Meaning of Alienation," *American Sociological Review,* XXIV, 6 (December 1959), 783–91, and Dwight Dean, "Alienation: Its Meaning and Measurement," *American Sociological Review,* XXVI, 5 (October 1961), 753–58.

[47]Blauner, *Alienation and Freedom,* pp. 16–22.

The second component of alienation is *meaninglessness*, the situation when a person experiences the lack of a sense of purpose in his work.[48] He feels no connection between the parts (his own work) and the whole (the complete product or service). Meaninglessness comes about with standardized production techniques and with division of labor, which reduces the size of the individual worker's contribution to the total product. Blauner suggests that in small factories, in situations where team production was utilized, and where the technology was such that the work was highly integrated, there would be less meaninglessness than under conditions where a worker was concerned with a single small unit and where he could not see the relationship between his unit and the whole.

The third component is social alienation or *isolation*,[49] a feeling of not belonging to effective social units. The individual has little chance for self-expression. The presence of informal work groups would, of course, reduce the likelihood of this form of alienation, but as Blauner suggests, not all factory work allows the emergence of these work groups. Some workers are physically isolated from others, while in other situations the noise level might preclude the development of such groups. Widely diverse backgrounds on the part of the workers might also operate to produce alienation if the diversity prevents the development of meaningful social relations on the job.

The final component of alienation to be considered is *self-estrangement*,[50] the alienation of a person from himself. The worker is depersonalized and detached. Self-estrangement would be most evident when the individual feels a need for exercising control and initiative but cannot because of the conditions of his work. Work that is boring and monotonous is most likely to cause this form of alienation. The self-estranged worker is detached from his work, viewing it as a means to an end and having no sense of pride in what he is doing nor any feeling of intrinsic satisfaction from it.

Blauner's primary purpose is to delineate those conditions under which the various forms of alienation are most likely to occur. In the course of so doing, he points out the rather obvious, but often ignored, fact that although the majority of research on industrial work has been concentrated on the auto worker, who appears in most analyses as the archetype of the alienated man, assembly-line work, as characterized by the auto worker, comprises only five percent of all industrial work. Industrial work is, in fact, highly varied. This variation, according to

[48]*Ibid.*, pp. 22–24.
[49]*Ibid.*, pp. 24–26.
[50]*Ibid.*, pp. 26–31.

Blauner, should be and is accompanied by variations in the types and degrees of alienation present among the workers.

The first source of this variation is the type of technology in the industry. By technology Blauner means the complex of physical objects and technical operations, both mechanical and manual, regularly employed in turning out the goods and services produced by an industry. The type of technology is affected by the overall state of the industrial arts, the economic and engineering resources of the specific firms involved, and the nature of the product being manufactured.[51] The impact of these sources of technological differentiation can be seen in the types of industries that Blauner considers in his analysis. The printing industry is characterized by a craft technology that has been minimally affected by technological change. At the same time, the product is unique for each day's work as the material to be printed changes. The textile industry, in which machine tending is a major component of the production process, has a more advanced technology and a more standardized product. The auto industry is characterized by standardized products and great variety in the production process, which itself is rather technologically advanced. Finally, the industrial-chemicals and petroleum-refining industries are highly advanced technologically with continuous-flow production. These industries engage in continual research to improve the production process. The product here is also standardized in terms of the batches of particular substances that are refined.

The second major source of variation is the nature of the division of labor within a particular organization.[52] While this is clearly affected by the technology involved in the production process, it also varies independently according to the manner in which the particular organization assigns the men and machines at its disposal to the individual tasks. The division of labor can vary from high differentiation, in which each man and machine combination works only on a minute part of the whole, to situations in which both systematically contribute to a wider portion of production. The attempts at job enlargement, which have been noted at organizations such as International Business Machines, exemplify the ways in which the division of labor can be altered within an industry.

The social organization of the particular industry itself provides the third source of variation.[53] This involves the degree to which either traditional or bureaucratic standards are employed in organizational operations. By this Blauner means the degree to which rules are present and enforced, the amount of emphasis on following standard operating

[51]*Ibid.*, p. 6.
[52]*Ibid.*
[53]*Ibid.*

procedures, and the extent to which personal considerations are rejected. Organizations can vary from highly bureaucratic to highly traditional along the various subdimensions of bureaucratization.

The final source of variation is in the economic structure of the industry.[54] Blauner points out that marginal industries with smaller profit margins generally push their workers harder and engage in tighter supervisory practices.

These sources of variation affect the settings from which the various forms of alienation may emerge. As will be noted below, there are variations among and within the four major industries to be analyzed. Some organizations within the textile industry, for example, are probably less bureaucratic than others and have a more advanced technology, a less intensive division of labor, and a more secure economic position. Although further analyses of these intra-industry variations would be profitable, our concern, at the present time, will be focused on the broader patterns of differences among the various industries. An additional point, which should be added before Blauner's findings in this regard are considered, is that the workers in the various industries bring expectations with them to the job; their backgrounds affect their reactions to the diverse situations that confront them on the job.

The diversity of the industrial settings becomes very evident as the types and extent of alienation among the workers are analyzed. The printer works in a craft industry with a craft technology. He feels little powerlessness since he can set his own work pace, can move about, and is relatively free from supervisory control. The constantly changing product and the readily seen results make his work meaningful. Since a printer is a part of a strong occupational community, he has few feelings of isolation. Similarly, he is not self-alienated because of his pride in his work and his involvement in what he is doing. The printer is thus not alienated in his industrial work. This is not to suggest that he does not suffer dissatisfactions on the job. Doing a poor job or working with people whom he finds unpleasant certainly would yield dissatisfactions, but he is relatively free from alienation as the term is being used.[55]

The textile worker provides some contrast to the printer. His work is essentially that of tending looms; a weaver can tend from forty to sixty. He thus is controlled in terms of the degree to which he can move about; though he has to move to tend the looms, he has little or no opportunity to go beyond specific locations. The rhythm and pace of his work are also controlled, and he is tightly supervised both by his immediate superior and by the nature of the work itself. As a consequence

[54]*Ibid.*, p. 10.
[55]*Ibid.*, pp. 35–37.

he experiences a rather high degree of powerlessness. He feels somewhat less meaninglessness because he can see the finished product and understand the processes designed to produce it. Since there is little variety in his work, some meaninglessness is, however, present. The setting of the particular textile workers studied, a small town in the South, coupled with some company pride and homogeneity of backgrounds of the workers, created a situation in which isolation was not felt. It was eliminated by a common residential and cultural community rather than by an occupational community, such as was evident among the printers. The backgrounds of the workers also affected the degree of self-alienation; being from the rural South, with little education, and placing minimal emphasis on self-expression, they experienced minimal self-alienation.[56]

When the auto worker is considered, the level of all four types of alienation is found to be high. Blauner concentrates on the assembly-line worker in his analysis, noting that not all of the work in automobile factories shares the characteristics he discusses. Powerlessness is high for the auto worker. The assembly line keeps moving with a constant flow of work designed to keep him busy all the time. The quantity, quality, and techniques of the work are predetermined and are not under his control. There is little freedom of movement from the line. The worker is controlled quite impersonally, the assembly line itself becoming a control mechanism. The auto worker has, and feels that he has, little power.

He also experiences a high degree of meaninglessness. His work is only a small part of the whole. Furthermore, there are other workers doing exactly the same thing that he is; as Blauner points out, a person cannot be *the* left hubcap assembler. While the worker may know a lot about automobiles from his leisure activities, his level of meaninglessness is still high. The heterogeneity of backgrounds reduces the chances for the development of a cohesive occupational or residential community, which would reduce the feeling of isolation. The factories are large, contributing to a person's feeling "like a number." Further contributors to the feeling of isolation are the compressed wage and skill distributions in the plant and the fact that there is little chance for advancement. Self-estrangement is also present because of the monotony of the work and the lack of challenge on the job. Money becomes the principal work motivation. While the auto worker is perhaps the classical alienated man, it should again be noted that his type of work comprises only a small fraction of all industrial work.[57]

[56]*Ibid.*, pp. 58–88.
[57]*Ibid.*, pp. 89–123.

The final type of worker to be considered is the chemical operator who works in the continuous-process chemical refinery. Most of the work is skilled maintenance, involving mental and visual, rather than manual, skills. The worker is responsible for the smooth and continued flow of the product and usually must move about as part of the job. Blauner suggests that the management of chemical and other such continuous-flow production organizations is usually progressive, with few ties to traditional management practices. The chemical operator experiences little powerlessness because of his freedom of movement and control over the quality of production. He is able to set his own pace of work and, to some degree, the order in which some procedures are followed. Since the work is largely team work and the workers understand the contribution each makes to the total process, little meaninglessness is felt. Similarly, little isolation is experienced because of the closely knit work groups. The supervision is relatively loose, and there are enough status differentials to make the possibility of advancement a reality for most of the workers. The opportunity to experiment with new jobs and the level of involvement in the work lead to little self-estrangement.[58]

Blauner's conclusions are supported by a number of other studies. In a study of the mental health of the industrial worker, Arthur Kornhauser found the mental health of the worker directly related to the skill level of his job.[59] Kornhauser goes further than Blauner in attributing good mental health among workers to on-the-job situations. Blauner, it may be remembered, suggested that the background of the worker in the community, as in the case of the textile workers, was a key factor affecting the amount of alienation experienced. Although Blauner's and Kornhauser's central concerns are different, Kornhauser's evidence suggests that such factors are not really central. He states: "Differences in mental health are not accounted for by the amount of education or other prejob characteristics of the men in different job categories."[60]

An interesting side issue here is the degree to which previous experiences predispose a person to experience job satisfactions or dissatisfactions. Blauner, Presthus, and others take the position that background characteristics are quite important, while Kornhauser's evidence indicates that they are less important than the job situation itself. While there is an unfortunate lack of correspondence in the kinds of data the various authors have used, the evidence seems to suggest that the background and personality factors interact with the work situation to yield reactions to the work. The relative weight of background, personality, and situa-

[58]Ibid., pp. 124–42.
[59]Mental Health of the Industrial Worker (New York: John Wiley & Sons, 1965).
[60]Ibid., p. 261.

tional factors in bringing about particular responses is an issue that is not yet resolved. Kornhauser himself, however, while generally discounting the importance of the background and personality variables, notes:

> Generally advantageous or disadvantageous social and economic influences in childhood exert effects on personal development and self-feelings that carry over directly as determinants of subsequent mental health. Later conditions of work and life provide gratifications and impose frustrations in relation to established wants and expectations in a manner that fosters or impairs self-esteem and overall mental health. Disparity between aspiration and achievement, with resultant sense of failure, is one important aspect of this total process.[61]

What Kornhauser appears to be saying is that background and personality factors are important but that they only make a difference in the context of the actual work situation and that particular types of work situations are more likely to lead to good mental health or to feelings of alienation. Given a particular work situation, in other words, healthy or alienative responses will probably ensue, regardless of the particulars of a person's background. This position is strengthened by Arthur G. Neal and Salomon Rettig's findings in regard to alienation among manual and nonmanual workers.[62] They find little relationship between the mobility values (the expressed amount of desire to advance in the stratification system) of their subjects and the subjects' feelings of alienation. They suggest that the opportunity structure, career history, and place of a person in an organization are the key factors leading to differing degrees of alienation. Along the same lines, Leo Meltzer and James Salter suggest that job satisfaction is related to freedom on the job, lack of close supervision, opportunity to use one's own abilities, etc.[63] Both of these studies reinforce the idea that background and personality factors interact with the work situation to yield the varying levels of satisfaction or alienation. The crucial variable is the work situation, in the sense that the personal factors would not matter at all unless they were placed in a work situation, and because the research evidence indicates that similar work situations yield similar responses.

Before examining an approach to occupational stresses and tensions among executives, an additional point about alienation should be made. Although the concept has most often been applied to the blue-collar worker, it is evident that alienation can be experienced at all levels of

---

[61] *Ibid.*, pp. 154–55.

[62] "Dimensions of Alienation Among Manual and Non-manual Workers," *American Sociological Review*, XXVIII (August 1963), 599–608.

[63] "Organizational Size and Performance and Job Satisfaction," *American Sociological Review*, XXVII (August 1962), 351–62.

the occupational structure. Michael Aiken and Jerald Hage, for example, found that relatively high levels of alienation are present among a professional group (social workers) when the organizational environment in which they work is characterized by high degrees of centralization and formalization.[64] High centralization and formalization lead to a lack of participation in decision making and an absence of discretionary power on the part of the persons involved, who are confronted with a situation in which their expectations are not met, causing a high level of alienation. Approaching the problem from a different perspective, one might expect that job satisfaction for social workers would be higher in those agencies where centralization and formalization are low. This assumes, of course, that the desire for autonomy and decision-making power is relatively high throughout the various agencies.

EXECUTIVES AND WHITE-COLLAR WORKERS

That executives and other white-collar workers are not immune to tensions and conflict in their occupations is evident from the works of Presthus and Saunders, which were mentioned earlier. A systematic overview of both the types and sources of conflict for white-collar workers is provided by Robert Kahn et al. in their analysis of the stresses confronting the personnel employed in large organizations.[65] A basic assumption in this study is that many persons are continually engaged in a quest for identity, which is congruent with the earlier discussion of work motivations in that identity can be achieved through achievement of status, the production of goods or services, or rewards from social interaction. The authors of this study contend that, while the quest for identity may be central for many persons, the organization confronts a person with conditions of ambiguity and conflict rather than clarity and harmony. This is not meant as an attack on the large organization but rather as a statement of the facts of modern organizational life as they perceive them.[66]

The basic model in this analysis is that of the role set, following the lead developed by Robert K. Merton.[67] This model begins with the idea that a person (the focal person) has his own perceptions of his role. At

[64]"Organizational Alienation: A Comparative Analysis," *American Sociological Review*, XXXI (August 1966), 497–507.

[65]Robert Kahn et al., *Organizational Stress* (New York: John Wiley & Sons, Inc., 1964).

[66]*Ibid.*, pp. 4–6.

[67]*Social Theory and Social Structures*, 2nd ed. (New York: Free Press of Glencoe, 1957), pp. 368–80.

the same time, the members of his role set also have expectations regarding his behavior. The role set is composed of those persons with whom he systematically interacts: his superiors, peers and, in many cases, his subordinates. Their role expectations take the form of sent roles that are transferred to the focal person in the form of role pressures, which can be legitimate or illegitimate and which can vary in strength, direction, specificity, and in the range of conditions under which they are applicable. A person's behavior is thus based on the interaction of his role perceptions and the pressures from the members of his role set.

When role pressures and person's own role perceptions coincide, ambiguity and conflict will not be present. As might be expected, this coincidence occurs only in the minority of occupational situations. Kahn *et al.* state that a national survey shows that only one-sixth of the labor force reported being free from tension on the job,[68] and some thirty-five percent of the labor force experienced real ambiguity in their roles.[69] This conflict and tension result in tensions on the part of the organizational members and in less effective work on their part, thus affecting the organizational output. While not all conflict has negative consequences, in this case the conflict and ambiguity are rather clearly detrimental to the organization and the individuals involved.

A series of factors contributes to the conflict and ambiguity experienced. In the first place, many organizations contain built-in conflict. Subsystems or departments may be engaged in activities that are incompatible unless the coordination of the total organization approaches perfection. For example, personnel, production, purchasing, sales, and research and development departments often are in conflict because of the nature of their activities. The personnel and production departments often work most effectively by maintaining equilibrium, while sales, purchasing, and research and development departments often are sources of change for the organization.[70] Another such source of built-in conflict exists in those situations where subsystems of the organization are engaged in essentially the same functions and utilize essentially the same facilities. The various automotive divisions of some of the major manufacturers are an example of this, as are the various departments within a university. Conflict arises over the allocation of scarce resources within the organization. This conflict can be viewed as conflict between subsystems, but also as conflict that affects the individuals within those subsystems.[71] The reward system established by the organization can

---

[68]*Organizational Stress,* p. 55.
[69]*Ibid.,* p. 74.
[70]*Ibid.,* p. 99.
[71]*Ibid.,* p. 100.

serve as an additional source of built-in conflict. When the status system is rather rigidly defined, groups or individuals with entrenched positions are in conflict with those who believe the system should be altered to enhance their own positions. Whether or not the entrenched status system is rational or the demands of those who wish to alter it are legitimate is actually irrelevant, since the conflict will exist in any case.[72] These built-in conflicts affect the individuals in that part of their role expectations, from others and usually from themselves, is to support the subsystem of which they are a part.

In addition to these types of conflicts, the organization itself contributes to conflict and ambiguity on the part of individuals through the job descriptions (role expectations) that are formally or informally developed from particular positions. One type of position within the organization that is particularly susceptible to such conflict is the "boundary position," which entails contacts with persons or groups outside or in other parts of the organization. According to Kahn *et al.*, the holders of such positions are prone to experience chronic conflict because of the differing role pressures on them from the multiple sources of pressure with which they must deal.[73] Those in innovative roles in the organization, such as in research and development departments, many engineering departments, and in situations such as converting hand operations into computer-based operations, face conflicts between themselves, the new guard, and the old guard, who have vested interests in the maintenance of the *status quo*. Similarly, those whose roles demand creativity often are in conflict with those whose role expectations are to maintain routine procedures.[74]

An additional organizational basis of stress is the status of the people in the organization. As noted earlier, those of higher status are likely to experience greater job satisfaction and greater tension. Higher status roles usually involve both boundary relationships and demands for innovativeness. In addition, the organizational demands on such individuals are greater in terms of the quantity of expectations. Those in middle management may also face tensions engendered by their own mobility aspirations. The same factors that contribute to job satisfaction and that are a part of the original motivation to work thus contribute to these occupationally related tensions and conflicts.[75]

In addition to these organizationally based situations, the nature of the interpersonal relationships on the job can also contribute to stress

[72]*Ibid.*, p. 100.
[73]*Ibid.*, pp. 102–24.
[74]*Ibid.*, pp. 125–36.
[75]*Ibid.*, pp. 137-49.

situations. Members of the focal person's role set exert direct pressures on him to conform to their expectations. The closer the relationships, the greater the pressures become. The very facts of organizational life, the presence of superiors, peers, and subordinates, suggests that incompatible expectations from these people are almost built into the situation.[76]

Similarly, the focal person's own personality can contribute to conflicts, tensions, and ambiguities. Kahn *et al.*, for example, suggest that the introverted individual may experience tensions because his tendency to withdraw from interpersonal relations leads to antagonisms on the part of members of his role set. In addition, many organizations appear to expect some degree of extroversion among their employees. In terms of flexibility and rigidity, the authors found that the flexible person is subject to more tensions because he tends to reach out for more role expectations as he attempts to expand his own range of activities. He can thus experience what could be termed "role overload." Similarly, the person who is highly motivated to increase his expertise or his status is liable to face high levels of conflict and tension as these needs are not constantly met. The more security-minded individuals will experience less such tension, in that they will tend to withdraw from the competition and be satisfied with somewhat blunted role relationships.[77]

SUMMARY AND CONCLUSIONS

The focus in this chapter has been on the individual. We began by examining some of the alternative explanations of why people work, concluding that the individual carries a set of expectations about work and about specific jobs into the work setting. These expectations are *learned*, whether they involve money or more social factors. It is these expectations as they interact with the realities of specific occupational conditions that give rise to the patterns of satisfaction and dissatisfaction that have been discussed.

While the focus has been on the individual, two other elements have been of critical importance in the discussion. The *organizational setting* and the *technology* employed are the fundamental elements that confront the individual. People work in organizations and work with the technology that is presented to them or that they themselves have a hand in deciding upon. The combination of individual characteristics (including here the variables of experience, training, age, sex, minority group status, and so on) and organizational and technological factors con-

[76]*Ibid.*, pp. 185–222.
[77]*Ibid.*, pp. 225–333.

fronted gives rise to the particular set of expectations and the resultant patterns of satisfactions and/or dissatisfactions.

At this point we leave the specific focus on the individual and consider the occupational structure itself. In the discussion that follows, the individual will again be considered, but not as the central concern.

part **II**

Types of
Occupations

A person's occupation is the role that links him to the employing organization or that, increasingly rarely, gives him independent status. The occupation is also a major linkage for the individual to the total society. From the previous discussion it is obvious that there are differences among occupations. Our problem here is how to conceptualize these differences. There is no generally accepted typology of occupations. Indeed, the various approaches to the study of occupations are in no way unified. One of the earliest students of occupations, Karl Marx, for example, utilized the occupation's relationship to the means of production as the major classificatory basis. In large part, we will agree here. The important addition that we wish to make to the Marxian notion is that the occupation is the link for the individual to the total social structure. It is thus the nature of these broader linkages that are important here.

Everett C. Hughes and his students have provided an alternative method of viewing occupations in terms of similar elements and processes. Thus Hughes and his students have examined such elements as the "dirty work" that every worker must perform and, similarly, the notions of a "fair day's work" in all occupations.[1] Unfortunately, the elements

[1] This point is developed more fully in Julius A. Roth, Sheryl K. Ruzek, and Arlene K. Daniels, "Current State of the Sociology of Occupations," *The Sociological Quarterly* 14 (summer 1973), 311.

studied and the processes examined are not sufficient to permit a broad theory of occupations or an adequate typology. While very insightful in terms of analyses of specific occupations, the approach has so great a number of "missing links" that no comprehensive conclusions can be reached.

Another approach to this issue has been implicitly suggested by Chris Argyris, who urges that organizational analysts use a "model of man" in their studies.[2] Argyris suggests several dimensions along which people vary, suggesting that these are crucial in understanding behavior in organizations. While this is an important point, it ignores the equally important point that the organization sets the limits on most of the behaviors within it.

This negative approach to possible ways of viewing occupations can perhaps be turned in a more positive direction by noting that in order to understand occupations, one must include the types or models of the men and women who are in the occupations, also understand the characteristic stresses, tensions, and satisfactions that they derive from their occupations, be aware of the differing processes of socialization that they undergo, and be able to capture the relationships between the occupations and the employing organizations and the total social structure.

Obviously, there is not enough information about all occupations to permit total knowledge in all of these areas. The most fruitful approach seems to be to cluster occupations into types that seem to have some homogeneity, especially in terms of the place of the occupation in the social structure and the relation of the occupational type to organizational work. With this in mind, we will use a classification scheme that is a modified version of the one that has been used by the U.S. Bureau of the Census. The categories are:

1. Professionals
2. Managers, proprietors, and officials
3. Clerks and kindred workers
4. Skilled workers and foremen
5. Semiskilled workers
6. Unskilled workers (including farm and nonfarm workers)

[2]"Personality and Organization Theory Revisited," *Administrative Science Quarterly* 18 (June 1973), 141–67.

4

THE PROFESSIONS

Doctor, lawyer, nurse, teacher, policeman, and professor—all of these occupations, plus a myriad of others, have at least one thing in common. All are concerned with various aspects and phases of professionalism. In this chapter, we are going to examine the nature of the professions, concentrating on the characteristics of professionals. These characteristics will be related to the nature of the people who are in various professions, the work settings of professionals, and the impact of professionals on their clients and the wider society.

Profession is probably the most widely used and commonly known occupational category and refers to the occupational class most readily identified by the public at large as a type of occupation. From the sociologist's perspective, profession and many similar "types" are misused at times. For example, the fact that an athlete is no longer an amateur, in the sense that his payments are larger and more open, does not make him a professional in the limited sense the term implies here. The "world's oldest profession," prostitution, similarly would not qualify from the perspective of the sociologist. At the outset, then, it should be clear that an occupation is not a profession simply because its members are being paid. The concept of profession has come to have a rather specific meaning, which allows determination of the degree to which a specific occupation can be considered a profession.

Before proceeding with the discussion of the exact nature of professions, the reasons for the prominence of this occupational type should be explored. An obvious point is that many professions have high status; doctors and lawyers have high visibility and images that are consistently developed and reinforced through literature and the mass media. They are also very close to being true professionals from the technical standpoint. A second point is that the growing number of persons in the professional category and the growing number of occupations that have become, or are attempting to become, professions are increasing occupational specialization. A member of an occupation that becomes specialized as he carries on his work will increasingly identify with and share the values and behaviors of his fellow specialists. An occupational community will develop, fostering solidarity among its members and excluding those who are not part of it.[1] Concomitant with specialization is the greater amount of training needed to become a specialist; persons undergoing training in a particular area tend to experience increased solidarity with those with a similar experience. And as more knowledge becomes available in most areas of human endeavor, more extensive and intensive training is needed for even minimal competence. Those who undergo this training become experts and, at least in one sense, professionals.

In addition to this rather general social change, some occupationally generated factors, both selfish and altruistic, contribute to the growth of the professions. On the selfish side, the motive of groups to improve their status within the occupational structure is served by their becoming regarded as professions, since the label has an honorific connotation. At the same time, the occupation's economic position can often be strengthened by the bargaining position of a united group of practitioners. A profession also can often exclude persons who are deemed unqualified, which allows control over the labor market, thus again enhancing the group's position. On the altruistic side, there is an evident desire on the part of many occupations to improve the services and performance levels of their members by the establishment of stricter entrance requirements, ethical codes, and certification statutes. The exact degree to which either selfish or altruistic factors operate in specific cases is subject to empirical determination, but in a real sense, it does not matter which type of motivation is dominant in the drive toward professionalization, for both selfish and altruistic motives yield occupationally beneficial consequences.

Aside from the visibility of professionals and the interest on the part of professionals or would-be professionals for the maintenance or acquisition of particular professional characteristics, there is an overriding social reason for the importance of the professionals. *Professionals have*

[1]See William J. Goode, "Community Within a Community: The Professions," *American Sociological Review*, XXII, 2 (April 1957), 194–200 for a discussion of the community-like aspect of the professions.

power. This power can be seen in control over clients. It can also be seen in the role of professionals in the decision-making processes of government and business. It can further, and perhaps most importantly, be seen in terms of the direction that the total social structure is taking. If the previous discussion of the postindustrial society is recalled, with its emphasis on knowledge and services, then the role of professionals stands out in clear relief. Professionals are the ones who deal with this knowledge, developing and interpreting it, and making it available for common use. The professionals also are at the center of the delivery of many services, particularly those in the area of social and intellectual concerns.

Eliot Freidson has noted that professionals are at the very center of the "knowledge industry."[2] If it is true that this industry is at the very core of modern nations, then the power of the professions becomes increasingly, and perhaps frighteningly, clear. In our analysis we will be concerned with some of the consequences of this growth of professional power.

There is still another way in which professionals have power and are thus important to the total society. Freidson has noted that the professions have led to a dramatic change in the manner in which work is organized.[3] Instead of organizing work on an "administrative" or bureaucratic principle, Freidson suggests that the "occupational" principle has now come to be a major alternative. Simply put, this means that traditional principles of hierarchy in organizations may be obsolete and that the total work environment may change to reflect a different means of controlling work. The professionals in organizations are able to determine what they do and how they will do it. The contents of the work are thus in the hands of the professionals, rather than the organization. Evidence will be presented later in this chapter that suggests that professionalized organizations are indeed different from those that have few or no professionals.

While there may be disagreement over the extent to which the professionals will "rule the world," there is probably little in the way of disagreement that the professionals are a distinct and important professional type. It is time now to examine the characteristics of the professions. The best place to begin is with a consideration of the attributes of the *professional model.* There have been strong criticisms of the use of this type of model in recent years.[4] These criticisms are basically correct in that probably no profession and certainly no individual professionals

---

[2]"Professions and the Occupational Principle," in Eliot Freidson, ed., *Professions and their Prospects* (Beverly Hills, Calif.: Sage Publications, 1974).

[3]*Ibid.*

[4]For a discussion of many of these criticisms, see Roth, Ruzek, and Daniels, "Sociology of Occupations."

behave in exact accordance with all of the attributes to be discussed.[5] At the same time, this professional model can serve as an "ideal type" that permits comparisons between the ideal and reality and among professions in general. After discussing this model, some of the negative consequences of some of the characteristics will be considered. Our first task, however, is to understand the nature of the professions.

THE PROFESSIONAL MODEL

The components of the model have been approached somewhat differently by different authors, but there is a strong thread of common ideas throughout. A. M. Carr-Saunders and P. A. Wilson suggest that the major criterion for professional status is the presence of an intellectual technique, acquired by special training, that performs a service for society and is unavailable to the laity.[6] In their analysis of the historical development of the professions, Carr-Saunders and Wilson note that licensing, by the profession itself or by the state with the profession establishing the criteria, follows the development of this intellectual technique. This allows the profession to determine if potential members have in fact acquired the specified training and intellectual techniques. The term intellectual techniques raises an important question, since technique suggests an application of knowledge, while intellectual connotes a more theoretically oriented approach. Talcott Parsons recognizes the apparent incompatibility of these two terms when he points out that professions such as medicine are primarily applied, while scientific disciplines, such as sociology or biochemistry, are primarily dedicated to the advancement and transmission of empirical knowledge, with only a secondary emphasis on its utilization.[7]

Parson's definition of a profession makes this point explicit:

> I conceive a profession to be a category of occupational role which is organized about the mastery of and fiduciary responsibility for any important segment of a society's cultural tradition, including responsibility for its perpetuation *and* for its future development. In addition, a profession may have responsibility for the application of its knowledge in practical situations.[8]

[5]See George Ritzer, *Man and His Work: Conflict and Change* (New York: Appleton-Century-Crofts, 1972).

[6]"Professions," *Encyclopedia of the Social Sciences* (New York: Macmillan Company, 1944), XXII, 476–80.

[7]"Some Problems Confronting Sociology as a Profession," *American Sociological Review*, XXIV, 4 (August 1959), 547.

[8]*Ibid.*

The stress on intellectual techniques and important segments of cultural tradition runs through every definition of the professions and can perhaps be restated by saying that professions are organized around bodies of knowledge. Whether this knowledge is gathered and transmitted in the form of a scientific discipline or is applied in the form of a service is not the central issue at this time. The issue of pure (scientific inquiry) versus applied knowledge can become important within particular professions but, for our purposes, an occupation involved in either or both can be considered a profession if it meets certain other criteria.

The characteristics discussed thus far are probably central to the nature of the professions, but they are also rather general; additional criteria or attributes of professionalism should be added to clarify further the nature of this occupational type. Ernest Greenwood has suggested five major professional attributes.[9] First, as might be expected from the previous discussion, is the presence of systematic theory. Greenwood also notes that this can be intellectual as well as practical, and adds that it is based on research.[10] This is, of course, congruent with Parsons's emphasis on the perpetuation and development of a profession's knowledge base. Greenwood's emphasis on research appears to overlook a minor, but interesting, point. While most professions in fact rely upon research as a contribution to the base of knowledge, two of the most easily identified professions, the law and ministry, apparently do not. Their knowledge base depends on lore rather than on science. Various sources of knowledge are available for the development of the systematic theory that underlies a profession. While most professions do rely on research, other approaches are feasible.

A second professional attribute, according to Greenwood, is professional authority.[11] The professional can dictate what is good or bad for his client, who gives him this authority in the belief that the professional's knowledge will enable him to make the correct judgment in matters affecting the client's life. Professional-client relationships will require more extended discussion at a later point, but at present they can be taken as a regular professional attribute.

Greenwood's third attribute is formal and informal community sanction of the profession, its powers and privileges.[12] Formal approval can be seen in the manner in which the profession itself is given the power to determine the appropriate character and curriculum of the training process. While state accreditation and licensing procedures may follow

[9]"Attributes of a Profession," *Social Work*, II, 3 (July 1957), 45–55.
[10]*Ibid.*, pp. 46–47.
[11]*Ibid.*, pp. 47–48.
[12]*Ibid.*, pp. 48–49.

the training period, the standards are set by the profession itself, since the state or its functionaries do not have the knowledge to set standards. Another aspect of the sanctions given to professions is in the area of professional confidence; the information given to a professional by his client is privileged communication, thus protecting the rights of the client but also reaffirming the authority of the professional.

Another attribute is a regulative code of ethics in the form of codified statements of the appropriate behavior of the professional toward his clients and toward fellow professionals.[13] These ethical codes are both formally and informally enforced, through censure, removal from the professional association, or ostracism from interaction systems. There is some indication that increased specialization within professions leads to difficulties in the enforcement of ethical codes and that these codes are violated in practice. It is clear, however, that occupations that are aspiring to be known as professions usually develop ethical codes as part of what they envision as the process of professionalization.

Greenwood's final attribute is a professional culture, which involves norms governing membership in professional associations, organizations that are qualified to provide training, and appropriate sites for professional practice.[14] In addition, the professional culture contains the language and symbols of the profession. A professional culture is a means of differentiating between professionals and outsiders, since only insiders are privy to the meanings of the symbolic system of the profession. It could be hypothesized that the greater the development of the professional culture, the greater the social distance between the profession and the laity.

Greenwood's set of attributes is largely concerned with the way an occupation is linked to the social structure. If an occupation has these characteristics, according to this type of formulation it can be considered a profession. A profession's knowledge base is part of the wider society, its ethical codes are utilized by the wider society as the means of controlling professional behavior, and its power and authority are granted to it by the community. However, in a sense, whether or not an occupation is a profession depends on the way in which it is viewed by society. The occupation may have all the other attributes thus far discussed, but if it is not given community sanction, it will not be considered, and cannot operate as, a profession.

Further insights into the nature of the professions are provided by Edward Gross.[15] While some of the characteristics to be treated below are similar to those already discussed, Gross adds another dimension to

[13]*Ibid.*, pp. 49–51.
[14]*Ibid.*, pp. 51–54.
[15]*Work and Society* (New York: Thomas Y. Crowell Co., 1958), pp. 77–82.

the professional characteristics. Some of the attributes, which he discusses, are clearly attitudinal. That is, the characteristics appear as the direction and strength of the orientations of the persons involved, rather than as structural characteristics that may be present or absent. For example, a central characteristic in this formulation is the degree of personality involvement.[16] The professional is characterized by a high level of involvement, which is transmitted to his clients in the form of their belief that he will consistently act in their best interests. The professional also has a well-developed sense of obligation to his art; he wants to do the best job he possibly can. Gross notes that the professional "is not supposed to be interested in sordid money."[17] While this supposition is probably unwarranted in practice, the point is that the professional is thought to be one who would work just for the intrinsic rewards of his occupation. Another attitudinal component is the closeness with which the professional identifies with his colleagues through formal and informal professional associations.[18] This close identification is a source of attitudes governing his own orientations as well as source of control over his behavior.

In addition to these attitudinal components, Gross notes some of the same general structural characteristics which have already been discussed. For example, the professional is viewed as working with an unstandardized product.[19] His knowledge is applied to solving particular problems, each of which, though unique, fits within his general body of theoretical knowledge. Related to this is the idea that the source of the professional's power is his knowledge. Since the client is usually ignorant in the field of the professional's competence, the professional has power over him through his advice and suggestions. In this sense, the idea of community sanctions, suggested by Greenwood, is given further support, since the wider community itself is similarly ignorant and must give the professional the right to make decisions in important areas of life.

A final characteristic, again related to those being discussed, is that the service provided by the professional is essential to the health and welfare of the individual and of society.[20] It is clearly very difficult to determine exactly why one service is more essential than another, but the implication here is that there is some societal consensus in this regard. Even if there were no consensus, the fact is that the laity does not have the prerequisite knowledge to replace the professional; thus the professional is able to attain and maintain his position by an essentially

[16]*Ibid.*, p. 78.
[17]*Ibid.*, p. 79.
[18]*Ibid.*, pp. 79–80.
[19]*Ibid.*, pp. 77–78.
[20]*Ibid.*, p. 80.

monopolistic control over the knowledge. Obviously, this knowledge must be considered important for individuals or society, or the monopoly would have no impact, since a monopoly of trivia would not be too marketable.

Another sociologist, William J. Goode, has suggested some additional characteristics of professions, which provide further insights into the nature of this occupational type. In addition to some of the points already noted, Goode suggests that the student of a profession undergoes a more far-reaching adult socialization process than the person learning other occupations.[21] By this, Goode indicates that professional training not only consumes more time in the formal school setting but also involves socialization into appropriate attitudes and behaviors. While Howard S. Becker and Blanche Geer suggest that the major impact on the medical student is from his peers, with the faculty having a lesser role in the formation of professional attitudes, the crucial point is that an attitudinal consensus is achieved.[22] Such a consensus is a hallmark of professionalism, regardless of its source.

Although the extensive socialization brings about common sets of knowledge and attitudes, it should not be assumed that graduates of professional training are a totally homogeneous group who march through life in a sort of conceptual lockstep. As will be demonstrated later, wide variations in performance and attitude exist within any profession. Nevertheless, professions appear to have more homogeneity than most other occupational types.

Goode also suggests that the profession is a powerful force in society and over the individual, in that most legislation concerning the profession is generated by the profession itself.[23] This relates to Gross's point about the ignorance of the general public, including legislators, of the work of the professional, so that legislative efforts must be turned over to the profession in the absence of alternative sources of knowledge. Goode also suggests that the norms developed by professional groups to govern their conduct are more stringent than those with a legal basis.[24] Thus, the real source of control over an individual professional lies in the hands of the profession, with society's (legal) control being weaker. This mechanism allows the profession to maintain its autonomy.

A final point made by Goode is that a profession is typically the terminal occupation for members.[25] The trained professional does not

---

[21]"Encroachment, Charlatanism, and the Emerging Profession: Psychology, Sociology, and Medicine," *American Sociological Review*, XXV, 6 (December 1960), 903.

[22]Howard S. Becker and Blanche Geer, "The Fate of Idealism in Medical School," *American Sociological Review*, XXIII, 1 (February 1958), 50–56.

[23]"Encroachment, Charlatanism, and the Emerging Profession," p. 903.

[24]*Ibid.*

[25]*Ibid.*

leave the profession, in contrast to many occupations in which a change in jobs is quite normal. The professional has both a financial and temporal investment in the occupation. Additionally, the long socialization has made him, in many ways, incapable of changing occupations, since both his skills and his attitudes are relatively fixed.

Thus far the discussion has been concerned with the development of a set of attributes characterizing professions. Before proceeding further, it would be useful to introduce certain distinctions among the terms that are being used. In their book, *Professionalization*, Howard Vollmer and Donald Mills note:

> In our discussion of the readings, for example, we avoid the use of the term "profession," except as an "ideal type" of occupational organization which does not exist in reality, but which provides the model of the form of occupational organization that would result if any occupational group became completely professionalized. In this way, we wish to avoid discussion of whether or not any particular group is "really a profession," or not. In accord with Hughes' experience, we feel that it is much more fruitful to ask "how professionalized," or more specifically "how professionalized in certain identifiable respects" a given occupation may be at some point in time.
>
> We suggest, therefore, that the concept of "profession" be applied only to an abstract model of occupational organization, and that the concept of "professionalization" be used to refer to the dynamic *process* whereby many occupations can be observed to change certain crucial characteristics in the direction of a "profession," even though some of these may not move very far in this direction. It follows that these crucial characteristics constitute specifiable criteria of professionalizaton.[26]

The authors further specify that the term professionalism should be used to refer to the ideology found in many occupational groups in the process of professionalization. Although professionalism may not lead an occupation very far down from the professionalization in every instance, it is an integral part of the process. Further distinctions are that professional groups are those associations of colleagues found in occupational contexts in which a high degree of professionalization has occurred. The noun professional refers to those who "are considered by their colleagues to be members of professional groups."[27] These distinctions should add clarity to the discussions that follow and also suggest, as Vollmer and Mills intended, that professionalization is a dynamic process, linked to the wider social structure and to the occupational groups themselves.

We have now covered most of the attributes that are contained in

[26]*Professionalization* (Englewood Cliffs, N.J.: Prentice-Hall, Inc., 1966), pp. vii-viii.
[27]*Ibid.*, p. 8.

the professional model.[28] No occupation is totally professionalized, and no individual in a profession acts totally professionally. In the next section, we will examine some of the negative aspects of the attributes that we have been discussing. We will then turn to the nature and sources of variations within and between professions.

THE NEGATIVE SIDE OF THE PROFESSIONAL MODEL

The discussion thus far has portrayed professionals as altruistic, dedicated, highly trained, and performing critical services for humanity. This is only partially true. We have presented the professional model as an ideal type. The expectation is thus that no profession or professional would really have all of the characteristics described to the highest degree. Later we will discuss sources of variation in the performance of professions and professionals, but we now turn to a critical analysis of the model itself.

Julius A. Roth has provided some important insights into the negative side of the professional model.[29] Roth's discussion is based primarily on the attributes suggested by Greenwood. The first attribute discussed is the body of systematic theory. Roth notes that some professions have created a body of theory in order to justify their own existence: "For example, social work has fought to lengthen its university program to prove that a masters degree is necessary to produce qualified practitioners, yet the relationship of this training to social work practice has never been demonstrated."[30] The extent to which a given profession has this theoretical basis may be due more to the politics of higher learning and what is recognized as theoretical than any concrete demonstration of theoretical impartance. In addition, while all professions engage in periodic professional meetings with the avowed purpose being to keep

[28]This discussion has by no means covered all of the literature dealing with professional attributes. Other important works that can be consulted include: Wilbert E. Moore, *The Professions, Roles and Rules* (New York: Russell Sage Foundation, 1970); Bernard Barber, "Some Problems in the Sociology of the Professions," *Daedalus,* 92 (fall 1963) 669–88; J. A. Jackson, ed., *Professions and Professionalization* (London, Cambridge University Press, 1970); and Philip Elliott, *The Sociology of the Professions* (New York: Herder and Herder, 1972). Elliott's work does an excellent job of linking the professions to the total society, noting historical patterns in the emergence of particular professions. Professions apparently emerge within the dynamics of a changing society, such as the emergence of the practice of law when the separation of church and state occurred.

[29]"Professionalism: The Sociologist's Decoy," *Sociology of Work and Occupations* 1 (February 1974), 6–23.

[30]*Ibid.,* p. 7

the members abreast of new theoretical development, most of the activity
of professional meetings is actually social or related to changing individual's employment in the job market.

Another aspect of the issue of theoretical knowledge is that the
knowledge base itself is not totally consistent. Every professional field
has deep and sometimes bitter disputes regarding the appropriate theoretical perspective. Medicine, for example, today uses the "germ theory"
of disease, but this has not always been so. The recent introduction of
and controversy surrounding acupuncture is indicative of the absence
of theoretical closure in medicine.

Another aspect of the knowledge base of the profession involves the
question "whose knowledge?" Stewart, Manasse, and Hall have noted that
pharmacy students are confronted with different knowledge paradigms
from the faculty, peers, and practitioners within the schools of pharmacy
themselves.[31]

The second attribute discussed by Roth is professional authority.
The fact that many clients are free to ignore professional advice and that
many professionals can be fired by their clients (architects, lawyers, engineers) reduces the absoluteness implied in the notion of professional
authority. In addition, many semiprofessionals or aspiring professionals
are continually under question regarding the extent of professional authority. School teachers, for example, are rather frequently under attack
for their professional selection of books that are viewed as undesirable
by some members of the community.

The third attribute is community sanction or the power that professions are given over their own affairs by the community. Roth notes
that the real question is not whether or not there is such a sanctioning,
but the conditions under which such sanction is gained. Clearly, professions vary widely in the extent to which they, the clients, employing
organizations, competitors, or governmental regulatory agencies control
professional behavior. The gaining of such control is a political matter.

The fourth attribute involves the code of ethics. In discussing this,
Roth concludes:

> The evidence we do have about realtors, lawyers, psychologists, insurance
> agents, physicians, and other occupational groups with codes of ethics
> shows overwhelmingly that, although these codes sometimes serve to curb
> competition among colleagues, they have almost no protective value for
> the clientele or the public. Indeed, the existence of such codes is used as
> a device to turn aside public criticism and interference.[32]

[31]Jesse Stewart, Henri Manasse, and Richard Hall, "Inconsistent Socialization in
Pharmacy: A Pattern in Need of Change," *APHA Journal* (Forthcoming).
   [32]"Professionalism," p. 10.

Roth further notes that while professional codes of ethics demand equal service to all,

> there (is) a mass of evidence already publicly available on the bias of professional workers and their service organizations against deviant youth, the aged, women, the poor, ethnic minorities, and people they just didn't like the looks of.[33]

As we will see later, enforcing codes of ethics is highly problematic even when the desire to do so is there.

Roth's final point is that while professions do generally have an occupational culture, so does every other occupation. Even though the professions' cultures are very well developed and often distinct, so are those of occupational groups such as circus performers, professional athletes, dock workers, seamen, and so on. This attribute thus does not really distinguish a profession from other occupational groups.

Roth concludes that listing professional attributes and determining whether or not a particular occupation is professionalized in the sense of a "scorecard of professionalization" is fruitless. The author agrees. How then, can we use the professional model? First of all, even though the attribute approach has its pitfalls, when taken as a totality, the elements of the professions do provide a distinction between professions and nonprofessions. They also provide the imagery that occupations aspiring to professionalism observe in their political attempts to gain recognition. The professional model is thus a basis of operations for occupations. It is also an imprecisely used set of criteria that the public utilizes in its view of the professions. This is the second major usage of the professional model. Implicit or explicity, public acceptance of an occupation as a profession is critical. While the public does not rate each occupation on each element of the professional model, there does appear to be an imagery of occupations in the public's mind. Our later discussion of occupational prestige will deal with this issue in depth, but here it is sufficient to note that the very term "professional" is widely used in discussions of occupations. Thus Haug and Sussman are correct in noting that *public acceptance* is crucial in determining whether or not an occupation can be called a profession.[34]

The professional model is thus used casually in the actual determination of whether or not an occupation is a profession. Occupations attempt to adopt the elements of the model, and the public employs the model in its assessment. The model cannot be thought of as a precise list of all-or-nothing attributes. It does, however, serve to set off the

[33]*Ibid.*, pp. 10–11.
[34]Marie Haug and Marvin Sussman, "Professionalism and the Public," *Sociological Inquiry* 39 (1969), 57–67.

professions from other occupations. Thus our approach to the professions is like that of Freidson, who suggests that this type of occupation is "a special status in the division of labor supported by official and sometimes public belief that it is worthy of such status. . . ."[35]

If there is agreement about the general dimensions of the professional model and how and why the model is applied to various occupations, the issue still remains in regard to the sources of differentiation and variation in professional practice, and it is to this issue that we will presently turn. Before doing so, however, the exact nature of the variations and differentiations to be discussed must be specified. In a study of 11 different occupations at various levels of professionalism (according to the professional model), Hall found that the occupations varied in their degree of professionalization. There is thus *inter*professional variation. There is also *intra*professional variation in terms of the way individuals and groups of practitioners operate.[36] We now turn to these sources of variation.

SOURCES OF INTRA- AND INTERPROFESSIONAL VARIATION

In this section we will examine some of the sources of variations in behavior within and between occupations at varying levels of professionalization. The first point to be discussed is the variety of settings in which professionals work. We will then examine how the development of knowledge affects professionals. Women as a source of differentiation among professions will then be examined, and their place within the professions will be noted. The role of peers and then the role of clients will be considered as they affect the professionals' behavior. Finally, we will look at some recent developments that have begun to affect the traditional role and life of the professional—the paraprofessional, the altered role of government, and unionization.

THE SETTINGS OF PROFESSIONAL WORK

The work of the occupations we are considering is carried out in three basic settings. The first is that of the individual practitioner. This

[35]Eliot Freidson, *Profession of Medicine* (New York: Dodd, Mead, and Co., 1972), p. 187.

[36]See Rue Bucher and Anselm Strauss, "Professions in Process," *American Journal of Sociology*, LXVI, 4 (January 1961), 325–34, and Jack Ladinsky and Joel B. Grossman, "Organizational Consequences of Professional Consensus: Lawyers and Selection of Judges," *Administrative Science Quarterly*, XI, 1 (June 1965), 79–106, for a discussion of this type of variation. Ritzer, *Man and His Work*, also contains an extended discussion of this point.

setting often serves as the major model in discussions of the nature of professions. In this setting the professional is seen as a free, autonomous individual. The country doctor heeding the call of the sick or working in his laboratory, the individual lawyer searching for support for his client's position, or the architect developing original and controversial designs have been discussed and celebrated in fact and fiction. Although central to many conceptualizations of the nature of professional work, this type of setting is in actuality a disappearing phenomenon and, in addition, may contain elements dysfunctional for the professionals involved.

A second basic setting is the professional organization, such as the law firm, medical clinic, social work agency, or library. This type of setting is probably that of the majority of the occupational groups being considered. It should be divided into two subtypes, on the basis of W. Richard Scott's suggestion.[37] He notes that, on the one hand, there are autonomous professional organizations, in which the members of the profession determine the norms governing their behavior with administrative tasks, which are of course necessary for the operation of any organization, essentially separate from professional tasks. The architectural firm, law firm, or medical clinic are examples of this subtype. The second subtype, according to Scott, is the "heteronomous" professional organization, in which the professional employees are at least partially subordinated to an externally imposed administrative framework. Examples are public schools, libraries, and social work agencies. These externally imposed norms, which often have a legislative origin, serve as a set of general or specific guidelines within which the professionals must operate, thereby lessening the amount of professional autonomy. Obvious examples of reduction of autonomy are the legal stipulations of welfare eligibility or the statewide selection of textbooks for schools. In both cases, the individual professional or the professional group as a whole has greatly diminished authority to choose clients or work materials.

The third basic setting is the professional department within a larger organization, such as engineering, legal, or research and development departments. In this setting the professional and his department are merely a part of a larger organization. It is often assumed that this setting confronts the professional with many situations in which organizational and bureaucratic norms conflict with professional standards. Scott, for example, has suggested that there are four basic sources of professional-organizational conflict.[38] The professional desiring to utilize his own internalized normative system may resist bureaucratic rules because they

---

[37]"Reactions to Supervision in a Heteronomous Professional Organization," *Administrative Science Quarterly*, XX, 1 (June 1965), 65–81.

[38]W. Richard Scott, "Professionals in Bureaucracies—Areas of Conflict," in *Professionalization*, eds. Vollmer and Mills, pp. 265–75.

constrain the methods normally used to solve problems. A second source of conflict is the professional's resistance to bureaucratic standards. For example, a physician in an industrial setting may be asked by his employer to minimize time lost by getting workers back on the job as quickly as possible, but his professional standards demand a time-consuming complete diagnosis and treatment of each case. A third source of conflict is the professional's resistance to bureaucratic supervision. In this case the professional is asked to subordinate himself to a system in which his superiors are likely not to have expertise in his specialty. In reality, it would probably be impossible for a person in a position of authority over a group of professionals to have competence in all areas in which his subordinates are operating. As Scott suggests, when "professionals enter bureaucratic organizations conflicts in the area of authority relations are widespread if not ubiquitous."[39] These same kinds of conflicts could conceivably be present in the two types of professional organizations previously discussed.

The final source of conflict is the professional's conditional loyalty to the bureaucracy. If he uses his professional organization as a major reference, he is likely to view his employing organization simply as one of many potential employing organizations. If conditions arise that make his present situation undesirable, he will seek employment elsewhere, using his professional colleague group as a means of locating a new position. The employing organization is thus a means to an end. But Scott notes that although a number of studies have shown professionally oriented workers to have low loyalty to their employing organization, the organization itself often has a reward system based upon successive advances within the organization. Thus for the organization, advancement depends on the employee's not changing organizations. The "visible" professional, however, can advance within or without a particular organization.

While the existence of such professional-organizational conflict is indisputable, it is not clear whether professionals in the organizational setting experience more conflict than those in the other two kinds of settings. Furthermore, most of the analyses of the conflict appear to assume that the professionals are the "good guys" and that the organization blocks the "higher ideals" of professionalism, an assumption that would be most difficult to substantiate.

Regarding the relative potentials for conflict within the various types of settings, the author found that while the autonomous professional organizations, discussed above, tended to be less bureaucratic than the heteronomous professional organizations or the professional departments

[39]*Ibid.*, p. 274.

within large organizations, the reverse was sometimes true on particular bureaucratic dimensions and within particular organizations.[40] For example, some legal departments were less bureaucratic than some law firms, which suggests that the potential for conflict for lawyers is at least as great within some law firms as it is within some legal departments. In this study it was also found that professional departments tended to be less bureaucratic than the heteronomous professional organizations. It would thus appear that those professionals in larger organizations do not necessarily confront situations that contain inherently more conflict potential than their colleagues in other types of settings.

One further point on professional-organizational conflict is relevant. While the kinds of conflicts that Scott and others have described have some negative consequences for both the organization and the professionals involved, there is no clear evidence suggesting that the consequences are wholly negative. Lewis A. Coser, for example, has suggested that conflict per se may be positively functional by creating solidarity within the conflicting groups while the conflict persists and by opening communications channels during its resolution.[41] For these reasons, it will not be assumed in the discussions that follow that a professional person or group experiences more conflict or more gratification in any one type of setting. With this in mind, we will examine the settings more intensively.

THE INDIVIDUAL PRACTITIONER

While the individual, "free" professional appears to be the ideal type and has served at times as a sort of cultural hero, relatively little is actually known about his type of professional work. At best, perhaps, much of the data available is in the form of impressions about the individual practitioner, with only a few empirical studies to serve as points of departure. The general conclusion that will be drawn in this analysis is that this type of professional may in fact not be as professionalized as his counterparts in other settings; an even broader conclusion, which will be reached at the conclusion of the analysis of the work of professionals in the various settings, is that the professional model is not fully realized in practice by any of the groups involved.

Most of the occupations involved in individual practice fall in Wilensky's "established" category. The architect, lawyer, dentist, or physician

---

[40]Richard H. Hall, "Professionalization and Bureaucratization," *American Sociological Review*, XXXIII, 1 (February 1968), 92–104.

[41]*The Functions of Social Conflict* (New York: Free Press of Glencoe, 1956), pp. 72–148.

in practice by himself is a clear example of this. At the same time, some of the occupations in the "process" category, such as optometrists, pharmacists, or veterinarians, can and do operate on an individual basis, although there is a strong tendency for pharmacists to work under the auspices of large, multipurpose drug-store chains. Relatively few of the "new" or "doubtful" occupations are found in individual practice. Some funeral directors operate their own establishments, but the trend toward larger organizations is evident here. Marriage counseling, where it is carried out as a separate occupation, is often done on an individual basis. Other professionalizing occupations also appear at times in the individual-practice setting, but the previously noted trend toward organizational work appears to be a major factor operating against individual practice. The place of scientists of various kinds along the professionalization continuum is still somewhat unclear, but if scientists are considered professionals to any degree, they are almost totally employed by industry, government, or academic institutions. The lone scientist working in (and blowing up) his basement is a product of literary imagination.

If the ranks of individual practitioners are thinning in comparison to those of professionals in other settings, the question remains, what are the unique characteristics of the solo practitioner? Does he vary in terms of his background? Are there any special characteristics about the kinds of work he does? Where does he fit into the overall professional structure?

Among the various occupations found in this setting, lawyers have been the most intensively examined. In *Lawyers on Their Own*, Jerome Carlin analyzed a sample of individual practitioners in Chicago.[42] Carlin points out that over half of all lawyers are in individual practice, regardless of the size of the community in which they practice. Since the majority of lawyers are found in cities with populations in excess of 200,000, this study can be taken as at least partially representative of the majority of individual practitioners, although the Chicago situation may be somewhat unique. Later studies in Detroit and New York, to be noted below, seem to confirm the Carlin findings regarding the characteristics of the urban individual practitioner.

The most striking finding in the Carlin study is that the individual practitioner is separated, both in terms of the kinds of legal work performed and in terms of social status, from the rest of the legal profession. Part of the reason for this is the background of lawyers in individual practice. They tend to be self-made men, who have risen the hard way from lower- or working-class backgrounds and immigrant parents.[43] Their

---

[42]*Lawyers on Their Own* (New Brunswick, N.J.: Rutgers University Press, 1962).
[43]*Ibid.*, p. 3.

rise is into the ranks of a profession, even though their status within the profession is quite low. The majority of this group did not attend full-time law schools but received their legal training in Catholic night law schools or proprietary law schools, which have no university affiliations and are sometimes operated for profit.[44] At the time these lawyers attended them, the part-time schools were clearly inferior to the full-time, university-affiliated law schools; entrance often demanded little more than a high-school diploma, and a much smaller percentage of the graduates passed the bar exam. Nevertheless, the lawyers who made it through such schools and passed the bar exam have all the rights and privileges of other lawyers, at least at the formal level.

The background of these lawyers reveals another interesting fact. Many of them entered the field of law by default; originally wanting to pursue another professional career, they found the training too difficult or too expensive or thought that their background would serve as a basis for discrimination against them. They thus did not have a sense of calling to the field, but rather a sense of calling to become a professional person.

Despite the high hopes they often had for their careers as professionals, many of these lawyers engage in the most marginal areas of the law, such as personal-injury cases, collections, rent cases, and evictions. One of their major problems is simply getting business, as direct and severe competition from other occupations is beginning to undermine their work in many areas. Thus accountants and real-estate brokers are increasingly able to handle the tax and real-estate work, traditionally done by the solo practitioner. Carlin notes that the pressures to earn a livelihood may force the solo lawyer to submit to pressures to violate legal ethics[45] and in a later study, to be discussed below, suggests that this is in fact the case. The financial incentive may also force the individual lawyer to become a middleman or broker between clients and other lawyers in order to receive referral fees. The decision to refer a case is often not based on the best interests of the client but on the lawyer's desire to obtain the largest settlement or recovery, and hence the largest commission. The solo lawyer thus may become a businessman rather than a lawyer, defeating his own purpose in becoming a professional in the first place.

Carlin summarizes his findings by stating:

> In considering the work of the individual lawyer in Chicago, one is drawn to the conclusion that he is rarely called upon to exercise a high level of professional skill. This arises in part from the generally low quality of his professional training, but even more from the character of the demands

[44]*Ibid.*, pp. 6, 18.
[45]*Ibid.*, p. 209.

placed upon him by the kinds of work and clients he is likely to encounter. Most matters that reach the individual practitioner—the small residential closing, the simple uncontested divorce, drawing up a will or probating a small estate, routine filings for a small business, negotiating a personal-injury claim, or collecting on a debt—do not require very much technical knowledge, and what technical problems there are are generally simplified by use of standard forms and procedures.[46]

This pessimistic conclusion about the solo practitioner says little about the way the individuals in this type of work feel about their own existence. Carlin notes that these lawyers tend to deny their low status by stressing their independence and the fact that they are in the general practice of all facets of the law. This feeling of autonomy, however, does not overcome the fact that these lawyers also feel insignificant in the overall legal structure and are frustrated because their high ambitions have not been realized, even though they are professionals. Carlin suggests that these individual practitioners, like general practitioners in medicine, are "most likely to be found at the margin of [their] profession, enjoying little freedom in choice of clients, type of work, or conditions of practice."[47] Furthermore, their verbalizations of autonomy do not correspond to the facts, and they appear to realize that individual practitioners have little freedom. They only get the business that comes their way or that they can bring in. Their cases usually are in one type of legal practice, such as personal injury or small-business taxation, and they are generally geographically limited to their immediate neighborhoods.

This picture of the individual lawyer is strengthened by Jack Ladinsky's findings regarding a sample of lawyers in Detroit.[48] These data reveal that solo lawyers come from minority religious and ethnic backgrounds, have parents of entrepreneurial or small-business status, and receive qualitatively and quantitatively inferior educations more often than the lawyers in law-firm practice included in the study.[49] Ladinsky suggests that these lawyers select this role for themselves, to a degree, in that the minority background of many of them has taught them to expect discrimination in the hiring policies of firms and to avoid it by entering individual practice. At the same time, overt discriminaton is a reality, and the lawyer with this type of background who tries to get into firm practice will have a difficult time. Ladinsky suggests that discrimination and self-selection interact to perpetuate the situation. Like Carlin, he also suggests that the work of the solo practitioner is being eroded by

---

[46]*Ibid.*, pp. 206–7.

[47]*Ibid.*, p. 206.

[48]"Careers of Lawyers, Law Practice, and Legal Institutions," *American Sociological Review*, XXVIII, 1 (February 1963), 47–54.

[49]*Ibid.*, p. 49.

outside agencies, such as automobile clubs, insurance and real-estate companies, abstracting firms, banks and savings-and-loan associations, and accounting firms. Thus, the "minority lawyer, then, inoculated with the ethic of entrepreneurship, goes solo to remain 'free'—only to discover that freedom to practice the rounded kind of law he desires has eluded him."[50] Though he may work outside of bureaucratic organizations, he finds that organizations not belonging to the profession have taken over many of his functions.

One further note about the metropolitan individual practitioner should be made. Carlin, in following up some leads from his earlier work, examined the degree to which a sample of lawyers in New York accepted and conformed to ethical norms.[51] He found that the individual practitioner was the most likely to violate these norms, with the nature of the client and type of case being important contributing factors in the violations. Both Carlin and Ladinsky suggest that their findings have real importance for the practice of law. Since these lawyers often represent individuals, as opposed to corporations, which are represented by the larger law firms, the quality of the lawyers involved adversely affects the legal representation that many individuals receive. Since these lawyers are often from minority groups, minority clients are the ones who are adversely affected. Furthermore, many of the larger, more prestigious and more ethical firms will not accept the kinds of cases the solo practitioner confronts and, in fact, refer these cases to him, so that the organization of the bar is such that ethical violations and ineffective legal practice are almost built into certain situations.

The discussion thus far has concentrated on the metropolitan bar. Certainly many of the findings would be inapplicable to the legal profession in smaller cities and towns, although Carlin suggests that even here the individual practitioner is at a disadvantage. Spatial isolation from research centers often puts a professional at a disadvantage in terms of access to new developments in his field, and the problem is intensified if he is in private practice. But the solo practitioner in these settings is unlikely to be a minority group member and is probably no more or less likely to be unethical than members of small firms in the same setting.

Rather obviously, everyone has known individual practitioners in law or medicine in either smaller or larger communities who are dedicated to their field, its ethics, and their clients and who try, despite the difficulty, to keep up with the rapid developments in their field. What is being suggested here is that such factors as the growth of group practice of various sorts, limited access to communication processes and to

[50] *Ibid.*, p. 54.
[51] *Lawyers' Ethics* (New York: Russell Sage Foundation, 1966).

financial rewards, and the growing complexity of the professions themselves militate against the solo practitioner. For most fields, therefore,
individual practice is probably just an image of the past and like many
such images, revered, but somewhat irrelevant.

Some professions, both established and otherwise, such as dentistry
and optometry, still appear to be largely practiced individually. But the
trend toward organizational work may involve professions such as these
when the desirability of specialization, leading to a need for a coordinated group of specialists in the clinic setting, and the financial and
temporal advantages of group practice become more apparent. A higher
volume of clients can probably be handled in group practice, and the
practitioners can rotate the time allotted for being "on call," thus leaving
more time free for other activities. This is not meant to suggest that
group, firm, or organizational practice is a panacea for professional problems or that problems in the areas of ethics and the place of the individual client in the system can be solved by a more organized kind of
practice. Extensive changes toward more organized practice would pre-
suppose that discrimination on grounds other than professional competence would be eliminated, since one of the key factors in keeping people
out of group practice, at least among the lawyers, seems to be actual or
perceived discrimination on the basis of race, religion, or ethnicity. Since
the total elimination of such discrimination is rather unlikely, the solo
practitioner will probably remain in the system as a minority professional. Even if discrimination were to be limited to professional competence, with those who are less competent not admitted to organized
practice, the persons discriminated against might still filter down to individual practice, thus maintaining its low status.

Two additional and somewhat related points should be raised before
turning to an examination of the professional in the organized setting.
In the discussion of the reasons for the relatively low quality of the solo
lawyer, the role of the inferior part-time law school in producing such
lawyers was mentioned. The part-time law school is a type of professional training institution that is unique to the legal profession, although
many students attend graduate schools on a part-time basis. It has served
as a means of social mobility for many persons who do not have the
financial resources for full-time study or who prefer to work and study
part-time. Thus, though these schools give inferior training when compared with full-time schools, they appear to serve an important function.
One obvious solution to this dilemma is to improve the quality of the
part-time schools, thus maintaining a source of legal training for those
who would otherwise be unable to acquire any, while providing them
with training that would be at least roughly comparable to that received
from full-time schools. This, of course, is more easily said than done.

The second point is related to the place of the person seeking good legal representation within the legal system. If Carlin is correct in his assertion that law firms tend to deal with corporate clients, which seems to be the case at least in metropolitan areas, trends toward even more such organized practice in law, as well as in the other professions, may create a situation in which the individual has little access to professional services. This would appear to be particularly true in situations wherein a client must be understood on more than the basis of particular legal, medical, or social symptoms. The recurring concern of the medical profession about the disappearing general practitioner and the steps it has taken to create a "family physician" specialty exemplify this trend. Here again, the development of techniques to deal with these individualized problems is probably up to the professional organizations involved since, as we have seen, they tend to exercise the major control over the profession. Organized professional practice need not be concerned with highly specialized problems, even though this has been the tendency, as will be seen in the next section.

THE AUTONOMOUS PROFESSIONAL ORGANIZATION

As previously stated, the autonomous professional organization is one in which the members of the profession determine its structure. Consequently, norms and sanctions are established in keeping with the expectations of the professionals involved. Decisions in regard to type of practice, criteria for selection and advancement of members, distribution of income, etc., are made by the professionals in the organization. The organizational structure is thus in a sense imported from the outside in terms of the norms of the profession itself. The organization is designed to accomplish the goals of the profession.

In the discussion of the individual practitioner, it was apparent that his type of professional practice contained elements leading to deviations from the ideal-type professional model. The autonomous organizational setting also contains such elements, although they take a very different form and produce correspondingly different results. The autonomous setting is most clearly exemplified by the law or architectural firm or the medical clinic, which are organized around established professions. Organizations such as advertising agencies, management-consultant firms, or marriage-counseling clinics are also autonomous professional organizations, but their professional basis is less well developed in terms of traditions or acceptance. They appear to lack the normative base that the established professions have. Unfortunately, comparative data are not available to assist in the analysis of the differences between types of autonomous professional organizations. Data are available regarding some such organizations, however, and the contrasts with individual practice can easily be seen.

One of the most thorough analyses of the autonomous professional organization is Erwin O. Smigel's *Wall Street Lawyer*. The legal profession has perhaps been the most comprehensively examined profession because of its centrality to the wider social structure. Although the Wall Street law firm is not typical of the majority of law firms in the United States, because of its size and type of practice, the contrast between this type of legal practice and that previously discussed illustrates the immense diversity within the legal profession and suggests that such intra-professional differentiation is not unique to the law.

The law firms studied by Smigel perform a number of functions.[52] First and foremost, they are spokesmen for much of big business in the United States. Not only do they represent business, but many members of the firms serve as members of the boards of directors of the corporations they represent. While such membership might be viewed as an impediment to professional judgment, it is generally assumed that the Wall Street law firm will serve as the legal conscience for the corporations. These lawyers also develop much of the business law in the United States through their intellectual and financial resources. Smigel suggests that many judges rely upon the briefs prepared by respected firms as the bases for their own decisions.

A second major function of these firms is that of recruiting centers for government service. Members of the firms are appointed to important governmental positions and seek national political offices; prominent examples are Adlai Stevenson, John Foster Dulles, Thomas E. Dewey, and Senator Clifford Case of New Jersey. Many other members of the firms are active in various capacities for national, state, and local governmental agencies. Wall Street lawyers also participate in civic and philanthropic activities, such as the Metropolitan Opera, various art museums, and other cultural and charitable affairs. Here again the national impact is great, since many of these organizations and activities have a scope much wider than the New York metropolitan area. The Wall Street law firms also are important in international relations, since many of their corporate clients deal extensively with foreign governments. The Wall Street lawyer is thus an important figure not only as a type of profes-

[52]The following material is a condensation of the material in Erwin O. Smigel, *The Wall Street Lawyer* (New York: Free Press of Glencoe, 1964), pp. 1–14, 38–40, 47–100, 296–307, and 343–50. Some of the findings reported, particularly in regard to recruitment practices, are no longer operative. The Wall Street firms have opened up their hiring, both in terms of the law schools from which people are selected *and* in terms of admitting more women and minority group members.

sional, for the purposes of this analysis, but also in his own right. Smigel's analysis is concerned primarily with how the law firms operate and the impact this has on the individuals involved and the legal profession. Our concern is similar, with particular emphasis on the effect of this kind of organizational setting on the idealized professional model.

These law firms are large, the smallest one considered having 50 lawyers on the staff and the largest having 125. Smigel had some difficulty in gaining entree into the firms because most of the lawyers felt that professional and organizational ethics would be violated when clients and their cases were discussed. Many also felt that the profession itself was rather sacred and should not be investigated. Gradually Smigel was able to persuade most of the firms that his research would not threaten them or their clients and that the results might well be beneficial to the profession.

The lawyers involved have personal backgrounds that are in direct contrast to those of the solo practitioners. The most striking fact is that over 70 percent of the lawyers had attended Harvard, Yale, or Columbia law school—in most assessments the elite schools of the nation—and had been top students. The Wall Street law firms actively recruit these top men and would prefer all their lawyers to have these credentials. The firms also look for the "correct" family background, which is viewed as being important in the development of the proper social graces and for contacts to bring business in the future. The recruit should also have the type of personality that fits with those of the members of the firm.

Lawyers with this set of credentials, which the potential recruit should have, are obviously in short supply. Since competition among the firms is keen and there is increasing competition for top law-school graduates from firms outside of New York and from various governmental units, the firms are being forced to look beyond the Ivy League schools for their recruits. They are apparently hiring Jewish graduates more frequently, a practice that was rare in the very recent past. As more and more Jewish students are able to enroll in the prestige law schools and as the performance level of these students puts them near the top of the class, the trend will probably increase. Relatively few Catholic lawyers are found in the Wall Street firms because of what are considered to be lower class origins, poorer education and, often immigrant parents. Since few blacks attend Ivy League undergraduate or law schools, the pool of potential candidates here is low. Additionally, it is thought that the black lawyer would not "fit in" in dealing with most clients. As Smigel suggests, from the point of view of the law firms themselves, this seems rational. As might be expected, there are very few women attorneys in the Wall Street firms. Smigel notes that there is greater discrimination against women than against Jewish recruits. The law firms believe that clients would object to women lawyers and that the women are likely to get married and leave. In addition to these reasons for the exclusion of women, which seem rational from the point of view of the firm, an antiwomen bias is also evident in many firms. Smigel notes that one firm "still elects to employ male stenographers when it can get them."[53]

The differences in background between these Wall Street lawyers and their colleagues in individual practice is so great that the term colleague itself is probably inapplicable. The Wall Street lawyer has a superior education, both quantitatively and qualitatively. The individual practitioner often is a member of a minority group, a fact that has no effect on his ability to practice law but which puts him into contact with minority, hence less powerful, clients, while the Wall Street lawyer deals with the corporate and governmental seats of power. As will be seen below, the kind of law practiced by the Wall Street lawyers is also clearly different.

Before turning to an examination of the work of the Wall Street lawyer, it should be pointed out that not every graduate of the prestige law schools desires this type of practice. An additional fact the firms have to face is that they do not always appear to law students to be the most desirable places to work. Many potential employees believe that the specialization in the large law office is so great that they would soon become limited in their abilities. Others feel that they would be lost in such a setting and would have a greater chance for advancement elsewhere. The hiring practices of some firms are hindered by having, for one reason or another, the reputation of being cold and unfriendly "law factories." Since the firms are competing for the same men, they try to build their images as good places to work. They try to de-emphasize their departmentalization and emphasize the opportunities to work at all phases of the organization's activities. They also stress the excellent training the graduate will receive in the firm. Many graduates in fact look upon experience in a Wall Street firm as an excellent postgraduate training period, which will serve as a basis for future positions in industry or government. The competition between firms is a controlled competition in the sense that there are unwritten rules regarding the kinds of inducements offered, with all firms offering the same starting salaries and other benefits; but they compete strongly at the symbolic level of the attractiveness of working in one firm as opposed to another. The hiring process has become routinized to the extent that specific persons are designated as "hiring partners," whose function is to seek out top prospects and to screen applicants. These men become personnel men

[53]*Ibid.*, p. 47.

as well as lawyers, with visitations to the law schools and routinized interview procedures.

The selection process for the Wall Street firms in reality is highly structured and programmed. Minority lawyers, graduates of less desirable law schools, and poor performers are automatically excluded. The combination of the proper preparatory school, undergraduate college, and law school puts a candidate who is interested in this type of practice into contention for an associate position in a Wall Street firm. As the competition becomes more severe for these people, the requirements themselves will probably change, with more minority lawyers being considered, if they are the "right type," and a broader range of law schools being regarded as appropriate.

The careers of the men who join a Wall Street firm are not locked into a set pattern once the hiring process is completed. Several career patterns can be identified. Some graduates plan to use the Wall Street firm solely as postgraduate training for positions in big business. The pay offered by corporations is a great deal more than the relatively low pay that beginning firm lawyers receive. Thus some men who did not intend to go into corporate practice do so because of the financial inducements. This, of course, is a slight, but normal, variation from the idealized professional person, who is dedicated to his work and has relatively little interest in the material advantages it can bring. Others who leave the Wall Street firm after a relatively short internship do so for family reasons, finding the time demands from the firm too severe for their wives and children. Smigel notes that the firms actually encourage such "dropping out," since they do not want lawyers who are not devoted to this type of practice.

Another interesting pattern is found among those lawyers who realize that they will not be chosen for partnership in the firms. For some, this constitutes a form of failure, even though they take rewarding and important jobs in industry or in smaller firms. Failure is thus a highly relative thing, since these failures are professionally and financially in much stronger positions than the solo practitioners discussed previously. Others who are not accepted into partnership remain with the firms as permanent associates, a position that is usually viewed by incoming associates as another form of failure. The permanent associates are typically specialists in particular areas who are secure in their positions. They are important to the law firms, despite their lack of success by the firms' standards.

For the incoming associate, the patterns discussed above are discernible career paths, and if the new associate has a strong desire to move into a partnership position in the firm, they are paths to be avoided. For such a person, competition with his cohorts is very strong. Smigel discusses the various systems of cues by which the associates can judge their progress. These cues range from the amount of responsibility and the difficulty of the assignments given to the associate to the relative size of his end-of-the-year bonus. The average amount of time spent at the associate level for those who become partners is eight and one-half years but, as some men move up to the partnership level as early as the sixth year, the period of real tension for the aspiring associate begins rather early in his career. The competition, though keen, is gentlemanly; the associate is judged on the basis of his ability and personality. If he is perceived as pushing too hard, this will operate against him. Both partners and associates stress the fact that hard and good work are the keys to advancement into the partnership position.

Definite patterns exist in the kind of work performed by the lawyers at particular phases of their careers. The beginning associate is viewed as having limited skills, even with his elite education, and is put to work preparing briefs and engaging in legal research under the supervision of a partner or a senior associate. Since the cases handled by these firms are usually very complex, the associate works on only a small segment of the overall problem. As he is doing this, he learns legal and social skills. His interactions with the various partners to whom he is assigned have a great deal to do with his future in the firm.

As his tenure with the firm continues, he is given more and more responsibility. He begins to have contact with clients. While his work is still specialized, his area of responsibility in particular cases is broadened. As associates move toward partnership positions, some assume supervisory positions over beginning associates. Once partnership is achieved, even more client contacts are maintained. The new partner still performs specialized work, but as time passes he assumes broadened responsibilities over cases. The senior partner is an advisor and administrator; he does little research on his own but is very knowledgeable about the entire range of the particular cases he is handling. Smigel suggests that the senior partner becomes a general practitioner in the area of business law. He manages and coordinates the work of his subordinates, and his role of advisor is based upon his knowledge and experiences.

The Wall Street law firm is somewhat unique in that it specializes in business law. At the same time, Smigel notes that its organization and practices are very similar to those of other large law firms, whether in New York or elsewhere. If this is the case, the large law firm, like solo practice, creates conditions that are clearly deviant from the idealized professional model. In the first place, the associate is an employee rather than a free professional; he works on a salaried basis and is thus rewarded like any other employee. He takes orders and works under supervision. Indeed, this is an additional reason for some associates' decisions to leave this type of practice. While the legal profession as a whole places a high value on disputation, the associate is expected to dispute tactfully and only up to the point a partner expects. He is in fact not autonomous. In addition, strict, but unwritten, standards of dress and decorum are upheld.

The partner does not escape from this deviation. A great amount of his time is spent in bringing in and maintaining business for the firm. With large overhead expenses, the firms must maintain a dollar volume in order to survive. Since they do, the efforts of the partners must be viewed as successful, but at the expense of the practice of the profession. In addition, the complexity of the cases involved requires the specialization and coordination discussed above. The partner thus becomes a caller of committee meetings, further dissipating the amount of time devoted to legal practice.

Despite these variations from the professional model, Smigel suggests that the Wall Street firm contains elements essential to the model. Extremely high ethical standards are maintained. The emphasis on performances as the basis for advancement is central to a rational profession. Specialization itself is required when complex issues are confronted, for without specialization, the answers to complex problems could not be found.

Smaller law firms in and out of metropolitan areas have not been systematically investigated. It would appear that these smaller firms and their members escape some of the problems of specialization and lack of autonomy noted previously. At the same time, similar pressures to bring in business operate. Also, these lawyers probably, although not necessarily, have received inferior training, both in law school and in practice. If they are in the general practice of law, their knowledge base and facilities, such as libraries, appear to be inferior.

But the concern of this chapter is not with lawyers per se, and the problems confronting the practice of law in the various settings thus far discussed appear not to be unique to this profession. If we take the Wall Street firm as the elite of its profession, as Smigel believes we can, then it is clear that the autonomous professional organization, like solo practice, confronts the professional with a setting in which the ideal form of professional practice cannot be achieved.

Freidson and Rhea's analysis of a large medical clinic provides additional insights into the nature of professional practice in the autonomous setting and into an important issue in the general area of professionalization.[54] This study was concerned with the self-regulation of professionals. Freidson and Rhea note:

---

[54]See Eliot Freidson and Buford Rhea, "Knowledge and Judgment in Professional Evaluation," *Administrative Science Quarterly*, X, 1 (June 1965), 107–24.

Professionals have the special privilege of freedom from the control of outsiders. Their privilege is justified by three claims. First, their work entails
such a high degree of skill and knowledge that only fellow professionals
can make accurate assessments of professional performance. Second, a high
degree of selflessness and responsibility characterizes professionals, so
they can be trusted to work conscientiously. Third, in those rare instances
in which individual professionals do not perform with skill or conscien-
tiousness, their colleagues may be trusted to take the proper regulatory
action.[55]

These claims and the privilege that they support were verbalized by
many of the lawyers interviewed by Smigel. The issue of self-regulation
is also central to Carlin's analysis of lawyers' ethics. He suggests that the
large firm is better able to enforce ethical standards on its members than
is the bar itself on its individual and group members. But Freidson and
Rhea's findings suggest that, while group practice may enhance the level
of adherence to ethical and performance standards, the self-regulation
system in such a setting is less than perfect.

Many of the doctors in the clinic studied were unable to rate some
of their colleagues' competence levels. The rating process in the clinic
was structured according to specialties; those specialties that do not refer
clients to each other (pediatrics and ophthamology, for example) have
very little knowledge about each other. The knowledge level was relatively high, however, within specialties. Systematic differences also appeared in the competence rating according to age and length of tenure
in the clinic. Younger doctors consistently gave lower ratings to their
colleagues. Newcomers to the clinic were rated lower than oldtimers,
regardless of their age. Other aspects of the organizational structure
also affected the rating process. For example, physicians in obstetrics-
gynecology were rated as quite competent by pediatricians, but as having
much less competence by specialists in internal medicine. As the authors
point out, the pediatricians only see the successful products of the ob-
stetricians' work—healthy babies. The physicians in internal medicine, on
the other hand, share the gynecologists' problems.[56]

Freidson and Rhea suggest that their findings indicate that the "prerequisites for regulation do not seem well enough developed to allow
an extensive and coherent process of professional regulation."[57] Despite
the fact that the process is less than perfert, gross or potentially danger-
ous misconduct would be rather quickly handled, in the opinion of these
authors. The lack of information about colleagues does not appear to
affect evaluations on serious matters. Nevertheless, these findings suggest
that this type of autonomous professional organization does not lend it-

[55]*Ibid.*, pp. 107–8.
[56]*Ibid.*, pp. 116–20.
[57]*Ibid.*, p. 122.

self to a comprehensive evaluatory system. This clinic, like the Wall Street law firm, relies upon the records of its recruits as evidence of competence, and a person, once admitted, is assumed to be competent. The question that remains unanswered concerns the manner in which self-regulation occurs for professionals outside the rather elite establishments discussed. If the communications processes contain blockages in the organized setting, they are undoubtedly also present in other types of practice.

THE HETERONOMOUS PROFESSIONAL ORGANIZATION

The autonomous professional organization is characterized by many elements that allow the professionals operating in it to exercise a great deal of personal and collective autonomy. Professional judgment is maximized, and the individual is expected to reach his own conclusions regarding the appropriate disposition of the various issues he confronts. Despite the conformity of dress and decorum demanded of the Wall Street lawyer, he is expected to remain "creatively conformist" in his thoughts. The conformity is limited to certain generally accepted legal and firm-based standards. In the heteronomous type organization,

> professional employees are clearly subordinated to an administrative framework, and the amount of autonomy granted professional employees is relatively small. An elaborate set of rules and a system of routine supervision control many if not most aspects of the tasks performed by professional employees, so that it is often difficult, if not impossible, to locate or define an arena of activity for which the professional group is responsible individually or collectively.
>
> Examples of professional organizations often corresponding to this type include many public agencies—libraries, secondary schools, social welfare agencies—as well as some private organizations such as small religious colleges and firms engaged in applied research.[58]

In his development of the nature of the heteronomous professional organization, Scott does not attempt to explain why these external constraints are present in these organizations. He suggests that, in general, the stronger professions, such as medicine and law, enjoy mandates allowing them greater autonomy. This argument is weakened by the existence of autonomous organizations, such as advertising or management consulting, among the less professionalized occupations. He also notes that a majority of the occupations found in the heteronomous setting are composed largely of women, a fact that apparently hinders

[58]Scott, "Reactions to Supervision," p. 67.

professionalization. But, while these factors are certainly operative, two additional considerations appear to be of even greater importance.

In their book, *Formal Organizations*, Peter M. Blau and W. Richard Scott develop an organizational typology based on the principle of *cui bono*—who benefits? This typology is designed to demonstrate that the nature of the public served by an organization has a strong impact on the kinds of problems it confronts. The four basic types are the "mutual benefit" organizations, in which the membership is the prime beneficiary; the "business" concerns, in which the owners are the prime beneficiaries; "service" organizations, in which the client group receives the major benefits; and "commonweal" organizations, in which the public at large is the prime beneficiary.[59] Blau and Scott argue that organizations that fit the heteronomous category are service organizations, since the client group, such as the student or the welfare case, is the prime beneficiary of the services provided. While it is hoped that the clients do benefit from the services, a strong case can be made for labeling these organizations as commonweal types. The public at large benefits from the educational process and, in fact, is highly dependent upon it. The public also benefits, socially and financially, from the work of social welfare agencies. Since the public has such a stake in the results of the work of these organizations, it is understandable that community members also want a role in their organizations' operation. Obviously, the extent to which the public, through controlling boards, should control such organizations is difficult to determine. Many teachers and social workers would suggest that lack of professional knowledge on the part of the controlling public actually is detrimental to the operation of such organizations. Nevertheless, the fact remains that these organizations are at least partially "commonweal" in their outputs and orientations.

This is related to the second factor that probably exerts pressure toward external controls on the professionals in the heteronomous organizations. The general public, in addition to having a stake in the operation of the organization, also has strong opinions and a belief in its own knowledge about the actual work done by the professionals involved. Most parents, for exaxmple, believe that they know their children better than the teachers and many probably feel that they would be effective teachers. Social welfare programs are controversial for many reasons; many lay people obviously believe that their own solutions to the problems of the indigent and the unemployed would be superior to those of the social workers trained in the area. In short, the public appears to believe that the professionals do not have any particular knowledge that

[59] *Formal Organizations* (San Francisco: Chandler Publishing Company, 1962), pp. 45–57.

is not available to the general masses.[60] Critics of the education of teachers have probably added fuel to this argument by their insistence that teacher education itself is not intellectually demanding.

For whatever reasons, the heteronomous professional organization has externally imposed rules and standards. These can range from legislatively developed laws regarding welfare eligibility or child adoption procedures to the selection of textbooks by state boards of education. The professional person in such an organization cannot exercise professional discretion in any area where these external norms prevail. If he does so, he violates the norms and is potentially subject to censure. As Harold L. Wilensky and Charles N. Lebeaux note in regard to public welfare workers,

> public welfare programs are framed in law, and the agency operates in a "goldfish bowl." The basic law setting up a program is usually brief; administration of the program requires an endless flow of regulations which comprise the everchanging "Manual." Operation in the glare of publicity may create an atmosphere of insecurity which . . . tends to foster rigidity and proceduralism.[61]

In some ways, less conflict for the professionals in such settings would be generated if they held weaker ideals of professionalism or professional attitudes. Blau and Scott, for example, found that the professionally oriented social workers in the agency they studied were much more likely to be critical of the agency and the laws and procedures governing it than were the less professionally oriented workers.[62] Scott's further analysis of data from the same study found that the professionally oriented workers were also more likely to be critical of their supervisors and the overall organizational system.[63]

In his analysis of the role of the teacher, Ronald G. Corwin suggests:

> Teachers have virtually no control over their standards of work. They have little control over the subjects to be taught; the materials to be used; the criteria for deciding who should be admitted, retained, and graduated from training schools; the qualifications for teacher training; the forms to be used in reporting student progress; school boundary lines and the criteria for permitting students to attend; and other matters that affect teaching. Teachers have little voice in determining who is qualified to enter

[60]In Everett C. Hughes's terms, these professionals have neither "license nor the mandate" sufficient to command the amount of public respect necessary for them to carry out their own judgments. See Hughes, *Men and Their Work* (New York: Free Press of Glencoe, 1958), pp. 78–87.

[61]*Industrial Society and Social Welfare* (New York: Free Press of Glencoe, 1965), p. 246.

[62]*Formal Organizations*, pp. 71–74.

[63]"Reactions to Supervision," p. 81.

teaching. Nonprofessionals control the state boards which set standards for teaching certificates.[64]

In his own research, Corwin found that teachers who are highly professionally oriented are usually militant in their professionalism. They want to change the system. At the same time, these teachers experience the most numerous and intense conflicts in the schools, as evidenced by heated discussions or major incidents. They are the most dissatisfied with the system. Teachers who accept the status of an employee, as opposed to that of a professional, are likely to be satisfied with the system.[65] Here again, a high level of professionalism is dysfunctional for the smooth operation of the organizations involved. If it is assumed, however, that a high level of professionalism is beneficial for the client groups and for the public, then the external controls found in the heteronomous organizations are what is dysfunctional. These organizations are thus in an extremely difficult dilemma. Public control and accountability are probably necessary and worthwhile, as is a high level of professionalism. Procedures have yet to be developed that will allow the maximization of both sources of control. It is probably possible to devise a system where both can be optimized, but the centrality of the services performed makes it appear unlikely that the public would want to relinquish its role in the control process. It could be hypothesized, however, that increased demonstration of professionalization on the part of occupations involved would yield them greater controls.

An additional aspect of the heteronomous professional organization is that it is a rather "flat" organization; the professional members usually have exactly the same title, with relatively minor pay differentials if the qualifications for employment are enforced. If a person is to advance, he must do so by leaving the profession; that is, he must take a supervisory position in which he no longer engages in professional practice. While advancement in the autonomous type of organization does not involve a change in title (once a lawyer, a person remains a lawyer even though he may move up from associate to partner), the differentials in pay and status are wide and recognizable. In the heteronomous professional organization, this is not the case.

The heteronomous professional organization confronts its members with conditions far from optimal in terms of individual or collective professional advancement. While the individual can certainly improve his skills and knowledge, the organizational structure tends to prevent their effective utilization and may even provide a source of real stress for the professional. It would seem that if an occupation as a whole increases its

[64] A Sociology of Education (New York: Appleton-Century-Crofts, 1965), p. 241.
[65] Ibid., pp. 258–63.

degree of professionalization, employment in heteronomous organizations would lead to collective frustration. Maximal use of professional skills and knowledge appears to be contingent upon a work setting that allows their utilization. Therefore, increased professionalization should be accompanied by reduced external controls. Whether this is possible is difficult to assess, given the previously discussed lay concerns about the operations of such organizations.[66]

THE PROFESSIONAL DEPARTMENT

As mentioned above, the professional department is generally thought to be the setting wherein the professional is likely to be confronted with the most frequent and severe conflicts between professional and organizational norms and values. Occupations at various degrees of professionalization are found in larger organizations. The medical or legal staffs of private and public organizations, libraries in business firms or universities, or advertising or personnel departments exemplify the diversity of professionals found in this setting.

In an analysis of scientists in an industrial setting, William Kornhauser found that there are built-in strains between organizational and professional values. While such values may not be crucial in the professionalization process, they are important factors in everyday work situations.[67] Kornhauser suggests that there are four areas in which professional and organizational values are in basic conflict. The first is the nature of the goals sought. The professional scientist seeks excellence and adherence to scientific standards. The organization also seeks excellence, but wants its scientists to come up with profitable developments in a regular fashion. But the nature of science is such that the developments may not only fail to be profitable but also may not occur with any temporal regularity. It is important to note that both sets of goals are legitimate, but both cannot always be realized at the same time.[68]

The second area, involving several types of conflict, lies in the source of control over the scientists' work. The recruitment of new personnel

---

[66]Additional insights into the occupations of teaching, nursing, and social work and their place in heteronomous organizations are found in Amitai Etzioni, ed., *The Semi-Professions and Their Organization* (New York: Free Press of Glencoe, 1969).

[67]*Scientists in Industry* (Berkeley: University of California Press, 1965), pp. 12–13. The professional in the organization is not, of course, the only type of professional who faces conflicting value systems. The professional in the other types of settings may have clients who oppose his value system. The professional himself may hold conflicting values, as in the case of a person who wants to improve his economic position but also maintain the highest professional standards. These values may not always be incompatible, but at times they are.

[68]*Ibid.*, pp. 17–41.

and personnel policies in general operate on different premises. The organization wants to select persons it believes will benefit the organization in the long run. It may, for example, desire personnel who have potential to move into management positions. The sciences, on the other hand, demand that selection be based on scientific ability, and managerial and scientific skills are not necessarily the same. In addition, the organization may have personnel procedures inapplicable or inappropriate for scientists or other professionals.[69] Simon Marcson has noted that civil service regulations impede recruitment in a governmental research setting.[70] The actual organization of work groups is another example of conflicts over controls. Scientists desire work groups to be organized around scientific specialties, since this facilitates intensive investigations into specific areas of interest. The organization, on the other hand, prefers that work groups be organized around particular tasks, which involves mixing different types of scientists and engineers for the solution of a particular problem or the development of a particular product.[71]

Supervision is another problem within the general control area. Organizations rely upon legitimate hierarchical authority as the means of control; scientists and other professionals rely on expertise as the major control mechanism. Although movement up the hierarchy in an organizational setting is typically based on expertise, the kinds of expertise demanded for advancement in the hierarchy may not be the same as those demanded by science. In addition, as a scientist is placed in a supervisory positions are likely to be supervising scientists and engineers will have less time to spend on keeping up with his field. Also, those in supervisory positions are likely to be supervising scientists and engineers whose specialties are different from their own. In this case, expertise cannot be expected. Communications pose an additional problem. One of the strongest values of the scientific community is free communication among scientists in order to facilitate further developments. The organization, on the other hand, has a strong value of maintaining company secrets. A new product or process is no longer a secret once it is produced, but businesses like to achieve any competitive edge they can; thus they do not want their scientists to communicate significant findings if they are in any way a threat to secrecy.[72]

A third major area of value conflicts derives from the kinds of incentives sought. The scientist operates in a community that transcends

[69]*Ibid.*, pp. 49–50.

[70]*Scientists in Government* (New Brunswick, N.J.: Rutgers University Press, 1966), pp. 12–24.

[71]Kornhauser, *Scientists in Industry*, pp. 50–56.

[72]*Ibid.*, pp. 56–80.

organizational or geographical boundaries, and he is known by his contributions to this community. He is rewarded by the recognition that he has made contributions to knowledge. The organization uses advancement within it as its primary reward system. As discussed above, this creates conflict with continued scientific advances. The organization expects its members to be local in orientation, with loyalty to the organization and its purposes, but the scientist is cosmopolitan in that his rewards and references are in the wider scientific community. For the cosmopolitan, advancement in the local organization may not be an attractive incentive.[73]

The final conflict area concerns the matter of influence: Who has the ultimate power in decision making? Since the organization assumes the risks for its actions, it has the last word in deciding which course of acton to pursue. In this sense, the hierarchy has ultimate power over professional expertise, which puts the scientist in a rather awkward position. If he remains detached from the decision-making process, he has little impact on organizational matters. If he becomes involved in organizational matters, he in reality becomes part of the organization and moves out of the scientist role. His expertise does not give him influence except in his own limited area. Since everyone in the organization who is not in his specialized area does not understand his expertise, it has no influence over them unless they have requested his specialized knowledge.[74]

While these areas of value conflict are probably inherent in the situation, conflict need not result from them, either for the professional or the organization. Kornhauser points out that the organization adjusts to the presence of professionals. He states:

> In sum, the strain between professional autonomy and bureaucratic control is accommodated by the creation of new roles for research administration. Administrative matters are controlled on the basis of hierarchical principles of authority, while matters regarded by professionals as the primary responsibility of the individual are more subject to multilateral determination through colleague relations. Thus organizational controls are relied upon to a greater extent in the sphere of general policy, in research areas close to operations, and by top research directors, whereas professional controls are used more extensively in research assignments and procedures, in more basic research areas, and by first-line research supervisors.[75]

[73]*Ibid.*, pp. 117–55. See also Barney G. Glaser, *Organizational Scientists: Their Professional Careers* (Indianapolis: Bobbs-Merrill Co., 1964).

[74]Kornhauser, *Scientists in Industry*, pp. 158-91.

[75]*Ibid.*, pp. 201–2.

The accommodation of the organization to the presence of professionals is accompanied by accommodations on the part of the professionals. Multiple career lines develop for these people as some remain in research, some become research administrators, and some move into the higher levels of management. Kornhauser notes that these multiple career lines allow the research oriented person to receive more pay and freedom of investigation and those who choose the organizational route to receive more pay and new ranks. But, since not all professionals or organizations are willing to make these accommodations, the potential for conflict remains. Kornhauser's own data suggest that organizations vary rather widely in their adaptations to professional employees. A study by Todd R. La Porte suggests that accommodative mechanisms are generated within the organization as it seeks to maximize the research contributions of its scientists. In the organization he examined, La Porte found that the existing causes of strain and conflict came from sources external to the organization, in areas such as procurement and budgetary procedures.[76]

While the kinds of accommodations that Kornhauser and La Porte describe are important means of ameliorating some of the conflicts between organizational and professional norms and values, it is clear that such amelioration does not take place at all times and in all situations. Kornhauser notes that the organizations he examined varied in their success in accommodating the conflicts. The nature of accommodation itself is such that the bases of the conflicts remain, even though they may not always be in the open. The organization still maintains its purposes and the professionals still have their values. As will be suggested later, changes in the organization or among the professionals can alter an accommodative balance, thus creating new conflicts or demanding new accommodative techniques.

Conflict is not the only condition of imbalance between professional and organizational values. Ambiguities also are present, which can result in conflicts for the individuals involved. John D. Donnell, in a study that utilized the conceptual framework of Kahn *et al.* as discussed in chapter 3, noted a series of ambiguities in the role of the corporate lawyer. The number of lawyers employed by corporations has increased greatly in recent years. In the 12 years between 1951 and 1963, the number of lawyers in industry increased 127 percent, while there was only a 13 percent increase in the number of lawyers in private practice.[77] Donnell

[76]"Conditions of Strain and Accommodation in Industrial Research Organizations," *Administrative Science Quarterly*, XX, 1 (June 1965), 21–38.

[77]John D. Donnell, "The Corporate Counsel: A Role Study" (DBA thesis, Harvard University, 1966), p. 61.

notes that the large organization is the most likely to have a legal department. Since most organizations are increasing in size, the trend toward
increased use of corporate legal departments will probably continue. Like
the scientists discussed before, corporation lawyers are caught between
their professional norms and those of the organization. Donnell views
this as resulting in ambiguity, rather than conflict. The probable reason
for this difference in outcome results from the nature of the professions
involved. The law tends to operate on the basis of past precedent, while
science is in the business of developing new knowledge. In this sense,
law is conservative, while science is radical. The conservatism of the law
would appear to coincide rather closely with the purposes of corporations, while the radicalism of science may or may not so coincide. My
impression is that the backgrounds of lawyers also would lead them to
believe in the goals of business, while the same might not be true for
scientists.

Despite the more moderate nature of the outcome of the professional-
organizational relationship in the case of lawyers, the ambiguities, which
Donnell notes, have an impact on the professional services performed.
These ambiguities have three sources. The first is that the role of the
lawyer in private practice is itself ambiguous. Donnell states that the
"only activity of a lawyer in private practice which is exclusively his is
to represent a client in a court."[78] Other activities overlap with other
occupations and agencies, such as the services that realtors, bankers, and
accountants provide that could be and at times are performed by lawyers.
Lawyers themselves provide services that are in the province of other
occupations, such as marriage counseling or business management. This
ambiguity does not end when the lawyer enters the corporation, although
the potential range of his activities is greatly diminished, since he now
is a specialist in business law. In reality, the lawyer who enters the corporation undoubtedly had this specialty beforehand, as Smigel's evidence
on Wall Street lawyers suggests, but there was a potential for him to
practice in other areas of the law.

This general ambiguity is made specific for the corporate counsel by
the fact that he is likely to perceive most of the actions of the corporation
as involving potential legal problems. An absence of criteria for determining priorities among the legal issues that arise makes it difficult for the
lawyer to determine just where and how he should act. Donnell states
that even if such criteria are available, a large amount of time and energy
must be devoted to an investigation into a potential corporate action to
determine the potential legal problem involved and then to rank this
problem in the hierarchy of priorities. The lawyers resolve this dilemma

[78]*Ibid.*, p. 63.

by attempting to be on top of everything or by only giving advice when it is solicited.

The second source of ambiguity is similar to one faced by the organizational scientist. The lawyer must come to grips with the issue of whether he is a lawyer or a businessman.[79] He must often balance legal risks and business risks, since his job demands that he be familiar with each. The scientist, asked to come up with profitable developments, is in the same position in that he must weigh the merits of the development for his employer against the demands of his scientific discipline. As in the case of the scientist, appropriate legal actions may or may not be appropriate business actions. The lawyer also is often in the position where his knowledge of the business almost demands that he give business advice when he believes that an incorrect decision is about to be made, although the incorrect decision may be legally appropriate. If he gives the advice, he becomes a businessman; if he does not and acts exclusively as a lawyer, his employer is liable to lose money and the businessman's part of his knowledge is being wasted. If he chooses the businessman role, it may later be difficult to separate it from the lawyer role, thus limiting his effectiveness in his position. The latter role, if played exclusively, limits his effectiveness as an officer of the corporation. This particular dilemma is resolved in some instances by polarization at either extreme, but in most cases the lawyers attempt to play both roles, separating them where necessary and possible.

The third source of ambiguity is tied to the traditional role of the lawyer as an officer of the court. The lawyer is expected to uphold the law but at the same time to contribute to the profit making of the corporation. In most cases, corporate policy is to obey the law, incidents of white-collar crime notwithstanding. There are times, however, when actions of corporate personnel may come into conflict with the law. The lawyer may decide to act as a policeman, a role that involves knowing what the intended actions are to be and then acting to prevent them. This choice involves some betrayal of confidential information that the potential law violator, in many ways the lawyer's client, has provided the lawyer. This is in clear violation of general professional standards of confidentiality. If the lawyer does not attempt to prevent the illegal act, he is not serving the corporate interests, even though he keeps the information confidential. Another facet of this problem is that if the lawyer does decide to play the role of policeman and does reveal the potentially illegal action, his future relationships with other executives may suffer, in that they may be unwilling to reveal the exact nature of their plans for fear the lawyer will both pass information on to their

[79]Ibid., pp. 64–65.

superiors and prevent actions they view as organizationally beneficial.[80]

Additional insights into the problems confronted by lawyers in the corporate setting are provided by Quintin Johnstone and Dan Hopson, Jr. They note that some executives would like corporate counsel to act as a rubber stamp for their ideas.[81] When the lawyer, or any professional, is put in this position and acts according to the executives' expectations, he no longer operates as a professional. These instances are in the minority, but the potential for this kind of expectation is heightened by the pyramidal hierarchy of most business organizations. The corporation is likely to have a finely developed organization chart, with the relative positions in the hierarchy of professional and nonprofessional staffs clearly indicated. Johnstone and Hopson point out that corporate legal departments are likely to be highly differentiated in terms of multiple levels and corresponding to job titles. If an executive at a higher level in the hierarchy approaches a lawyer at a lower level, this type of relationship has a higher probability of existing. In most cases, however, relationships between lawyers and clients (executives in this case) appear to be among equals in the organizational hierarchy. The problem of rubber stamping appears not to be limited to members of professional departments. Smigel suggests that the younger associates in Wall Street law firms generally will dispute a point of law only to the extent of the expectations of partners with whom they are dealing.[82] The young lawyer soon learns when he is expected to cease disputation and yield to his superior. The Wall Street lawyer is disputing with other lawyers, but the structured form of the expectations is not dissimilar to that of the executive lawyer. In both cases, hierarchical factors can outweigh potential expertise.

An interesting facet of corporate legal practice discussed by Johnstone and Hopson is the tendency toward very low turnover rates. While this indicates satisfaction with the work and a stable situation for the organization itself, the authors suggest that it may also indicate that the "minimum tolerable level of performance is rather low."[83] While their evidence is rather weak, there is some suggestion that corporate lawyers do in fact operate somewhat below the highest standards of the profession. This, of course, is the same thing that Carlin and Ladinsky have suggested about the individual practitioners, while Smigel suggests the opposite in regard to the Wall Street lawyer. Good comparative data would be needed before firm conclusions could be drawn in this area.

Another problem for corporate counsels is that they are likely to handle only a narrow range of legal problems. This, according to most people concerned about the legal profession, is not as it should be, since

[80]*Ibid.*, pp. 65–66.
[81]*Lawyers and Their Work* (Indianapolis: Bobbs Merrill Co., 1967), p. 205.
[82]*The Wall Street Lawyer*, pp. 322–29.
[83]Johnstone and Hopson, *Lawyers and Their Work*, p. 235.

lawyers should be familiar with both the practice and implications of a wide range of legal problems. Here again, however, the picture of the corporate counsel is not clearly differentiated from that of the solo practitioner or the Wall Street lawyer, who also specializes to a fairly high degree. Again, good comparative data are needed for any conclusive analysis of the extent and consequences of extreme specialization.

The Johnstone and Hopson research indicates that the legal departments studied varied rather widely in the stress placed upon professional (bar) activities. The departments also varied in the degree to which they were hierarchically organized. The corporations themselves varied in the kinds of expectations they held for the departments. These findings raise an important issue for the general discussion of professionalization—the role of the setting of professional work on the behavior of the professionals involved. Four distinct settings of professional work have been discussed, the solo practitioner, the autonomous professional organization, the heteronomous professional organization, and the professional department. Each of these settings confronts the professional with a different working environment with differing sources of norms, career patterns, problems, and rewards. At the same time, the common characteristics, discussed before, exist in the variety of settings.

A major source of both the variations and the common characteristics is the organizational setting in which the professional is employed. Since the solo practitioner is not subject to this type of work structure, he will be ignored in this analysis. Any of the three types of organizational setting discussed may vary to the extent that professional behavior and values are affected. My analysis of the degree of bureaucratization of a group of professional organizations provides some indication of the manner in which professional work settings do vary and of the relationship between the setting and professional values and attitudes. In this discussion, the importance of varied professional training and of differing degrees of professionalization among the occupations involved in affecting behavior and values is not considered, even though these are undoubtedly important factors. The concentration on the setting assumes that differences in socialization in professional schools and differing levels of professionalization of the occupations involved do make a difference but that the effect of these variations will be randomly distributed among the occupational groups analyzed. The professions involved are analyzed on the basis of the distinction between structural and attitudinal components of professionalization.

In this phase of the research, the organizational settings were analyzed by determining the degree to which they were bureaucratized.[84]

---

[84]See Richard H. Hall, "Professionalization and Bureaucratization," pp. 95–104, for additional discussions of the techniques used and of the findings reported here.

The bureaucratization of the organizations involved was approached from a dimensional perspective, which involves the assumption that organizations will vary in their degree of bureaucratization along several dimensions of bureaucratization. Previous research in this area has suggested that organizations do not necessarily exhibit the same degree of bureaucratization on all of the dimensions, but this is not the central issue at this time. What is of interest here is the determination of the relationships between the degree of bureaucratization, as the measure of the organizational structure, and the degree of professionalism, as measured by attitudinal scales of professionalism developed in the course of research.

The components of the bureaucratic model used here are:

1. Hierarchy of authority is the extent to which the locus of decision making is prestructured by the organization and the extent to which it follows hierarchical principles. (Decisions of varying types are made at different levels in the organization with the assumption that decision-making ability and power are directly related to hierarchical position.)
2. Division of labor is the extent to which work tasks are subdivided into functional specialization as determined by the organization.
3. Presence of rules is the degree to which the behavior of organizational members is subject to organizational control.
4. Procedural specifications refers to the extent to which organizational members must follow organizationally defined techniques in dealing with the variety of situations they face.
5. Impersonality describes the extent to which both organizational members and outsiders are treated without regard to individual qualities. (All people are treated the same way without consideration of individual differences.)
6. Technical competence is the extent to which organizationally defined universal standards are utilized in the selection of personnel and in the advancement process.

In the research under discussion, these dimensions were measured by asking the professionals involved to respond to a series of statements about their organization. Their responses were tabulated to develop a score for each dimension. The average score for the respondents in a particular organization was then taken as the degree of bureaucratization on a particular dimension. The relationships between the scores on the bureaucratic dimensions test and the scores on the professional attitude scales were then determined as indicated in Table 4-1.

The most obvious general finding is that there is an inverse relationship between degree of bureaucratization and level of professional attitude. This implies, of course, that a highly bureaucratic organization tends to impede the development of strong professional attitudes. At the same time, an organization whose members hold strong professional

TABLE 4–1. Rank Order Correlation Coefficients Between Professionalism Scales and Bureaucracy Scales

	Professional Organization Reference	Belief in Service to Public	Belief in Self-Regulation	Sense of Calling to Field	Feeling of Autonomy
Hierarchy of authority	—.029	—.262	—.149	.148	—.767[2]
Division of labor	—.236	—.260	—.234	—.115	—.575[2]
Rules	—.144	—.121	—.107	.113	—.554[2]
Procedures	—.360[2]	—.212	—.096	.000	—.603[2]
Impersonality	—.256	—.099	—.018	—.343[1]	—.489[2]
Technical competence	.593[2]	.332[1]	.420[2]	.440[2]	.121

[1] = $p < .05$
[2] = $p < .01$

values may be difficult to bureaucratize, a point that will be discussed later.

When the specific relationships are examined, some interesting patterns emerge. With regard to the use of the professional organization as a reference group, there is a relatively small negative relationship between this variable and the presence of a rigid hierarchy of authority. It would thus appear to make little difference if there is extensive reliance upon such a hierarchy in professional organizations. The findings of Peter M. Blau, Wolf V. Heydebrand, and Robert E. Stauffer support this conclusion, which suggests that the presence of such a hierarchy may facilitate the work of professionals if that hierarchy serves coordination and communication functions.[85] This would be the case particularly when the hierarchy is recognized as legitimate. The professional may thus recognize and essentially approve of the fact that certain decisions must be made by particular positions in the hierarchy. Since many decisions are based on the suggestions of the professionals involved, this would further tend to minimize feelings that the hierarchical principals were in opposition to professional values. Conflict probably exists only in those cases where the decisions made in some way disagree with either the professional's own judgment or adversely affect his own work. As will be seen below, such hierarchies are not limited to professional departments, since relatively bureaucratic hierarchies are found in other types of organizations.

A stronger negative relationship is found on the division of labor dimension. If the division of labor is very intense, forcing the professional

[85]"The Structure of Small Bureaucracies," *American Sociological Review*, XXXI, 2 (April 1966), 179–91.

to work in only a limited area, the person may be forced away from his broader professional ties. This finding confirms the suggestion noted above by Johnstone and Hopson about extreme specialization among lawyers. It is clear that professionals can be highly specialized in their work. The issue here is the source of the specialization. If the source is organizational, professional identification is weakened; if the source is within the profession itself, such identification might not be affected.

The presence of the rules dimension is, to a limited degree, inversely related to the professional attitude. Organizationally developed rules about the behavior of members appear not to intrude too strongly on this or the other professional attitudes. It would appear that these rules are not too stringent in the organizations analyzed. A strong negative relationship exists between the procedural specifications dimension and the attitude of the professional organization as a reference group. This is expected, since strong professional orientations appear to be basically incompatible with organizationally developed techniques of dealing with work situations—the more procedures developed by the organization, the less room for professional discretion. This area would thus be a real source of conflict for professionals if they work in such procedure-laden environments. The presence of professionals in an organization in many ways demands that the organization not develop its own procedures, since one of the major elements in the nature of professions is professional judgment based upon the criteria of the profession.

The relatively strong negative relationship between this professional attitude and the impersonality dimension is not unexpected. The more professional groups apparently do not need or utilize impersonality in their organizational arrangements. If the organization itself stresses impersonality and contains a highly professionalized group, conflict again can ensue.

The strong positive relationship between the use of the professional organization as a reference group and the organizational emphasis on technical competence is, of course, predictable. Organizations that employ professionals by definition utilize competence criteria, rather than selecting personnel by nepotistic or particularistic means.[86] It is not clear, on the basis of this research, whose criteria of competence are being utilized. From the previous discussions it is evident that if the organization determines the criteria for personnel policies and if these policies contain elements inconsistent with the standards of the profession involved, a strong potential for conflict exists. This would be a strong possibility in the cases of the heteronomous organization and the professional

---

[86]Since this bureaucratic dimension is so strongly related to most of the professional attributes, it might even serve as an informal indicator of the level of professionalization of the members of an organization if other such indicators are not available.

department. In the research being discussed, the ratings of the degree of bureaucratization and the measures of the professional attitudes were gathered from the same persons. It would thus appear that such conflict is minimal in the organizations being examined here.

The findings concerning belief in service to the public, belief in self-regulation, and sense of calling to the field are essentially the same as those just discussed. The areas of congruence and conflict that might emerge also appear to be quite similar.

Strong negative relationships exist between the autonomy variable and the first five bureaucratic dimensions. This suggests, of course, that increased bureaucratization would threaten professional autonomy. It is in this set of relationships that the most evident source of conflict between the professional and the organization can be found. The drive for autonomy on the part of a professional may come into direct and strong conflict with organizationally based job requirements. At the same time, the organization, as such, may be threatened by strong professional drives for autonomy. If the professionals act in a totally autonomous fashion, the goals of the organization might not be served. In the ideal situation, professional and organizational goals are identical, so that the professional is fully autonomous and, at the same time, accomplishes the purposes of the organization. Since even the autonomous professional organization contains elements antithetical to some professional attitudes, this ideal state is not achieved in reality.

The preceding discussion suggests that the professional in an organization does not and cannot operate in a totally autonomous fashion and that the organization does set limits of varying degrees of stringency on him. The most obvious question at this point is, What factors contribute to the varying levels of bureaucratization and thus to greater or lesser levels of autonomy for the professional? Part of the answer may lie in the nature of the particular profession itself. When the occupations included in my study are grouped in accordance with their overall level of professionalization, some rather definitive patterns emerge, as Table 4-2 indicates.

The most evident finding is that the more professionalized groups are found in the least bureaucratized settings, which suggests that the more professionalized groups probably do not need the kinds of organizational controls required by less professionalized groups. If an occupation is self-regulating and its members can act autonomously, the organization does not need to provide an extensive control system. If, on the other hand, the occupation does not provide its members with sufficient controls in the form of self-regulation, and if the members do not or cannot act autonomously because of deficiencies in the knowledge base of the occupation, then organizational controls must be provided in the absence

TABLE 4–2. Average Ranks and One-Way Analysis of Variance *H* on Degree of Bureaucratization of Work Settings of Three Types of Professionals

	High Pro- fessionalization (Average Rank)	Medium Pro- fessionalization (Average Rank)	Low Pro- fessionalization (Average Rank)	H Value (2 df)
Hierarchy of authority	9.5	18.9	14.1	6.14[1]
Division of labor	9.2	17.8	15.7	5.57
Rules	7.9	19.1	15.9	9.65[2]
Procedures	7.3	18.5	17.3	10.96[2]
Impersonality	11.2	16.2	15.1	1.65
Technical competence	16.5	14.7	10.2	2.02

[1] $= p < .05$
[2] $= p < .001$

of alternatives. This suggests that an equilibrium can be achieved between professional and organizational control systems. The equilibrium comes about when organizational controls are present in those areas where the professional, for whatever reason, lacks the prerequisites for autonomous performance.

Just as the potential for equilibrium is present, this relationship between professional and organizational control systems is an important source of conflict. As soon as the equilibrium is upset, either the organization or the professionals will react. An example of this would be the case of an occupation that attempts to professionalize and does achieve a greater degree of authority for its professional organization. The members then believe that they should have a stronger role in determining who should be employed by the organization (the technical competence dimension of bureaucracy). If they press for their demands at all, conflict is likely. Another situation that disturbs the equilibrium is organizationally based, as when an organization attempts to establish new procedures regarding the procurement of office supplies for all departments, including the professional departments. If the latter departments' members' needs are not as well met by the new procedures, conflict would again result. These examples suggest that changes in the professional groups or the organizations can destroy an existing equilibrium. Since levels of professionalization and bureaucratization are not static, the potential for conflict is great.

An additional source of tension between professionals and organizations is the situation in which there are not *enough* organizational rules for the professionals, leading to a state of *anomie*. This situation could arise when the organization does not provide sufficient structuring for the professionals. This assumes, of course, that the professionals involved do not have the equipment for the structuring of their own work. This type

of condition would probably occur most often among the less professionalized types of professions. This discussion has assumed that individual
contributions to the structuring of work situations, above and beyond
those of the profession or the organization, are important but also randomly distributed in the population involved so that their effect is not
central.

The discussion thus far has been focused on two alternative sources
for the structuring of the work of the professional—the profession and the
organizational setting. It has been suggested that the organizational setting can have a powerful influence on the work of professionals, as can
the degree of professionalization of the group itself. It has also been
noted that little can be gained from an a priori assumption that professional departments differ from autonomous professional organizations,
which are, in turn, inherently different from heteronomous organizations
in terms of organizational structure. Nevertheless, the organizational or
nonorganizational setting in which professionals are found exerts a profound influence on the behavior of the professional in his work. This
influence is so profound that we must now ask, Is an altered professional
model needed?

AN ALTERED PROFESSIONAL MODEL?

A general theme that runs through the discussion regarding the
settings of the work of the professionals is the variations in the manner in
which the work itself is organized and controlled. Indeed, autonomy in
this sense appears to be the crucial issue. Moore explicitly states that
autonomy is the "highest" point on his scale of professional attributes.[87]
Our approach here is slightly different from Moore's in that we will concentrate on the autonomy of professional work groups, rather than on
the professional as an individual or as belonging to a distinct occupational category.

*The degree of professionalization depends on the extent of autonomy
exercised in the work (usually organizational) setting.* Support for this
conclusion can be seen in the studies already discussed. Different occupations were found to be more or less professional in a variety of organizational settings. In another study, George A. Miller and L. Wesley
Wager found that the type of training (length of education and type of
education) a person obtained was related to placement in units of an

[87]Moore, *Professions, Roles and Rules*, p. 6. Moore's scale consists of the following
elements, in ascending order of importance: the professional practices a full-time
occupation, has a commitment to a calling, is in an organized occupation, has received specialized training, exhibits a service orientation, and enjoys autonomy.

American aerospace company.[88] While not dealing directly with the autonomy issue, the findings indicate that the nature of the training was related to the type of role orientation the engineers and scientists studied had—the more extensive and professionally oriented the training, the more the employing organization reinforced the professional orientation, presumably through encouraging autonomy.

Gloria V. Engel has dealt directly with the autonomy issue. In a study of physicians, she found that the physicians in moderately bureaucratized settings experienced the greatest amount of autonomy.[89] The minimally bureaucratized setting (solo practice) did not provide sufficient resources and facilities, while the highly bureaucratized setting (a government-associated medical organization) had a rigid administrative structure. The moderately bureaucratized setting (a privately owned clinic and hospital) provided the practitioners with the greatest opportunities for autonomy.

Engel and Hall and Freidson have suggested that professionalism itself may be an alternative way of organizing work.[90] Instead of relying on bureaucratic forms, more and more work may come to be organized according to the professional or autonomous perspective. Again, autonomy here involves the ability of the occupational group to determine its own work patterns in an organization. The emphasis here is on work groups and not on individuals. In another paper, Engel and Hall have noted that there is a strong tendency for professionals to work in teams.[91] Because these teams are typically composed of people in the same profession with different specialties, they are able to bring more knowledge and expertise to bear on a problem than a single individual. This lowers the autonomy of the individual but can increase it for the group. Thus groups of doctors, lawyers, or accountants engage in autonomous work. These same occupations can be found in settings that provide less autonomy. It is thus not the title of the occupation that is important but the extent of the autonomy that its members can exercise in the work setting. This is what appears to be critical in understanding the nature of the contemporary professional model.

In the sections that follow, we will be examining additional sources

---

[88]"Adult Socialization, Organizational Structure, and Role Orientations," *Administrative Science Quarterly* 16 (July 1971), 151–63.

[89]"Professional Autonomy and Bureaucratic Organization," *Administrative Science Quarterly* 15 (March 1970), 12–21.

[90]Gloria V. Engel and Richard H. Hall, "Professions, Professionals, and Professional Autonomy," and Eliot Friedson, "Introduction," in Eliot Friedson, ed., *The Professions and Their Prospects* (Beverly Hills, Calif.: Sage Publications, 1974).

[91]Gloria V. Engel and Richard H. Hall, "The Industrialization of the Professions: A Reorganization of Professional Work Patterns," in Phyllis L. Stewart and Muriel G. Cantor, eds., *Varieties of Work* (Boston: Schenkman Publishers, 1974).

of variation in professional work. Most of these have important implications for autonomy.

KNOWLEDGE AND KNOWLEDGE OBSOLESCENCE

Knowledge is a key factor in professional autonomy. If the professional has specialized knowledge to "sell" and this knowledge is valued, he is given autonomy in his work as he pursues this knowledge. The professional must convince either an employing organization or clients that this knowledge is worthwhile and not in the possession of other people. Professional work groups depend on the fact that the employing organizations need their inputs. When there is this dependence, the work groups are expected to provide the knowledge involved while being given control over the manner in which the development and dissemination of this knowledge occurs.

Knowledge is most commonly thought of as that that is learned in professional school. This is not the case. As with all socialization, acquiring knowledge is a life-long process. For the professional, the acquisition and sorting out of knowledge is a continuing endeavor, and most professions maintain a systematic set of mechanisms for helping their members keep abreast of recent developments. As will be indicated later, keeping up with the field is of critical importance for the professional, yet it is no easy matter. Perrucci and Rothman note, for example, that in metallurgical engineering there are 600–900 journals and 35,000 papers annually and in aerospace science there are 1,500 journals and 45,000 papers.[92] It is obviously impossible for an individual to digest all of this material. Nevertheless, it is important.

For the individual, keeping up with developments in a field is important in that there is sometimes an objective threat of loss of job if knowledge becomes obsolete. For the organization, obsolete knowledge is useless. Perrucci and Rothman note that "many organizations apparently find it more advantageous to bring in new talent than to provide an opportunity for established professionals to keep abreast of new developments."[93] The old, "unabreast" professional is clearly under some threat in this kind of situation.

In an analysis of data from a sample of engineers, Rothman and Perrucci found that there were important career consequences associated with knowledge obsolescence. They suggest:

[92]Robert Perrucci and Robert A. Rothman, "Obsolescence of Knowledge and the Professional Career" (Institute for the Study of Social Change, Department of Sociology, Purdue University), n.d.
[93]*Ibid.*, p. 4.

In general, the data lend support to the contention that technical obsolescence and emerging career patterns are interrelated. On the one hand, positions involving narrow technical activities, extensive administrative responsibilities, application rather than research, and organizational situations involving relatively stable technologies are conducive to the weakening of professional expertise. The common attribute of these positions would seem to be that the technical demands neither require nor stimulate the maintenance of such expertise. On the other hand, such positions may offer the less knowledgeable an acceptable career adaptation to the pressures produced by obsolescence.[94]

In a very real sense, the professional must struggle to "keep up" with the field. The consequences for the individual who does not keep up may be a move out of the profession into administrative work or, in the extreme, out of a job.

For professions themselves, the issue of knowledge obsolescence is more difficult to see. At the same time, every occupation has to demonstrate in some way that it remains important, and a major way to do this is through continued development of new information, which keeps nonprofessionals "away" from the knowledge of the professionals. Esoteric and exotic knowledge does provide a social distance mechanism of great importance for professional groups. It serves as a major basis for autonomy.

At this point the discussion will take a quick and, at first glance, puzzling turn to the analysis of women in professions and women professionals.

WOMEN AND THE PROFESSIONS AND PROFESSIONAL WOMEN

Our focus has been on the sources of variation in professional practice. The initial point to be made in this section is that women are a major source of such variation in particular cases. We will then briefly examine some of the factors that affect the behavior of women in the professions.

Richard L. Simpson and Ida Harper Simpson have argued that the presence of a large proportion of women in certain professions has actually contributed to lowered autonomy and hence less professionalization of the occupations.[95] Using teaching, nursing, librarianship, and social work as the basis for their discussion, Simpson and Simpson suggest that there are characteristics of women that have impeded the de-

[94]Robert A. Rothman and Robert Perrucci, "Organizational Careers and Professional Expertise," *Administrative Science Quarterly* 15 (September 1970), 292.

[95]"Women and Bureaucracy in the Semi-Professions," in Amitai Etzioni, ed., *The Semi-Professions and Their Organization* (New York: Free Press of Glencoe, 1969), pp. 196–265.

velopment of these semiprofessions into full professions. In the first place, many women experience real conflicts in their home and family versus professional role expectations. This can find expression in felt role conflicts in which the person is torn between two conflicting and legitimate demands. It can also find expression in the fact that many women experience discontinuous or part-time careers. Such discontinuity and part-timeness have consequences for the practice of the profession and the manner in which the practitioners are perceived. A person who only works part-time or is in and out of a career because of family responsibilities is not viewed as seriously as one who works full time. This factor, of course, is linked to rates of turnover. Younger females have higher turnover rates than older females or males, according to most studies. Where male and female turnover rates are the same, as they are in many instances, the "women tend to leave jobs for family reasons; men, for professional advancement."[96] Simpson and Simpson suggest that one consequence of high turnover rates is for the employing organization to increase its level of bureaucratization. If this is true, then there would be a corresponding decrease in professionalization, if our previous arguments are correct.

Simpson and Simpson suggest that there are additional female characteristics that diminish the professionalization of the occupations involving women. These involve the deference of women to men, the stronger desire among women for pleasant social relations on the job, a desire to relate to people on a total, rather than a depersonalized and fragmented, basis, a lower drive toward intellectual mastery, an absence of long-range ambition, a lack of occupational communities, and the compliant predisposition of women.[97]

Obviously, these are not inherent traits of women. Furthermore, factors such as deference to men or compliant predispositions may no longer be operative as a consequence of alterations associated with the women's movement. In terms of the professionalization of the occupations in question, of course, the past history is important and the fact that most of the members of an occupation have been women has been a factor hindering the professionalization process. As has already been noted, there are other strong impediments above and beyond the gender of the occupational members.

There are women in many other professions besides the semiprofessions. Indeed, professional women have been at the forefront of the women's movement. It is worthwhile at this point to examine the place of women in the professions in general. Athena Theodore has assembled

[96]*Ibid.*, p. 220.
[97]*Ibid.*, pp. 232–43.

a good amount of the recent literature on professional women.[98] A major conclusion is that there is a great deal of "sex-typing" in the professions. "Medicine, law, science, engineering, dentistry, and the ministry are sex-typed as male occupations; and nursing, grade-school teaching, librarianship, and social work are sex-typed as female."[99] This is obviously culturally bound, since it is clearly demonstrated that this sexual distribution is not found in many other societies at an equal stage of development. The sex-typing is linked to the more general sex-type expectations. "The female professions developed as extensions of the traditional role functions of the female in the family in tasks requiring nurturing, socializing, and helping. Interestingly enough, the married female, with her presumably greater expertise in these areas, was until recently completely excluded from employment."[100]

It is interesting to note that, with the exception of nursing, the higher administrative positions in these semiprofessions (principals, social work supervisors, etc.) have increasingly gone to men as men have entered the semiprofessions. In the established, full professions there is also sex-typing when women are admitted. In the ministry, women are still almost totally excluded, while in medicine and law, women are concentrated in lower status specialties that have some sort of "family" orientation (obstetrics and gynecology in medicine and domestic relations in law).

The female professional faces dilemmas not encountered by her male counterpart. Traditional (and still strong) expectations exist in regard to a married woman's responsibilities regarding her children and husband. In most cases, for example, the husband's career is given first priority, and thus a professional woman may find herself entertaining, traveling, and offering general occupational assistance around the husband's occupation rather than her own. Very obviously, if the husband's occupation involves moving, any wife in a profession that requires the development of a clientele is severely hindered. The physical fact of childbirth and the social expectations regarding children introduce occupationally relevant factors for a woman. These family events have almost no occupational impact on the male.[101]

One of the most interesting characteristics of the professions is the identification of professionals with their fellow professionals. The professions are *organized* occupational groups. This organization is both offi-

[98]Athena Theodore, ed., *The Professional Woman* (Cambridge, Mass.: Schenkman Publishing Co., 1971). This is a collection of sociologically based studies of women in the total variety of professional situations. It contains discussions of career choices, adult socialization, career patterns and marriage, and the implications of women in the professions for social change.
    [99]*Ibid.*, p. 4.
    [100]*Ibid.*, p. 5.
    [101]*Ibid.*, pp. 20-21.

cial, through professional associations, and unofficial, through friendship patterns and informal communications networks. In the established professions, these groups have been and generally remain male dominated.

> This occurs through the elaborate structure of both formal and informal networks of tightly knit professional communities that stretch across the entire country. Male professionals exert tremendous power over every aspect of professional life, from recruitment into professional schools, the curriculum, residencies and apprenticeships, grants for scientific research, and even the income of professionals through consultations, referrals and the disposition of honorific rewards.[102]

Cynthia Epstein has provided several insights into the interpersonal dynamics that can be so frustrating to the woman professional. She notes, for example, that there is a disjuncture between "appropriate" sexual roles and appropriate occupational roles.[103] The occupational roles do not contain the elements that women have been socialized into following in interpersonal interactions. In addition, sexuality and the traditional norms regarding male-female interactions can enter the picture. Epstein notes that if a male professional accepts a female protégé (such sponsorship is common in many professions), the sponsor's wife may object on grounds of the intimacy involved in such a relationship, and the protégé's, husband, child, or father will possibly raise similar questions.[104] Such issues would not be raised in a male-male relationship.

There will undoubtedly be some improvements in the situation of women professionals. Given the power of the existing arrangements, however, how rapidly these improvements will occur is very questionable. It appears that there are rapid changes in the admission of women to professional schools. More and more women are entering the established and powerful professions. It will take another twenty to thirty years to determine if these changes are more than tokenism and if women who opt for the professional life will be able to experience careers that are similar to those of their male counterparts.

There are certain situations that help the woman professional in adjusting to the strains in the role. If a woman shares statuses other than sex with her colleagues, as in the case of a female Wall Street lawyer who has a similar background to her male counterparts or a female black dentist who practices in the black community, colleagues and clients

---

[102]*Ibid.*, p. 28.

[103]"Women Lawyers and Their Profession: Inconsistency of Social Controls and Their Consequences for Professional Performance" (Paper presented at the 1969 Annual Meetings of the American Sociological Association, San Francisco).

[104]Cynthia Fuchs Epstein, "Encountering the Male Establishment: Sex-Status Limits on Women's Careers in the Professions," *American Journal of Sociology* 75 (May 1970), 965–82.

alike will likely be less resistant. If a woman is married and can share a practice with her husband or collaborate on research, strain can be eased. Similarly, if a married couple are in the same field, each marriage partner can support the other. Both of these last situations involve other aspects of the marital relationship, of course. (These situations will be dealt with in more detail in Chapter 10.) Having friends in the same field also helps reduce the extent of the strain that the woman can experience as a professional.[105] These conditions, of course, are not available to all female professionals. The woman may be the only woman in her field at the particular place of employment, may not have the same background as her colleagues, and may not be married, or, if married, may have a nonsupportive husband or children.

The evidence on women in the professions also suggests that the professions are not as universalistic and fair as their proponents and many analysts have suggested. There is both official and unofficial discrimination against half of their potential membership. There are mechanisms to deal with this discrimination at the individual level (individual women can resolve some of these dilemmas through their career choice patterns and, where relevant, through mate-choice patterns). A critical factor is the determination of whether or not the changes that appear to be happening are superficial, or whether or not the professional world is in fact changing.

We now move to a consideration of influential factors that come from outside a profession's own ranks—governmental regulations.

REGULATIONS AND THE PROFESSIONS

To some people, the whole notion of governmental control of the professions is irrelevant. The irrelevancy is based on the well-known fact that governmental certification and licensure is almost totally based on the professions' own wishes, rather than on those of the public. It certainly is correct that local, state, and federal legislative bodies defer to "professional judgment" when it comes to determining qualifications for practice.

At the same time, the role of government is important, if unappreciated. This can be seen in two cases. In the first place, while the established professions use the government to their own advantage, the government may in turn impede the activities of professional groups in domain conflicts with the established professions. Organized medicine,

[105]Cynthia Fuchs Epstein, *Woman's Place: Options and Limits in Professional Careers*, (Berkeley: University of California Press, 1970), pp. 140–42.

for example, successfully blocked the efforts of osteopaths and chiropractors seeking extended limits to their practice. Likewise, clinical psychologists, in their attempts to deal with nervous and mental disorders, have been blocked by organized medicine.[106]

Since these are interprofessional boundary disputes, the government becomes an important mediating party. For the occupational groups known as paraprofessions (to be discussed below), the established professions determine, through the government, the courses of training and behavior permitted. The government thus does regulate many professional activities, even if it does so on the basis of a more established and powerful profession's bidding.

The second important role of government is an emergent one. This involves a more active regulatory stance over human service delivery areas, such as medicine or welfare. As the federal and state governments assume increasingly important financial roles in the service delivery arena, it can be expected that government regulation will also increase. A hint of this can be seen in the medical field. The 1972 United States Social Security Act included provisions for the establishment of Professional Standard Review Organizations (PSRO's).

> The function of these organizations will be to review the necessity, quality, and appropriateness of professional health services paid for by the government and provided by either individual professionals or institutions.[107]

Since the government is so important in the provision of such funds, the implications for professional practice may be great. To be sure, much of the review of the PSRO's will be based on judgments from the profession of medicine. At the same time, it can be expected that statisticians, accountants, and social scientists will also have an influence in the review process. While it is premature to speculate on the exact impact of PSRO's, some potential can be seen in John Wennberg and Alan Gittelsohn's conclusion that

> the PSRO's can evaluate the wide variations in the level of services among residents of different communities. Coordinated exercise of the authority vested in these regulatory programs may lead to explicit strategies to deal directly with inequality and uncertainty concerning the effectiveness of health care delivery.[108]

[106]Freidson, *Profession of Medicine*, p. 30.

[107]Mary E. W. Goss, "Needed Sociological Research on Professional Organization and Control in Medicine" (Paper prepared for the 1973 Annual Meetings of the American Sociological Association, New York).

[108]"Small Area Variations in Health Care Delivery," *Science* 182 (14 December 1973), 1107.

Programs such as the PSRO's may be a prototype for regulatory programs in areas such as welfare, education, law, and other human services. If the current wave of consumerism continues and the government (at all levels) responds to this wave, then one could expect more government regulation of professional practice. This is, of course, no guarantee of better professional practice, but it does represent a real and potential source of variation from the traditional forms of practice. The traditional form of regulation, of course, is the use of the profession itself as the regulatory body.

PROFESSIONAL SELF-REGULATION

We have already noted that the norm of professional self-regulation does not work as well as its proponents would argue that it does (in the section on autonomous professional organizations). According to Freidson, a major reason for this is the absence of observability of much professional work.[109] He suggests that more administratively oriented professional practices with an established hierarchy may offer more of a review possibility.[110] At the same time, he concludes that professional self-regulation tends not to penalize general incompetence or shoddy work. While a professional may be ostracized or be denied referrals, neither type of censure prevents a person from practicing the profession. These more social sanctions are extremely weak when compared with more bureaucratic control mechanisms. Since, of course, professions are being practiced in organizations to an increasing extent, professional self-regulation may actually increase. It may well be that some professions may decide to regulate themselves more realistically rather than face the "threat" of governmental regulation.

Official self-regulation is just one way in which professionals are influenced by their peers. Interaction with peers is just as important for professionals as for any other type of worker. In this regard, Johnstone and Hopson note:

> In addition to groupings of lawyers in clearly delineated formal organizations such as law firms and legal departments, regular cooperative relationships sometimes develop among particular lawyers in different formal organizations and these become so close that in effect they evolve into informal work units of the lawyers concerned. This can happen between inside corporate lawyers and the outside counsel they consistently use,

[109]Freidson, *Profession of Medicine*, chap. 7.

[110]See Mary E. W. Goss, "Influence and Authority Among Physicians in an Outpatient Clinic," *American Sociological Review* 16 (February 1961), 39–50.

between private firm lawyers in one city and those in their correspondent firm in another, or between a highly specialized practitioner and those lawyers in other firms who frequently draw on his services.[111]

A similar point is made by Oswald Hall in his analysis of the informal structuring of medical practices. Hall notes that factors such as race, religion, and ethnic background play a role in acceptance into the "inner fraternity" of physicians who dominate the medical profession in the community he examined. Hall stresses that competence is vital to acceptance, but so is the proper personality. Nonacceptance can lead to a situation in which the possibilities for financial and professional advancement become blocked.[112] Here again, the work of the professional is structured, in this case by social factors.

The effects of this structuring may have little to do with the performance of the professional in his work, or they may enhance or detract from his performance. If the peer group expects consistently high performance levels, then the consequences will be positive for both the professional and his clients or employing organization. On the other hand, if the expectation level is low, as Johnstone and Hopson suggest that it is for some corporate counsels, or if potentially well-qualified practitioners are excluded from memberships in inner circles, law firms, or other professional organizations because of racial or religious factors, the effects will be negative.

A further, and perhaps obvious, point about the impact of peer structuring should be noted. The professional who is for one reason or another excluded from an informal group that is significant to him, as in the case of a physician who is not admitted to practice in a prestigious hospital or a teacher who is placed in the position of an isolate in the sociometric structure of a school, will probably still react to the group from which he is excluded. The form of the reaction could range from bitterness to attempts to behave in ways so that he would be accepted. Whatever the form of the reaction, the group still has an impact on his behavior.

In both official and unofficial ways, the life and work of the professional are affected by his peers. Since two important characteristics of the professions are that a profession is a major point of reference for its members and that professional organizations are important, the notion of professional self-regulation cannot be dismissed simply because self-

[111]Johnstone and Hopson, *Lawyers and Their Work*, p. 33.

[112]Oswald Hall, "The Informal Organization of the Medical Profession," *Canadian Journal of Economics and Political Science*, XXII, 11 (February 1946), 30–44, and "Stages of a Medical Career," *American Journal of Sociology*, LIII, 5 (March 1948), 327–36.

regulation does not operate at an optimal level. It is important for the professions and the individual professional as yet another source of variation in behavior. We turn now from a consideration of the profession and professional to a major component of the social situation of the professional—the client.

THE CLIENT

The client is an important part of the role set for almost all professionals.

> The professional renders his expert services for clients. Those clients may be individual or collective; they may actively seek professional advice and help, or have the service provided as a sort of by-product of their position in some social organization.[113]

Perhaps because of their presumed subservience to the professional, clients have not been intensively examined in terms of their impact on professional practice. There is a growing concern with the impact of the professional on the client, a topic we will turn to later, but less interest has been shown in the reciprocal effect.

Some indication of the importance of the client for the professional can be seen in Mark Lefton and William Rosengren's analysis of the impact of clients on organizations.[114] Lefton and Rosengren point out that hospitals (a professional organization) vary in their concern about clients along two dimensions—lateral and longitudinal. The lateral dimension involves the extent to which the hospital must deal with the total life of the patient. High laterality would mean an involvement in all phases of the person's life, as in many psychiatric facilities. Low laterality involves just a concern with a limited aspect of the person's life, as in an emergency room or in some surgical wards. The longitudinal dimension is the time frame involved. While Lefton and Rosengren's concern is with organizations, their implications are important for the professions. The professional must act differently toward clients with differing lateral and longitudinal dimensions. A long, intense legal case involves more of the lawyer's professional time than a simple probate hearing or the like. The professor behaves differently with his own Ph.D. students (high longitudinality and laterality) than with a single student out of a class of 500 whom he will never see again. Thus the role relationships with clients at least partially structure the activities of the professional.

The professional-client relationship is often thought to be at the

[113]Wilbert E. Moore, *Professions, Roles and Rules*, p. 87.
[114]"Organizations and Clients: Lateral and Longitudinal Dimensions," *American Sociological Review* 31 (December 1966), 802–10.

heart of the role of the professional. Moore suggests that the client comes to the professional in a spirit of *credat emptor*—let the buyer (client) trust.[115] The client is in a position where he needs the services of the professional, or at least believes that he does, since he is unable to supply the answers to his own problems. The professional is expected to deal with the client to the best of his ability, using his judgment for the client's benefit. The professional is also expected to be loyal to his client, not betraying the trust the client has demonstrated by coming to him. The client contributes to the one-to-one relationship by paying a fee directly to the professional for his services. In this form of relationship, both the client and the professional are characterized by high levels of individual freedom. This is the idealized description of the client-professional relationship in popular and some professional literature.

There is growing evidence that this image does not correspond to reality in many cases. Although complete evidence is not available, it is probable that this idealized image is realized in some proportion of professional practice. In many cases, however, the client relationship becomes a limiting or structuring factor for the professional. Hughes, in discussing Carlin's study of individual lawyers in Chicago, states:

> As a matter of fact, there are some indications in recent studies of a great paradox. Part of the cherished freedom of a professional worker is not merely to do his work according to his own best judgment and conscience, but also to choose his own style of work and economy of effort. Lawyers who practice alone—at least in a sample of them taken in Chicago—are utterly captives and choreboys of their clients. They have no freedom to choose a branch of law and make themselves expert or learned in it. Most of them, in time, do find their practice narrowed to a special line of chores: they have become specialists by default.[116]

Oswald Hall's analysis of medical careers supplies additional evidence that the client is in many ways a structuring agent. He notes that the doctor must adopt the appropriate strategy to attract and keep clients. Since the attraction of clients takes place in a competitive environment, "intelligent enterprise may be more important than medical knowledge and skill."[117] Hall suggests that the attraction of clients, particularly for specialists because of the referral system, requires relationships with other medical practitioners, thus linking the doctor to another social structure. This attraction and maintenance of clients requires the doctor to conform to his clients' expectations as well as to those of his colleagues.

The importance of clients was stressed in Smigel's examination of

[115]Wilbert E. Moore, "Economic and Professional Institutions," in *Sociology: An Introduction*, ed. Neil J. Smelser (New York: John Wiley & Sons, 1967), p. 322.

[116]Everett C. Hughes, "The Professions in Society," *The Canadian Journal of Economics and Political Science*, XXVI, 1 (February 1960), 60–61.

[117]Hall, "Stages of a Medical Career," p. 322.

the Wall Street lawyers. The initial selection of the lawyers was based to some extent on their probable abilities in client relationships. As the beginning associates sought to advance into partnership positions, they were assessed on the basis of their ability to interact with, and later attract, clients. The partners in the firms suggested that relationships with clients occupied more of their time in many instances than the practice of law. In the case of these lawyers and the doctors discussed by Hall, the ability to relate to clients was not held to be more important than the professional competence but rather an additional factor to be considered in analyzing professional work. Again, the exact amount that relationships to clients contribute to a structured work situation for the professional, as opposed to the factors already discussed, cannot be determined without additional evidence.

The discussion thus far has centered around the way in which relationships to clients affect the daily work of the professional. The evidence suggests that neither the client nor the professional is totally free in this relationship and that both must conform to the other's expectation. There is another, and somewhat neglected, sense in which the professional, who is dependent upon clients, is limited by his clients. It is extremely difficult for such a professional to be geographically mobile. Jack R. Ladinsky found, on the basis of his analysis of census data, that *Professions that demand costly equipment purchases and close cultivation of clienteles block migration.*[118] Ladinsky also found that salaried professionals (those with a direct client group) were more likely to move within and between states. The self-employed, client-oriented professional is essentially locked into a location, unless he wants to risk building a clientele again.

Hughes's words succinctly summarize the points made thus far:

> And here we are at a paradox of modern professional freedom. The effective freedom to choose one's special line of work, to have access to the appropriate clients and equipment, to engage in that converse with eager and competent colleagues which will sharpen one's knowledge and skill, to organize one's time and effort so as to gain that end, and even freedom from pressure to conform to the client's individual or collective customs and opinions seems, in many lines of work, to be much greater for those professionals who have employers and work inside complicated and even bureaucratic organizations than for those who, according to the traditional concept, are in independent practice.[119]

Thus far we have been treating the client as an individual who interacts with the professional. In an increasing number of cases, clients are

---

[118]"Occupational Determinants of Geographic Mobility Among Professional Workers," *American Sociological Review,* XXXII, 2, (April 1967), 257, italics in original.

[119]Everett C. Hughes, "The Professions in Society," p. 61.

organizing and presenting professionals with a united front, frequently threatening many of the traditional professional tenets. This can be seen in such diverse organized groups as welfare recipients, students, a divorcing couple, rape victims, pregnant women, and organizations of lay people in religious bodies. According to Haug and Sussman, this involves attacks on a professional's expertise and altruism and on the system of delivery of services.[120] Such attacks are threats to a professional's autonomy. What the clients are saying is basically that the professional does not know all of the answers and does not take the clients' characteristics or wishes into account. This is true whether or not the clients are poor or rich or educated or uneducated. The development of new careers in the paraprofessions is an attempt to bring the client perspective into the delivery system, but by and large the paraprofessional "movement" has not had as great an impact as its supporters had hoped.

If the client movement does in fact continue and grow, the implications for the professions could be enormous. The discussion of government regulations can be linked to this section at this point. One reflection of client concerns is the growing potential for government regulations. Clients no longer believe in "doctor's orders" or other such manifestations of the belief in the omnipotence of professionals. At the same time, as was suggested at the outset of this book, there continues to be an increasing need for such professional occupations. What will probably happen is that the professions will continue to be important, but the social status differentials and general social distance between the professionals and their clients will be reduced. The increasing usage of the idea of service delivery systems, with citizen inputs, is indicative of this potential.

There is still another aspect of the professional-client relationship. Our focus has been on the professional, but the client must also be considered. By implication, the client has been considered in our discussion of the client movement. Many clients are dissatisfied with the services they receive. By definition, of course, the clients are less powerful than the professional in this relationship, and probably in the vast majority of the cases the client willingly submits to the professional since the client seeks out the professional in the first place in a one-to-one professional-client relationship.

The greatest conflict between professionals and clients comes when the clients are most different from the professional—when they are non-upper middle class, poorly educated, minority group members, etc. In this regard Emil Berkanovic notes:

---

[120]Marie R. Haug and Marvin Sussman, "Professional Autonomy and the Revolt of the Client," *Social Problems* 17 (fall 1969), 153–161. See also *Journal of Social Issues*, 26, No. 3, *Professionals and the Poor*, Marcia Guttentag, Issue Editor.

It would appear, however, that the three requirements of universalism, functional specificity, and emotional neutrality reflect value choices which are more compatible with the rationalistic and non-expressive value systems of the ethnic groups which come from northwest Europe than with the values of people from elsewhere. Further there is evidence that many non-white, non-middle-class groups find the services organized around these ideals often fail to meet their needs. . . . Thus, many non-whites feel that service professionals do not care about them, do not listen to them, and do not understand their problems. Indeed, many appear to feel that their problems are not easily categorized into the various cubbyholes which make up the professional division of labor, and that they want their problems treated as they experience them, rather than as the professional chooses to fragment them.[121]

This expresses an inherent conflict in that there is little reason for optimism over either short or long time frames. If people of increasingly diverse ethnic and racial backgrounds are in fact admitted to professional schools, it would be predicted that, as graduates, they would behave more like their fellow professionals, rather than like their age cohorts who did not receive such training. The socialization process in professional schools would tend to "wash out" ethnic and racially based behaviors and substitute the behavior and values of the profession. Some slight amelioration of the problems, which Berkanovic discusses, may occur over time with more and more non–northwest European background people in professional schools, but the progress will be slow. (We will deal with the issue of minority group professionals below.)

Clients have a direct face-to-face impact on the professional. The client movement may have important indirect impacts through the legislative process as the whole delivery of services becomes reshaped over time. Here again we see threats to the autonomy of the professional. In some ways, the fact that we have been discussing the sources of variation in professional behavior as threats to autonomy is indicative of the continued autonomy of the professions. *If the autonomy were not there in the first place, these variations would not be threats.* We now turn to the last source of variation, the unionization of professional work.

UNIONIZATION

Members of all professions belong to unions, even though to some professionals unions are the very antithesis of professionalism. This apparent paradox can be resolved by noting that there are large differ-

[121]"Some Implications of Professionalism for Institutional Racism" (Paper prepared for the 1973 Annual Meetings of the American Sociological Association, New York), p. 5.

ences within each profession as well as between professions. At the same time, unionization of professionals is a major issue in many work locations. Everett Carll Ladd, Jr., and Seymour Martin Lipset provide good insights into the nature of this paradox and the present situation when they note:

> Perhaps the principal reason, then, for the long standing aversion of college professors and other professionals to trade unions lies in the fact that the latter have been nourished by a condition of dependence—the need to organize and act collectively to achieve some measure of standing and voice vis-à-vis the dominant 'outside' party, usually management of the large-scale business enterprise, whereas the former have operated in a situation of substantial independence or autonomy. The factor of social status is closely associated here. Members of an occupation characterized by a high degree of self-regulation draw from that position a sense of individual standing and importance that they guard jealously. The collectivism and accompanying equalitarian norms of trade unionism, in contrast, are acceptable, if not always appealing, to those whose personal status and freedom of action in any case must be low. . . . The egalitarian norms of unionism would appear to clash much more sharply with standards and expectations that have prevailed in the professions than with those of the 'semi-professions,' such as public-school teaching and nursing.[122]

Ladd and Lipset's own data confirm this last comment. Among the college faculty surveyed in their study, it was the lower status, younger, and more poorly paid faculty members who most favored unionization (holding constant the faculty members' general orientation toward unions, which is not of concern to us here).

For nonacademic professionals, there is a rather obvious linkage between employment in bureaucratized organizations and unionization. There is also a clear linkage between economic conditions and unionization. When states pass legislation that enables collective bargaining for public employees, there is another strong potential for unionization of professionals employed in the public sector. There are thus several factors that, when combined, appear to lead toward increasing unionization of professionals.

Our interest here is not in unionization per se, but in professional autonomy. The evidence is unclear in this regard. Advocates of unionization argue that professional autonomy would be enhanced by unionization, because economic and job security issues would be enhanced and the professional could concentrate on the tasks to be performed. Indeed, some professional unions have pushed the idea of client concerns and

---

[122]*Professors, Unions, and American Higher Education* (Berkeley, Calif.: Carnegie Commission on Higher Education, 1973), p. 3.

care much more than some of the traditional professional associations.[123] On the other hand, the opponents of unionization argue that unionization means leveling at the lowest or middle level, with "brilliant" work neither rewarded nor sought. They also argue that union contracts would define the work to be performed to such an extent (based on analyses of more traditional industrial union contracts) that the professional would not be able to exercise independent judgement.

There is little evidence available to determine or predict the impact of unionization on the professions. Those professions that are moderately unionized, such as teaching or nursing, had so little autonomy to begin with that any conclusions based on their current lack of autonomy under unionization, are not definitive. Unionization thus exists as a potential, though not necessary, threat to professional autonomy.[124] It is an additional source of variation of professional practice. Before concluding this chapter, two unconnected but relevant topics will be considered—professionals who are also minority group members and paraprofessionals.

THE MINORITY PROFESSIONAL

Much of what was noted in regard to the treatment accorded women in the professions can be applied, even more strongly, to minority group members. Discrimination is evident from primary school on through professional schools and into practice. Documentation of this comes most heavily from studies of black physicians.

There is a long history of restrictive quotas on racial, religious, and ethnic minorities in medical (and other professional) schools. While this pattern is at least overtly ended, its presence until the very recent past has had the effect of greatly diminishing the number of minority professionals and also limiting the likelihood that minority professionals could serve as role models for succeeding generations. Even admission to and graduation from professional schools is no guarantee of full admission to professional practice. Our discussion of the importance of peers and of sponsorship should suggest that minority group members would have many problems

[123]Gloria V. Engel and Marion L. Schulman found that advocacy of unionization among a sample of physicians was associated with strong patient care orientations. They also found that lower perceptions of autonomy were also associated with a pro-union attitude. Engel and Schulman, "The Relationship of Unionization to Professionalism" (Paper prepared for the 1973 Annual Meetings of the American Sociological Association, New York).

[124]Marie R. Haug and Marvin B. Sussman argue that *job* autonomy may actually be enhanced by unionization, partially because of unionization itself and partially because of the growing rejection of professional expertise by clients. In Haug and Sussman, "Professionalization and Unionism: A Jurisdictional Dispute?" in Eliot Freidson, ed., *The Professions and their Prospects* (Beverly Hills, Calif.: Sage Publications, 1973).

entering professional practice. For black physicians, obtaining hospital appointments has been an extremely difficult task. Lack of access to facilities and interactions with fellow professionals has the inevitable consequence of diminishing the professional's competence *and* income.

According to Ritzer, the black professional can act in one of three ways—work on "black" problems, as a number of noted academic professionals have done; work in the black community where the economic rewards will be slight and social rewards may be negative because of the relative success of the black professional; or try to compete in white society, which again has been successfully done in a large number of cases.[125] In the last case, the black community may in turn be resentful.

As minority group solidarity increases and more open-admissions policies in professional schools begin to bear fruit, it can be expected that more minority professionals will practice in and focus on minority-related areas. Again, these changes have occurred so recently that no definitive statements can be made. It is probable that the increasing number of minority professionals will be distributed at all levels and in all types of professional practice, if the informal patterns of discrimination do in fact cease to be important.

PARAPROFESSIONALS

Paraprofessionals are those workers who assist professionals in their work and are controlled by the professionals. We have paramedical personnel, such as pediatric nurse practitioners, physician assistants, and certified nurse midwives.[126] There are also social worker and teacher aides and a large number of other paraprofessional occupations.

The growth of the paraprofessions has occurred for two major reasons. The first is the overload that many professionals experienced as case loads and general work loads increased. The second reason is more social and involves attempts to bring community members into health and social service delivery systems. Relatively poorly educated people were brought into "new careers" programs in order to provide minority- or poverty-based perspectives on service delivery.

[125]Ritzer, *Man and His Work*, pp. 110–12. See also David Howard, "An Exploratory Study of Attitudes of Negro Professionals Toward Competition with Whites," *Social Forces* 45 (September 1966), 20–27, and Michael Richard, "The Negro Physician: Babbitt or Revolutionary?," *Journal of Health and Social Behavior* 10 (December 1969), 265–75.

[126]Jane Cassels Record and Merwyn R. Greenlick, "New Health Professionals at Kaiser: A Question of Role Ambiguity" (Paper prepared for the 1973 Annual Meetings of the American Sociological Association, New York). Freidson, in *Profession of Medicine*, pp. 48–49, correctly emphasizes the fact that the control of the paraprofessional lies in the hands of the professional. Record and Greenlick document this by noting the importance of the receptivity of the professional staff in a group health plan.

The work of the paraprofessional is the more routine aspects of professional practice, answering phone calls and responding to routine questions, recording biographical data, maintaining discipline in the classroom, and so on. The major issue for the professional is the amount of responsibility to give the paraprofessional. This is also the major issue for the paraprofessional. The paraprofessional is trained to offer rather limited technical assistance but, as is the case with much training, the paraprofessional may want and be able to learn more on the job. It is very conceivable that a paraprofessional could learn medicine, law, or social work, just as earlier professionals did before the advent of professional schools. Thus the paraprofessional could become an apprentice and eventually know as much about day-to-day practice as the professional (the issue of theoretical knowledge as a basis of the professions is interesting in this light).

Professionals strongly resist this sort of perceived encroachment, maintaining that their expertise is required for the difficult decisions. This can be viewed, cynically, as an attempt to maintain one's economic position or, more charitably, as an attempt at maintaining high standards and theoretically-based decisions. In either case, there are continual jurisdictional disputes between paraprofessionals and professionals and between paraprofessions. The physician's assistant represents a threat to the nurse, as does the legal assistant to the legal secretary.

For the paraprofessional, there is little hope for advancement, unless some sort of promotional and salary hierarchy is introduced that permits the person to advance without changing his basic status. There is the other alternative of returning to school and becoming a full-fledged professional. This, of course, is difficult to do at middle age.

The ideal situation, from a rational point of view, would be for services to be delivered with inputs from the paraprofessional where needed in terms of the nature of the clientele or community being served. The tasks in the delivery of services would be divided and assigned according to ability and training, and there would be complete service for all of the needs of the clients. This remains an ideal, of course, because the professionals' power is such that control will remain with the established professions and professionals. It is impossible to determine if this professional control does or does not guarantee quality.

SUMMARY AND CONCLUSIONS

This has been a long chapter. There is a vast body of literature on the professions and professionals. These occupations are important for society and are also highly visible, and thus the length seems warranted.

The first order of business was to indicate the important characteristics or attributes of the professions. While the professional model can serve as a mechanism to obscure variations in professional practice, it does serve to differentiate professions from other occupations and also to highlight why the professions have achieved the status and autonomy that they enjoy. A modified professional model was suggested that focused on the extent of autonomy in the work setting.

The work setting, be it in solo practice, autonomous or heteronomous professional organizations, or professional departments is a critical component in differences among and within professions. While there is good evidence to suggest that professional and bureaucratic modes of organization are antithetical, it was stressed that organizations typically accommodate to their memberships, typically permitting professionals more autonomy than other employees.

While the setting of professional work is important, there are other sources of variation in professional practice. In this regard, we discussed the role of knowledge obsolescence, the presence of women, clients, peers, government regulations, and unionization. These were all discussed from the standpoint of their impact on the autonomy of the work of the professional. We did not specify the relative strength of each of these factors in affecting professional work, as that is a task for research not yet undertaken. The professions are thus not set in concrete. There are threats to autonomy from outside the professions and within. The place of any single profession in society is affected by the factors that we have discussed. Thus the professional model, so disarmingly simple in its original statement, becomes a complex and dynamic ideal type—not achieved in real life and changing in its composition over time. The professions themselves are the same—not ideal and rapidly changing.

5

MANAGERS, PROPRIETORS, AND OFFICIALS

The key occupational group in industrial society is management. Effective direction of human efforts—whether in the public or private sectors of an economy—is central to the wise and efficient utilization of human and material resources.[1]

Whether this same importance is found in the postindustrial society may be open to some question, but the fact remains that the occupational types to be considered in this chapter are important decision makers, policy setters, and direction givers for the organizations that so shape our lives. This set of occupations contains the richest and most powerful people in the society. It also contains people who are virtual captives of their employing organizations or their surroundings.

The discussion of the professions proceeded from the relatively simple professional model to the conclusion that neither professions as a whole nor the individual professions are homogeneous. The discussion

---

[1]John P. Campbell et al., *Managerial Behavior, Performance, and Effectiveness* (New York: McGraw-Hill Book Company, 1970), p. 1. This book contains an excellent overview of the problems associated with management selection, training, motivation, and performance. Much of the work on management has been done by psychologists. We will pay relatively little attention to the psychological aspects of the occupations to be discussed, focusing instead on the relevant *sociological* variables. While this focus does not permit a complete picture of the topic, the author believes that the sociological focus contains sufficient strengths to justify its seemingly provincial presentation here. The sociological focus, like its psychological or economic complements, is obviously incomplete for a total perspective.

of managers, proprietors, and officials will begin with the same conclusion. The very name of the category suggests the heterogeneity of this group of occupations. Perhaps the only truly common characteristic within this category is the relatively high socioeconomic status the members of the category enjoy. Another characteristic, but one that is not unique to this or most of the other categories, is that the members of the category occupy positions in organizations. The term "manager" refers to business executives, itself a very broad category. Proprietors are owners of businesses and, in the majority of the cases, they are also managers, performing the same kinds of functions and occupying the same positions as top executives. Proprietors also perform a wide variety of other nonmanagerial roles. Officials are in many ways identical to managers, the major difference being the fact that officials are employed in nonprofit organizations, such as governmental agencies, school systems, hospitals, business and professional associations, etc. They are administrators in nonbusiness organizations. The simplest description of this category is that managers, proprietors, and officials occupy *middle to high positions in organizations of all types.*

It is important to note at the outset that there is no model, such as the professional model, by which the occupations can be analyzed. In some cases, the professional model itself can be a useful analytical tool in examining similarities and differences between this set of occupations and the professions. Since both occupational categories occupy roughly equivalent positions in the social-stratification system, such an analysis is of some use. Inevitably, however, it leads to the relatively useless conclusion that these occupations are not as professional as the professions in terms of the components of the professional model. Application of the professional model in this way is inappropriate because of the implication that those occupations that do not approximate it are somehow inferior to those that do. Despite the sometimes fevered strivings of some occupations to achieve correspondence with this model, for most there is little in the way of inherent goodliness or Godliness in corresponding with the model. This is not to suggest that there is a paucity of models for executives. Writers from Frederick W. Taylor and the scientific management school to Rensis Likert and Douglas McGregor to the human relations school to current theorists have provided models of how to be better executives.[2]

[2]See Frederick W. Taylor, *Scientific Management* (New York: Harper & Row, Publishers, 1911). See also Rensis Likert, *New Patterns of Management* (New York: McGraw-Hill Book Company, 1962) and Douglas McGregor, *The Human Side of Enterprise* (New York: McGraw-Hill Book Company, 1960). For a review and critique of both of these management models, see Amitai Etzioni, *Modern Organizations* (Englewood Cliffs, N.J.: Prentice-Hall, Inc., 1964), pp. 20–49. More recently, Camp-

While it is easy to say that these works, mostly by psychologists, have not really gotten very far in informing scholars or practitioners about the "true" nature of the work of managers, proprietors, and officials, sociologists have not been much help either. In fact, there is a real absence of research on these occupations. The reasons for this range from difficulties in gaining access to the occupational members to politically based biases against research on this segment of the population to a concern with the organizations in which these occupations are found, rather than the occupations themselves. For these and other reasons, there is incomplete sociological information and an absence of a sociological perspective on these occupations.

What does emerge from our present state of knowledge is that these are organizationally based occupations (with a major exception in the case of proprietors). The organizations in which the occupations are found determine the occupational title—personnel manager or industrial relations manager or salesman or sales engineer. The organization also provides most of the rewards and most of the focus of activities for the individual. The organization thus shapes the occupation and individuals. Much of our interest in this chapter will be focused on this individual-organizational nexus. It is hoped that this focus will add to our knowledge of this heterogeneous occupational category. We will begin our discussion with the subcategory of executives.

EXECUTIVES

Many writers suggest that an important difference exists between managers and executives. Executives are those near or at the top of their organizations, while managers occupy lower positions in the hierarchy. This distinction will be maintained in this analysis, although it is useful only in the limited way. The ranks of executives are filled by those moving up from management so that the characteristics of the two groups cannot be totally different, except insofar as those who do move into executive positions may have measurably different characteristics from those who do not move up. Whether they do or not has been the subject of a rather large quantity of writing but is still unresolved. While executives are those higher in the organization, the characteristics of the work performed and the performers themselves will generally be viewed as similar except for the status difference.

---

bell *et al.*, *Managerial Behavior, Performance, and Effectiveness* and Chris Argyris, *Management and Organizational Development* (New York: McGraw-Hill Book Company, 1971) have provided models for reaching and measuring effective executive behavior.

An important statement on the functions of the executive was provided by Chester I. Barnard, a former president of the New Jersey Bell Telephone Company, in his book *The Functions of the Executive*. A major contribution to organizational theory, the book views the organization as a decision-making system and also provides an overview of the work of executives. According to Barnard, executives perform three major functions. The first is the maintenance of communications within the organization, which involves the establishment of positions in the organization to form a communications system and the filling of these positions with personnel who are capable of performing the required communications functions.[3] According to Barnard, those filling these positions should be loyal to and dominated by the organization. This loyalty and domination is brought about by creating the proper incentives for the incumbents, such as interest and pride in the work, prestige, and material rewards, the last of which is the least important in this regard.[4] Barnard suggests that those lower in the hierarchy need more specific abilities than their superiors. The latter, the generalists, acquire their abilities through experience, while the former can be given specific training in their specialties. The effective organization matches the abilities of the executive with the communications requirements of the position to be filled.

The second major function of the executive is the securing of essential services from individuals, which involves bringing people into cooperative relationships with the organization by promotional techniques and propaganda and eliciting the required services from the individuals once they are willing to cooperate. The services are elicited by maintaining morale and inducements, developing norms and sanctions, supervision, and socialization into the jobs.[5]

The third executive function is the formulation and definition of the purposes, objectives, or goals of the organization. More than simply stating that the goal is profit, service, or whatever, this involves the translation of the organizational goals into specific activities that are carried out all the way down the hierarchy, with the activities becoming more specific as the hierarchy is descended.[6] Barnard states that these functions are "merely elements in an organic whole. It is their combination in a working system that makes an organization."[7]

A more recent but quite similar, view of executive functions is pro-

[3]Chester I. Barnard, *The Functions of the Executive* (Cambridge, Mass.: Harvard University Press, 1947), pp. 217–18.
[4]*Ibid.*, pp. 220–22.
[5]*Ibid.*, pp. 227–31.
[6]*Ibid.*, pp. 231–32.
[7]*Ibid.*, p. 233.

vided by the editors of *Fortune* magazine. From a compilation of definitions provided by executives, the following composite self-portrait
emerged:

> An American executive is a person paid for a full-time job in which he:
> (1) directly helps to set his company's objectives and over-all policies;
> (2) is required to make or approve decisions that significantly affect profits
> and future plans; (3) coordinates several major corporate functions, or
> those of a major division or department; (4) maintains and develops an
> organization of trained subordinates to achieve the company's objectives;
> *and* (5) delegates responsibility and authority to the organization, and
> controls performance and results through at least one level of supervision.[8]

This last point is the simplest means of differentiating between executives and managers. The executive has a wider span of control, both
in terms of personnel and policy. While many managers perform some
of the functions, the true executive performs them all. In addition, the
authors suggest that executives are only found in relatively large organizations of 1,000 employees or more. While the size is certainly arbitrary,
the differentiation itself is not. The manager performs narrower and more
specific functions, with relatively little impact on policy formulation,
while the executive has a broader impact.

If this is an accurate picture of what the executive does and how the
executive is differentiated from the manager, we can now turn to the
questions of *who* it is that does these things, *how* an individual reaches
an executive position, and *what difference* the behavior of an executive
makes for the organizations involved and the society as a whole.

The answer to the first of these questions is rather easy and is
already known to most people. The executive is well educated, frequently
with an advanced degree.[9] The executive is well paid, with some salaries
reaching the startling and seemingly exorbitant two to three hundred
thousand dollar annual level or higher. The executive is almost exclusively white and male. These well-known facts don't tell us very much,
since they do not differentiate the executive (with the exception of the
pay issue and the power that executives are believed to have) from many
other members of the labor force. The executive does work long hours,
but so does the professional. He is dedicated to his work, but so are
many other workers. The executive interacts with other executives on and
off the job, but again most other people in occupations interact with

---

[8]The editors of *Fortune Magazine, The Executive Life* (New York: Doubleday,
1956), pp. 17–18.
[9]The editors of *Fortune Magazine, The Executive Life* (New York: Doubleday and
Company, 1956) note that quite frequently the executive's advanced training has little
to do with his eventual executive position.

those on the same level as themselves. What then is so different about the executive?

Some answers to this may be seen in analyses of careers of executives. These analyses are handicapped by the fact that they have concentrated on successful executives (there are very few analyses of losers in any sphere of life), but some insights can be gleaned. W. Lloyd Warner and James Abegglen studied the backgrounds of some 8,000 business leaders.[10] They distinguished between a "birth" elite and a "mobile" elite, with the former being sons of successful fathers and the latter moving into executive positions from lower status backgrounds. Both are characterized by *early* success in their work. Similarly, David E. Berlew and Douglas T. Hall report that challenges in an executive's first year of employment and success in meeting difficult assignments lead to continued success, in terms of both intrinsic satisfactions and extrinsic achievement.[11]

Elliott A. Krause extends this time period, suggesting that it is the first decade and a half that are crucial, noting that within this time period, "those who are definitely on the way up have been clearly separated from those who have peaked."[12] There are two elements to these considerations, regardless of the time span involved. The future executive learns how to be successful early in his career, *and* the parameters of this success are defined by the organization in which the person is employed. While most executives change jobs over the years, their success is defined by some organization along the way. A person's reputation is built within the organizational setting and is carried with the individual up his own organization or to another organization.

These elements—success early in the career and organizational definition of success—are both problematic. In the author's opinion, the organizational definition of success is the more crucial element. The reason for this is that there have not been any validated and usable predictors of success on the part of individual actors.[13] That is, there is no set of attributes that successful people have and unsuccessful people don't have. To be sure, intelligence is always a major characteristic, but many unsuccessful people are also very intelligent. What seems to be important, then, is the organizational definition, for the individuals who come into the organization, of behavior that is recognized and rewarded as successful. The question now becomes, what do organizations want their successful younger personnel and future executives to be like? The answer here, unfortunately, is most unclear.

[10]*Big Business Leaders in America* (New York: Harper & Row, 1955).
[11]"The Socialization of Managers," *Administrative Science Quarterly*, XI, 2 (September 1966), 207–23.
[12]*The Sociology of Occupations* (Boston: Little, Brown and Company, 1971), p. 236.
[13]Campbell *et al., Managerial Behavior, Performance, and Effectiveness.*

This lack of clarity is due to the contrasting pictures of organizational executives. On the one hand, there are those who portray the executive as a nonthinking yes-man who accepts and believes in the organization over himself. Robert Presthus' description of the "upwardly mobile" person in the organization exemplifies this approach. According to Presthus, the upwardly mobile person has the following characteristics:

1. He accepts the organizational goals.
2. He submits to and accepts the collective values of the organization involving power, survival, and growth.
3. He is obedient, accepting authority as proper and legitimate.
4. He attaches himself personally to his superiors but remains detached and impersonal toward his subordinates.
5. The organizational norms become his personal norms.
6. He exhibits high morale and job satisfaction and does not question the system and, if and when failure comes, it is a personal failure, not one of the system itself.
7. He is highly involved in the organization, which contributes to organizational effectiveness.
8. He is action oriented and tends to ignore conflicting alternatives and ambiguities.
9. When hostility and resentment arise, they are not voiced. He does not show anger at his superior. He tries to be "other-directed," playing the role required for success.
10. When he feels anxiety, it is not admitted. Presthus notes that a high ulcer and hypertension rate is a consequence of this.
11. He is a local rather than a cosmopolitan.
12. He shies away from controversial causes and dissent.
13. He suffers a great deal of status anxiety and is very aware of status symbols. For this reason, organizations attempt to insure that the office furnishings for executives of equal rank are identical, so that unintended distinctions are not imagined.
14. Status achievement becomes an end in itself rather than the result of significant achievement.
15. He is a joiner in community activities.
16. The rewards for the upward-mobile individual are not found in the intrinsic value of the work being performed but rather in the effect that the work will have for his position in the organization.[14]

A drastically different picture is presented by Walter Guzzardi, Jr.[15] Innovation, dissent from established practices, confidence in -decision-

---

[14]Robert Presthus, *The Organizational Society*, pp. 164–204. See also Whyte, *Organization Man*.

[15]*The Young Executives* (New York: New American Library, Inc., 1964). Courtesy of *Fortune Magazine*,© 1965 Time Inc.

making powers, avid reading, and independence characterized the successful young executives whom Guzzardi studied. Guzzardi's men are practically the antithesis of Presthus' or Whyte's organization men.

What sense can be made of these contradictory findings? What do organizations expect? The answer, as could be expected, is that it depends on the organization. Guzzardi himself provides part of the answer when he notes that the innovative executive can only be successful in an innovating organization.[16] In organizations that are not innovative and see no need to become so, the more compliant, nonquestioning approach would undoubtedly be more successful. The literature on organizations contains many indications that organizations that are in rapidly changing environments and that deal with complex and changing technological problems are most likely to be innovative.[17] Thus even the organization itself is in no way free to decide independently if it is to be innovative or not and which type of behavior to reward as successful. It should be fairly clear that if an organization views itself as being in a placid environment and promotes and rewards people on that basis and the environment is actually very different, then the organization and its executives are in for a surprise and shock. Obviously, a major task of the executive is to avoid such surprises and shocks.

In many ways, the executive is like the professionals whom we have discussed at length. The similarity is primarily that the executive also uses his mind to make decisions. These decisions are on behalf of the organization and are clearly affected by organizational procedures and precedent. They are also based largely on experience, rather than abstract theory but, as we have seen, the professional's decision-making autonomy is not very theory based either.

Much of contemporary decision-making theory is organized around mathematically based models. These assume that the knowledge of the origins of the situation about which the decision is to be made, its current status, and the probable outcomes of alternative choices is quite complete. The advent of computers and other data-processing devices has contributed to the development of this approach, which assumes rationality on the part of the participants as well as complete knowledge. There is, however, some evidence that decision-making models ignore important components of reality.

James G. March and Herbert A. Simon, whose theory of organizations is based on decision making, point out:

Most human decision making, whether individual or organizational, is

[16]*Ibid.*, p. 69.

[17]For a recent review of this literature, see Gerald Zaltman, Robert Duncan, and Jonny Holbek, *Innovations and Organizations* (New York: John Wiley & Sons, 1973).

concerned with the discovery and selection of satisfactory alternatives; only in exceptional cases is it concerned with the discovery and selection of optimal alternatives.[18]

These *satisficing* decisions are based on criteria that describe minimally satisfactory alternatives and that rely on less than perfect knowledge. Optimal decisions must be based on criteria that allow all alternatives to be compared, thus being dependent on perfect knowledge of the antecedents, current status, and expected outcomes of a particular case in the decision-making process, a set of conditions unlikely to occur in reality.

In the same vein, David Braybrooke has suggested that executives do act on the basis of nonrational decisions. The successful executive has a repertoire of responses to situations, unpremeditated in their application and not fully recognized by the executive himself. The response strategies are based upon resources such as the amount of energy and its application, the air and style of leadership, skill in bargaining, and universal connections (access to sources of information and assistance) that a particular person possesses. These resources are transferable from situation to situation or organization to organization. Relatively nontransferable are such resources as mannerisms appropriate to a particular setting (the differences in approach of the stereotyped public-relations man as opposed to that of the conservative banker), local connections within an organization and with its affiliates, and knowledge of, and judgment about, the men with whom the executive interacts. The executive also has information from a variety of sources at his disposal. Braybrooke suggests that these elements are combined into stratagems that are employed in the decision-making process. Some stratagems become habitual, part of a particular executive's style. In some cases, new or novel stratagems are employed, based upon some new mixture of the resources available. Whether habitual or new, the stratagems are not recognized as such by the individuals involved and are not necessarily based upon rational criteria. Any strategy employed, if it is used at all consistently, while predictable, will not be, at times, rational.[19]

Braybrooke states:

A perfect organization would leave the executive paradoxically little to do; an imperfect organization, in an imperfect world, creates so many diffi-

---

[18]*Organizations* (New York: John Wiley & Sons, Inc., 1958), pp. 140–41. For a comprehensive overview of the limitations of the assumption of pure rationality on the part of organizations and their participants, see James G. Thompson, *Organizations in Action* (New York: McGraw-Hill Book Company, 1967).

[19]David Braybrooke, "The Mystery of Executive Success Re-examined," *Administrative Science Quarterly*, VIII, 4 (March 1964), 533–60.

culties for him that even sober observers are liable to credit his successes to intuitive wizardry.[20]

Braybrooke believes that executives combine resources, rather than such intuitive wizardry, into the stratagems discussed above that allow him to proceed, but in a less than totally rational way.

Implicit in many discussions of executives (and managers) is the question of just how much the executive must be a conformist. That is, how much does the individual have to act in accordance with the wishes of his peers, superiors, and subordinates and those of the organization, rather than acting as an independent individual? Popular belief tends to support the notion that the executive is highly conformist, but research findings indicate otherwise. John B. Miner, for example, found that executives and professors exhibited essentially identical patterns on a test of conformity. Among both groups, conformity decreased with age, and both groups exhibited wide ranges of conformity and deviance at the various age levels. Miner also suggests that demands for conformity or innovation may vary with the type of industry and with the orientation of the academic discipline.[21] In the same vein, Renato Tagiuri found little difference in the ordering of values among groups of scientists, executives, and research managers. Using the Allport-Vernon-Lindsey value questionnaire, which measures interest in theoretical, economic, aesthetic, social, political, and religious pursuits, Tagiuri found essentially the same ordering of these values; theoretical (discovery of truth), political, and economic values ranked highest for all. He suggests that some of the professional-organizational (scientist-executive) conflicts, which have been discussed, may be based on misperceptions of other groups' orientations.[22] In this case it is the research manager, as a middle man, who must mediate between the groups, ideally allowing each group to be seen in its true light. In terms of the present discussion, Miner's findings and the fact that values are shared between the different groups suggest either that executives are not the organization men they have been portrayed to be or that these other occupations are equally composed of organization men. Stated more positively, samples of executives indicate that executives' values and orientations toward their work and life are essentially similar to those of other highly trained members of the occupational world.

From these pieces of research, the suspicion grows that the stereo-

[20]Ibid., p. 560.

[21]John B. Miner, "Conformity Among Professors and Executives," Administrative Science Quarterly, VII, 1 (June 1962), 96–109.

[22]Renato Tagiuri, "Value Orientations and the Relationship of Managers and Scientists," Administrative Science Quarterly 10, (July 1965), 39–51.

type of the conformist executive is wrong. This suspicion is aggravated even further when Melvin Kohn's research is examined.[23] Kohn compared employees of bureaucratized organizations with employees of nonbureaucratized organizations. In discussing his findings, he notes:

> Observers of bureaucracy, impressed by its need to coordinate many people's activities, have assumed that a primary effect of a bureaucratization must be to suppress employees' individuality. We have found, to the contrary, that bureaucratization is consistently, albeit not strongly, associated with greater intellectual flexibility, higher valuation of self-direction, greater openness to new experience, and more personally responsible moral standards.[24]

Part of the reason for these findings was the higher educational level of the bureaucratically employed workers, while greater job protection, higher income levels, and more complex work also contributed to the results. This was a study of some 3,101 male respondents in a national survey. The workers represented all levels of the hierarchy of the organizations in which they were employed. While these findings do not deal with executives per se, they strongly reinforce the point that organizational employment does not create a set of highly conformist people.

The executives we are discussing are important for the organizations in which they work. The functions they perform are central to the success of the organizations, even though they may not have as much impact on the organizations as many would like to believe. In an interesting study, Stanley Lieberson and James F. O'Connor found that the impact of executives, as measured by leadership change in 167 large corporations over a twenty year period, was not as great as the impact of forces over which the leadership (executives) have no control.[25] The industry in which the corporation operated, the year, general economic conditions, and the company's original position within its industry had a far greater impact on sales, net income, and profit margin than did leadership changes. Leadership changes did affect profit margins strongly over a two or three year period, but the constraints on the organization's activities imposed by the general economic conditions, the organization's industry, and place in the industry were found to be more important than leadership.

Lieberson and O'Connor note that the constraints on leadership vary. In some cases the leader is virtually powerless, while in others there is

[23]"Bureaucratic Man: A Portrait and an Interpretation," *American Sociological Review* 36 (June 1971), 461–74.

[24]*Ibid.*, p. 472.

[25]"Leadership and Organizational Performance: A Study of Large Corporations," *American Sociological Review* 37 (April 1972) 117–30.

much more room maneuvering. Nevertheless, the executive cannot realistically be viewed as the autonomous "captain of the ship" who makes or breaks the organization. Instead, he is severely limited by the conditions in which his organization is operating.

The executive is also constrained from within the organization. Every organization has traditions and precedents. It also has friendship patterns, sponsorship norms, and other informal mechanisms that limit the extent to which any one individual or set of individuals can have an enormous influence. Organizations also have established chains of command, divisions of responsibility, procedural specifications, etc., which further limit what executives can do.

Much of the work of the executive is therefore resolving conflicts among the competing demands on the organization. If an organization has more than a single goal (note that the goals of sales, net income, and profit margin may themselves be incompatible), and almost every organization does, then the executive must also resolve conflicts between goals as well as between the myriad of alternative means to achieve these goals.

The executive brings with him to his job his individual characteristics. These include intelligence, aptitudes, knowledge, temperament, preferences, and expectations.[26] He then behaves in the work situation, based on the opportunities available to him, the situation in which he finds himself, and his abilities. His behavior, in turn, has consequences for the organization, in terms of the organization's performance (within the limitations noted from the Lieberson and O'Connor study). His behavior is an input for future behavior in that there is constant learning based on the feedback from past performance. All elements of his individual characteristics, his behavior on the job, and the impact on the organization are restricted by the organization in which this behavior occurs. The executive is thus in the same relationship to his employing organization as all of the other workers. There is more autonomy and power and greater consequences for the organization than for the executive. The constraints faced and the conflicts encountered by the executive are different only to a slight degree from those faced by the other workers.

MANAGERS

The discussion thus far has been focused on top executives. These personnel are the visible group within the overall managerial hierarchy

---

[26]This discussion follows the model suggested in Campbell *et al.*, *Managerial Behavior, Performance, and Effectiveness*, p. 11.

of the corporate world. Top executives are drawn from the broad group of management roles that are above first-line supervision in organizations (first-line supervisors will be considered in the section on foremen). Managers share most of the characteristics of the executives already discussed, such as education, varying aspirations, functions performed, etc. Since managers' positions are lower in the hierarchy, their work is more specialized and involves less responsibility and authority. Examples of such roles are production managers, sales representatives, industrial relations or personnel managers, public relations officials, accountants, maintenance superintendents, and data analysts at various levels in the hierarchy. Some of the managerial roles involve professional or professionalizing occupations, such as engineers, accountants, and public relations officials. Others are more traditional managerial roles. A major factor in the behavior of managers is that they are *specialists*, occupying well-defined positions. Their training and the nature of their work limit the scope of their activities. Their positions in organizations define their interaction patterns on the job. The functions they perform are similar to those of executives, but on a smaller scale. They make decisions on policy, but only insofar as it affects their limited sphere of endeavor and within the framework of overall corporate policy. Their performance is subject to more direct scrutiny, since they themselves are supervised. The possibility for innovation or experimentation depends on the amount of autonomy given to them.

For the manager who is a specialist, there can be conflict between his occupational specialty and organizational demands. A study of personnel managers demonstrates this point well.[27] In this study it was found that these specialist-managers frequently felt the pressures of demands from one part of their organization that conflicted with what was expected on the basis of their judgment as specialists (professionals).

Conflicts between specialty and organizational expectations were not the only ones confronting managers. Delbert C. Miller and William H. Form have identified several such conflict situations.[28] First, there can be conflict between top management (executives) and a manager over such things as production quotas. The manager sees the day-to-day problems, while the executive takes a more distant and abstract view of the whole thing. A second source of conflict is the inevitable conflict between departments. Organizations can be viewed as arenas of conflict, with departments as major participants in this conflict. Managers are de-

---

[27]George Ritzer and Harrison M. Trice, *An Occupation in Conflict: A Study of the Personnel Manager* (Ithaca, N. Y.: Cornell University Press, 1969).
[28]*Industrial Sociology* (New York: Harper & Row, Publishers, 1964), pp. 192–94.

partmental representatives and are thus parties in the conflict situation.[29] Obviously, also, managers must deal with subordinates, and there is thus conflict between subordinates' expectations and those of superordinates.

While the manager is certainly in a conflict situation, there is little indication that this is either unexpected or debilitating. On the contrary, the evidence discussed earlier about job satisfaction suggests that the managerial stratum in the labor force is in fact the most satisfied with its work. Charles M. Bonjean has suggested that managers have strong, favorable self-images and believe that their occupational roles permit "relatively full expression of their individual potential as well as opportunities to expand this potential."[30] Bonjean also found that the managers in his study did not feel powerless in their large organizations and were in general less alienated than samples of small businessmen and workers included in the study.

A major factor in this positive orientation toward their life and work may be that managers are in the mainstream of contemporary society. As will be discussed below, it is the small business owner and others who are most adversely affected by the trends toward large corporations and large organizations in general. Another, and more negative, view of the middle manager is provided by C. Wright Mills. He suggests that, while middle management contains technically specialized personnel, the major concern of this group is the management of people rather than the utilization of technical skills.[31] This is the same point made by Dalton and Miller and Form in their analyses. The person must be accepted before his ideas can be put into practice. If the manager includes the management of people as part of his repertoire of skills, then he will feel that he can achieve his potential in the large organization. Contrary to Mills's implication, it is difficult to demonstrate that the management of people is in any way less self-realizing or moral than the utilization of material, technical skills. It certainly can be, but there is little evidence to suggest that management of people has consistently negative results for those managed or for the manager himself.

Managers also believe in their work. In a major study of men in middle management in several British firms, Cyril Sofer found that for

[29]For an extensive treatment of conflict among management personnel, see Melville Dalton, "Conflict Between Staff and Line Managerial Officers," *American Sociological Review* 15 (June 1950), 342–51. Dalton also considers and demonstrates the importance of background differences between staff and line managers. These differences may not be as pronounced today as they were at the time of this study.

[30]"Mass, Class, and the Industrial Community," *American Journal of Sociology,* LXXII, 2 (September 1966), 154.

[31]*White Collar* (New York: Oxford University Press, 1956), p. 86.

the most part these men in mid-career were satisfied with their work and their employers.[32] He notes that "'the company' plays a crucial role in the psychological life space of the executives and technical specialists whom it employs."[33] While these people in mid-career (age 35–40) all had their worries about promotion potential, bright younger men coming into the firms, lack of recognition and appreciation, and so on, for the most part they identified with their employer, not in the sense of total acceptance, but in the sense that the company was their work and work was central to their life. The organization thus serves as a major point of reference for the manager, a focus for life and a means of providing order.

While managers are oriented toward their employing organization, they also have a career anchorage point for themselves. Curt Tausky and Robert Dubin have noted that this career anchorage may be downward or upward.[34] What this means is that the person with an upward career anchorage looks to further, and at times unlimited, advancement within the company. The downwardly anchored person, on the other hand, looks back to where he has been, noting the movement that has already taken place. A person's view of his own success is thus dependent on where he anchors his career. The downwardly anchored person may have already achieved success while, for the upwardly anchored individual, success is yet to be achieved. These dual anchorage points can exist in people with the same tenure in the organization and at the same age.

Before proprietors are analyzed, an additional point about both managers and executives should be made. The evidence presented thus far has shown that the latter are oriented toward upward mobility, regardless of the point of anchorage. It is obvious that there are limits to such mobility, given the nature of organizations. Nevertheless, the occupational group being examined is characterized by the fact that the vast majority of its members are at least somewhat mobile in their careers. Unlike in the world of nature, in the organizational world, what goes up generally stays up. Demotions do occur, however, with ramifications for the individual and the organization. Organizations must at times eliminate incompetent incumbents by demotion or discharge. According to Fred H. Goldner, this forces the organization to legitimize at least a significant proportion of this failure so that deviant acts and withdrawal on the part of the participants do not ensue.[35] The participants in the

[32]*Men in Mid-Career: A Study of British Managers and Technical Specialists* (Cambridge: Cambridge University Press, 1970).

[33]*Ibid.*, p. 338.

[34]"Career Anchorage: Managerial Mobility Aspirations," *American Sociological Review* 30 (October 1965), 725–35.

[35]"Demotion in Industrial Management," *American Sociological Review*, XXX, 5 (October 1965), 714–24.

system should not become alienated or have their motivation destroyed. For the individual, problems of redefinition of the self-concept become paramount.

Goldner's analysis of the demotion patterns in one organization exemplifies the issues in the demotion process. The organization in the study is a diversified industrial firm with widely dispersed sales, research, and production facilities. The organization has expanded rapidly, and great upward mobility has resulted from its policy of promoting from within. The organization has adopted the policy of rewarding excellence by promotions that, at the same time, creates an atmosphere wherein merely adequate or inadequate performances are organizationally nonrational. In this firm, the general policy has been to retain those who are performing at the adequate level, which in turn creates security for the employees at the expense of having positions filled by the most qualified personnel. In this organization, the motivation for advancement on the part of those interested in and able to achieve upward mobility is maintained, while those who are no longer performing above the adequate level are retained in the organization by demotion. The majority of the executives and managers interviewed believe that there is a good chance of their being demoted, since a belief has developed in the organization that demotion is a "normal phenomenon."[36] Those who believe that they may be demoted also believe that they may be promoted. This paradox is explained by the fluidity in the organizational structure and the manner in which the organization has handled the demotion process. A major part of the demotion system is that it is obscure. Demotions are relatively invisible because of the high rate of lateral movement in the organization. A person can be transferred to another location without others knowing that he has been demoted. According to Goldner, some executives who are demoted do not realize that this has happened. Additional ambiguity is introduced by similar positions being filled by those on the way up and on the way down. Training sessions outside the company are used for those who are being advanced and to help adjustment of those being demoted. Another pattern is zig-zag mobility, where a person is changed to a lower-status job and then changed again to a position of equal or higher status than his original job. This increases the ambiguity in that neither the person himself nor others can be sure whether his move is an actual demotion.

These arrangements allow the organization to maintain the norm that excellence is rewarded and at the same time provide a source of personal redefinition for those who are demoted. Since it is anticipated,

[36]*Ibid.*, p. 718.

demotion is not so personally damaging as it might be. Similarly, the pressures and long hours of higher positions serve as a "sour grapes" rationale for those not promoted. The organization, with its pattern of geographically shifting demoted personnel, provides additional techniques of redefinition. The individual is not forced to face friends and subordinates who knew him "when." He can turn his energies to nonwork activities in a new location, compensating for his lack of interest in his work. This particular organization attempts to protect its employees and itself by this demotional system. Although Goldner does not suggest this, it is logical that not all accept demotion gracefully and with a solid personal redefinition, nor is it probable that high motivation levels are maintained for all of those who have not yet been demoted. The organization itself, while altruistic in these patterns, also gains by not losing trained and experienced men. While they are demoted, these men still are useful in many corporate positions.

The analysis of demotion, while interesting in its own right, also illustrates a major concern of this section. The world of the executive and manager is *not* filled with one type of person with one career pattern. The analyses of the innovator versus the organization man and of the demotion process illustrate this. Similarly, pictures of this group as either constantly making decisions without regard for the interests of other people or as an unhappy cog in a large corporate machine are inaccurate. In short, except in terms of factors such as educational level and relative affluence, managers and executives are a heterogeneous lot. The most important common feature of this group, perhaps, is the fact that they do work in organizations and thus must adapt to the particular organizational requirements. They do face conflicts in their position, are subject to pressures from above and below, and are demoted and fired. They also accept the purposes of their employer and are motivated to achieve within the organizational framework. It is a group that also has received relatively little systematic attention from social scientists.

PROPRIETORS

Proprietorship is an important element of the "American Dream."[37] To be one's own boss, to have a farm or store or motel of one's own is a continuing, and increasingly impossible, desire on the part of many parts of the occupational world. To be sure, all of today's corporations that are not the product of a merger or a spinoff from some larger

[37]Ely Chinoy, *Automobile Workers and the American Dream* (New York: Doubleday & Co., 1955).

company started as a proprietorship or small business. The family farm, another form of proprietorship, is also a dominant force in our historical tradition.

This element of the American Dream is rapidly becoming myth, and disappearing with it is the possibility of realizing the character traits of independence and autonomy by going into business for oneself [there are other sources of these character traits—author]. The trend of the past seventy years or more, and particularly in recent years, has been a decrease in small independent enterprises and self-employment, and an increase in the domination of large corporations and government in the workforce. In the middle of the 19th century, less than half of all employed people were wage and salary workers. By 1950 it was 80 percent and by 1970, 90 percent. Self-employed persons dropped from 18 percent in 1950 to 9 percent in 1970.[38]

This now small category of proprietors (owners of businesses) has undergone significant changes during the twentieth century. With very few exceptions, proprietorship today is limited to small businesses. The owners of large businesses are the diffuse stockholders, and the separation of ownership from management has been almost total. Although the owners in some cases may participate in the management of their businesses and indeed may comprise much of the top echelon of the executive hierarchy, in the large organization such a person would have the characteristics of an executive. The proprietor today is self-employed, gains at least half of his income in the form of profit or fees, and works in an organization having two, or fewer, levels of supervision.[39] Examples of such proprietorships are watch repair shops, beauty shops, delicatessens, hardware stores, and small manufacturing firms. For the most part, proprietors are found in retail and service businesses, since the opportunity in production organizations is limited by the economics of large-scale production.

Walter L. Slocum suggests that most proprietorships have the characteristics of a family farm in that most of the necessary work is done by the proprietor and members of his family.[40] In addition, the proprietor performs multiple occupational roles, such as bookkeeping, cleaning, inventorying, buying and, most important, selling. Slocum maintains that the most important facet of the proprietor role is the maintenance of good customer relationships, since most small businesses cannot meet the

[38]*Work in America: Report of a Special Task Force to the Secretary of Health, Education and Welfare*, prepared under the auspices of the W. E. Upjohn Institute for Employment Research (Cambridge, Mass.: M.I.T. Press, 1973), p. 21.

[39]Bonjean, "Mass, Class, and the Industrial Community," p. 152.

[40]*Occupational Careers* (Chicago: Aldine Publishing Co., 1966), p. 58.

prices or variety of products of chain or department stores.[41] The successful proprietor usually works long hours at a relatively low rate of pay. An additional feature of at least some forms of proprietorship is that the owner is not truly independent. Caplow, for example, points out that the veteran's legislation after World War II was directed toward the establishment of small businesses, such as filling stations, groceries, and dry-cleaning shops.[42] The products distributed to these operations are controlled by the producers and wholesalers. In many cases the prices charged for merchandise and services are set for the proprietor, so that he is not in fact an independent businessman. In many proprietorships, the individual is forced by contract to purchase his materials from one source, further reducing his independence. Caplow suggests that the unit managers of the larger organizations that supply the small businesses are more adequately rewarded than those who function as owners. The owner typically must depend on corporate advertising to get the public's attention. According to Smelser, advertising has become a functional equivalent for personal contact between buyer and seller. While the small businessman does rely upon good customer relations to maintain a regular flow of business, the products purchased or used are standardized. The standard for trustworthiness, Smelser notes, has become standard prices, guarantees, brand names, and so on.[43] The only real entrepreneurship the proprietor can exercise is in the area of customer relations, since the rest of his business is in reality out of his control.

Another similarity between business proprietorship and contemporary farming is that there is a high rate of occupational inheritance. Most farmers are sons of farmers. The easiest means of entering small business is also through the family, either by blood or marriage. Small businesses require a substantial capital investment, in most cases, making it difficult, if not impossible, for potential proprietors to enter this occupation given the difficulties in amassing capital. In those instances where a small business is franchised as part of a larger organization, the lessee becomes a relatively poorly paid manager, subject to the policies of the franchising organization. As in the case of farming the opportunities for the children of proprietors are limited, contributing to the movement away from this occupation on the part of the children.

The description thus far has suggested that proprietorship is in many ways a marginal occupation. This conclusion is strengthened when evidence regarding some personality and attitudinal characteristics of small businessmen is examined. In Bonjean's study of a Texas community, it

[41]*Ibid.*

[42]Theodore Caplow, *The Sociology of Work* (Minneapolis: University of Minnesota Press, 1954), p. 46.

[43]*The Sociology of Economic Life* (Englewood Cliffs, N.J.: Prentice-Hall, 1969).

was found that the independent businessmen, unlike the managers discussed above, exhibited relatively high degrees of alienation in terms of
feeling powerless, normless, isolated from society, and low self-esteem.
The businessmen also tended to rank higher on scales measuring social
isolation, which involves membership in organized groups, visiting neigh-
bors and relatives, attending religious services, and general social participation. Part of this can, of course, be explained by the long work hours
that do not allow time for such social participation. On most of the
variables included in the study, the businessmen ranked very close to a
sample of blue-collar workers. Bonjean attributes the reactions of the
businessmen to the fact that their position in the Texas community had
slipped with the arrival of industry after 1950. According to Bonjean,
these are reactions to the "mass society" of which the businessmen do
not feel a part.[44]

Martin Trow and later Norbert Wiley suggest additional factors that
lead to the alienation of the proprietor from society. Trow notes that
small businessmen in a New England community are hostile toward both
big business and labor unions, two of the legitimate power sources in
society.[45] Wiley interprets the small businessman as one with inconsistent
class attributes.[46] Utilizing Weber's distinctions of three attributes of the
social-class system, the labor market (employer-employee), the credit or
money market (debtor-creditor), and the commodity market (buyer-
seller), Wiley notes that two consistent sets of class attributes can be
identified. Big business is the employer-creditor-seller, while labor is the
employee-debtor-buyer. Small businessmen and farmers comprise

> classic mixed types, for while both make their living by selling, they also
> do capital buying from powerful sellers, and their incomes are often
> affected as much by buying as selling. In addition, they are often heavily
> in debt and may be employers of labor, at least sporadically. Both groups,
> consequently, are affected with economic cross-pressure and cannot iden-
> tify their interests with either big business or labor unions.[47]

Both Trow and Wiley support their conclusions by the fact that
small businessmen and farmers alike have shown strong support for
extreme right-wing political groups. Unable to identify with the major
power blocs, identification with these extremist groups is a means of

[44]Bonjean, "Mass, Class, and the Industrial Community," p. 155.
[45]"Small Businessmen, Political Tolerance, and Support for McCarthy," *American
Journal of Sociology*, LXIV, 3 (November 1958), 270–81.
[46]"America's Unique Class Politics: The Interplay of Labor, Credit and Commodity
Markets," *American Sociological Review*, XXXII, 4 (August 1967), 529–41.
[47]*Ibid.*, p. 536.

attacking the threatening forces of big business and big labor. Since, on the basis of census data, the proportion of the labor force in these occupations has declined, it would be expected that their political and social impact would do likewise.

The analysis of the proprietor has focused on the marginal character of his occupation. A number of exceptions to the points made above can be found. In farming, for example, large farms now supply the majority of food. Whether in dairy, wheat, or produce, the large profitable farm resembles the modern organization more than the traditional family farm. Slocum notes that the farm manager is now typically a college graduate who performs many of the functions of managers in nonagricultural industries.[48] Similarly, other occupational roles, such as equipment maintainers and agronomic or horticultural specialists, involve a much sharper division of labor than traditional farm occupations. They also involve an important change in the manner in which the occupation is entered. While the majority of agricultural experts, whether farm managers or some type of agricultural specialist, usually have a farming family, their skills are acquired through the educational system, rather than through family socialization. On the basis of these characteristics, there is little differentiation between farming occupations and those of the professionals and managers already discussed.

Another exception to the points made above is that there are a number of extremely lucrative small businesses. In the fashion and advertising industries, for example, there are many cases of startling successes for very small enterprises. (There are probably many times more cases of startling failure in this type of endeavor, but these do not receive as much notice.) Once such success is achieved, however, there is an overwhelming tendency for the enterprise to enlarge or be absorbed into a larger organization, so that the instances of small businesses staying small and highly profitable are very few.

While self-employment or proprietorship is of limited importance in the overall occupational structure, it is also part of the American Dream. Chinoy found that the major preoccupation of the automobile workers he studied was starting their own small business.[49] While an unrealistic dream, it remains part of the culture. As was the case with the professional, however, the reality of contemporary occupations is that they are found in the organizational setting. As Caplow notes, "for the majority of the labor force, and in most modern occupations, self-employment is not a plausible alternative."[50] For those people who continue to enter the

---

[48]*Occupational Careers*, p. 57.
[49]Chinoy, *Automobile Workers*, p. 82.
[50]Caplow, *The Sociology of Work*, p. 83.

ranks of proprietors, however, the question is not really one of alternatives, since the majority of those who enter this type of occupations do
so from the family setting, where the formal and informal socialization
processes may limit the perception of alternatives. As has been mentioned, many children of proprietors do not follow in their father's foot-
steps, but those that do, learn the occupation in a situation where the
consideration of possible alternatives is limited by family pressures to
engage in this line of work. Since there is often only room for one offspring in such an endeavor, siblings are to a great extent forced out of
this occupation. For the balance of the labor force and those about to
enter, Caplow's point is correct, given the problem of capitalization and
the nature of the socialization process.

OFFICIALS

Like the occupational types that have already been discussed
in this chapter, officials are a heterogeneous grouping containing a wide
variety of specific occupations. City managers, federal, state, and local
administrators, hospital administrators, school superintendents, and administrators of fund-raising organizations or religious groups are part of
this category. More than in the case of the business executive or manager,
the official category is comprised of occupations that are sometimes considered or consider themselves professionals. Since their work tasks are
almost identical with the executive functions, it is appropriate to place
hospital administrators, city managers, school superintendents, etc., in the
category of officials.

In general, the functions, orientations, aspirations, and conflicts of
the executives and managers are applicable to the officials. Officials work
at various levels in organizations of varying sizes. The distinctions made
between executives and managers hold for the officials, also, since the
areas of responsibility and authority vary similarly. Like executives or
managers, officials may work in specialties where their training is particularly relevant. Academic training in administrative science or behavior) is designed for potential practitioners in and out of the business
sector. In sociology, courses in complex or formal organizations have developed from an earlier interest in industrial sociology, based on the
realization that organizations have important common characteristics, regardless of their particular goal or sponsorship. In sum, the work that officials perform is almost identical to that of the executives and managers.

Despite these strong similarities, the category of officials remains
distinct. Mills suggests that the government official suffers from a lack of

income and prestige when compared with the business executive.[51] This would be true for almost all members of the category. Without considering for the moment whether or not officials are worth as much as business executives, the important implication is that such officials are given a lower position in the social-stratification system, with correspondingly less power and privilege. The major factor that accounts for this situation is that officials are at least one step removed from the income-generating source within a capitalistic system. Whether in a public organization, such as a governmental unit, or a private organization, such as a religious organization, hospital, or professional association, the official and his organization are dependent upon secondary sources of income in the form of taxes, contributions, or dues. While the potential for high organizational and individual incomes exists in such situations, this potential is seldom realized, since the taxpayers, contributors, or dues-payers have at least some control over the amount they give to the organization. Cases of government or labor-union officials who become inordinately rich at the expense of their constituents are actually rare, despite the publicity given to such cases. We frequently think of officials in terms of offices such as president or vice-president of the United States, where there have been obvious cases of the accumulation of seemingly inordinate and possibly illegal wealth. The vast majority of officials, in the public and private sectors, do receive less income and other such rewards than their counterparts in the business sector.

Since man does not live by bread alone, however, other motivational factors and rewards must be considered. A study of upper-level federal executives conducted by W. Lloyd Warner *et al.* suggests that these executives emphasize intelligence, general intellectual values, culture, restraint, respect from others, and respect from themselves.[52] The Kilpatrick, Cummings, and Jennings study found essentially the same concerns among their sample; involvement in their work, devotion to duty, and the need for challenge characterized the sample in that study. Both studies emphasize that the upper-level personnel in federal service believe in what they are doing, and this belief serves as an important motivator.[53] It is probable that officials in other areas have rather strong beliefs in their organization and its purposes, especially those near the top of the hierarchy. As was the case for certain of the professions, for these people, dedication to a purpose or cause may, in some ways, compensate for lower levels of financial rewards.

[51]Mills, *White Collar*, p. 83.

[52]*The American Federal Executive* (New Haven: Yale University Press, 1963), p. 235.

[53]Franklin P. Kilpatrick, Milton C. Cummings, Jr., and M. Kent Jennings, *The Image of the Federal Service* (Washington, D.C.: Brookings Institution, 1964), pp. 56–85.

Other studies give somewhat the same picture. Andrew Sikula found that a sample of federal officials valued accomplishment, self-respect, and freedom and equality (family security was ranked the highest in importance, but this is outside of our current interests) most highly in their value system.[54] In his study, Kohn found that

> employees of government (and of nonprofit organizations) do exemplify the social psychological characteristics associated with bureaucratization: they are more tolerant of nonconformity, have more personally responsible moral standards, evidence greater flexibility in dealing with ideational problems, and make more intellectually demanding use of their leisure time than do employees of equally bureaucratized profit-making firms.[55]

The discussion thus far has centered around the financial and motivational characteristics of officials. An important additional component of the status of officials is the prestige they are accorded. As Mills notes, government employees are generally given less prestige than those in business, and this is true for other officials, according to national surveys of occupational prestige. Government officials have been the subject of more intensive examination than other members of this category and will serve as the basis for the discussion of prestige. The Kilpatrick, Cummings, and Jennings study found that high-status persons outside of federal employment viewed the civil servant as "security conscious, lacking in ambition, adaptable to a routine, a poor worker, and noncreative and dull."[56] The federal employees themselves stress the importance of security as a positive factor in their employment. The general public sees the civil servant as honest and devoted to his duty. The general picture seems to be one of a person locked into an organization that does not allow creativity and that permits performance at a minimal level. The term "public servant" seems to express part of the image of many officials, since the idea of the servant is one of low status, serving the needs and desires of masters. Nongovernment officials are in a similar position, serving the needs of their constituents. While they may have power in their own organizations, officials are in the position of being subservient to an external power group that, at least theoretically, can recall the official when it so desires. While business executives are in the same position in relation to stockholders, they are given more autonomy in their operations. The official is more subject to the pressures of being in the public's eye and suffers in prestige because of his servant position, regardless of his work and other motivations.

---

[54]"The Values and Value Systems of Governmental Executives," *Public Personnel Management* (January–February 1973), 16–22.

[55]Kohn, "Bureaucratic Man," pp. 466–67.

[56]Kilpatrick, Cummings, Jr., and Jennings, *Image of the Federal Service*, p. 240.

While the rewards and prestige of the official are generally less than those of the executive in business, on other characteristics the official is much like his counterpart in business. The Warner *et al.* examination of federal executives, for example, found that on almost every background characteristic the government officials were very similar to the big business leaders studied by Warner and Abegglen. An interesting difference was that the federal executives were more educated than their business counterparts.[57] Since the official's category is comprised of many professionalizing occupations for which the educational requirements are becoming increasingly stringent, the same is probably true for most of the particular occupations in this category. There are strong indications that businesses are facing increasing difficulties in the recruitment of trainees from colleges, and it would seem that the official's category is recruiting personnel who are not easily differentiated from those going into the business world. Of course, competition for well-trained personnel is intense in all areas, including the professions, which compete among themselves for potential members. The point is that officials probably cannot be differentiated from business executives and managers in terms of training and ability. More empirical evidence is necessary before the image of the official as being noncreative and lacking in ambition can be demonstrated. Like most stereotypes, that of the official is probably incorrect.

While strong similarities exist between officials and executives, except for the pay and prestige factors, for some officials an additional component of the work situation provides an important source of strain above and beyond that faced by most members of this category. Occupations such as the school superintendent, city manager, or hospital administrator are confronted with demands from the environment from which other members of the category are largely insulated. The business executive and the government official must be cognizant of the environment, but in most cases they are separated from it by personnel whose specific function is to deal with outside demands. To be sure, top executives in business must make decisions in the face of environmental pressures. The goals of business, however, are generally quite explicit, and decisions can be made, at least partially, on the basis of a clear conception of the goals.[58] For the type of official under discussion, however, the

---

[57]Warner *et al., The American Federal Executive*, pp. 400–407.

[58]Most analyses of organizations suggest that environmental pressures are ubiquitous. For the kinds of organizations under discussion and their officials, however, environmental pressures would be directly felt. Moreover, decisions are generally not based on pure rationality in any organization. Where the goals are less specific and, at times, in conflict with each other, the decision-making process becomes even more difficult. For a discussion of the nature of decision making based on goals (rational model) and the effects of the environment on the decision-making process, see Alvin Gouldner, "Organizational Analysis," in *Sociology Today*, eds. Robert K. Merton,

situation is less clear-cut. Gladys M. Kammerer, in a discussion of the role of the city manager, points out that the role is not played in a vacuum but must take into consideration the institutional-structural arrangements of the community, the style of politics, the local economy, and demographic characteristics.[59] As was seen in the discussion of officials' pay, their position in this case is subject to direct pressures from constituents. While the organization the official is heading may itself have quite specific goals, the environmental pressures are such that decisions based on the goals may conflict with the interests of significant groups in a community. The official in this case must mediate between conflicting interests in the relevant environment as well as within his own organization. If he makes decisions that are rational on the basis of his assessment of the situation, he risks offending significant groups in the community, thus jeopardizing effective implementation of the decision and, at the extreme, his own position. If he is too cognizant of the conflicting demands, he may not act at all or act so indecisively that the organization becomes ineffective. This type of position thus becomes one of balancing between alternative pressures, pressures that may be very diffuse in their range but intense in their force.

The theoretical perspective most commonly applied to these conflicting pressures and the mechanisms designed to deal with them is role conflict.[60] The official, like all occupational role incumbents, is faced with conflicting demands—from multiple constituents, from peers, and from any relevant role sender. The individual's own preference and value system may conflict with expectations that he receives from others. The individual can conform to either of a set of conflicting expectations, attempt a compromise solution, act independently of the expectations, or withdraw from the situation.[61] The specific resolution pattern is based on the strength of the demands. While such role conflict is not at all limited to the official, the visibility and constituent dependence of the official make him particularly vulnerable to role conflict.

Leonard Broom, and Leonard S. Cottrell, Jr. (New York: Basic Books, 1959); James D. Thompson, *Organizations in Action* (New York: McGraw-Hill Book Company, 1967); and Hall, *Organizations: Structure and Process* (Englewood Cliffs, N.J.: Prentice-Hall, 1972).

[59]"Role Diversity of City Managers," *Administrative Science Quarterly*, VIII, 4 (March 1964), 423.

[60]The major statements of the role conflict theory are found in Neal Gross, Ward Mason, and Alexander McCeachern, *Explorations in Role Analysis* (New York: John Wiley & Sons, 1958) and Robert Kahn *et al.*, *Organizational Stress: Studies in Role Conflict and Ambiguity* (New York: John Wiley & Sons, 1964). Ritzer, *Man and His Work:Conflict and Change* (New York: Appleton-Century-Crofts, 1972), contains an excellent summarization of role conflict in specific occupations, pp. 116–67.

[61]Ritzer, *Man and His Work*, p. 140.

WOMEN AND MINORITY GROUP MEMBERS

It is undoubtedly self-evident by now that we have been speaking of a largely male and non-minority group set of people in these occupations. Since almost all of the occupations discussed in this chapter involve supervision of others, women and minority group members are placed in the position of supervising people who may and frequently do think of them as inferior. When these disadvantaged groups are found in this occupational category, it typically is in situations in which they deal with "their kind" of people and problems. Thus there are women executives in fashion and cosmetics, women officials in sororities and women's associations (Camp Fire Girls, Girl Scouts, etc.), black union leaders and black managers in black-dominated industrial plants, and so on.

Again, as with the professionals, these patterns seem to be changing. Recruitment is much more open than in the past, with even active or compensatory recruitment occurring in some situations. Any prognosis of a limited revolution for women and minority group members in the ranks of management or officialdom must be tempered by the fact that the real proof of change will be seen over the next twenty to forty years. Since advancement is a very important part of the occupations under discussion, it is at midcareer and later that the evidence of changed patterns should be most evident. Recruitment changes are important, but the long-run changes will be even more important.

It must be remembered that, except for proprietors, these are organizational occupations. Organizations change slowly, frequently retaining patterns long after individual organizational members may themselves have changed. Personnel practices in organizations can unintentionally discriminate against minority groups. Discrimination can take various forms: "not even thinking of" someone as a promotional possibility or excluding someone from promotional consideration because the person does not interact "well" with fellow employees (women and minority group members are systematically excluded from informal work groups for a variety of reasons; they also seldom are able to engage in such activities as car-pooling because of residential discrimination) or overt discrimination based on sex, race, or ethnicity.

The impact of this on an individual's career is obvious—lack of advancement. This can be neatly seen at the collective level in a study of the Canadian federal system conducted by Christopher Beattie and Byron G. Spencer.[62] They contrasted the salary levels of French- and

[62]"Career Attainment in Canadian Bureaucracies: Unscrambling the Effects of Age, Seniority, Education, and Ethnolinguistic Factors on Salary," *American Journal of Sociology* 77 (November 1971), 472–90.

English-oriented (Francophones and Anglophones) members of the Federal bureaucracy. They found that the Anglophones with seniority had significantly higher salaries than Francophones with similar seniority. While there were some differences in the quality of education between the groups and many Francophones left the federal service to work in Quebec, the most powerful explanation for the differences found was career discrimination. Career discrimination operates against the minority group members. It also operates against the employing organizations as they lose able personnel.

The occupations we have been discussing affect minority groups in many ways. These occupations are the important decision makers in the organizational society. The role of large organizations is probably already clear. Small organizations or proprietorships have only recently been analyzed in terms of their impact on minority groups. Howard Aldrich, and Albert Reiss, Jr., and Aldrich have recently examined the social and economic consequences of white and black ownership in black ghettos.[63] They found that white proprietorships are usually larger than black-owned businesses. In addition, the white-owned businesses were more likely to employ outsiders—whites—thus lowering the economic opportunities in the black community. While proprietorships are a small part of the labor force, they thus contribute to the nature of the social organization and disorganization found in the communities of which they are a part.

The Aldrich and Reiss studies also document the marginality of the proprietors in terms of their susceptibility to crime. It is the proprietors who are among the most frequent crime victims. They must depend on police for protection, further lowering their autonomy. This is true whether the proprietor is white or black.

SUMMARY AND CONCLUSIONS

The managers, proprietors, and officials are obviously a heterogeneous lot in terms of the organizations in which they are found, the auspices under which they work, their level in the various hierarchies, and the tasks performed. At the same time, with the exception of proprietors, they share high socioeconomic status, educational backgrounds, and the constraints of organizational life. While proprietorship may be an element of the American Dream, the contemporary American and Western image is probably best portrayed by managers and officials. For

---

[63]Howard Aldrich, "Employment Opportunities for Blacks in the Black Ghetto: The Role of White-Owned Businesses," *American Journal of Sociology* 78 (May 1973), 1403–25 and Albert Reiss, Jr., and Howard Aldrich, "Absentee Ownership and Management in the Black Ghetto: Social and Economic Consequences," *Social Problems* 18 (Winter 1971), 319–39.

college graduates this kind of organizational work is the only viable alternative, with the exception of the professions. Members of the latter group often become executives or officials as they move into supervisory positions in their employing organizations. For the less well educated, organizational life is probably the only career choice in most cases.

While central to the contemporary occupational world, the many facets of this category do not allow crystallization into a coherent model as with the professions. The conformist-innovator and the dedicated-opportunistic axes of the descriptions of this group suggest both the relative paucity of information available and varieties of behavior exhibited. The array of literary and scholarly descriptions of this category is probably accurate in that it leads to the conclusion that the category itself is multidimensional. As a broad grouping of people with relatively similar socioeconomic characteristics, the category is useful; as a distinctive group of occupations, it is not. The most important common denominator of the category, again with the exception of the proprietors, is that these are organizationally based occupations. This means that the members of the category are filling positions that contain built-in obligations, rewards, and relationships. The contents as well as the incumbents of particular positions are determined by the organization. The question of the criteria upon which the positions are filled, whether by innovators or conformists or by dedicated or opportunistic actors, has not yet been answered. Undoubtedly a wide range of behavior is both permitted and rewarded; yet what is permitted and rewarded in one setting may lead to dismissal, demotion, or lack of advancement in another. It is thus the organization that determines the kinds of, and routes to, success or failure for its members. The role of the individual is vital but only within the limits set by the organization, even when minority group status is considered.

6

WHITE-COLLAR WORKERS

White-collar workers are significantly different from workers in the occupations we have thus far discussed. The differences are of two types—the sexual composition of the occupational members and the amount of power that they have. White-collar work is the first type of work in which there is a heavy representation of females. It is also the first type of work in which decisions are followed, rather than made. There is no causal link in either direction between these two phenomena.

Specific groups included in this category are secretaries, stenographers, typists, telephone operators, receptionists, and airline stewardesses, predominantly women's occupations. More sexually mixed groups in this category are bookkeepers and cashiers, shipping and receiving clerks, office machine operators, and mail carriers. The latter are called clerical and kindred workers in the census. Another major group in the white-collar category is the retail sales worker. The sales worker operates at the individual customer level rather than at the corporate sales level, as do sales executives. The white-collar worker, almost by definition, is an organizational employee, and individual work, either as a solo practitioner or as a proprietor, does not exist for this group.

This is a growing occupational category. The number of white-collar workers exceeded the number of blue-collar workers for the first time in 1960. While the census category includes professionals and managers, proprietors, and officials, the shift to white-collar work is a major alteration in the labor force. Everett M. Kassalow comments:

Yet, one must note that while the percentage of white-collar workers in the labor force has increased steadily for decades, the nature or source of this increase has changed in the past ten years. Until 1950, gains in the white-collar sector reflected declines in extractive employment, such as agriculture and mining; other manual percentages were still advancing slightly or holding even. Between 1900 and 1930, for example, the farm-work force declined from 37.5 percent to 21.2 percent as a percentage of the total civilian labor force. Correspondingly, white-collar workers advanced from 17.6 percent to 29.4 percent of the total; manual workers also increased moderately as a relative share of the labor force, rising from 35.8 percent to 39.6 percent. Between 1930 and 1950, the share of manual workers in total employment continued to rise slightly, and the percentage of farm workers fell once more. The number of white-collar employees once again increased on a relative as well as an absolute basis.

The trend in the 1950/1960 decade, however, was of a different nature. Farm employment continued to decline, but so did manual or blue-collar employment. The upsurge of white-collar workers in the 1950s was a result of a relative decline in the number of both farm and manual workers. Employment in the service industries also showed an important relative increase in the 1950/1960 period.[1]

Kassalow attributes much of the increase to the shift in consumer demands. While the level of commodities sought probably has actually increased, commodity consumption has declined relative to the consumption of services. Kassalow correctly notes that the service industries, which include governmental agencies at all levels, tend to employ a higher proportion of nonmanual workers than do industries producing goods.[2] If the trends projected in chapter 2 are correct, white-collar employment should continue actual and relative growth with regard to the labor force. An additional factor is the growth of organizations. Some evidence indicates that as organizations grow in size and complexity, the number of personnel in administrative work (white-collar work) grows disproportionately to the number engaged in production work.[3] If this is the case, further growth from this source should remain important over the long run. Changes in the production process itself, such as the introduction of automation, are having an impact on the labor force, although the importance of computers and other equipment designed for speeding the administrative process will probably substantially alter white-collar

[1]Everett M. Kassalow, "United States," in White Collar Trade Unions, ed. Adolph Sturmthal (Urbana: University of Illinois Press, 1966), p. 306.

[2]Ibid., p. 308.

[3]See William A. Rushing, "The Effects of Industry Size and Division of Labor on Administration," Administrative Science Quarterly, XXII, 2 (September 1967), 273–95. After reviewing the literature and his own data, Rushing has concluded that increased complexity (greater division of labor) is the major factor in the growth of clerical personnel. Growth in size without increased complexity appears to have the opposite effect.

employment in the long run. The impact of technological changes on the production and administrative process will probably continue to increase the relative size of the white-collar category, but the composition of the category will change as fewer persons are engaged in routine information-handling chores, such as simple clerical tasks (filing and preparing customers' bills, for example), and as more personnel are needed for the equipment that takes these tasks over and for direct interaction with organizational customers and clients in a service capacity.

BACKGROUND

A perceptive analysis of the history of white-collar work and its impact on contemporary practices and images is offered by C. Wright Mills. Early offices were small, as were the businesses they serviced. A dominant figure in the nineteenth- and twentieth-century office was the bookkeeper, essentially the hub around which the owner and other workers revolved. According to Mills, the bookkeeper was an

> old-young man, slightly stoop shouldered, with a sallow complexion, usually dyspeptic-looking, with black sleeves and a green eye-shade. . . . Regardless of the kind of business, regardless of their ages, they all looked alike. . . . He seemed tired and he was never quite happy, because . . . his face betrayed the strain of working toward that climax of his month's labors. He was usually a neat penman, but his real pride was in his ability to add a column of figures rapidly and accurately. In spite of this accomplishment, however, he seldom, if ever, left his ledger for a more promising position. His mind was atrophied by that destroying, hopeless influence of drudgery and routine work. He was little more than a figuring machine with an endless number of figure combinations learned by heart. His feat was a feat of memory.[4]

While the work of the office worker has changed drastically, the probability of advancement out of this position has not. In many ways, the tasks performed, while changed in content, seem to have the same kind of effects.

Major changes in white-collar work occurred concurrently with changes in technology and in organizational forms, as the processes of growth and bureaucratization continued. As organizations became larger, administrative demands became more compelling, leading to increases in

---

[4]C. Wright Mills, *White Collar* (New York: Oxford University Press, 1956), p. 191. While written some twenty years ago, Mill's analysis is very similar to that of more recent critics of the conditions of contemporary work. See Stanley Aronowitz, *False Promises* (New York: McGraw-Hill Book Company, 1973).

the size of office staffs. Large offices departmentalized and rationalized emerged. The growth of banking, financial, and insurance industries created "office industries," according to Mills.[5] The growth of government as an employer had a similar impact. The development of office machinery, from typewriters, through duplicators, collators, and comptometers, to computers, has subdivided the work performed, so that specialization and work flow patterns make the office work increasingly like factory production processes. A major factor in the changing nature of office work is the trend toward centralization. While much of the production process and the provision of organizational services can be decentralized, administrative processes are increasingly more centralized, a trend greatly facilitated by information-handling machines, such as the computer. This further increases the size of offices and the potential for standardization of office work. Mills suggests that standardization is facilitated by decreasing the number of private offices and opening up the office setting into almost floor-wide work units.[6]

These changes have had a drastic effect on the nature of office work. Where a distinct hierarchy of prestige, if not pay, once existed, standardization has minimized status differences. Once the private secretary was the pinnacle of success for the office girl. She "takes care of his appointments, his daily schedule, his check book—is, in short, justifiably called his office wife. If her boss's office warrants it, she may even have stenographers and typists working for her."[7] Next in the hierarchy was the stenographer, who could take dictation as well as type. The typist, who worked only with the machine, copying matter where speed and accuracy were the most important skills, had a position higher than that of simple clerks. Remnants of his hierarchy remain, of course, but the pooling of typists and the advent of dictating machines have flattened the skill differentials and the corresponding status differences. For the male white-collar worker, a similar flattening process has occurred.

Not all white-collar workers are found in the office. Mail carriers, sales workers, and shipping and receiving clerks, for example, are neither predominantly feminine nor in office occupations. At the same time, they are affected by the processes discussed above. Mechanization and routinization have shrunk the range of skills required (the sales clerk does not bargain, nor does he have control over the amounts or the prices of the goods for sale). Status differentials have similarly become flattened in these occupations.

The objective conditions of white-collar work have changed mark-

[5]*Ibid.*, p. 192.
[6]*Ibid.*, p. 197.
[7]*Ibid.*, p. 207.

edly, and to a large extent the workers themselves also have. Mills notes that in American folklore the white-collar girl is usually born of small-town, lower-middle-class parents. After graduation from high school or a year or so at a business college, she goes to the big city. She views her job as a move up in the status hierarchy.[8] While the majority of white-collar workers today come from an area contiguous to the urban area, the idea of mobility remains an important component of the occupation.[9]

In a 1953 study, Nancy Morse found that while there was less migration from rural areas to the cities for white-collar jobs than Mills suggested, the white-collar workers were generally satisfied with their work and their employers.[10] Morse's study emphasizes the homogeneity of white-collar workers. Great similarities in background and experience characterized the workers studied. More recent studies are beginning to indicate that the white-collar workers are neither so mobility oriented, nor satisfied, nor homogeneous.

The reasons for these changes lie in changes in the nature of the work and of the workers. The work has changed due to the automation of the office; the workers have changed due to altered patterns of women workers and women's attitudes about work.

CHANGES IN WHITE-COLLAR WORK

Clerical workers will be the basis for discussion here. They comprise the largest segment of the while-collar workers.[11] Sales workers will be dealt with in a later section. It is overwhelmingly clear that the greatest change in clerical work has been the introduction of the computer. This is simply a continuation of the technological changes that have been in progress for some time. Jon M. Shepard notes four stages of technological change in the office.[12] The first stage of technology was "craft accurate work," in which the work was like that previously described by Mills—the accurate and rapid shorthand of the private secre-

[8]*Ibid.*, p. 202.

[9]In contrast, Michael Crozier notes that in a French governmental clerical agency he studied, the majority of the women employees come from the provinces because the agency cannot compete for local (Parisian) girls. Since the employment opportunities are limited in the rural areas, the positions are accepted despite the relatively low pay. The idea of mobility appears to hold even there. Crozier, *The Bureaucratic Phenomenon* (Chicago: University of Chicago Press, 1964), p. 16.

[10]*Satisfactions in the White-Collar Job* (Ann Arbor: Survey Research Center, University of Michigan, 1953), p. 8.

[11]Sar A. Levitan and William B. Johnston, "Job Redesign, Reform, Enrichment—Exploring the Limitations," *Monthly Labor Review* 96 (July 1973), 40.

[12]*Automation and Alienation: A Study of Office and Factory Workers* (Cambridge, Mass.: M.I.T. Press, 1971), pp. 41–47.

tary, precise accounts of the bookkeeper, and, the perfect penmanship of the ledger clerk. The second stage was that of "early mechanization," in which typewriters, dictating machines, adding machines, and the like were introduced. While all of these machines require some skills, there is less of a "craft" to the work. Indeed, it is this form of mechanization that can turn white-collar work into factorylike conditions, as with "pools" of typists. The next stage was "punched-card data processing." The now universal IBM card and the machinery that handles it introduced a new form of semiskilled work—key punching, verifying, and business machine operation. These new machines replaced many skills needed in the earlier phase, such as the use of adding machines. The final stage (up to this point) is that of electronic data processing—the computer. Computers handle complex masses of information rapidly. They can also store and retrieve information. In terms of work, the impact of the computer is that computer operators monitor the machinery, making certain that all things are running properly. In addition, of course, a great deal of the work involves preparation of work for the computer. This is an activity that is largely like that in the earlier, punched-card era.

The impact of computers on office work is generally thought to be one of upgrading, with lower skill requirements reduced or eliminated and the number of higher skill requirements increased.[13] What seems to be happening is that a new level of white-collar workers, the programmers and systems analysts, are being introduced as upgraded workers. At the same time, many workers remain at the lesser skilled positions associated with traditional clerical tasks and the newer machine technology tasks, such as key punching. Shepard notes that many of the new computer-based occupations carry managerial-level salaries, even though the workers are engaging in work that is "neither supervisory nor managerial."[14] Blum notes that this will create a sharp gap among white-collar workers.[15] We will thus have the elite, who interact with the computers, while the rest (a large majority) will continue to operate as they have in the past, with perhaps more of a factorylike atmosphere.

THE CHANGED WORKER

No type of worker is the same over time. The professional of today is different from his counterpart a decade or a century ago. The

[13]*Ibid.*, pp. 50–52.
[14]*Ibid.*, p. 61.
[15]Albert A. Blum, "White Collar Workers" (Document D 1-68 of the Third International Conference on Rationalization, Automation and Technological Change, sponsored by the Metalworkers' Industrial Union of the Federal Republic of Germany, Oberhausen, Germany, 1968), p. 75.

same is true for white-collar workers. Many of the changes among white-collar workers are linked directly to changes in the nature of practice and attitudes regarding women and work. The changes also reflect age differences among the white-collar workers. The basic pattern is that younger workers, both male and female, are more dissatisfied with their work than are their older counterparts. Both the findings reported in *Work in America* and those of Harold L. Sheppard and Neal Q. Herrick suggest that younger workers have different expectancies about their work than their older counterparts.[16] Sheppard and Herrick note that older workers are concerned about their pay and their (slim) chances for promotion. Younger workers have these same concerns, but to an even stronger degree: "But their prime dissatisfaction centered around something quite different: the work itself."[17]

Younger workers, both male and female, are apparently taking expectations into their work that contain elements of intrinsic enjoyment of the work itself. When this does not occur, the alienation and dissatisfaction discussed in chapter 3 appear. Shepard's data suggest, however, that alienation among white-collar workers has not increased to the level experienced by lower level blue-collar workers; rather, it is at about the same level as that of more skilled blue-collar workers.[18] Nonetheless, the young white-collar worker is not a person who thinks of himself as directly involved with the management phase of organizational operations, as was the case in the past.

The evidence in regard to women among white-collar workers is much less clear. It is clear that women tend to get less pay for equal work, in all types of occupations.[19] What is not clear is the extent to which this is both perceived and felt among white-collar workers. Subjective impressions suggest that white-collar workers are a segment of the population that is least likely to be involved in women's movements. Union membership is lower, and there is just much less participation in the women's movement. This would appear to contribute to lower levels of awareness of economic discrimination and less militancy about it than

[16]*Work in America: Report of a Special Task Force to the Secretary of Health, Education, and Welfare*, prepared under the auspices of the W. E. Upjohn Institute for Employment Research (Cambridge, Mass.: M.I.T. Press, 1973), pp. 44–51, and Harold L. Sheppard and Neal Q. Herrick, *Where Have All the Robots Gone?* (New York: Free Press, 1972), pp. 113–21.

[17]Sheppard and Herrick, *Where Have All the Robots Gone?*, p. 119, italics in original.

[18]Shepard, *Automation and Alienation*, pp. 108–14.

[19]*Work in America*, pp. 61–64. See also John E. Buckley, "Pay Differences Between Men and Women in the Same Job," *Monthly Labor Review* 94 (November 1971), 36. Buckley finds that the pay differences are the greatest between enterprises that employ just men or just women doing the same job. Where enterprises employ *both* men and women on the same job, the differences are much less.

in professional occupations. Nevertheless, the extensive publicity given to sexual equality has undoubtedly affected the white-collar female worker, so that more militancy than in the past could be expected.[20] White-collar work and workers are changing. At this point, it is time to look more closely at the sort of work that white-collar workers actually do.

THE NATURE OF WHITE-COLLAR WORK: MULTIPLE SETTINGS

The standardization and routinization of much white-collar work is evident. So also is the fact that it is carried out in the organizational setting. Less apparent is the fact that white-collar workers occupy two different positions within the organizational framework. Some, like the salesclerk, receptionist, or mail carrier, are at the boundary of the organization and have contact with customers or clients. The other type of position is within the organization where the contacts are only with others performing essentially the same function. Clerks and typists are typical of this group. The most obvious difference between the groups is that the former deals with unstandardized humans in the form of customers or clients, and the latter group does not.

Those in boundary positions are at times the first, often the last, and sometimes the only contact outsiders have with an organization. For organizations that must rely upon good public relations, it becomes imperative that persons in these positions present a good image. Thus attractiveness in looks and personality become important prerequisites for positions such as the receptionist or airline stewardess. While such occupations do deal with a heterogeneous client or customer group, their interaction patterns are in reality very standardized. The bureaucratic norm of impersonality is extremely evident in these occupations. While the smile and welcome to an office or airline might well be genuine, it is the same for all who enter. Universalistic standards thus prevail in this boundary position. The same is true for the mail carrier, who has quite different physical and personality prerequisites. The mail carrier obviously is not expected to show any favoritism in his work. While there is not the same kind of expectation for the carrier as there is for the re-

---

[20]Elliot A. Krause, *The Sociology of Occupations* (Boston: Little, Brown and Company, 1971), pp. 240–41, suggests that white-collar workers and particularly women do not have a career orientation toward their work, but rather utilize their work as a means of obtaining other goals—the utilitarian orientation. The sexual difference here appears to be misleading, especially based on the findings of Joan E. Crowley, Teresa E. Levitin, and Robert P. Quinn, "Facts and Fictions about the American Working Woman" (Survey Research Center, University of Michigan, 1974). This research, based on a large national sample, finds few differences between men and women in their orientations toward their work.

ceptionist, the carrier has an image (through rain, sleet, and snow . . .) he is expected to portray.

These boundary positions are quite different from the boundary position of the sales person. Contemporary economic conditions are such that the person who interacts with the salesclerk comes to the clerk with a predisposition to purchase at a price that is already fixed. An exception to this would be the case of the major appliance or the automobile, where some bargaining does occur but within limits set by the selling organization. Even here, the customer comes with the desire to purchase. The fact that those with whom the sales person has contact come to him to make a specific purchase allows a wider range of behavior than is allowed the receptionist or stewardess. The customer's needs can only be met by dealing with the sales person. The customer has the option of choosing among several organizations selling the same commodity or service, but he cannot control the type of sales person with whom he deals. It is obvious, of course, that if a sales person drove potential customers away, he would not earn a living, if he were paid on a commission basis, or would not be retained by the organization, if he were paid a straight salary.

Analyses of the behavior of sales personnel have been relatively limited and are rather dated. The work that has been done suggests that the general motivational framework used in previous discussions is relevant here. Many types of sales personnel are on a direct or partial commission basis, which emphasizes economic motivations. The commission serves as a motivator, but not in a direct way and not in the same way for all sales personnel. Judson B. Pearson, Gordon H. Barker, and Rodney D. Elliott, for example, found that the direct commission served as an incentive only for the most successful salesmen. These salesmen, engaged in direct sales from truck routes, were ranked according to their sales performance. For those with very high performance records, the incentive system was a source of satisfaction; for the balance of the salesmen, the commission incentive did not affect satisfaction. The authors inferred that the system also did not provide a strong source of motivation for the balance of the personnel.[21]

In a related study, Nicholas Babchuck and William J. Goode found that a sales group that had been highly competitive changed to a cooperative work organization. Production (sales) levels remained high. At the same time, hostility within the group decreased and morale increased.[22]

[21]"Sales Success and Job Satisfaction," *American Sociological Review*, XXII, 4 (August 1957), 424–27.

[22]"Work Incentives in a Self-Determined Group," *American Sociological Review*, XVI, 5 (October 1951), 679–87.

Here again, motivations other than strictly economic ones played a role in the overall motivational system.

The conclusions for these white-collar jobs are, of course, congruent with the findings from studies of the production process, which have systematically found quota restrictions in effect when incentive (piecework) systems are in effect. Thus the findings in regard to sales workers are not surprising in light of the general knowledge available about work. What is important is that this group of white-collar workers, probably typical of the class that espouses middle-class values and mobility aspirations, does not respond to the incentives that are thought to be central in the upper-middle-class world. Values other than the purely economic ones intrude in the motivational framework at this level. The question these findings raise is, To what degree are the kinds of responses found among these sales personnel typical of the occupational structure in general? Since there is evidence that blue-collar workers respond in much the same way, the focus of the analysis should be on those higher in the occupational hierarchy. It could be hypothesized that since white-collar workers in general and probably sales workers in particular do reflect the general value orientations of the American middle and upper-middle classes, the members of higher status occupations would engage in similar kinds of practices. That is, executives, officials, and professionals respond to more than the economic motivation and therefore do not always work to maximize this particular reward. Thus the members of these occupations could well engage in "quota restrictions" when other values are of greater importance. However, this type of analysis has not been attempted.

Since sales work involves a direct presentation of self before a customer, the reactions to this component of the work should be examined. According to Stephen J. Miller, the salesman attempts to control the customer to protect his self-concept as well as to facilitate the sales process. Using automobile salesmen as the basis for analysis, Miller found that the salesmen prefer having customers that they have recruited, because such customers give the salesman the advantage of knowing what the customer wants in the situation. The potential customer who drops in off the street is threatening to the salesman, since he is in an unstructured situation. The salesman does not know if the person is merely trying to get warmed up, is browsing around for a car, or is actually a real prospect. The salesman also knows nothing about such a customer and thus has no leads by which the situation can be controlled. Miller points out that the salesman has economic and noneconomic interests in the transaction. In addition to his self-concept, his status as a salesman is affected by the outcomes of the various transactions in which he is engaged. Regardless of the outcome, he wants to be known as a good salesman.[23]

The nature of the sales process is such that not every customer is a purchaser. This is a fact of life to which the salesman must adjust. F. William Howton and Bernard Rosenberg suggest that salesmen adjust to this situation by defining rebuffs in their work in terms of accepting humiliation as part of the work, but they do not define the occupation itself as humiliating.[24] Rebuffs thus become part of the day's work, not especially enjoyable, but still acceptable. Since rebuffs are given this social meaning, it would follow that success in the form of sales are also given a social meaning.

A related, but more critical, view of the salesperson is taken by Mills in his analysis of saleswomen in department stores. He points out that a wide status discrepancy exists between the saleswoman and her customers on most occasions. The contact between customer and saleswoman is usually so brief that meaningful interaction is impossible. While surrounded by attractive goods the customers can afford, the saleswoman is limited in her own purchasing power, which makes deprivation even more evident.[25] At the same time, the relationship between customer and saleswoman is one in which the saleswoman is put in the position of "waiting on" the customer, which in and of itself has negative status consequences.

Mills suggests that the role of saleswoman can be performed in a variety of fashions. The "wolf," for example, pounces on customers as they appear in her area. More aggressive is the "elbower," who pushes through her sales colleagues in an attempt to monopolize as many customers as possible. The "charmer" relies upon her personal attraction to lure potential customers, with the goods being sold of lesser importance. The "ingenue" is self-effacing and looks for support from colleagues and customers. While not as effective in the sales process, the ingenue receives socioemotional support. The "collegiate," as the name implies, is a part-time worker who makes up in eagerness what she might lack in other skills. The "drifter" moves around gossiping with colleagues. She is highly concerned with social interaction at the expense of sales volume. The "social pretender" attempts to create an image of herself as coming from a high socioeconomic status background. This can be an effective

[23]Stephen J. Miller, "The Social Bases of Sales Behavior," *Social Problems*, XII, 1 (summer 1964), 15–24.

[24]"The Salesman: Ideology and Self-Imagery in a Prototypic Occupation," *Social Research*, XXXII, 3 (autumn 1965), 277–98.

[25]Mills, *White Collar*, p. 174.

approach for certain kinds of customers. The "old-timer" has made a career out of this occupation. She has her own approach to customers, a routine developed through years of practice. This type approaches all customers in the same way, and does not rely on the gimmicks of the other types.[26]

While this categorization of the saleswoman cannot be taken as an exhaustive typology, it does illustrate the fact that a variety of behaviors are possible in the sales process. Mills tends to assume that economic motivations are dominant for the salesperson. An examination of the types such as the drifter or the charmer suggests that the economic factor may be less important than social responses for some engaged in sales work.

The sales roles discussed by Mills reinforce the idea presented earlier that these boundary positions in organizations are important for the organizations involved. For this reason, sales personnel, like the receptionist discussed above, do act according to regularized patterns. They may be friendly, appealing, or even hostile toward potential customers. Whichever pattern is followed, the fact that it is followed is further evidence of the impersonality built into the contemporary sales process. Mills quotes from an observation of a salesclerk in a department store:

> I have been watching her for three days now. She wears a fixed smile on her made-up face, and it never varies, no matter to whom she speaks. I never heard her laugh spontaneously or naturally. Either she is frowning or her face is devoid of any expression. When a customer approaches, she immediately assumes her hard, forced smile. It amazes me because, although I know that the smiles of most salesgirls are unreal, I've never seen such calculation given to the timing of a smile. I tried myself to copy such an expression, but I am unable to keep such a smile on my face if it is not sincerely and genuinely motivated.[27]

The implication here, of course, is that the salesperson is alienated from her- or himself. While there is the evident impersonality Mills discusses, caution must be exercised in assuming that the salesperson is self-alienated. It is very conceivable that he may not feel self-alienation, a serious condition in and of itself, or that if he does feel it, it is confined to the work situation, with other outlets provided for self-expression off the job. A complete analysis of the situation would require data that would describe the varying amounts of alienation felt, the sources of such alienation, and consequences of alienation for the individuals involved. The approach taken by the Morse study is relevant here. If the sales-

[26]*Ibid.*, pp. 174–75.
[27]*Ibid.*, p. 184.

person, or any other person for that matter, takes expectations of social interaction into the job and such expectations are not met, alienation and dissatisfaction are likely to ensue. On the other hand, the absence of such expectations would have different consequences when the same situation is confronted. As is so often the case, the impact of the mass society on the individual has been widely, and often polemically, discussed but has been inadequately researched.

The white-collar worker on the organizational boundary is confronted with an additional job component that affects his behavior. He is the contact between the outside world and the organization. As such, he receives pressures, which can be incompatible, from both sources. Whyte's analysis of waitresses in the restaurant industry vividly shows the kinds of problems this can create. Waitresses are generally considered semiskilled service workers rather than white-collar workers, but the situations they face are analogous to those being discussed. The restaurant industry itself is somewhat unique in that it is both a production and service organization confronted with a largely unpredictable market. The waitress is under pressures from customers who want food and service to their individual demands. At the same time, the waitress depends upon the customer for tips, which in this case serve the same function as commissions. She must also interact with the rest of the organization, the pantry, kitchen, and bar workers. They have power over her in the sense that their lack of cooperation can make it very difficult for the waitress. The waitress can be put into the position of demanding things from the rest of the organization that cannot easily be delivered, such as changed or special orders or volume of demand too large for the facilities. The real problem for the waitress, however, appears to be her relationship to the customer. If she can control the situation by holding the initiative in the customer-waitress relationship, she can reduce the amount of pressure on herself by providing the customer's order at her own pace. If, on the other hand, the customer gets control of the situation or the relationship is ambiguous, the waitress is under more pressure, leading to maladaptive practices such as anger toward the customer or other personnel in the restaurant, poor relationships with supervisors, or nervous reactions such as crying or getting the shakes.[28] Whyte suggests that since control of the situation at all times is impossible to achieve, a component of the occupation is unresolvable pressures from customers and from other segments of the organization. The same general condition confronts white-collar workers in boundary positions. Thus, while

[28]William F. Whyte, "When Workers and Customers Meet," in *Industry and Society*, ed. William F. Whyte (New York: McGraw-Hill Book Company, 1946), pp. 123–47.

the impersonal component can serve as a control mechanism, situations are still diverse enough to bring about pressures and pleasures in the occupation.

These boundary positions have another component that must be noted. They are extremely sex typed. Who has ever seen a car sales*woman* or a male receptionist? Similarly, in restaurants catering to an elite clientele, there are waiters, while in less elite places there are waitresses. Even within an organization like a department store, sex typing occurs. There are very few female major appliance or carpet salespersons, and few males are found in notions or toiletries. This situation effectively yields pay differentials, since the male sales and waiting positions are those with greater financial reward. The bases for this distinction lie in sex-typed exceptions, since women are the major users of major appliances as well as notions and toiletries, and females are no better receptionists, except perhaps where older style "sex appeal" is a prerequisite for the job.

For white-collar workers not in boundary positions, the component of customer or client is missing. The central parts of the occupation are the work itself; the organizational structure, which defines the work process, prescribes the directions of social interaction and outlines the nature of the expected social interaction and the work group. Before examining these components, it is necessary to point out that the organizational structure is a given in the occupation. While cliques, work quotas, and social interaction are important in the analysis of this form of white-collar work, the work itself is carried out within a structure set down by the employing organization. The assignment of a new employee to a position in effect defines the work performed, the individuals with whom it is possible to interact, and the probable directions of the interaction. This same process operates for others in organizations, but for the white-collar worker in this setting and for many blue-collar workers the fact of the organizational structure is the basic framework for analysis. The other components of the white-collar position are variations from the theme set by the organization. This is not to imply that such variations do not take forms widely divergent from the official organizational structure but that the structure is the point of origin for such variations.

With this in mind, a description of the nature of these internal white-collar occupations can begin. Technological changes have a tremendous impact on these occupations. In order to understand the nature of the impact, a series of studies dealing with nonautomated white-collar work will be examined.

Crozier's analysis of a French governmental clerical agency, which is perhaps atypical in its factorylike atmosphere, illustrates the fact that white-collar work is not inherently dissimilar from factory work, despite the status difference ascribed to it. The particular agency studied employed about 4,500 workers, divided into four main work sections for administrative purposes. The work was largely repetitive and self-supervising. The workers were expected to accomplish all of the work that came in on a given day, and the load was such that the workers were forced to keep busy or fall behind, reducing the need for close supervision. Thus the majority of the workers were at the same level and performed the same duties. "The technology of the Agency's work is simple, and it has remained basically unchanged for 35 years. The employees, all female, work in production units on heavy cross tabulating accounting machines (with six or two tabulators)."[29] The organization reflects the nature of the technology in its simplicity.

> The basic units of work organization are the four-girl work teams. These teams, to which more than 60 per cent of the employees belong, are in charge of the direct productive function of the Agency—ie., the carrying out and accounting of the customers' orders. . . . The Agency as a whole . . . remains a rather rare example of a large modern organization in which everything still revolves around a large set of autonomous and parallel productive units, working independently of one another. . . . Work therefore, does not depend on supervisory decisions and group relationships, but on the impersonal pressure of the public at large. . . . Within the work team . . . there are division of work and a great deal of interdependence. Two girls work at the tabulating machines and two at checking. The work process begins with a check of the customer's credentials, then the girl at the first (six-tabulator) machine types, at one time, all documents necessary for carrying out the order. The figures are then checked by the third employee; and they are finally tabulated again, for balancing the accounts, by the fourth.[30]

This same process is repeated throughout the day and day after day.

A very similar picture is drawn by George C. Homans in his description of "cash posting" in an American organization. He states:

> The cash-posting job was essentially as follows: Bundles of bill stubs, representing paid bills, came from the cashier's office to the desk of the poster's supervisor. A cash poster took one of these bundles, went to the right "ledger" [file] and pulled out the cards whose numbers corresponded to those on the stubs. . . . When a cash poster had finished one bundle she started on the next one, while the "pulled" cards were sent to another room to be tabulated against one another. . . . The supervisors expected

---

[29]Crozier, *The Bureaucratic Phenomena*, p. 14.
[30]*Ibid.*, pp. 17–18.

each poster to "pull" an average of at least 300 cards per hour, and each one did. This was the "quota." But aside from this there was no group norm of output and no incentive pay, and individual posters varied from just over 300 to almost 500 cards per hour.[31]

In this case the cash posters were not a majority of the clerical workers of the organization. Others performed duties that required more discretion and involved less repetition. For these duties the process still involved handling a large volume of work in a systematic way.

An analysis of telephone operators provides much the same picture of white-collar work. The operators sit in front of switchboards in rows, completing calls and writing out tickets in accordance with company policies. The work requires discipline and is performed under conditions of close supervision unusual for white-collar employment. The operator cannot normally leave her switchboard without being replaced, nor can she talk with her fellow workers. The work of the operator is clean and of the white-collar variety, but the supervision is as close and discipline as exaxcting as one can find in a factory.[32]

The discussion thus far has concentrated on the more repetitive of the internal white-collar occupations. The work of key-punch operators or typists in typing pools shares many of the characteristics discussed above. There are other internal occupations that do provide more variety and freedom from close supervision. The secretary, whether private or shared among a number of executives, enjoys a higher status and a greater diversity in the work performed. Shipping and inventory clerks are more closely linked to changes in organizational demands and generally have more freedom of movement and interaction. It would appear, however, that the majority of these internal white-collar workers are engaged in repetitive and stationary work. This, at first glance, seems incompatible with the findings reported earlier that such workers are more satisfied with their work than are blue-collar workers.

The incompatibility can be resolved when a number of factors are examined. In the first place, white-collar workers do tend to believe that they are part of the management process and are thus important for the functioning of the organization. This belief apparently carries over into the general assessment of the job to the extent that their own importance is imagined, even though it is not real in terms of individual contributions to the system. A second factor is that the work is clean and in the office area of an organization, a positive attribute in the assess-

---

[31]"Status Among Clerical Workers," *Human Organization*, XII, 1 (spring 1953), 6–7. This type of work was among the first to go with the arrival of automation. It still exists, however, in this and other forms.

[32]See Joel Seidman *et al.*, *The Worker Views His Union* (Chicago: University of Chicago Press, 1958).

ment of an occupation.[33] A third factor is that this type of office work has traditionally permitted meaningful social relationships, which apparently tend to overcome some of the objective components of the situation. Homans, for example, notes that the work of the cash posters did allow for social interaction and much of the meaning of work for these girls was derived from such interaction.[34]

An extended analysis by Gross suggests that "cliques" or interaction patterns in the office perform three major functions for its members. First, cliques provide a source of information for their members. This is especially true when they cross specific work group lines, allowing different perspectives to be brought into discussions. In this sense they provide the worker with information about what the larger organization is doing. Although there is no guarantee that the information shared in cliques is always correct, it does tend to integrate the individual into the larger whole. The second function of cliques is simply providing a source for congenial social interaction, which, as can be seen from the discussions above, is not present within the formal structure. The final function is perhaps the most important. Gross suggests that work in an office has less meaning to the worker than does work in a factory. The cliques provide personal response and satisfaction for the worker. The worker is responded to as a person by other workers, who also provide him with a basis for seeing the relationship between his work and the whole.[35]

The nature of this internal white-collar work is such that social interaction may provide the *only* source of positive satisfaction for the individuals beyond the minimum provided by the money earned and the idea of keeping busy.[36] If this is actually the case, or if social interaction is even a moderate contributor to work satisfaction, then the limitation of possibilities for interaction should reduce satisfaction levels. Crozier's evidence supports this interpretation in that a generally low level of satisfaction was found. The workers were restricted to the four-member work team. The pressures for productivity were very strong and the organization of work was such that there was little interdependence between the units. Crozier found that in such situations the "amount of interaction will be rather low and solid supportive cliques will be rare."[37]

This last point illustrates one of the major considerations for white-collar work. In the French situation, it was the organization that deter-

---

[33]For a discussion of this point, see Theodore Caplow, *The Sociology of Work*, (Minneapolis: University of Minnesota Press, 1954), p. 46–47.

[34]"Status Among Clerical Workers," p. 7.

[35]Gross, "Characteristics of Cliques in Office Organizations," *Research Studies of the State College of Washington*, XIX (1951), 131–36.

[36]Some evidence suggests that clerical work has now fallen behind blue-collar production work in terms of pay. *Work in America*, p. 39.

[37]*The Bureaucratic Phenomena*, p. 37.

mined the size and composition of the work groups. In almost every white-collar situation, the organization places workers in an office or at a sales counter. This means that there is organizational control even over the formation of cliques insofar as who will become a member is considered. A person cannot become a member of a clique if he or she has not even met the members of the clique because of physical separation. In the last section of this chapter, we are going to examine some elements of the organizational control of white-collar work.

THE ORGANIZATIONAL CONTROL
OF WHITE-COLLAR WORK

The plan for this last section is to look briefly again at automation in the office, paying attention here to the role of the organization in relation to the white-collar worker in the introduction and utilization of automation in the office. We will then look at some other aspects of organizational control of white-collar workers. Finally, we will examine the manner in which white-collar workers can and do respond to this organizational control.

We have already noted that the most important factor for internal, clerical-type white-collar occupations is the introduction of technological change through automation and computerization. A point so obvious that it is often overlooked is that this is an *organizational decision*. The managers and executives make the decision to introduce these massive technological changes. The decision is made and then presented to the white-collar workers. While there is ample evidence that suggests that participation by the workers will facilitate the implementation of the change, the actual decision to change is outside of the hands and minds of the workers.

Even the decision to introduce computers can have an impact. Mann and Williams report the widespread rumors that followed an organizational decision to bring in computerized processes.[38] These rumors ranged from massive layoffs to forced early retirement. The point is that the white-collar workers' responses were touched off by the organizational decision.

Once technological change has occurred, there is likely to be more organizational control of the work itself. Ida R. Hoos describes the work and the control system for key punchers as a

---

[38]Floyd C. Mann and Lawrence K. Williams, "Observations on the Dynamics of a Change to Electronic Data-Processing Equipment," *Administrative Science Quarterly* 5 (September 1960), 217–56.

dead-end occupation, with no promotional opportunities. The work is simple, monotonous, and repetitive, but requires a high degree of accuracy and speed. The pressure for great speed, coupled with the demand for precision, creates much tension, especially since practically all organizations maintain an objective count of production. Although measurement of clerical output is not a new practice, the simplification and routinization of office tasks which accompany EDP (electronic data processing) have provided further incentive for applying production room thinking to office operation.[39]

Hoos further notes that the "former occupations involved a certain amount of moving about the office and contact with other employees or customers. The workers now complain of 'being chained to the machine.' "[40]

Shepard notes that even the relatively high-status computer operators are restricted in their movements, having to insure that someone will cover the work if the operator must leave the room for any sort of critical need, even going to the bathroom.[41]

Computerization of office work introduces additional controls in the form of quality controls. With computers, it is easy to detect when, where, and by whom an error is made. The computer determines the sequence of job operations and the amount of time it takes to complete them. It also detects errors before they interfere with its operations on specific programs. A commonly used set of programs in the social sciences uses the straightforward term "fatal error" to indicate to the unfortunate person who submits a program exactly what and where the error is.

For the office worker, then, organizational control over behavior increases with technological change. Behaviors both directly work related and those that are more social come under more direct organizational determination.

For the boundary white-collar worker, the control issue is different. In most boundary positions there is very little likelihood of automation having much impact.[42] At the same time, organizational control is exerted through several mechanisms. William Ouichi has identified two mechanisms by which department stores can control the behavior of their sales personnel.[43] "Behavior control" involves determining the behavior that is desirable and then monitoring the behavior of sales people through direct supervision. "Output control," on the other hand, requires the

[39]"When the Computer Takes Over the Office," *Harvard Business Review*, XXXVIII, 4 (July–August 1960), 105.
[40]*Ibid.*
[41]Shepard, *Automation and Alienation*, p. 71.
[42]Levitan and Johnston, "Job Redesign," p. 40.
[43]William Ouichi, "Organizational Control and the Management of Salespersonnel," Management Report Series, Report #1, Graduate School of Business, University of Chicago.

organization to have measures of the output of each individual, such as sales volume or sales volume minus returns. In a study of seventy-eight department stores, Ouichi found that a combination of these approaches was most commonly used, subjecting the sales people to oversupervision and control.

There is still another aspect of organizational control that is important. Since these are organizational jobs, the organization controls the careers of the individuals. Such control at the present time takes the form of limiting, even precluding, upward mobility in the organization. Shepard notes the tendency for middle-level positions to disappear after the onset of computerization of offices. There are no positions for the clerical personnel to move into.[44] Ritzer makes much the same point when he notes that the major problem for white-collar occupations is status insecurity.[45] There is little or no place to move up in the status hierarchy; at the same time, many blue-collar workers are moving up and passing the white-collar worker, at least in terms of pay. The white-collar worker is thus locked into the organization with little hope for advancement and with few skills or other abilities to take into another occupation.

What is the reaction to all of this? How do white-collar workers cope with what can only be viewed as a dismal picture? There are several individual and collective responses. Individually, people can quit the jobs. White-collar workers have very high turnover rates.[46] Much of this turnover is "natural" to the extent that people opt to move to a new location, marry, have children, and so on. Much of it must also be attributed to the conditions of work. Since many white-collar workers are young single women who retain the notion that getting married and leaving work for the home is a desirable end in and of itself, turnover here is as much a pull to a new situation as a push from the old. For the majority of men and women for whom marriage is either not possible or not desirable, this turnover explanation is not viable. When turnover occurs in this latter segment of white-collar workers, the job change is typically to another white-collar job where the conditions are not all that different.

Another individual response, pointed out by David Mechanic, is to work oneself informally into a position of power within the organization.[47] Mechanic argues that by becoming expert in something not available to superiors, by exerting effort and interest, by being attractive in

---

[44]Shepard, *Automation and Alienation*, p. 81.

[45]George Ritzer, *Man and His Society: Conflict and Change* (New York: Appleton-Century-Crofts, 1972), pp. 182–84.

[46]*Work in America*, p. 39.

[47]"Sources of Power of Lower Participants," *Administrative Science Quarterly* 7 (December 1962), 349–64.

the eyes of superiors, by being in a central position in an organization, and by participating in selected coalitions within the organization, a person, such as a secretary, can become extremely powerful, even indispensable, within the organization. This can have the obvious impact for the individual of increased feelings of meaningfulness, power, and prestige. While others in the organization, such as junior-level managers and executives and fellow clerical personnel may resent such situations, for the individual it is a means of achieving identity and purpose within the white-collar situation.

A collective response to the work situations is unionization. Although white-collar workers have traditionally been difficult to organize,[48] there has been an increase in the unionization of white-collar workers in recent years.[49] As the work becomes more like that of the factory and as economic conditions worsen, the appeal of unionization may also increase.

For some white-collar workers, those in government employment, unionization may become an increasingly viable option. Recent legislation has been critical in authorizing union activities among public employees.[50] Since this is a major area of white-collar work, we may anticipate increased unionization among these workers.

Another important trend is the stance of women in regard to unionization. It had long been thought that white-collar women resisted or did not concern themselves with unionization because of their assumed short-term job orientation. Recent evidence suggests, however, that women do not differ significantly from men in their preference for union representation.[51] The unionization of women in general has been hampered by the fact that unions are male dominated,[52] even where membership is preponderantly female. If women rise to positions of leadership within

[48]Dick Bruner, "Why White Collar Workers Can't Be Organized," *Harper's*, August 1957, 44–50 suggests that white-collar workers still look to and identify with management. He also suggests that white-collar workers believe that they can take their skills from employer to employer. With technological change, this may become less likely. The backgrounds of white-collar workers also would play a factor in attitudes toward unionization. For persons who come from blue-collar backgrounds, white-collar work may be perceived as being mobile for the individual, with blue-collar work and unionization something to be escaped. For someone from a white-collar background, prounion sentiments are not likely to be too strong, at least within the present generation. Despite these considerations, there are several old and strong white-collar unions such as retail clerks, postal employees, and railway clerks. Presently there is a rapid increase in unionization among government employees at all levels. Albert A. Blum *et al.* deal extensively with white-collar unionism in *White-Collar Workers* (New York: Random House, 1971).

[49]*Work in America*, p. 39.

[50]Joseph Goldberg, "Public Employee Developments in 1971," *Monthly Labor Review* 95 (January 1972), 56–66.

[51]Lucretia M. Dewey, "Women in Labor Unions," *Monthly Labor Review* 94 (February 1971), 42–48.

[52]Stanley Aronowitz, *False Promises* (New York: McGraw-Hill Book Company, 1973), pp. 297–98.

unions, white-collar unionism will probably increase. The factors of changing technology and changing state laws and the potential of more women-oriented unions probably will combine to increase white-collar unionization.

Another collective response, this time from the organization itself and, at times, from unions, is job enrichment programs. This is a topic that will be dealt with in some detail in chapter 11. Such programs involve trying to alter the work conditions, content, and responsibility to permit the individual worker to have more control over his or her work. Such programs are also part of the blue-collar world, of course, and should be considered in the broader context of technological change to be discussed in the later chapter.

SUMMARY AND CONCLUSIONS

We have been discussing a type of occupation whose members are subject to strong organizational control and vitally affected by technological change. It is also an occupational category that is rapidly increasing in size. The white-collar workers are in boundary positions in organizations, as in the case of salesclerks, or in internal organizational positions, as in the case of clerical personnel. Women are a major component of this occupational category. Many of the aspects of pay and job discrimination against women are found here, but at the same time there appears to be a low realization of the discrimination and little militancy about it. Part of the reason for the low militancy may be the low organizational positions of all white-collar workers, which puts people in some jeopardy. White-collar work is becoming more factory-like, particularly for the internal organizational positions. While the pay levels have slipped somewhat in respect to some blue-collar work, it is still viewed as a viable short- and long-run career alternative by many people. White-collar work is a "job" in the sense that the skills can be easily transferred from employer to employer, with little retraining required.

With the growth of services and information handling, we can anticipate that white-collar work will continue to increase. It will probably be increasingly undifferentiated from blue-collar work, the elite of which —foremen and craftsmen—we will now consider.

7

CRAFTSMEN
AND FOREMEN

We now make our shift from white- to blue-collar occupations. Our discussion thus far has followed a descending order in terms of socioeconomic status. This pattern is broken at this point, particularly in regard to craftsmen. These are the elite of blue-collar workers. In terms of income, it is not uncommon to hear of interstate truck drivers earning over twenty thousand dollars per year. Other skilled workers earn comparable salaries. These occupations engage in manual, rather than mental, work and dirty, as opposed to clean, work. These factors detract from the socioeconomic status. Within organizations, these occupations are frequently more highly rated than lower-level white-collar occupations. As we will see, craftsmen's power in the organization is quite high, with organizations conforming to craft-based organizational forms. When occupational prestige is considered, however, blue-collar prestige is somewhat lower than that accorded white-collar workers.[1]

Socioeconomic status and prestige are not the only elements of interest about these occupations. We will examine the nature of the occupations and look closely at what the occupational-organizational intersection is for these top-level blue-collar positions. Since the combination of these two types of occupations within one classification is largely based

[1]For a comprehensive discussion of the components of occupational prestige and general socioeconomic status, see Albert J. Reiss, Jr., *Occupations and Social Status* (New York: Free Press of Glencoe, 1961).

on their common socioeconomic situation, it conceals the fact that craftsmen and foremen are distinctly different in terms of the content of their occupations. For this reason, the two types will be discussed separately.

THE CRAFTS

While the position of the crafts in the labor force has remained relatively constant over the years in terms of the proportion of the labor force in the category, new crafts have emerged, such as TV repairing, as old ones, such as blacksmithing or wheelwrighting, have largely disappeared. The U.S. Bureau of Labor Statistics projects that the crafts will decline slightly in the next decade.[2] Technological developments will undoubtedly affect the uniqueness of some craft work and economic demands for mass-produced goods will probably continue to make inroads. Within the crafts there is currently a shift away from production crafts to more service-oriented functions, such as auto repair work. Despite the decline, the crafts will undoubtedly retain their position in the labor force.

The position of the crafts within the occupational structure can be attributed largely to their possession of scarce skills. This is, of course, the position of professionals and executives and, in many ways, the crafts share other characteristics with the professions. Caplow has provided an insightful analysis of these similarities. His focus is on building craftsmen, such as carpenters, masons, steamfitters, or electricians, but can probably be extended to certain other craftsmen, such as printers or railroad engineers. The similarities are less true of many of the newer, service-oriented crafts.

The first similarity is in the manner of recruitment to the occupation. Caplow states:

> As in the case of professions, the rights and duties of candidates are specified with precision at each stage of their advancement, and the power of the state is often invoked to prevent outsiders from practicing the occupation. The most important differences are that the ultimate judges of competence are members of "higher" occupations, such as engineering, and that governmental authority cannot be overtly exercised by the occupational association. The control of recruiting is seldom complete—apprenticeship has partly given way to trade schooling organized by outsiders; effective occupational monopoly is usually limited to a local community and ceases abruptly at the urban limits; and the penalties for violation are nominal,

[2]"The U.S. Economy in 1980: A Preview of BLS Projections," *Monthly Labor Review* 93 (April 1970), 22–23.

unless they are reinforced by personal violence or by agreements with employers or suppliers.[3]

This recruitment pattern serves a number of purposes. It allows the occupation to establish a monopoly of the skills involved. By limiting the number of practitioners, it ensures greater rewards for those in the field, if there is a demand for the product or service. Some people argue that this type of monopolization of skills is based entirely on the desire to restrict or eliminate competition and thus optimize the earning power of the members of the occupation. Another explanation is that the recruitment pattern serves to protect the occupation from incompetent practitioners and thus raise the quality of the performance of duties. Both factors are probably operative for the professions and the crafts. The fact that the crafts have a more limited control system in recruitment than the professions should not obscure the fact that the system is *occupationally* controlled, a factor not present in the majority of nonprofessional occupations. This occupational control has, of course, been the major source for excluding minority groups from the crafts.

An additional common characteristic of professions and crafts is the lifelong involvement in the occupation. Once in the occupation, it is extremely unlikely that an individual will change jobs. Seniority provisions in craft unions strengthen the position of the older worker and ensure, insofar as possible, that the individual has security in his field once he is accepted. Caplow suggests that the involvement of the craftsman is not as strong as that of the professional, since the craftsman is faced with seasonal fluctuations and occasional opportunities or desires to go into business for himself or to assume supervisory positions.[4] The identification with the specific occupation does, however, tend to remain. The involvement is strengthened by the fact that the craftsman passes through a series of stages in training and apprenticeship to reach his position. Once he is a full-fledged member of the craft, his income is maximized; however, there is little improvement in status or income after occupational membership is achieved. The potential income of the craftsman is achieved earlier in his career than in the case of the professional, but the likelihood of changing occupations is equally slight for both groups.

Another similarity, which exists in principle for both professions and crafts, is the occupation's control over evaluation of merit and performance. As was the case with the professions, the reality of the situation

---

[3]Theodore Caplow, *The Sociology of Work* (Minneapolis: University of Minnesota Press, 1954), pp. 102–3.
[4]*Ibid.*, pp. 107–98.

is such that evaluation is difficult, if not impossible. Moreover, an additional evaluatory agent is almost always present in the form of the employing organization and its engineering staff. In the crafts there is the general assumption that journeymen are in a position to judge apprentices and that masters are in a position to judge both journeymen and apprentices. As this traditional relation breaks down in the face of trade-school education and technological development, evaluation becomes more difficult for members of the craft and is increasingly in the hands of the employing organization.[5] Caplow points out that a strong craft union can retain a good deal of control in the face of these developments. If the traditional apprentice-journeyman-master distinctions are retained and the union has been able to standardize production rates, materials, and techniques, the employing organization is unable to distinguish between the different categories within the craft in terms of performance, since it is standardized by level, which allows the union to retain control. Such practices are given the negative connotation of featherbedding or stalling, but from the union's point of view they are necessary for continued power of self-control.[6] This form of standardization creates a situation in which members of the craft at the various levels are viewed as being interchangeable and retains the power of work assignment for the union.

In addition to the power of evaluation of merit and performance, some craft unions have succeeded in obtaining contracts covering all employers in an urban area. These contracts are designed to allow craft control over a wide variety of activities of concern to both union members and the employing organizations. In some ways these contracts contain elements analogous to the codes of ethics of the professions; the codes include provisions to protect outsiders from incompetence and unqualified practitioners and provisions designed to "safeguard the socioeconomic position of insiders."[7] The provisions include, in addition, such things as specifications of standard hourly wages together with provisions for overtime and other special conditions; rules of eligibility and ineligibility, which include the number of apprentices allowed per job and hiring and seniority standards; specifications of safety rules and acceptable tools and methods; and clauses pertaining to the union's right to a monopoly over certain activities. This allows occupational self-control to the extent that outside influence from employing organizations is unlikely to intrude except during contract negotiations. As is true of the

[5]Edward Gross, *Work and Society* (New York: Thomas Y. Crowell Co., 1958), p. 57.
[6]Caplow, *The Sociology of Work*, pp. 111–12.
[7]*Ibid.*, p. 113.

professions, the actual extent of such self-control is likely to be rather limited.

Caplow's analysis is primarily concerned with, and relevant to, the building trades, which have been affected by technological changes to the extent that standardization of techniques and output is an evident component of the work. Other occupations included in the crafts have been or will be so affected. At the same time, the crafts contain elements that allow the worker to view his individual contribution to the whole. He can see what he has done, making his contribution somewhat unique and providing the opportunity for intrinsic satisfaction because of this ability to identify with a completed product or service. This again is similar to the work of the professional. Blauner's analysis of the printing craft is instructive in this regard.

Printing involves an unstandardized product, the printed page, with which the individual can identify, since each member of the craft can see what his individual contribution is. In addition, this type of craft involves

> the freedom to determine techniques of work, to choose one's tools, and to vary the sequence of operations. . . . Because each job is somewhat different from previous jobs, problems continuously arise which require a craftsman to make decisions. Traditional skills thus involve the frequent use of judgment and initiative, aspects of a job which give the worker a feeling of control over his environment.[8]

Blauner's analysis of alienation suggests that this feeling of control contributes to the lack of feeling of powerlessness among the printers. In this sense, the craftsman, like the professional, has control over his work and its environment even with the standardization noted above. There is freedom to vary the rate of performance and its sequence. The judgment factor enters the picture in terms of decisions regarding appropriate tools and techniques.

Another important consideration, suggested by Blauner, is that printers form an occupational community in that they identify strongly with the occupation.[9] He notes:

> Craft identification, a product of socialization, sometimes begins early in life, since there is a strong tendency for sons to follow fathers into the

---

[8]Robert Blauner, *Alienation and Freedom* (Chicago: University of Chicago Press, 1964), p. 43.

[9]For an extensive analysis of the printing craft and the relationship between it and union structure, see Seymour M. Lipset, Martin A. Trow, and James S. Coleman, *Union Democracy* (New York: Free Press of Glencoe, Inc., 1956).

same skilled trade. The long apprenticeship period is the formal process through which a craftsman learns occupational norms as well as proficiency in work. Craft identification and loyalty is further reinforced through membership in craft unions.[10]

This is very similar to the "use of the professional organization as a major reference" as discussed in the section on professions.

The salience of this occupational community can be seen in William F. Whyte's analysis of a group of glassworkers. The glass factory studied made fine crystal, which requires largely hand technology. Aside from changes in the composition of the basic materials and methods for handling them, the overall technology has changed little over time. A hierarchy of skills exists within the work group, and tradition and union provisions require that a person work his way up through the hierarchy. At one time, only workers of Swedish extraction reached the top position, because of the communal belief that the Swedes were the only group that had the requisite skills and artistic sense for the job. This pattern created an even stronger occupational community. The Swedish dominance declined when the sons of the older workers did not continue in the glass industry because of continued education. The unionization of the total plant and the entire glass industry in the urban area also had an impact, since seniority provisions replaced ethnic ties as the major factor in advancement.

Despite these changes, the sense of community remained, which was evident in the traditions and lore surrounding the work situation. The most skilled of the workers were constantly being compared to famous old-timers. In the case of non-Swedes, the comparisons were usually negative, at least from the perspective of the older workers. The composition of the work groups helped retain the sense of community, since a strong tendency existed for workers to belong to the same work groups for a length of time. This strengthened the social ties within the group, leading to some competition between groups and also to a more general identification with the occupation. Whyte notes that the movement of younger workers into top positions did create friction between the younger and older workers. The older workers believed that the young men in top positions did not have the all-round skills characteristic of top men in the past. The fact that there was friction reinforces the idea that the occupation is a central focus for these workers. Rather than being apathetic, they appear to feel strong emotional involvement in the work. Whyte's analysis also suggests that these craftsmen were also highly involved in their personal performance on the job; pride in craftsmanship

[10]Blauner, *Alienation and Freedom*, p. 47.

was an important component of the job. All of these factors contribute to the high level of identification with the occupation.[11]

It would be useful to have data comparing levels of involvement in the occupation among a variety of crafts in a variety of settings, as was the case for some of the professions. Such data are unfortunately not available. It would seem that the sense of community or involvement would be greater in those cases where workers systematically interact, as in the case of the glassworkers or printers, and less in some building trades where the work group composition changes with particular projects. Another factor tending to affect this variable is technological change. Change of this sort probably has a dual impact. The threat of technological change, with the possibility of lost jobs, changed working relationships, weakened craft unions, and lowered skill requirements, may increase the level of involvement and create heightened solidarity. Once changes are instituted, the level of involvement would probably decline over a period of time, as skill requirements became less rigorous, remaining vestiges of the apprentice-master system disappeared, and the work contained fewer elements allowing individual discretion.[12] If this is the case, the long term trend for the crafts would appear to be a decline in the occupational community, since technological changes, while often resisted, are largely inevitable in the crafts.

Further inroads into the sense of the community may develop as restrictions on recruitment into the crafts are eased. In the case of the glassworkers, for example, the union represented all of the workers in the particular glass factory. This weakened the grip of the Swedes on the top positions and allowed non-Swedes access to these positions. When unions are organized along strictly craft lines, as is the case in most of the building trades, ethnic solidarity remains but is threatened by demands for equal employment opportunities for all eligible applicants. As these threats become reality, the ethnic base of a good deal of the solidarity is weakened and this, coupled with changing technology, probably diminishes the level of involvement.

The crafts, however, do have a stronger sense of occupational identification than other manual and many white-collar occupations. Richard R. Myers's study of the building industry suggests that personal ties together with ethnic, religious, and racial considerations play an important role in the hiring process. The actual work groups tend to be composed of craftsmen who know and like each other.[13] Within any work situation,

[11]William F. Whyte, *Men at Work* (Homewood, Ill.: Richard D. Irwin, 1961), pp. 149–78.

[12]Gross notes this change in *Work and Society*, p. 57.

[13]Richard M. Myers, "Interpersonal Relations in the Building Industry," *Human Organization*, V, 2 (spring 1946), 1–7.

cohesive work groups are likely to be based on common background characteristics, such as race, religion, or ethnicity, as well as on such factors as sex, age, or educational level. The important finding in the Myers's study is that the initial composition of the groups is almost totally based upon such factors. Personal acquaintance is the key to the hiring process, creating a situation in which the solidarity is likely to be heightened and outsiders effectively excluded.

A study by Harold L. Sheppard and A. Harvey Belitsky, concerned with the nature of job seeking in Erie, Pennsylvania, substantiates the importance of the craft as a major reference point. The community and its metropolitan area were faced with a declining economy, which was further depressed by the departure of a major employer. A comparison of skilled, semiskilled, and unskilled workers was undertaken to determine the techniques utilized in finding employment by the workers who had been laid off. Skilled workers generally had a higher rate of reemployment in their old jobs as economic conditions improved. An exception to this was older workers, a group that generally faces more difficulties in finding employment. There were no skilled workers under 38 still unemployed at the time of the study. Since there is a tendency for skilled workers to be older, their chances in the labor market are adversely affected by the age factor but are enhanced by their skills.

The actual techniques used in seeking new jobs for those workers not rehired by their original employer varied by skill level. The union was an important source of information about new jobs for skilled workers but not for other groups. The union was also an effective means of locating new positions for the skilled group. The other groups had more success from information from friends and relatives or by applying directly to companies that were hiring at a particular time. At the same time, skilled workers who applied directly to companies had good success; their skills were a marketable commodity.[14]

The skilled worker has a distinct advantage in the labor market as compared with blue-collar workers of lesser skill levels. The importance of skills is not, of course, limited to the blue-collar world. What is important for the discussion is that the union is an important factor in the labor market for the skilled worker, even in times of high unemployment rates. The craftsman, however, looks to his colleagues as a resource. Here again the orientation may not be as strong as among some professions, but it is an important source of differentiation from other occupational categories in both blue-collar and white-collar occupations.

The importance of the union for the craftsman is further shown in

[14]Harold L. Sheppard and A. Harvey Belitsky, *The Job Hunt* (Baltimore: Johns Hopkins Press, 1966), pp. 31–100.

Caplow's discussion of the total labor market for the crafts. To some extent the supply of craftsmen is fixed by the recruitment patterns into the occupation, which tend to limit the number of persons in a particular craft within a geographical area. The control of the labor supply is not absolute, however, since noncraftsmen can attempt many of the jobs normally performed by craftsmen. Caplow points out that there is a rather constant supply of amateur or marginal painters, ready, willing and, to varying degrees, able to undertake painting projects of differing magnitudes.[15] The same is probably true for many other craft skills, such as plumbing, electrical work, or roofing, despite the personal and financial risks involved in such do-it-yourself projects.

> The union, on its side, has recourse to a number of familiar devices to preserve its monopoly. Employers who hire nonunion labor for craft work may be permanently boycotted by all the crafts. Personal violence against these competitors is not unheard of. The most effective controls are embodied in local ordinances and agreements [Note the close similarity of this practice with the professions' control over licensing and certification procedures], so that in many cities building permits, permits to operate machinery, and other necessary licenses will be revoked if inspection discloses the use of nonunion labor. While this control often ceases at the city limits, it is sufficiently effective in most communities to restrict the use of nonunion labor on craft work to small projects of no economic importance. There are, of course, some conspicuous exceptions in either direction: entire villages have been built by large scale contractors with nonunion labor; while in other places, private householders have been effectively prevented from doing plumbing or wiring on their own premises.[16]

The supply of labor can thus be controlled to some extent; the demand, on the other hand, is often highly variable. In the building and construction trades, climactic changes have an important effect. In addition, in the building trades and many other crafts, the employers are likely to be small and relatively insecure, lending further instability to the demand factor. These conditions create real problems for the craft unions in that they must somehow provide for their members during slack periods and face the situation of not having a fixed entity with which to bargain. The most effective technique, which the unions have developed, is the establishment of a fixed or just price for the work performed, high enough to allow earnings during full-employment periods to cover those periods when seasonal or industry declines occur. At the same time, the unions seek to become the only source for hiring, so that

---

[15]*The Sociology of Work*, p. 165.
[16]*Ibid.*, p. 165.

potential employers must come to the union for their workers. This gives the union power over the employers and its own members. Caplow points out that the unions are most successful in these practices during times of full employment. During periods of low employment their control over potential employers and their own members is lessened as the individual members use their own resources in trying to find work.[17] Except in times of low employment, the union is a powerful force for the craftsman and his employer. This power would tend to strengthen the union's position as a major reference for its members.

The discussion thus far has suggested that crafts and professions share a number of characteristics. To use the approach taken in the section on the professions, on both structural and attitudinal character- istics, the crafts in many ways approximate the professional model. Major differences exist between the groups, however, that prevent the two occupational types from being viewed as one. The basic difference is that the professions stress mental prowess, while the crafts stress manual dexterity. Some professions, such as surgery and some forms of engineering, require dexterity; nevertheless, the basis for the work is the exercise of mental skills. The simple mental-manual differentiation is based upon a more fundamental difference. The professions are built around a body of theoretical knowledge that can be applied in specific situations. Professionals contribute to the knowledge base and apply the knowledge that is available. In practice, the professional may not always refer back to the theoretical underpinnings of a case. He may simply prescribe, decide, or advise, in a mechanical way, on the basis of the simple facts presented to him; when a particular symptom appears, a standard remedy is suggested. At this level, his actions are little different from the craftsman. The differentiation is based on the assumption that the professional can back up his decision with the theoretical considera- tions on which the simple mechanical decisions were based. Whether or not every practicing professional can do this is subject to investigation, but professional training is designed to allow the person to do so.

The craftsman, on the other hand, is trained in techniques without the theoretical background. He may, in many instances, apply principles from theoretical sciences. The tool and die maker, for example, utilizes principles from trigonometry and analytical geometry in his work, but he does so without realizing it. Theoretical knowledge allows operation in situations that have not previously been experienced, but for the craftsman such knowledge is unavailable. This is not to suggest that the craftsman is unable to adjust to new problems and situations. He does so on the basis of his experience and by trial and error.

[17]*Ibid.*, p. 168.

Another difference between professionals and craftsmen is the colleague group. As Caplow notes, craft unions are locally based, and community boundaries are usually the limit of jurisdiction. Professional associations, on the other hand, are organized on a local, state, regional, and national basis, and some professionals utilize the national group as their reference. More important, the regulative power of the associations is much more broadly based than the local community.

Training for skilled work takes three basic forms. The traditional apprenticeship is still the most visible technique, but the number of apprentices has declined in recent years. The major source of training at the present time is the vocational school, particularly for the newer crafts. Vocational curricula in the past have been severely criticized because they have emphasized skills that are in low demand and do not adjust to changes in technology.[18] Presently, the high school and post-high-school vocational technical schools appear to have moved away from this problem. The true test of the impact of the vocational schools' training will come in fifteen to twenty years as their graduates are well into their careers. The growth of the vocational schools does suggest continued interest in and demand for the crafts.

A third method for learning a craft is on the job. In this case the worker picks up the skills while assisting a skilled worker or on his free time. Here again, union contract provisions may prevent this if the contract contains clear specifications of who is to do what kind of work. Governmental and private programs have been developed to increase the number of skilled workers and to upgrade the skills of members of the labor force. The success of such programs depends on union and employer cooperation as well as the willingness of a segment of the labor force to undergo additional training. Preparation for the crafts, while longer and more intensive than for many white-collar occupations and for most other blue-collar occupations, is not comparable to professional training. The diversity of the programs and their relationship to unions suggest a less coordinated approach to training for crafts.

The discussion thus far has suggested that the craftsmen are the elite of the manual workers and that they share a number of characteristics with the other elite, the professionals. The position of the craftsmen results in part from their traditional role in the labor force and also from their ability to demand and receive rewards, in the form of income, recognition, and autonomy, that are higher than those received by other workers in both the blue- and white-collar groups. The orientation of the craftsman, however, tends to be toward the other blue-collar workers,

[18]Grant Venn, "Man, Education, and Work," in *The Manpower Revolution*, ed. Garth L. Mangum (New York: Doubleday & Co., 1966), pp. 406–7.

rather than toward those of equal or higher status in the white-collar category.

Richard F. Hamilton's examination of the behavior and values of skilled workers provides some important insights into this relationship. Using data from a national survey that grouped craftsmen with foremen, a combination that is common but unfortunate for our purposes, he found that craftsmen's membership in voluntary associations was more like that of semiskilled workers than of white-collar workers (clerical and sales personnel). The craftsman and the semiskilled worker both belong to fewer such organizations than the white-collar workers. Similarly, the skilled workers' reading patterns were closer to the semiskilled than to the white-collar group. An important exception is that the skilled workers did read more trade magazines than either of the other groups. Hamilton suggests that this is further evidence of the independence of the crafts. At the same time the other reading patterns are closer to the other blue-collar patterns.[19]

In other areas, the relationship is maintained. The similarity of political and educational beliefs and attitudes on foreign policy and domestic issues reflect the proximity of the craftsmen to other blue-collar workers. An interesting finding in regard to the life style of the craftsmen is that they are more likely to own their own homes than the white-collar workers. Hamilton suggests that skilled workers actually comprise a semi-autonomous status group, closer to the balance of the blue-collar category than to the white-collar group. They are not "interstitial" in the sense of standing between the other status groups but instead lean toward the rest of the blue-collar group while retaining independence in certain areas.[20]

Hamilton attributes the autonomy of the skilled workers partially to the high rate of occupational inheritance within the group. There is some mobility into the crafts from the lesser skilled categories, but this is largely among workers who are already of the appropriate background, since the crafts can control entrance. At the same time, those who are downwardly mobile from the white-collar group tend to bypass the crafts, entering the labor force at the semiskilled level and not bringing their values into the crafts.

Most of the discussion thus far has been oriented around the traditional crafts. The growth of the craftsman category is based on the emergent service crafts, such as television or automobile repairing, and the behavioral and attitudinal characteristics discussed may not be rele-

[19]Richard F. Hamilton, "The Behavior and Values of Skilled Workers" in *Blue Collar World*, eds. Arthur B. Shostak and William Gomberg (Englewood Cliffs, N.J.: Prentice-Hall, 1964), p. 49.

[20]*Ibid.*, pp. 55–56.

vant for the newer craft occupations. Similarly, the discussion of the professionlike nature of the building and printing crafts may be inapplicable. Certainly the new crafts do not have the common ethnic, racial, and religious backgrounds of the older groups. Other traditions are also probably absent. Whether they model themselves on the other tradition of craft occupations would have to be determined by research, but it seems somewhat unlikely, since the social origins of the new craftsmen are not in the old crafts (the rate of occupational inheritance is such that the sons of the old-style craftsmen would either go into the same craft or attain higher educational levels and leave the craft system). Part of the reason Hamilton found relatively close identification of craftsmen with semiskilled workers may be that the newer crafts recruit from the semiskilled worker level. If this is the case, there would tend to be some carry-over of attitudes and behavior into the new occupation. This again is a topic for additional research.

The new crafts are similar to the new professions in their partial conformity to the traditional conceptualization of what a craft or profession is. While the crafts have not been investigated as intensively as the professions, some factors in the differences are evident. The new crafts do not have the long tradition of apprenticeship. Skills are acquired in vocational or training schools or on the job. Entrance is thus less structured, and there are fewer controls on the number entering the field and the nature of the prerequisites for entry. This could lead to a diminished emphasis on racial or ethnic considerations. At the same time, the differentiation between crafts and noncrafts becomes more difficult because training periods are less formalized and comprehensive. It is difficult to determine, for example, exactly which auto mechanics are skilled workers and which are semiskilled; no clear criteria exist. The simplest differentiation would probably be whether or not the individual can sell his skills on the labor market. If he can be hired as a mechanic, rather than as an employee, he would be considered skilled. Such a differentiation may be oversimplified, but it does represent much of the essence of the crafts. As was the case with the professions, however, the line between members and nonmembers of the occupational category cannot be drawn with certainty.

We have noted that there are many similarities between the crafts and the professions. This fact is not lost on the employing organizations. Arthur Stinchcombe, in a study of construction workers, notes that construction firms are much like professional organizations.[21] While Ritzer argues that Stinchcombe carries his argument too far by making an

[21]"Bureaucratic and Craft Administration of Production: A Comparative Study," *Administrative Science Quarterly* 4 (.September 1959), 168–87.

almost exact equation between professionals and craftsmen,[22] the fact remains that those parts of organizations or total organizations in which craftsmen work are less bureaucratic than either white-collar or lower-level blue-collar parts of organizations or total organizations. Craft unions negotiate working-condition and decision-making clauses into their contracts, thus preventing organizational rules from overcoming craft conventions. There are thus intraorganizational variations in structure when the crafts are part of the workforce.

This does not mean that the crafts are totally free to do as they like in an organization. Indeed, Ritzer believes that the greatest problem for the crafts is threats to their autonomy. In an important study of a sample of British workers by Goldthorpe *et al.*, increased autonomy was the *major* job change that the craftsmen desired in their present job.[23] Here, increased autonomy involves the workers' capacity for doing work in ways different than those established by their predecessors as correct. Autonomy is threatened by the organizations because organizations would probably like to do away with the work of craftsmen, which is specialized hand work. Whether the activity is welding, plumbing, or auto repair, organizations would like to find more economical production or service techniques. The potential for setting type by computer threatens the printer, just as preassembled brick walls threaten the bricklayer. It is in the autonomy area that unions fight the hardest to retain the traditional power of the craftsman.

As has already been suggested, the power of the crafts has enabled them to exclude persons deemed undesirable. As is well known, this has worked to the severe disadvantage of minority groups. Until very recently, there has been almost total exclusion of blacks in the building trade unions. As it is, there are only 4.2 percent blacks in crafts.[24] The exclusion of blacks and other minorities has been accomplished in the past by formal rules that only opened union membership to whites. With this sort of rule now illegal, the informal social mechanisms that are inherent in such closely knit groups still operate.[25] This is an important point, of course, since the crafts represent an alternative route for social mobility for minority group members. The crafts remain, of

[22]George Ritzer, *Man and His Work: Conflict and Change* (New York: Appleton-Century-Crofts, 1972).

[23]John H. Goldthorpe *et al.*, *The Affluent Worker: Industrial Attitudes and Behavior* (Cambridge: Cambridge University Press, 1970), pp. 20–21.

[24]Theodore V. Purcell and Gerald F. Cavanagh, *Blacks in the Industrial World* (New York: Free Press of Glencoe, 1972), p. 38.

[25]See Ritzer, *Men and Their Work*, pp. 203–5, and Ray Marshall, *The Negro Worker* (New York: Random House, 1967).

course, an almost totally male world. This is due to both exclusionary practices and female resistance to entering these particular occupations.[26]

FOREMEN

Foremen, although a relatively small proportion of the total labor force and of this occupational category, have been the subject of intensive analyses because of their pivotal positions in organizations. The foreman is at the bottom of the managerial hierarchy and at the top of the blue-collar segment of the organization. He can be called foreman, first-line supervisor, chief, or group leader. The position is one filled from below, and people are promoted out of the ranks to the position. Miller and Form describe the position as follows:

> . . . an office that requires supervision of the actual production or service as a full-time job. The person filling this office must have official contacts with both supervisory officials and the operators or clerks on the job. He must spend most of his time on the plant floor supervising personally, or supervising people who are part-time supervisors and part-time workers. Paper work must not occupy so much of his time that he has to have a secretary. He does not spend more than one-third of his day on it. In fact, paper work irritates him and keeps him off the floor. Further, he does not participate in policy-making. In short, his orientation is downward toward the workers and their problems. He must have enough authority so that workers obey his technical commands.[27]

The foreman's position is ubiquitous. At some point in most organizations (extremely small organizations in which members perform highly specialized functions would be the most obvious exception), such supervision is vital to the work process. Joan Woodward has noted that the ratio of supervisors to supervisees varies according to the technology of an industry, but even in those industries where human supervision is minimized, foremen are still present and have a wide span of control.[28] Charles R. Walker, Robert H. Guest, and Arthur N. Turner suggest:

> In a sense, the *foreman* is one species in a very large genus of human beings. The genus may be said to include all who directly supervise men

[26]For an extensive discussion of the general life-style of skilled workers, see Gavin Mackenzie, *The Aristocracy of Labor* (London: Cambridge University Press, 1973).
[27]Delbert Miller and William Form, *Industrial Sociology* (New York: Harper & Row, 1964), p. 206.
[28]*Industrial Organization: Theory and Practice* (London: Oxford University Press, 1965), pp. 55–56.

and women, such as the lower ranks of officers and noncommissioned officers in the armed services, head nurses in hospitals, senior clerks in banks and law offices, and many others.[29]

The foreman's position is thus one of coordination of workers' efforts to accomplish the goals of the organization. Such a position is obviously vital. It is also subject to a variety of conflicting pressures and to the impact of change.

A basic source of conflict for the foreman is that he is caught between his superiors' demands that he identify with them and embody organizational authority to his men and the worker's demands that he assist them in evading the rules and maintaining work group solidarity. Caplow notes that the resulting marginality or ambivalence is inherent in the position and is a major reason for the fact that foremen have been the principal targets for "supervisory training, conference systems, performance appraisals, and so on. . . ."[30] Caught between these conflicting demands, the foreman has four alternative identification patterns that he can assume, according to Miller and Form.

He can identify with his superiors and adopt the management ideology.[31] Miller and Form believe that pattern is especially likely when the foreman is brought in from outside the work group and expects that the position of foreman is a prelude to advancement into higher management positions. Since there appears to be a tendency to hire college-trained junior-executive types for the foreman's position, this type of identification should become more dominant.[32] The obvious problem with this form of identification is the social distance that develops between the foreman and his workers. "The latter will not confide in him or have much to do with him outside of work. On the contrary, they will withhold information, restrict their work, and use the union to make his life uncomfortable."[33] Such relatively dire consequences undoubtedly occur, but if the pattern of "imported" foremen continues, it would seem that such management orientation would come to be expected. The social distance need not necessarily lead to organizationally dysfunctional behavior. Miller and Form's point about social distance is relevant, however, to the extent that such distance affects the relationship between

[29]*The Foreman on the Assembly Line* (Cambridge, Mass.: Harvard University Press, 1956), p. 3.

[30]Theodore Caplow, *Principles of Organization* (New York: Harcourt, Brace, and World, 1964), p. 247.

[31]Miller and Form, *Industrial Sociology*, pp. 215–16.

[32]This tendency will be discussed in more detail below. For a general discussion of this trend, see Whyte, *Men at Work*, pp. 382–89.

[33]Miller and Form, *Industrial Sociology*, p. 215.

worker and foreman. In some cases, however, greater social distance could be organizationally useful and personally satisfying to both parties.

A second form of identification for the foreman is with the workers. This is particularly likely when the foreman has risen from the ranks and is viewed as still "one of the boys." This identification tends to lead a foreman to "cover up for his men, resist changes imposed from above, understand the union's demands, and modify his orders to fit the local situation."[34] He is also likely to have friendly relations with the workers on and off the job. As the upwardly oriented foreman suffers in his relationship with his men, this type suffers in his relationship to superiors. Rather obviously, this type of orientation, like that of the upwardly oriented, can have functional or dysfunctional consequences for both workers and the organization. The employee-oriented foreman can maintain a system wherein the workers have few grievances and maintain production schedules. At the same time, such an orientation can obstruct the organization in times of innovation or of crisis. For the worker, such a situation could lead to lessened earnings, if the basis for solidarity is restriction of output. This could be individually dysfunctional over a period of time if other bases for cohesion are not developed.

The other two forms of identification are less common. The foreman can try to straddle the barrier between management and labor and maintain a dual loyalty. Miller and Form suggest that this is reasonably likely to occur among those who have recently been appointed foreman from the ranks. Sympathy for, and allegiance to, the workers' points of view are retained. At the same time, the fact of promotion leads to the orientation toward management. Foremen can retain this dual orientation until a crisis occurs, at which time a position must be taken. Miller and Form believe that the choice will be with management. Once this move is made, the identification is likely to be maintained. The fourth form of identification is with other foremen through foremen's unions or associations. This is a result of realization by the foreman of his marginal status and an attempt to strengthen his position through common actions. While unions lead to solidarity, the chances for development of real power are minimal.[35]

The marginal position of the foreman leads to the alternative identification system. Since he is at the bottom of the management hierarchy, he must accomplish the difficult job of supervision by translating organizational policies and purposes into coordinated action by his workers. At the same time, his direct contact with the workers, regardless of his

[34]*Ibid.*, p. 216.
[35]*Ibid.*, pp. 218–19.

orientation, makes him susceptible to their reactions to the work and his supervision. Since he is responsible for work output, he is dependent upon the workers. Too great a dependence, however, diminishes the little power he has. He is caught between two systems that contain contrasting and occasionally conflicting orientations toward work.

The position of the foreman contains an additional element that leads to further power reduction. Many functions, once performed by the foreman or at least part of his responsibility, have been taken over by other personnel within the organization. In theory, at least, the foreman should know

> . . . not only (1) the company's policies, rules, and regulations and (2) the company's cost system, payment system, manufacturing methods, and inspection regulations, in particular, but also frequently (3) control, and time and motion study in general. He also has to know (4) the labor laws of the United States, (5) the labor laws of the state in which the company operates, and (6) the specific labor contract which exists between his company and the local union. He has to know (7) how to induct, instruct, and train new workers; (8) how to handle, and where possible, prevent grievances; (9) how to improve conditions of safety; (10) how to correct workers and maintain discipline; (11) how never to lose his temper and always be "fair"; (12) how to get and obtain cooperation from the wide assortment of people with the shop steward. And in some companies he is supposed to know (13) how to do the jobs he supervises better than the employees themselves. Indeed, as some foreman training programs seem to conceive the foreman's job, he has to be a manager, a cost accountant, an engineer, a lawyer, a teacher, a leader, an inspector, a disciplinarian, a counselor, a friend, and above all, an example.[36]

A person possessing all of these skills and the related knowledge would be a rare individual indeed. Rather obviously, many of these functions are the responsibility of staff departments within the organization. The foreman's position is further weakened if the staff is more expert than he in these areas. The staff departments responsible for these areas transmit their ideas of appropriate actions, and the foreman must carry them out, even if he disagrees with the plans. He is lower in the organizational hierarchy than the staff officials and may lack the specialized knowledge necessary for instituting his own ideas. He is surrounded by experts with power who make decisions regarding the work that he supervises. He is put in the position of carrying out policies and procedures he has had no role in forming. Figure 7-1 indicates the nature of the erosion of the foreman's position.

This analysis suggests that the principal role of the foreman is super-

[36]Fritz J. Roethlisberger, "The Foreman: Master and Victim of Double Talk," *Harvard Business Review*, XXIII, 3 (spring 1945), 283.

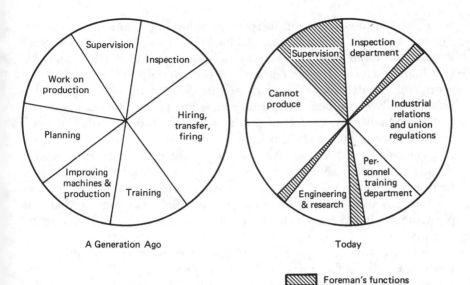

Figure 7-1   The Foreman's Functions: A Generation Ago and Today.
Source: Delbert C. Miller and William H. Form, *Industrial Sociology*
(New York: Harper & Row, 1964), p. 211.

vision. In some ways the removal of other responsibilities and the concentration on direct supervision would seem to make the position less difficult. The foreman, however, is in the position of attempting to supervise with few resources. The supervisory function itself contains a strong potential for ambiguity, as Etzioni's analysis suggests. Following the work of Talcott Parsons, Robert F. Bales, and others, Etzioni notes that supervision contains two elements.[37] The *instrumental* aspect is the "need to acquire resources, or means, and to allocate them among the various role clusters in the system," while the *expressive* function involves the "need to maintain the integration of various parts of the system with each other as well as with its normative system."[38] The instrumental leader is task oriented, while the expressive leader is concerned with the social and emotional stability of the group.

Research evidence consistently indicates that the two functions are separated in practice. Where they are combined, as in the case of a few great men, the problems to be discussed are minimized. Etzioni suggests a division of workers into those who are alienated and those who are

[37]Amitai Etzioni, *A Comparative Analysis of Complex Organizations* (New York: Free Press of Glencoe, 1961), pp. 113–25.

[38]These definitions appear in a later work by Amitai Etzioni, "Dual Leadership in Complex Organizations," *American Sociological Review*, XXX, 5 (October 1965), 689.

committed to their work and to the employing organization. The alienative response is more likely among blue-collar workers. For this type of
worker, the foreman is able to play only an instrumental role and this
to a limited degree. He can enforce compliance only to the limits of the
contractual relationship. The work groups develop their own expressive
leadership. Even in the instrumental area, some of the foreman's prerogatives are removed by control of production rates and allocation of work
within the work groups. In this kind of situation, the foreman has minimal controls in either area. The worker-oriented foreman may hold a
slightly stronger position than the management-oriented person but,
according to this analysis, is still effectively barred from the exercise of
too much power.[39] The earlier analyses of alienation suggest that this
phenomenon is most likely to occur in the more routinized production
systems.

An exception to this would perhaps be in work on assembly lines.
In this case the highly routinized work requires very little instrumental
control. This gives the foreman the opportunity to engage in expressive
activities. If another informal leader is present in the work group, however, the foreman is likely to lose in the competition. In such a situation
the foreman's overall power is quite low.

Workers who are more committed to their work and organization,
such as skilled or white-collar workers, relate to their foreman in a slightly
different fashion. Even in these cases, however, the foreman can seldom
play more than an instrumental role, according to Etzioni's analysis. For
the committed workers, however, a useful distinction is introduced. Some
foremen, principally in low-productivity units, rely upon the *official* power
of their position. Those in high-productivity units have some degree of
personal influence over the workers in instrumental matters. Etzioni calls
the former "foreman-officials" and the latter "foreman-leaders."[40] The point
here is basically that the foreman-official relies solely upon his position
in the organization, while the foreman-leader utilizes personal relations
with the workers in realizing the instrumental goals. In a sense, therefore,
the foreman-leader does utilize an aspect of the expressive relationship.
This is only the case in instrumental activities. He can appeal to the
workers through personal ties in the area of work itself. The foreman-
official does not have this resource.

This distinction makes a difference in the foreman's actual operations
on the job. The foreman-official spends less time in actual supervision
than the foreman-leader. Etzioni suggests that the foreman-official is
likely to attempt to increase productivity by engaging in production him-

---

[39]Etzioni, *Complex Organizations*, pp. 113–15.
[40]*Ibid.*, p. 116.

self. The foreman-official also tends to supervise closely, when he engages in supervision, while the foreman-leader utilizes a more general supervisory style. The foreman-leader also engages in more teaching activities than the foreman-official. The foreman-leader is more likely to be found among the more committed workers.

While stressing the point that the foreman-leader utilizes personal influence in his supervision, Etzioni also suggests that this type cannot become an expressive leader for his work group. This leads to the conclusion that programs designed to develop the foreman's expressive leadership abilities (human relations training) may be doomed to failure. "Psychological and social tensions in the work situation will increase rather than diminish [as a result of this kind of training] because the average foreman is encouraged to attempt what is for him the impossible: to wear two hats at the same time."[41] In order to gain in terms of his expressive position, the foreman often must resort to activities that weaken his position as an instrumental leader, such as overlooking tardiness or ignoring deviations from official norms in terms of quantity or quality of the work. The suggestion here is that the two forms of activity are incompatible. Etzioni states:

> The foreman, expected to please two masters, or rather his masters and his "servants," is caught in the conflicting role-prescriptions. He cannot perform either of the two effectively. His level of dissatisfaction and personal strain increases, as does that of most persons who are in role-conflict. His relationship with the workers becomes strained because he cannot be consistently expressive and because he tends to threaten the informal leader of the group (to the degree that one exists) by his endeavors to build up his own expressive leadership. Relations with higher levels of management become strained as the foreman becomes less effective instrumentally. In short, we suggest that it is quite likely that this form of leadership training leads to results opposite of those expected by its advocates.[42]

The fact that most foremen are relatively dissatisfied with their position and undergo a considerable amount of psychological and social strain is taken as evidence for the validity of this position. Etzioni concludes that foremen who have had human relations training are more likely to suffer these negative consequences. If this is the case, then the orientation of the foreman to management or to the workers, as discussed previously, will be differentially affected by such training. The worker-oriented foreman, who already may have some expressive relationships with his workers, will be drawn further away from management, inducing more strain in that direction. The management-oriented foreman, on

[41]*Ibid.*, p. 119.
[42]*Ibid.*, p. 120.

the other hand, will probably find that his efforts in an expressive direction are rebuffed, again leading to stress and strain.

The analysis thus far has suggested that the foreman's role is demanding and inherently conflict laden. The actual job requirements and the alternative orientations available present the foreman with conflicts not easily resolved. These difficulties are evident to the analyst as well as to the potential foremen in the ranks of workers. Chinoy's findings in his study of automobile workers illustrate this point. Less than 10 percent of the workers interviewed expressed a desire to become foremen. Half of the men had not given any thought to the possibility of moving up to the foreman's position, one-sixth had given up hopes of becoming foremen, and almost a quarter of the men interviewed claimed that they *would not want to take such a position*.[43] These findings are particularly striking in light of Chinoy's conclusion that such a move is probably the "only way up for factory workers."[44] Movement into skilled or white-collar work or into a position out of the factory is very unlikely, thus foremanship is the most reasonable means of upward mobility.

The workers' own definition of the situation was that a foreman's position was unlikely and undesirable, in many ways an objectively correct view of the situation. There were relatively few openings for foremen. Those who held these positions were likely to keep them for some time. Opportunities were greater for skilled workers, since the work groups tended to be smaller, which lead to a higher ratio of foremen to workers. Another factor affecting outlooks of these workers was that the means of achieving foremanship were unclearly defined. Management, in this case, claimed that performance and ability were the major criteria for the positions but at the same time utilized education and training as the chief factor in promotions. This led to a preference for younger men who possessed a high school diploma and additional training. Older men who did not have these prerequisites thus felt that the situation was hopeless.

Many of the workers in this study believed that the promotion process was filled with uncertainty and favoritism. Merit and ability were not seen as the real paths to advancement. This outlook was compounded by the difficulties in demonstrating the kinds of merit and ability needed for the foreman's position. There was little opportunity to demonstrate "initiative, leadership, resourcefulness, and cooperativeness."[45] The workers also believed that pull and connections were major factors in the promo-

[43]Ely Chinoy, *Automobile Workers and the American Dream* (New York: Doubleday & Co., 1955), p. 49.
[44]*Ibid.*, p. 46.
[45]*Ibid.*, p. 54.

tion process and that the person who did move up was someone who had gained the personal interest and support of his foreman. Membership in the right religious and fraternal organizations was also felt to contribute to advancement. These social ties, if they were important in the promotions process, were themselves viewed negatively by most of the workers. Those who actively sought such ties were given clearly negative appellations, such as brownnose or bootlicker. Chinoy notes that this form of reaction may be only rationalizations of failure to gain advancement or expressions of lack of interest in the position. At the same time, such reactions also serve as mechanisms that "inhibit interest and stifle hope."[46]

The objective lack of opportunity and the subjective reactions to the situation served as impediments to advancement into foremanship. At the same time, the rewards of the position were sufficient to make it a desirable one for the workers. Greater pay and freedom were available to the foreman. This kind of attractiveness was counterbalanced by the negative components of the position, which have been discussed. The workers viewed the position as one filled with grief. They recognized the pressures coming down from management and staff experts. The uncertainty and difficulty of the position made it one that was not attractive to many of the men. In addition, the responsibility of the position was viewed by many as undesirable or beyond their competence. Chinoy notes that the modern mass-production factory gives little opportunity to learn how to handle responsibility, making positions that demand the handling of responsibility threatening to the workers.[47]

Goldthorpe et al. found very similar attitudes in their more recent study in Great Britain.[48] The British personnel did not aspire to become foremen for either the qualities of the job or the slight financial gain from the foreman's position. The foreman's role requirements were undesirable and the rewards insufficient to tempt or attract the majority of workers.

A contrasting view of the possibilities of becoming a foreman and the reactions of foremen to their position is offered by Walker, Guest, and Turner.[49] These studies, also carried out in an automobile factory, suggest that a greater proportion of the workers desire to become foremen and see the advantages in the position. The majority of the foremen studied liked their jobs and viewed the rewards they received and the challenges on the job as positive reinforcements. The stresses and strains

---

[46]Ibid., p. 57.
[47]Ibid., p. 59.
[48]Goldthorpe et al., The Affluent Worker, pp. 119–26.
[49]See Charles Walker, Robert Guest, and Arthur Turner, The Foreman on the Assembly Line and Charles Walker and Robert Guest, The Man on the Assembly Line (Cambridge, Mass.: Harvard University Press, 1952).

discussed above were present but were outweighed by the advantages. The differences between these findings and those of Chinoy are largely attributable to differences in the organizations studied. The Walker, Guest, and Turner studies were carried out in a new plant and opportunities for advancement were much greater than in the older, more stabilized plant Chinoy studied. The former plant also attempted to upgrade workers whenever possible, so that the workers learned new skills and the orientation toward advancement on the job. There was also an attempt to give the foreman as much authority as possible in personal relationships. He had a voice in personnel, in training, and in disciplinary matters.

It would be useful to know the extent to which the foreman's position in other kinds of organizations approximates that in the two auto plants studied. Both analyses suggest, however, that the position is ambiguous and difficult. The position is difficult to fill. From the standpoint of the organization, the position's crucial nature demands that it be occupied by the most qualified persons. From the standpoint of the workers, it may represent an undesirable move, since a man can lose the security of seniority and gain the headaches described, even in organizations such as that described by Walker, Guest, and Turner.

The problems and the changes confronting foremen have contributed to a growing tendency toward redefinition of the place of the foreman in the organization. The foreman has traditionally been viewed as being on the bottom of the management hierarchy and at the top of the worker level. The position has been traditionally filled by people moving up from the ranks of workers. The emerging view of the foreman, however, appears to be one that emphasizes the management aspect. The trend is to bring college graduates in from the outside to be foremen. These foremen are at the start of their careers in the organization rather than at the end, as is the case with foremen who have been promoted from the ranks. The foreman's position is part of the on-the-job training.

George Strauss has suggested that the growing interdependence of work processes and more complicated technologies are specific contributors to this trend.[50] Comprehension of the total situation is thought to require more education than is possessed by the old-style foreman. Walter S. Wikstrom found essentially the same factors operative in his analysis of the foremanship patterns in four organizations. Small organizations and organizations that produced special-order single-unit items tended to utilize the older pattern. Organizations based on mass produc-

---

[50]"The Changing Role of the Working Supervisor," *The Journal of Business*, XXX, 3 (July 1957), 204.

tion and continuous-flow technology were found to have the newer, managerially oriented foremen.[51] Melville Dalton found foremen possessing engineering degrees in a study of an electronics firm.[52] Here the production process itself required highly trained supervision.

Analyses of the change in the foreman's position have been limited to production organizations. The same conclusions are probably applicable in service organizations and in the administration of all organizations as technological sophistication becomes more widespread. Evidence is unfortunately not available in regard to the extent of this transition. The impact of the change will probably be that the foreman will play an even more instrumental role, if Etizioni's analysis is correct. Foremen who come from outside the ranks of workers will further minimize opportunties to utilize expressive relationships in the position. It is conceivable that the expressive or informal leader will play a more important role as an officially or unofficially defined "straw boss" in these cases. The rather vast amount of data regarding supervisory practices does suggest that the supervisor, in this case the foreman in the position of a potential higher level manager, should utilize expressive leadership in his attempts to achieve the organization's goals. Since he has not been and cannot be one of the workers, this role cannot be played by the foreman. At the same time, the structure that develops in work situations cannot be ignored and requires that the foreman utilize the resources available to him. Strauss concludes that the supervisory powers of the straw boss (working supervisor in Strauss's terms) have diminished with the advent of the new style foreman.[53] It is likely, however, that his informal position has not been affected, which presents the foreman with an existing social structure he must take into account.

Another potential change in the role of foreman is that the role could just disappear altogether. It has been suggested that if participative management were to become a reality, there would be little need for the foreman.[54] Workers would interact with higher management, eliminating the middleman role. Of course, if all workers were to become totally dedicated to all phases of their work, there would not be any need for foremen in the first place. That, of course, is an impossible dream for all occupational categories.

---

[51]Walter S. Wikstrom, *Managing at the Foreman's Level* (New York: National Industrial Conference Board, 1967), p. 205.

[52]"Changing Staff-Line Relationships," *Personnel Administration*, XXIX, 2 (March–April 1966), 3–5.

[53]"The Changing Role of the Working Supervisor," p. 206.

[54]*Work in America: Report of a Special Task Force to the Secretary of Health, Education, and Welfare*, prepared under the auspices of the W. E. Upjohn Institute for Employment Research (Cambridge, Mass.: M.I.T. Press, 1973), p. 104.

SUMMARY AND CONCLUSIONS

Foremen and craftsmen comprise the elite of manual workers. Their status derives from their hierarchical position and, in the case of foremen, the use of mental and interpersonal skills, and the possession of highly developed and scarce skills in the case of craftsmen. Both groups continue to be affected by technological changes, and the effects appear to be adverse for the traditional foreman and some of the traditional crafts. New crafts have emerged in response to technological and social changes, which accounts for the relative stability of this group within the labor force.

Both foremen and craftsmen are strongly affected by the social environment. Foremen must utilize the existing social structure of those they supervise in their work. Craftsmen gain entrance to their trades and specific jobs through the structure surrounding their craft. The craftsman is generally supported by his peers, while the foreman may be threatened by his former peers. Recruitment into both groups is similarly affected by these kinds of social considerations. The craftsman traditionally had to be a member of the correct racial or ethnic group. Potential foremen may decline the opportunity for advancement because of the definition of the position by their work group. At the same time, the presence of the work group, whatever its degree of cohesiveness, has an impact on the foreman's work.

Despite changes in the nature of the work and altered relationships surrounding these occupations, the foreman and craftsman will remain in their position among blue-collar workers. The need for scarce skills and the fact that first-line supervision must still be performed should guarantee the continued viability of these occupations.

8

SEMISKILLED
AND UNSKILLED
WORKERS

Here we have another "type" of occupation that really isn't a type at all. The present category of occupations, like all of those that have preceded it, is very heterogeneous. The work is heterogeneous, as are the people involved. As we shall see, however, there are some important common features among the variety of semiskilled and unskilled occupations that permit a more generalized discussion.[1]

A major difficulty in dealing with these occupations is that much of the literature is ideologically based. Actually, there are multiple ideologies represented, and these ideologies are typically imposed on the semiskilled and unskilled by writers and intellectuals who are themselves far removed from the occupations. Fortunately, there is a good amount of recent research that is based on the workers' own responses to their situation so that we can begin to move out of the ideological phase into a data-based one. The data certainly can provide a basis for ideologies, but the earlier ideologies bear little resemblance to the data-based ideologies that have recently emerged. The past ideologies took two basic positions.

---

[1]Descriptive materials about the semiskilled and unskilled abound. Probably the best recent work is Studs Terkel, *Working* (New York: Pantheon Books, 1974). Terkel describes many other occupations in this work. Other recent analyses are Jerome M. Rosow (ed.), *The Worker and the Job: Coping with Change* (Englewood Cliffs, N.J., Prentice-Hall, 1974) and Stanley Aronowitz, *False Promises* (New York: McGraw-Hill Book Company, 1973). These recent discussions do not alter the conclusions of the sociologists discussed in this chapter.

The first was that of workers of this category were basically dumb and lazy and could only work if the work was finely subdivided into extremely simple tasks that could be monitored by direct supervision or other control systems. The second ideology took the opposite tack: workers were suppressed by the working conditions, and every worker yearned to be able to express his total human potential in terms of designing and controlling work and sharing in decision making. This approach further assumed that all workers both perceived the oppression of the job and were alienated or worse by its consequences. Neither ideology is meaningful in and of itself.

Semiskilled and unskilled work is not increasing as rapidly, in terms of labor force participation, as are other occupational categories.[2] Production work is declining as technological change occurs. There will probably be an increase in the number of local truck drivers, as the demands for services continue, but the category of semiskilled and unskilled work as a whole will become a smaller and smaller proportion of the labor force. Despite the decline, however, this is still a large occupational category, comprising almost a third of both the male and female labor force. In order to understand this set of occupations, we will first examine the nature of the work and then look at the way in which people react to the work.

THE SEMISKILLED

The term "semiskilled" implies one of the important characteristics of this segment of the labor force. These workers do not possess the skills of the craftsman, but have skills more easily learned in shorter periods of time. Caplow writes of semi-skilled workers:

> Their common characteristic is that no lengthy experience is required to perform the work, and that movement from one occupation to another is easy and frequent. Indeed, the mark of a semiskilled occupation is its vagueness. . . . Lifetime involvement in a job is rare. Men and women perform comparable work under comparable conditions. Job titles do not correspond to organized social groupings; and each occupation merges into many others.[3]

This vagueness implies an important component of semiskilled work; the worker performs a job defined for him by the employing organization.

[2]"The U. S. Economy in 1980: A Preview of BLS Projections," *Monthly Labor Review* 93 (April 1970), p. 23.

[3]Theodore Caplow, *The Sociology of Work* (Minneapolis: University of Minnesota Press, 1954), pp. 84–85.

His title often reflects the particular machine with which he is working or the part of the production process in which he participates. Job titles thus vary from industry to industry. He may be working with no one with the same specific title, but all will be semiskilled workers. The titles themselves do not carry the symbolic meanings attached to many other occupations.

While there is vagueness, there is also variety. Blauner's discussion is indicative of this variety. He states:

> Even within the manufacturing sector (a declining component of the total economy in contrast to the growing and highly differentiated service industries) modern factories vary considerably in technology, in division of labor, in economic structure, and in organizational character. These differences produce sociotechnical systems in which the objective conditions and the inner life of the employees are strikingly variant. In some industrial environments the alienating tendencies that Marx emphasized are present to a high degree. In others they are relatively undeveloped and have been countered by new technical, economic, and social forces.[4]

A series of studies that have dealt with the semiskilled worker illustrates the variety of work performed within the semiskilled category. Many of the studies to be discussed were designed to demonstrate the importance of work groups, the presence of nonofficial patterns of performance, or the potential for alienative responses to the work situation. For the moment, they will be used simply as descriptions.

The automobile worker has been studied more intensively than other semiskilled workers, despite the fact that the nature of his work is not typical of semiskilled work. Nevertheless, he does exemplify work on an assembly line. On the automobile assembly line, the

> major operations are performed by the workers themselves rather than by machinery. Though the work is carried out by hand with the aid of small power tools, such as electric drills and ratchet screwdrivers, it is not craft work, since the highly rationalized organization of work assignments and work flow standardizes the basic manual operations.[5]

Technology divides the production process into small units. Each worker performs one or only a few of the basic tasks. The average task requires one minute for completion. The worker performs his task on parts of a car moving down the line. When he is finished, he moves back to the next car and performs the same task. The process is continued throughout the work shift.

[4]Robert Blauner, *Alienation and Freedom* (Chicago: University of Chicago Press, 1964), p. 5.
[5]*Ibid.*, p. 95.

Within the automobile factory a great variety of specific tasks are performed. In the factory studied by Chinoy, about 25 percent of the workers were directly on the assembly line. Here a variety of functions was performed, corresponding to the components of the automobile itself.

> Most line workers were engaged in the assembly of a major component, such as the motor or axle, of the finished product on the final assembly line, although other operations such as painting and finishing fenders and hoods were also performed by men who remained stationed in one place, doing their repetitive tasks while the materials moved past on an endless conveyor belt.[6]

Another 30 percent of the workers operated automatic or semiautomatic machines, such as grinders, drill presses, or boring machines. These were essentially repetitive tasks, in that the worker simply inserted the pieces on which the operation was to be performed, started the machine, and removed the parts when the operation was completed. Another 15 percent of the workers were engaged in production jobs, such as welding, riveting, or repair work. These last two jobs did not require traditional skills and could be learned in a short period of time. Twenty-five percent of the workers were in "off-production jobs." Some of this off-production work involved inspection, which, according to Chinoy, was also semiskilled. Inspection in this case involved the use of automatic or semiautomatic machines or visual or tactile examination. Others in off-production work had a variety of functions, such as stock pickers, stock loaders, trim shop attendants, conveyor attendants, power truck operators, stock chasers, and hand truckers. The off-production jobs were generally more highly regarded by the workers and had higher pay scales. The work was less repetitive and paced. The remaining 5 percent of the workers were craftsmen in skilled maintenance or in areas such as toolmaking or jig building.[7]

Even though 95 percent of the work in this factory can be labelled semiskilled, the wide variety of specific tasks performed exemplifies the difficulties in identifying a characteristic component of semiskilled work. Even on the assembly line itself, the complexity of the modern automobile requires great variation among the specific tasks performed. The variety of work is due to the extreme rationalization of the work process itself. The planning of each small contribution to the whole allows the intense division of labor. A specific individual is thus not central to the total process. He is rather easily replaced, since the jobs do not require a

[6]Ely Chinoy, *Automobile Workers and the American Dream* (New York: Doubleday & Co., Inc., 1955), p. 35.
[7]*Ibid.*, p. 36.

long learning process, and his contribution to the whole, while vital, is minimal in terms of the importance of the single individual. This, of course, contributes to the alienation felt by the automobile worker.

A quite different form of assembly-line work is described by Whyte. In this case the product was steel barrels.

> This line began where men known as rollers took sheets of steel and put them on a machine that shaped them in a circular form. The shells then rolled to the welders who welded the two sides together. Then the testers checked the welds for leaks. Next came the beader men, who put the shells on a machine that put the beads (protruding ribs) into them. The shells then rolled into a spray booth, where their insides were sprayed with paint or lacquer. The double seamer operators attached both ends of the barrel. The barrel might then go on to another spray booth where an outside coat of paint or lacquer would be applied. Some orders called for a baked enamel finish, and the barrels were carried through bake ovens on conveyors for that purpose.[8]

The significant difference between the barrel assemblers and the auto workers is that the former could control the speed of production. The workers worked in pairs on either side of the line and could pace their own work. Whether or not this necessarily led to any less alienation or greater satisfaction is impossible to determine. The work itself apparently required little difference in skill from that required of the auto worker.

A still different kind of semiskilled work is that of the worker in continuous-flow production. Blauner's description of the work of men in a chemical refinery exemplifies this. In this case,

> practically all physical production and materials-handling is done by automatic processes, regulated by automatic controls. The work of the chemical operator is to monitor these automatic processes: his tasks include observing dials and gauges; taking readings of temperatures, pressures, and rates of flow; and writing down these readings in log data sheets. Such work is clearly of a nonmanual nature.[9]

In addition to the different activities performed, a greater potential for self-pacing and widened scope of the work also exists for the chemical worker. The process operators' work cycle extends over a 2-hour period, rather than the 1 minute for the auto worker. In taking his readings, the operator may check on fifty different instruments located throughout his area of jurisdiction. For workers not involved in actual production, a similar variety and diversity exists. Maintenance workers, for example,

[8]William F. Whyte, *Men at Work* (Homewood, Ill.: Richard D. Irwin, 1961), p. 137.
[9]Blauner, *Alienation and Freedom*, 132–33.

who comprise 40 percent of the work force, react to emergent situations. There is no prescheduled program for maintenance needs. There is even variety for workers who load and unload trucks or railroad cars or work in pumping operations. As in the previous examples, the nature of the work is clearly affected by the technology involved.

Another case studied by Blauner is the textile worker. Here again the emphasis is on the impact of the technological component of the work situation.

> The job of the typical worker is to mind or tend a large number of spin-ning frames, looms, or similar machines. He may feed yarn to, and remove yarn from, the machines when necessary and watch out for and repair breaks in the yarn when they occur. He does not operate an individual machine, as is characteristic in the garment and shoe industries. Instead he minds or tends dozens of identical machines, lined up in rows in the carding, spinning, weaving, and other rooms of the textile mill.[10]

This work requires little training and a minimal amount of physical exertion. The jobs in a textile mill, other than skilled maintenance work, require little more than alertness and some dexterity and can be learned in a relatively short period of time. Here again, the emphasis is on the impact of technology on the work process and the workers.

A final example of semiskilled work is that of the cabdriver. This is a service occupation, which involves direct interaction with the public. It is also an occupation that is much less structured in terms of work pat-terns and social relationships. The cabdriver is dependent upon finding fares. Although there are some locations where fares are more likely to be found, such as at airports, hotels, railroad stations, near downtown shopping areas and entertainment, and so on, there is little predictability where the fares wish to be taken or if new fares will be found in the area. The nature of the work is such that there are almost no steady customers with whom established relationships allow some certainty of either income or social relationships. The cabdriver also suffers from the fact that his skills are rather difficult to distinguish from those of his customers. Most people can drive cars and many know exactly how to get to their destination. The cabdriver thus is a convenience and fre-quently a necessity, but not someone who will be admired for unique skills.[11]

Another interesting component of the cabdriver's job is the manner in which he relates to his fares. Davis mentions

---

[10]*Ibid.*, p. 59.

[11]This discussion is based on Fred Davis, "The Cabdriver and his Fare: Facets of a Fleeting Relationship," *American Journal of Sociology*, LXV, 2 (September 1959), 158–65.

the man and wife who, managing to suppress their anger while on the street, launch into a bitter quarrel the moment they are inside the cab; or the well-groomed young couple who after a few minutes roll over on the back seat to begin petting; or the businessman who loudly discusses details of a questionable business deal. Here the driver is expected to, and usually does, act as if he were merely an extension of the automobile he operates. In actuality, of course, he is acutely aware of what goes on in his cab, and although his being treated as a nonperson implies a degraded status, it also affords him a splendid vantage point from which to witness a rich variety of human schemes and entanglements.[12]

At the same time, other fares will pour out their problems and life histories to the driver, placing him in a position similar to some bartenders. Bartending, of course, is another semiskilled service occupation.

Another interesting facet of this type of work is the dependence upon tips as a major part of the income. Davis found that cabdrivers had a well-developed vocabulary that described the various types of tippers. The typology of fares that develops allows the driver to order his universe to some degree. The driver also can attempt to manipulate the situation by using techniques he has found effective in improving the amount of tips he receives. The power of such manipulating is generally slight, however.

While the majority of the cabdriver's social relationships are with his fares, the relationships themselves are not the most rewarding to the driver. At the same time, he is not in a position to establish other relationships while he is working. When idle, he can talk with other drivers, but he is not earning money while doing so. His work thus is largely solitary and does not contain the potential for supportive relationships on the job. Here the nature of the work is the important determinant of the occupational subculture.

The discussion and examples thus far suggest the great diversity of occupations included in the semiskilled category. The exact number of specific occupations that could be included in this category is probably limited only by the number of job titles used by the employing organizations. A more important conclusion to be drawn is that the *semiskilled worker has his work defined for him*. The structure of the labor market is such that the potential worker presents himself to the employer for a position but not for a specific job. Since semiskilled work assumes that the skills can be learned in a relatively short period of time, the potential employee essentially sells his ability to learn the techniques needed for the particular job in the particular organization. If he changes organizations, he generally learns new skills for a new job. This is not to say that he may not become highly skilled in and attached to his work. It does

---

[12]*Ibid.*, p. 160.

imply, however, that semiskilled work is highly structured and that the structuring is largely out of the hands of the worker himself.

Three factors have been presented as contributors to this structuring. First was the nature of the technology utilized in the industry, as in the case of Blauner's discussion of the chemical, textile, and auto workers. Here the work process provides limits on what the semiskilled person does. A second factor is the employing organization. This is not meant to imply that the organization can overcome the limitations set by the technological system in all cases. While an automobile firm can vary its production process, the complexity of the automobile and the economics of the production process put limits on the extent to which the work can be altered. Limitations on the extent to which an organization can enlarge or enrich jobs are part of the context in which the organizations operate. The third factor that structures the semiskilled workers' occupation is the nature of the work. Service occupations differ from production work. Social relationships as well as the specific functions performed are affected in this way. For all three reasons, the semiskilled worker's occupation is predefined for him. In terms of his specific job-related activities, he can exercise relatively little discretion.

The discussion thus far has been centered around the "formal" aspects of the semiskilled worker's occupation. This is obviously not the total picture. Extensive and intensive studies of the informal work group have clearly demonstrated that much more happens on the job than simply the officially prescribed activities in the officially prescribed ways. The influence of peers, as discussed in the chapter on professions, is relevant here, as it is for all of the occupations discussed. These work groups provide a source of meaning for the worker on the job and provide a major part of his definition of his work situation. They develop norms, which may deviate in a number of directions from those that are officially prescribed. Work groups provide a context in which meaningful social interactions can take place. All of these functions have been well documented in studies by industrial sociologists and psychologists.

Before examining some of the specific contributions made by these unofficial work groups, one point should be stressed. Walker and Guest and others have pointed out that the specific membership of such groups is in a large measure determined by the organization itself.[13] The organization cannot define who will like whom and who will be included in or excluded from participation. It does define, however, where the workers are placed in the organization. Since such groups must be formed through social interaction and such interaction can only take place among workers in contact with each other, the organization thus determines who will

[13]Charles Walker and Robert Guest, *Man on the Assembly Line* (Cambridge, Mass.: Harvard University Press, 1952), pp. 67–72.

interact with whom. The factor of spatial contiguity is also vital, since it is difficult if not impossible for such groups to form across distances. The shift a person works determines with whom he has the opportunity to interact. Other factors such as the noise level and the amount of attention demanded by the job will affect interaction patterns. In some jobs there simply is no opportunity for such patterns to develop, as for the cabdriver.

While these unofficial social relationships are strongly affected by official considerations, the informal work group does have an existence apart from official prescriptions. As new employees enter the situation, they are introduced to the unofficial norms, which persist over time and personnel changes. Miller and Form state:

> The new employee must learn many things about the social behavior in his work situation. He must learn *who's who* (the informal status pattern or pecking order), *what's what* (the "ropes" or how things are done), and *what's up* (the current situation in his work area). But most important of all he must learn how he fits in. He must learn to play an acceptable role and no formal organization chart or manual will help him very much. He must know how role boundaries are established by his associates.[14]

The impact of these work groups and their norms and values has been intensively examined, and the studies suggest that the behavior of work group members deviates from the officially prescribed patterns. From the organization's perspective, this deviation is generally in a negative rather than positive direction. From the point of view of the individual worker, such deviations give him some control over the work situation, allow him to protect his earnings potential, and allow him to have some control of the rate of and quality of his output.

The actual operation of these unofficial patterns is graphically illustrated in Joseph Bensman and Israel Gerver's analysis of "crime and punishment in the factory."[15] The study was carried out in an airplane factory. The specific instance examined was the use of a device called a "tap." The tap is a hard steel tool designed to redrill holes in nuts so that a bolt can be inserted and tightened.

> In wing assembly work bolts or screws must be inserted in recessed nuts which are anchored to the wing in earlier processes of assembly. The bolt or screw must pass through a wing plate before reaching the nut. In the nature of the mass production process alignments between nuts and

[14]Delbert Miller and William Form, *Industrial Sociology* (New York: Harper & Row, 1964), p. 231.

[15]Joseph Bensman and Israel Gerver, "Crime and Punishment in the Factory: The Function of Deviancy in Maintaining the Social System," *American Sociological Review*, XXV, 4 (August 1963), 588–98.

plate openings become distorted. Original allowable tolerances become magnified in later stages of assembly as the number of alignments which must be coordinated with each other increase with the increasing complexity of the assemblage. When the nut is not aligned with the hole, the tap can be used to cut, at a new angle, new threads in the nut for the purpose of bringing the nut and bolt into a new but not true alignment. If the tap is not used and the bolt is forced, the wing plate itself may be bent. Such new alignments, however, deviate from the specifications of the blueprint which is based upon true alignments at every stage of the assembly process. On the basis of engineering standards true alignments are necessary at every stage in order to achieve maximum strength and a proper equilibrium of strains and stresses.[16]

Since bolts and screws on aircraft are designed to prevent their backing out of the nuts due to vibration in flight and the use of the tap removes the holding power of the nut, tap usage is defined as a criminal offense. The mere possession of a tap is grounds for dismissal. Use of the tap also covers up structural defects in the plane in the form of deviations from standards. Despite the severity of the penalties and the seriousness of the offense itself, one-half of the workers in a position to use a tap own at least one.

The worker coming into this factory is gradually introduced to the use of the tap under the supervision of an older worker. He is instructed under what circumstances its use is justified and the conditions in which it is safe to use it. The foremen in this situation recognize the necessity of the tap and use it themselves when they believe the situation so demands. Another element of this unofficial practice is that indiscriminate use of the tap is frowned upon. The expectation is that the tap is to be used with good judgment and the proper etiquette.

Etiquette is vital in the relationship between workers and inspectors. The inspectors are in many ways dependent upon the workers. Inspectors realize that they must depend upon the workers to do a good job on parts that are inaccessible so that an inordinate amount of time is not spent on simple inspections. The inspectors also fraternize with the workers when they are waiting for work. The etiquette is that the inspector turns his back or walks away when the tap is to be used. When the inspectors get pressure from the Air Force, the purchaser of the planes, the workers respond by limiting their use of the tap. This results in a slowdown of the work until the pressure on the inspectors is reduced. When Air Force inspectors themselves are nearby, the word is passed down the line to cease the use of the tap. Relations with the foremen are similarly governed by such norms of appropriate behavior.

Aside from the fact that such deviations from the official norms are

[16]*Ibid.*, p. 590.

an important component of all work groups at every level in the occupational hierarchy, this case suggests two additional conclusions. The first point, while obvious, is often overlooked in analyses of unofficial behavior. The deviations discussed are based upon the *official* norms. These norms serve as the starting point from which deviation may or may not occur. The official structure thus sets the stage for the deviation by prescribing the amount of work to be expected, the technologies to be employed in achieving the qualitative and quantitative goals, and the sanctions for norm enforcement. If the parts of the wing to be assembled did not vary from the allowable tolerances, there would be no need to use the tap. If there were not production quotas to be met, parts could be returned or scrapped if alignments were not perfect. If the sanctions for using a tap were not so stringent, there would be little need for the involved system of etiquette surrounding its use. The deviations observed thus have their origins in and are judged by the official structure.[17]

The second conclusion that can be reached on the basis of this study is that not all instances of unofficial behavior are oriented toward quota or output restriction. In this case the deviations occurred in an attempt to meet the quota set by the organization and thus to contribute to the total system. A basic motivation here undoubtedly was to maximize individual earnings, rather than a belief in the appropriateness of the quota for its own sake, but the actions taken were in the direction of higher production rather than lower. Other studies have found restrictions placed on production by such work groups.[18] Such groups can thus either impede or contribute to the amount of work turned out in a specific work situation. The factors that influence the direction of the work group's own norms in relation to the official output expectations appear to be such things as the ease with which the quota is met; the likelihood, as perceived by the workers, probably correctly, of having the rate of pay reduced if the quota is systematically met or exceeded; and the perception of the appropriateness of the quota. Semiskilled workers, like all other workers, develop sets of behaviors and expectations surrounding their work. Like all other workers, they also react to their work.

REACTIONS TO SEMISKILLED WORK

We have been stressing the heterogeneity of semiskilled work. Similar stress must be given to reactions to this heterogeneity. Indeed,

[17]Walker and Guest, in *Man on the Assembly Line*, pp. 68–69, make this same point.

[18]See Donald F. Roy, "Quota Restriction and Goldbricking in a Machine Shop," *American Journal of Sociology*, LVII, 5 (March 1952), 427–42.

research in this area has come to rather contradictory findings. A great deal of recent attention has focused on "blue-collar blues." The implication of this term is that the blue-collar, semiskilled worker is bored and alienated with his job. Further, there is some research evidence that indicates that the worker who is alienated is likely to suffer mental and physical health problems,[19] participate less in community and other activities,[20] take problems home with him,[21] and, when he does participate in political activities, engage in extremist social and political movements.[22] There is evidence on the other hand, though, that paints the semiskilled worker as relatively happy and not all that concerned about the work.[23]

How can these paradoxical findings be resolved? The answer lies in our original discussion of work motivations. The expectations of the semiskilled (and all workers) are the key to the issue. Goldthorpe *et al.* found in their study that their affluent workers had an instrumental orientation toward their work. Work was a means to the end of receiving good wages. Wages were received, and the workers were not all that alienated. Sheppard and Herrick found that older workers, who found no possibilities for advancement, were alienated by the lack of opportunities. *Work in America* suggests that it is younger workers who are alienated, because of their altered expectations about work.

The issue basically is this: If a job presents a worker with a technology that delimits the extent of his personal inputs beyond that that he expects and desires and an organizational structure that is so bureaucratized that he cannot pursue his own desired courses of action, alienation, turnover, sabotage, and the like will ensue.[24] If, on the other hand, the worker is permitted to put his own thoughts into the work and utilize organizational flexibility to the desired point, the worker will be satisfied. The corollary issue, of course, is that semiskilled work typically does *not* provide conditions that meet workers' expectations. Older

[19]See *Work in America: Report of a Special Task Force to the Secretary of Health, Education, and Welfare*, prepared under the auspices of the W. E. Upjohn Institute for Employment Research (Cambridge, Mass.: M.I.T. Press, 1973), chap. 3, and Arthur Kornhauser, *Mental Health of the Industrial Worker* (New York: John Wiley & Sons, Inc., 1965).

[20]*Work in America*, p .31.

[21]*Ibid.*

[22]*Ibid.*, and Harold L. Sheppard and Neal Q. Herrick, *Where Have All the Robots Gone?* (New York: Free Press of Glencoe, 1972), pp. 133–37.

[23]John H. Goldthorpe *et al.*, *The Affluent Worker: Industrial Attitudes and Behavior* (Cambridge: Cambridge University Press, 1970). The workers studied in this research had little attachment to their fellow workers. There was little socializing off the job with co-workers. In addition, they were generally satisfied with their employers.

[24]The major theoretical statement of this point is found in Robert Kahn *et al.*, *Organizational Stress* (New York: John Wiley & Sons, 1964).

workers *are* blocked in advancement and younger workers *do* find repetitious and boring work alienating. In the later chapter on technology we will examine some of the suggested means by which this can be changed, but the fact remains that most semiskilled work contains features that lead to the negative consequences, *if* the individual worker expects something more from the work.[25]

There is yet another issue surrounding the findings in regard to workers' reactions to their jobs. Many of the findings in regard to the poor mental health of the blue-collar worker, low political participation, and general alienation in life make the assumption that work is the *cause* of these other reactions. The causal relationship might well be in the other direction—problems off the job being the cause of problems on the job. Problems on the job are certainly related to those off the job, but it is very questionable that the causality is just in one direction. It seems reasonable to believe that off-the-job reactions contribute to on-the-job reactions and vice versa.

This issue becomes even more problematical when the centrality of work for the individual is considered. If work is very important for the individual,[26] work-associated factors would be expected to be very important for "general" life satisfaction. If, on the other hand, work is not very central, then the flow may well be from off-the-job factors to the job. For the workers we have been discussing, it would seem that work would have less centrality than for craftsmen or professionals. Thus, some of the findings in regard to work alienation and dissatisfaction might well be thought out again.

One way in which semiskilled workers in the United States have not reacted is through collective social and political action. Labor unions in the United States have been basically concerned with wage and wage-related issues, rather than with more radical attempts to change the system.[27] This is not the case in many other countries. It is impossible to say if this means that workers in the United States actually are not extremely dissatisfied or that more radical alternatives to current working conditions are not that attractive to the workers.

[25]These conclusions are reached on the basis of the massive study *Survey of Working Conditions* (Ann Arbor, Mich.: Survey Research Center, University of Michigan, 1970). An ongoing replication confirms the persistence of the problem.

[26]Robert Dubin, in "Industrial Workers' Worlds: A Study of 'Central Life Interests' of Industrial Workers," *Social Problems*, III, 2 (fall 1956), 131–42, found that 85 percent of a sample of industrial workers derived their major satisfactions in life off the job. This is in contrast to Louis Orzack's finding that two-thirds of a sample of nurses found their major personal satisfactions *on* the job. See Orzack, "Work as a 'Central Life Interest' of Professionals," *Social Problems*, VII, 2 (fall 1959), 125–32.

[27]See Elliot A. Krause, *The Sociology of Occupations* (Boston: Little, Brown, 1971), pp. 253–54, and William H. Form, "Job vs. Political Unionism: A Cross-national Comparison," *Industrial Relations* 12 (May 1973), 224–38.

THE UNSKILLED

The final occupational type is at the bottom of the occupational hierarchy. Like the semiskilled, the unskilled are being affected by technological change, but in a very different way. The nature of the work of the unskilled has not changed very much, but the number of jobs available to this category of worker has been drastically affected. A related change is in the educational composition of the population as a whole and the educational requirements for positions in the occupational structure. As the general level of education has increased, so have the educational requirements for entry into the system. Those persons with minimal educational backgrounds are at an obvious disadvantage in the labor market. At the same time, there are fewer persons with such a minimal background. The unskilled worker category has thus decreased as persons with sufficient education move into more highly ranked occupations and, concomitantly, the number of jobs available at this occupational level decreases.

It is rather difficult to pinpoint exactly who the unskilled are. The most obvious characteristic is that the unskilled worker sells his personal labor to his employer and utilizes little in the way of technology or machinery in his work. Caplow notes:

> Although most occupational categories include a category of the unskilled, it is difficult to attach any precise meaning to the term. It is only careless usage which regards freight-handlers and farmhands in regular employment as less qualified than punch-press operators, and it is sheer snobbery that leads certain of the occupational classifiers to group all household servants as unskilled.[28]

Caplow suggests that a more accurate criterion for determining the unskilled is to use the regularity of employment. Those who are regularly employed in the same job would be classified as semiskilled according to this criterion.

Despite Caplow's imputation of carelessness and even snobbery, most classifications do include the farmhand, freight-handler, and household servant in the unskilled category. A more relevant criterion than Caplow's idea of regular employment would be the amount of training required for a job. The semiskilled do learn their jobs in a short period of time. The unskilled, on the other hand, are simply told to go to work, with the assumption that the skills required are in the possession of the total popu-

[28]Caplow, *The Sociology of Work*, p. 172.

lation and do not necessitate any training. Caplow himself states: "In-dustry, retail commerce, and even the private household maintain a continuous demand for 'hands,' hired on a day-to-day basis for clean-up jobs, moving, heavy construction, snow removal, digging, carrying, hew-ing of wood, and drawing of water."[29] While these jobs may be irregular, they also involve sheer physical labor together with almost no on-the-job learning. A person is hired simply because he is available, with little anticipation of permanence and few assumptions about ability to learn.

Some private household and general maintenance workers are un-doubtedly an exception to these conclusions, but not on the basis of lack of snobbery. Some maids or other household servants, for example, occupy positions of real permanence and perform highly skilled activities in the form of cooking and child rearing. The majority, however, prob-ably engage in simple cleaning chores. Maintenance or janitorial work is becoming increasingly complex as the composition of floors and walls varies widely and must be cleaned with only the appropriate agent. Reading and understanding the type, amount, and frequency of use of cleaning agents require at least skills in reading. Here again, however, the majority of such work is probably limited to such chores as sweeping, dusting, and window washing. Job titles at this level may thus be mis-leading.

The composition of the unskilled category is quite varied. Caplow suggests that the category is composed of

> the partly retired, the pensioners, and the partly unemployable, the drifters and drunks, the physically and mentally handicapped . . . those who normally belong to higher occupational categories but have been temporarily laid off or are waiting out a strike or an off-season, together with the migratory farm workers, and stranded travelers, the part-time students, the part-time criminals, and many others.[30]

This mixture of people has been approached from another perspec-tive by S. M. Miller. Miller's concern is with poverty, but the typology he develops in dealing with the poor is useful for clarifying the compo-sition of the unskilled. Miller utilizes two criteria in categorizing the American lower class. The economic factor is treated in terms of the amount and stability of the income, yielding categories of "high (security) and low (insecurity)."[31] The second factor is the general style of life of

[29]*Ibid.*, pp. 172–73.
[30]*Ibid.*, p. 173.
[31]S. M. Miller, "The American Lower Classes: A Typological Approach," *Social Research*, XLVIII, 3 (April 1964), 13.

TABLE 8-1. Types of Economic Security and Familial Stability

	Familial	
Economic	*Stability:* +	*Instability:* −
Security: +	++(1)	+−(2)
Insecurity: −	−+(3)	−−(4)

Source: S. M. Miller, "The American Lower Classes: A Typological Approach," *Social Research*, XLVIII, 3 (April 1964).

the groups involved. The basic component here is family stability or instability as an indicator of the manner in which the family copes with its problems. Though not our concern here, the family is an important indicator of the general style of life. Using the criteria of economic and family status, Miller derives a fourfold table (Table 8–1).

Cell 1 is the *stable poor*. They are characterized by regular but low-skill employment. According to Miller, they are predominantly farm, rural nonfarm, and small-town persons, from white rural Southern populations. The category also includes a good number of older people and urban blacks who have obtained steady employment. Given these conditions, either of location or minority group status, it is unlikely that these persons will move out of the unskilled category, although Miller suggests that there is a good likelihood that their offspring may.[32]

The second cell, the *strained*, is composed of low-wage unskilled workers. Their instability may result from "wildness," on the part of younger workers, or alcoholism, on the part of older persons. Members of this group are likely to have "skidded" into their positions as a result of the extra-occupational activities. These same activities are also likely to lead to decreased economic and job security over time.[33]

The third cell, the *copers*, "manifest economic insecurity and familial stability—families and individuals having a rough time economically but managing to keep themselves relatively intact."[34] This group's size increases during times of layoff or economic recession. It is composed of a large number of urban black families and probably also many Southern white migrants to urban areas. The skill level and patterns of discrimination are such that there is little likelihood of the parents moving out of the unskilled group, although here again the offspring might.

The *unstable poor*, the fourth cell, are obviously beset by economic and family problems. "Partially urbanized Negroes new to the North

[32]*Ibid.*, pp. 14–15.
[33]*Ibid.*, p. 15.
[34]*Ibid.*, p. 16.

and to cities, remaining slum residents of ethnic groups which have largely moved out of the slums, long-term (intergenerational) poor white families, and the *déclassé* of Marx" comprise this group.[35] They are unskilled and irregular workers. They are likely to suffer long-term unemployment and are the least able to find work when it is available.

Miller's analysis is useful in that it points out the variety found among the unskilled as well as suggesting the interplay between occupational and other social factors. The unskilled vary not only in terms of the nature and frequency of their work but also in their orientations toward it. Some take the position of the semiskilled and other more highly ranked categories that work is essential for security and that life should be at least partially oriented to one's occupation. Others become almost unemployable because of their skill levels and orientations toward work.

For the unskilled who are able to find employment in semiskilled types of work, the problems that many faced before finding work continue with them to the job. In a study of "unemployables" who were brought into industry through a job-creation program sponsored by the National Association of Businessmen, Harland Padfield and Roy Williams found that the men studied reacted well to the fact of their employment.[36] Jobs were learned readily and the men were enthusiastic about their work. Problems arose from factors *outside* of employment. In some cases the level of family strife was raised, as wives failed to adapt to the husband's new hours and life patterns. Use of drugs and alcohol did not stop with employment. Old friendships in ghetto society were not broken. Other factors were resistance on the part of the labor union in the plant studied and the factory management's inability to integrate the trainees with the experienced workers. In addition, older workers were laid off, due to a recession, just as the trainees entered the plant, and the trainees received incentives for their work, whereas nothing new was added for the older workers. The program was eventually terminated.

The study illustrates how work is imbedded in the larger social structure and how the ongoing social patterns in a work setting affect each new worker. This particular study also demonstrates that the so-called "unemployable" is in fact employable, *if* the external and internal situations are understood and, insofar as possible, dealt with through counseling and other assistance programs and altered incentive programs within the employing organization.

The discussion thus far has suggested that the unskilled range from

---

[35]*Ibid.*, p. 16
[36]*Stay Where You Were: A Study of Unemployables in Industry* (Philadelphia: J. B. Lippincott Company, 1973).

those with steady employment in manual or service work to the most marginal members of the labor force. The unskilled are also characterized by the high proportion of persons suffering personal or social handicaps. These factors contribute to the conclusions that many components included in the analyses of the other occupational types are somewhat irrelevant in this case. For example, the possibility of upward mobility, remote as it is for many white-collar and semiskilled workers, is almost out of the question for the unskilled, at least within the individual's own generation. Lack of skill coupled with frequent discrimination removes mobility from their realm of the possible. As Miller's analysis suggests, it may be possible for some offspring to be mobile, but only within certain settings.

In the occupational setting itself, clear differences between the unskilled occupations and the other types are evident. For the manual unskilled worker, there appears to be a greatly lessened potential for structured social relationships. This is the case particularly for those who are hired on a day-to-day basis for work crews with constantly changing compositions. For those in a stable situation, the likelihood of such relationships developing is as high as in other occupations. The stable unskilled worker is, however, much more subject to layoffs than workers with higher skill levels, which would tend to make any such work group relationship much more tenuous.

For the unskilled in service occupations, a different picture can be seen. In the case of workers in larger social structures, such as the busboy or dishwasher in a restaurant or the orderly or attendant in a hospital, the location at the bottom of the social structure generally precludes much interaction with those with higher status. At the same time, the possibilities for interaction or friendship with others with the same status are limited in small organizations where there may be few possible associates. In the larger organization, the same possibilities exist as for other occupations.

The domestic servant also faces problems in his or her interaction system. As the proportion of live-in servants decreases, the opportunity for interaction with family members decreases. Chaplin points out that labor-saving devices for the home and the presence of packaged home services have diminished the demand for full-time domestic help, forcing those in the occupation to serve a number of employers, as in the case of the cleaning woman who comes once a week, and further minimizing the opportunity for anything more than impersonal relationships.[37] The fact that many domestic servants are members of minority groups adds

[37]David Chaplin, "Domestic Service and The Negro" in *Blue Collar World*, eds. Arthur B. Shostak and William Gomberg (Englewood Cliffs, N.J.: Prentice-Hall, 1964), pp. 527–38.

an additional complication to the picture. Vilhelm Aubert, in an analysis of the housemaid, has suggested that the nature of the contemporary servant-mistress relationship makes it difficult or impossible for the servant even to evaluate her work, since the mistress sets the standards and there are no objective criteria.[38] When there are multiple mistresses, the problem is enlarged even further. The domestic servant faces the additional difficulty of working in isolation. Aubert points out that there are no informal emotional contacts with colleagues at the place of work. "She cannot satisfy her craving for companionship in this way, and she does not have a role in a work group as a possible substitute for direct work satisfaction."[39]

Like the cabdriver discussed above, these servants can engage in some manipulation of the situation, but the opportunities are limited in most cases. The permanent servant, on the other hand, can do much more in structuring his social relationships but is still faced with his low status, as Ray Gold's analysis of apartment-house janitors suggests. The janitor in this case may not actually fall within the unskilled category, in terms of his skills and his income, but he generally is given a very low status by the tenants. In this sense there is real incongruence between his status and his income. The unionization of janitors has led to a relatively secure economic position. In the case of the janitors Gold studied, they also were provided with an apartment in the basement of the buildings serviced, giving them additional security. At the same time, factors such as the frequent minority group status, generally dirty clothes as a "uniform," garbage removal as a duty, and living in the basement as a symbol of his position all contributed to the low status. Gold states: "In the public's view it seems that the janitor merely is a very low-class person doing menial work for the tenants."[40] The performance of such personal services is generally stigmatizing in terms of status.[41]

Gold found that the janitors were treated on the basis of their status, as defined by the tenants, rather than on the basis of their income. Those tenants with incomes below or at the same level as the janitor resented the fact that the lowly janitor could afford personal possessions, such as a new car or television set. The higher status tenants tended to treat the janitors as family employees or servants. The janitors themselves preferred having rich tenants, since rich tenants did not engage in attempts to demonstrate their own higher status. Lower status tenants constantly

[38]"The Housemaid—An Occupational Role in Crisis," *Acta Sociologica*, I, 3 (1956), 149–58.

[39]*Ibid.*, p. 198.

[40]Ray Gold, "Janitors Versus Tenants: A Status-Income Dilemma," *American Journal of Sociology*, LVII, 5 (March 1952), 487.

[41]Caplow notes in *The Sociology of Work* that this form of personal service is almost always thought to be degrading. See pp. 48–49.

were trying to demonstrate their superiority to the janitor by demanding additional services or by verbal comments. The janitors, unlike the house-maids, had a union whereby they could discuss their common problems and develop an occupational identity. Nevertheless, the status ascribed to them precluded meaningful relationships on the job.

The discussion thus far has indicated that in addition to the low status implicit in unskilled work, members of this category work in situations that do not provide the same kind of social rewards found in other occupations. This is consistent with Kornhauser's finding that mental health varies consistently with the level of job held—the lower the skill level, the poorer the mental health.[42] Although the exact processes leading to this relationship are not clear, social isolation in many of the jobs and lack of security in many areas are probably operative here. Urban unrest, as exemplified by rioting and looting, is undoubtedly partially a consequence of the marginal position of the unskilled within the labor force and their general lack of integration into the social system.

In a sense, the unskilled, while part of the occupational structure in terms of their performing work and receiving rewards, are outside of the structure in terms of the analytical considerations utilized for the balance of the occupational types. There is little, if any, potential for mobility, either individually or collectively. The impact of fellow workers in the same work organization or as colleagues is minimized. The unskilled worker does, of course, work within the social context of his background and current living conditions, which in the case of limited education and minority group status serve as occupational impediments. The utilization of knowledges or skills on the job is also minimized, particularly in the case of workers hired on a day-to-day basis.

Despite being cut off from the mainstream of occupations,[43] the unskilled apparently want to work and have the same aspirations as the balance of the population.[44] The conditions of the unskilled are such that what they have to offer is not in demand. Some research evidence indicates that youths who learn "street skills" very well and who are highly motivated in their usage may well not be able to make it in the "straight" occupational world.[45] This report notes, "But, paradoxically, the skills which may make a man an 'executive' on the street—hustling,

[42]Kornhauser, Mental Health of the Industrial Worker, pp. 76, 261.

[43]Leonard S. Silk, "Is There a Lower-Middle Class Problem?" in Sar A. Levitan, ed., Blue-Collar Workers (New York: McGraw-Hill Book Company, 1971) suggests that there is a growing gap between the poor or unskilled and the balance of the social system.

[44]Leonard Goodwin, Do the Poor Want to Work? (Washington, D.C.: Brookings Institution, 1972).

[45]"Street Skills of Many Hard-to-employ Youths May Hinder Success in Job Training Programs," ISR Newsletter 1 (autumn 1973), pp. 5, 7. See also the discussion by Padfield and Williams, Stay Where You Were.

rapping, signifying, gang leadership, psyching out people, fighting, athletics, and so forth—may also serve to make him a failure as a dishwasher, mechanic, or maintenance man."[46]

A further disadvantage for the unskilled is that they learn to expect failure. Goodwin's study of women on welfare suggests that those who have tried work, and failed, show a marked increase in their acceptance of welfare. He notes, "The picture that emerges is one of black welfare women who want to work but who, because of continuing failure in the work world, tend to become more accepting of welfare and less inclined to try again."[47] He goes on to suggest that forcing people on welfare to work at meaningless jobs is no answer to the welfare question and indeed may intensify problems with welfare. He also looks at the relationship between welfare mothers and their sons. When this important linkage is examined,

> the data suggest that poor black mothers have a substantial influence on the work orientations of their sons, including those measuring acceptability of welfare and lack of confidence, and that the sons' adherence to these two orientations may lead to both early school dropout and low work activity. Hence, stringent work requirements for welfare mothers, which are likely to lead to additional experiences of failure, can psychologically damage not only the mothers but also their children.[48]

The unskilled are out of the occupational and organizational mainstream. As would be expected, minority groups and women are heavily represented in these occupations. There is a huge overrepresentation of blacks and other minority group members among the unskilled. The case of women is somewhat different here, since American society has never expected or allowed women to participate in jobs requiring much physical strength. The household servant, of course, is typically a woman. All of the factors associated with discrimination, lack of schooling, learned expectations about work, and so on join here to continue to put the disadvantaged at a further disadvantage in the occupational world.

SUMMARY AND CONCLUSIONS

We have reached the end of our analysis of types of occupations. We have not included a discussion of "deviant occupations," such as prostitution, drug marketing, or pickpocketing because, while fascinating, the occupational characteristics of such occupations are quite like those

[46]*Ibid.*, p. 5.
[47]Goodwin, *Do the Poor Want to Work?*, p. 113.
[48]*Ibid.*, p. 115.

of standard occupations of the same status.[49] Be they criminal activities by government officials or corporate executives, or lower class prostitution, the activities of the individuals involved do not differ that much from those of their nondeviant cohorts.

In this chapter we have dealt with occupations that are low on social status and whose members are likely to be the least satisfied with or interested in their work. It has been argued that it is not the people that lead to this condition, but rather the nature of the technology used in the organizations in which the work is carried out. These occupations are also obviously low in economic status. It is for these occupations that inflation is most severe and the impact of recession most immediate (due to layoffs). Since there is little mobility out of these occupations, the individual usually ends up about where he or she started. This means that as children come, the economic situation is likely to worsen.[50] Here again, of course, these conditions are out of the control of the individuals affected.

The major defining characteristic for these occupations, as the title of the category suggests, is the amount of skill brought to the job. Once the person has taken a position, his specific job title is defined by the machine with which he works or his specific function within an organization. For both the semiskilled and the unskilled, the assumption is that no particular skills are brought to the job. The significant difference between the types is in the amount of training received after a position is obtained. Both types of occupations allow little discretion on the part of the individual in terms of the functions he performs while on the job, although deviation from the officially prescribed standards does occur. The semiskilled and the unskilled share the general orientation that their work is a means to an end, rather than an end in itself. Intrinsic satisfactions in life are generally found off the job or in non-job-related activities.

It has been shown that the actual work performed, the reactions to the occupation and its setting, and the social relationships surrounding the occupations vary widely. Neither the semiskilled nor the unskilled are a homogeneous group. At the same time, they are quite distinct from the other occupations discussed. One exception is the service occupations in which the line between white-collar service occupations and semiskilled service occupations must be arbitrary. If a waitress is a white-collar worker at an exclusive restaurant, her occupation at the local greasy spoon is not that different, even though her status is. The distinction between the unskilled and the semiskilled is itself unclear, although the criteria used above do seem relevant.

[49]Ritzer, *Man and His Work*, chap. 6, has a good discussion of deviant occupations.
[50]Jerome A. Rosow, "The Problems of Lower-Middle-Income Workers," in Levitan, *Blue-Collar Workers*, pp. 81–82, discusses this "economic squeeze" in some detail.

A major change occurring among the semiskilled is the shift toward service-based work, as the production process is increasingly affected by technological change. While this change is probably not extensively affecting individuals, in the sense that relatively few persons move from production positions into service positions, the occupational opportunities are increasingly in the service area. The movement into the service occupations is probably across generations. The major change occurring among the unskilled is the sheer decline of unskilled work. Increasing educational requirements for almost all positions will probably continue to diminish the number of unskilled jobs available. Whether this will create a situation of full employment, with the formerly unskilled upgraded, or a situation in which there is a permanent cadre of unemployed and unemployable persons is still an open question.

Occupations
and the
Social Structure

This final section will further develop the central theme of the book—occupations and the occupational structure are systematically related to the wider social structure. Examples of this relationship, which have already been discussed, are the formal licensing of some professions, the high rate of occupational inheritance among craftsmen and proprietors, and the impact of automation on white-collar workers. In this section, the focus will be shifted to the relationships between occupations and broad segments or institutions within the total social structure, and the implied relationship between occupations and social stratification will be examined in detail. The impact of, and relationships between, the familial and educational systems and the occupational structure will be similarly examined. Aspects of the relationships between technological change and occupations that have not previously been discussed will also be covered in this section. The final chapter deals with the relationships between occupations and politics. The emphasis here will be on the local and national political system, but some attention will be paid to the role of political relationships within occupations themselves.

Two such relationships not examined, for quite different reasons, are those between occupations and the economy and religion. In the case of the economy, the relationship is perhaps overly obvious. Occupations are the major link between the individual and the economy. Those not in the occupational system, such as minors or the aged, are vitally affected by the system, minors by their parents' occupations and the retired by their previous occupation, which determines their present economic situation. For those who are unemployed, their very status indicates the direct relationship between occupations and the economy. At the same time, the close relationship between occupations and social stratification reflects the link between occupations and the economy. Economic factors alone do not determine an individual's position in the stratification system. They do, however, play an important role. The importance of economic incentives also indicates the close relationship between occupations and the economy. The occupational system is not the same as the economic system; however, the relationship is clear enough that it does not require a separate analysis.

Religion is quite a different matter. The relationships between religion and occupations are much less clear. Lenski has suggested that the religious factor does play an important role in the development of occupational behavior as evidenced by attitudes toward work and leisure.[1] Weber, of course, suggested the importance of the Protestant ethic in the development of capitalistic, industrialized societies and the interplay between religion and other social phenomena.[2] The problem for this analysis is that it is very difficult to separate religious from other phenomena, such as socioeconomic status or the impact of the family on the individual. This difficulty plus the real absence of information on the subject leads to the omission of an extensive discussion of religion.

The relationships between occupations and the social structure take many forms. In some cases there is evident conflict between the demands of, for example, the family system and the occupational system. The conflict can take the form of occupational demands for a parent to travel away from home, while the family system demands the presence of the father or mother at home. Wives and mothers who work clearly feel the conflict between the roles they are asked to play. On the other hand, of course, there can be a nice functional "fit" between the systems. Analysts have long noted that the nuclear family is ideally suited to having one person, typically the male, leave the home and go to work. Similarly, technological change that reduces employment in one sector has been accompanied by other technological changes that increase employment in another sector.

It would thus be inappropriate to assume a perspective of either total conflict or complete equilibrium. The perspective that will be taken is that of change. The patterns to be described and analyzed are in the process of change and are themselves in the midst of change.

[1]See Gerhard Lenski, *The Religious Factor* (New York: Doubleday & Co., 1963), pp. 82–128, 213–55.
[2]See Max Weber, *The Protestant Ethic and the Spirit of Capitalism*, trans. Talcott Parsons (London: George Allen and Unwin, 1935).

9

SOCIAL STRATIFICATION, MOBILITY, AND CAREER PATTERNS

The analysis thus far has been partially based on the fact that occupations have varying statuses within the social system. In this chapter, the relationship between occupations and social stratification will be examined in detail. The examination will consist of an analysis of reasons for the close relationship between occupational rankings and the overall stratification system, an overview of some attempts to describe the relationship, and a discussion of approaches to the explanation of the existence of stratification within the total social system. The important issue of mobility will then be discussed, particularly the movement within and between generations as it is related to the occupational and wider social systems. Career patterns, as a component of intragenerational mobility, will then be considered.

OCCUPATIONS AND THE STRATIFICATION SYSTEM

The most untrained observer recognizes the close relationship between occupations and social status. When meeting someone for the first time, one of the most common questions asked is: "What do you do?" Knowledge of what a person does provides a handy indicator of where a person fits vis à vis one's self. The rather common and unfortunate phrase "I'm just a housewife" indicates both the status ascribed to that occupation and the importance of occupational identification and the resultant placement within the social system. This does not mean that the resultant placement is always consistent or accurate at this level. The author has been in situations in meeting people for the first time when the response "I'm a college professor" called forth reactions varying from "That's too bad" to "My, it must be nice." Also imputed to the occupation and thus to the individual are such characteristics as extremely high intelligence, radical political and social beliefs, impracticality, love of students, love of writing, disdain for material goods, etc., none of which is necessarily correct. The important point is that occupations are used in common social interaction as a major means of locating the individual within the social system.

Approached more analytically, a number of factors act in the close relationship between occupations and social status. Peter M. Blau and Otis Dudley Duncan note: "In the absence of hereditary castes or feudal estates, class differences come to rest primarily on occupational positions and the economic advantages and powers associated with them."[1] Approaching the issue from a different perspective, Albert J. Reiss, Jr., states:

> Both individual income and educational attainment, which are used as measures of socio-economic status, are known to be correlated with occupational ranks; and both can be seen as aspects of occupational status, since education is a basis for entry into many occupations, and for most people income is derived from occupation.[2]

Caplow notes that occupational identification has displaced other status-fixing attributes such as ancestry, religious office, political affiliation, or personal character.[3] These authors are saying that the occupation has become the most reliable indicator for placement in the stratification system *and* that occupation is indicative of and closely related to other indicators, such as education or income, that might be used. For research purposes, occupation has the great advantage of simplicity. In nonindustrialized societies, of course, occupation is generally less important than considerations of ancestry or caste.

In interpreting the reasons for this convergence upon occupation as the major indicator of social status and for the close relationship between occupational position and position within the stratification system, Caplow has suggested three factors as central for industrialized societies.

---

[1] *The American Occupational Structure* (New York: John Wiley & Sons, 1967), p. vii.

[2] *Occupations and Social Status* (New York: Free Press of Glencoe, 1961), pp. 83–84.

[3] Theodore Caplow, *The Sociology of Work* (Minneapolis: University of Minnesota Press, 1954), p. 30.

Aggregation, or the sheer increase in size in social groupings, has led to the substitution of formal organizations for informal groupings. The large work organization is characterized by greater anonymity and impersonality than the smaller family unit. A person's position is thus usually responded to more than the individual himself. The term "job description" indicates that duties are ascribed to an office or position rather than to the individual. At the same time, the growth of urban communities diminishes the extent to which social interaction based upon an individual's complete knowledge of others is possible. Caplow notes this when he states:

> The urban dweller tends to define his own relationship to his fellows in functional terms, since other means of identification with the community are attenuated. Then too, the separation of home from workplace and the necessity for casual interaction with many unrelated people require various shorthand methods for recognizing others, of which occupational designations are the most convenient, after sex, age, and race.[4]

A second factor is *differentiation,* or occupational specialization. As this occurs, the scope of each individual's activities is lessened and at the same time becomes more hidden from people in other occupations. According to Caplow, the requirements of each occupation, its responsibilities, and the evaluation of performance become more and more esoteric and removed from the area of a layman's judgment. The response is thus to the occupational title and not to the qualities of the individual in the occupation. Differentiation has also led to more highly developed authority systems within organizations, as additional specialties require their own hierarchies and each hierarchy requires coordination with the whole. Higher status is given to those occupations higher in the hierarchy, and again the response is to an individual's title rather than personal characteristics or performance.[5]

This is related to the third factor, *rationalization.* Rationalization refers to the substitution of formal controls of behavior for informal, personal, and spontaneous controls. This leads to the assumption that the occupational position of an individual has been decided by "scientific," "appropriate," and "efficient" techniques.[6] Caplow suggests that the modern reliance upon occupational position assumes that the occupation is indicative of a person's intelligence, ability, character, and personal acceptability. If a person is promoted to a better position, it is assumed that he has worked diligently and well, not that he is the son of the corporation president. If a person is not promoted, it is also generally assumed

---

[4]*Ibid.,* p. 30.
[5]*Ibid.,* p. 31.
[6]Caplow, *The Sociology of Work,* p. 31.

that he does not have what it takes. The process of rationalization thus leads to the important assumption that a person's occupation is an effective indicator of the kinds of attributes that would be brought into an assessment of his status if complete knowledge of these other attributes were available. The assumption is that the formal controls are themselves rational.

In particular cases there are undoubtedly variations from the primacy of occupation as the major status determinant. At the local community level, particularly in smaller communities, ancestry still plays a role. Factors, such as sex or race, can override occupation in many cases. Nevertheless, occupation stands out as the major status determinant in industrialized societies. The next question to be considered then is, What are the characteristics of occupations that contribute to the various rankings given the spectrum of occupations?

An important determinant of the status of a particular occupation is the specific nature of the work being performed.[7] A simple differentiation here is whether the occupation involves the manipulation of physical objects, symbols, or other people. In general, the manipulation of physical objects gives the least status, while the manipulation of symbols gives the most. There is some evidence to suggest, however, that social manipulation, as in the case of some executives, also gives high status. Those individuals engaged solely in symbol manipulation, such as artists or scientists, generally have lower status than those whose occupations involve both symbolic and social factors. The relationship between the physical and the symbolic-social forms of work is not perfect. Some craftsmen, for example, have higher status than lower level white-collar workers. At the same time, as Caplow points out, the manipulation of physical objects is a prized skill in many leisure activities, such as sports and many hobbies.[8] It could be hypothesized that the greater the involvement in symbolic-social manipulation in the occupation, the greater the concern with physical manipulation during leisure time. This relationship is affected, of course, by the greater access members of the more rewarded occupations have to such physical settings as sports facilities, gardens, or home shops. In terms of the status of occupations, the physical-symbolic-social differentiation does remain important, regardless of the relationship in nonoccupational activities.

Another factor affecting the status of an occupation is the prerequisites for entry: the amount of education or training required, the presence of certification or licensing procedures, and the experience needed. In general, the more stringent the entrance requirements, the higher the

---

[7]This discussion follows the suggestion of Reiss, *Occupations and Social Status*, pp. 10–11.

[8]Caplow, *The Sociology of Work*, p. 44.

status of the occupation. This accounts for the high status of the professions in the general white-collar category and that of craftsmen among blue-collar workers. There are some exceptions, as in the case of some professions that have not achieved public acceptance, but the relationship holds in most cases.

According to Reiss, an additional determinant of the status of an occupation is whether the task is performed on an individual or group basis. Although Reiss does not specify which type of social organization has the higher status yield, it appears that work carried out on an individual basis gives an occupation higher status, since individual work implies that the individual is capable of accomplishing the total project on his own. This is also reflected in the traditionally high status of the individual practitioner in the professions. As this image changes, the importance of this component of status determination may be lessened.

The place of an occupation within the interpersonal-relationship structure on the job also affects its status. Occupations involving supervision have higher status than those that are supervised. The position of an occupation in an organizational hierarchy has a similar status relationship. The important thing is the formal position of an occupation. Related to this are the demands made on an occupation by the work structure. The amount and type of responsibility are crucial. The more the responsibility, the higher the status in most cases. As was the case in terms of the specific task performed, responsibility for social or symbolic activities yields a higher status than responsibility for physical objects.

Reiss suggests that the work situation, as well as the characteristics of the work performed, plays a role in determining occupational status. One factor here would be the institutional setting of the work. A factory has a lower status than an office, and a research laboratory has a higher status than a machine shop. The work situation also determines the kinds of rewards earned from particular occupations, such as income, recognition, tenure, retirement programs, etc. It is obvious that work situations vary in terms of the kinds of rewards they offer. Persons with the same title and responsibilities can receive highly varied rewards, as was demonstrated in the section on executives. Related to this is the fact that, within a community, various employing organizations occupy different statuses. Workers in automated factories usually enjoy a higher status than their counterparts in nonautomated situations. A secretary may derive higher status from working at a university than at an automobile dealership. Industries themselves vary in the amount of status accorded them. At the present time, for example, the electronics industry appears to yield more status than the railroad industry, although these patterns change in time. A final consideration in the work situation is the nature of the employment itself, whether it is public, private, or self-employment.

The last type of employment has traditionally been given high status. In general, private employment has higher status than public, except among elected public officials in high positions, such as governors of states or congressmen.

The configuration of these work and work-situation attributes determines the status given an occupation. The work-related attributes tend to be more universal, in that the characteristics involved extend across a variety of work situations. The situational considerations operate most obviously at the local level, where knowledge of the differences between the work settings is most evident. The combination of the work and situational aspects is the basis for the evaluation of occupational status. The fact that there is this local variation is part of the difficulty in determining status in an objective manner. Every occupation, however, does possess characteristics that can be evaluated according to the criteria discussed above. Whether all of these factors are taken into consideration in the assignment of occupational status in concrete situations is another question.

The discussion thus far has centered around the reasons why occupation has become the major determinant of status and some of the factors that contribute to the differential status of occupations. Before delving further into the explanations that have been developed to explain why the stratification system takes the form that it does, we will analyze some of the techniques used to measure the status of various occupations. These techniques are designed to demonstrate the existence of a system of ranking and to serve as research tools for further analyses of the relationships between social status and other conditions.

One of the most commonly used measurement devices is that developed by Alba Edwards. The scale ranks occupations in the following manner:

1. Unskilled workers
    1-a. Farm laborers
    1-b,c. Laborers, except farm
    1-d. Servant classes
2. Semiskilled workers
3. Skilled workers and foremen
4. Clerks and kindred workers
5. Proprietors, managers, and officials
    5-a. Farmers (owners and tenants)
    5-b. Wholesale and retail dealers
    5-c. Other proprietors, managers, and officials
6. Professional persons

Edwards suggests that these occupational groupings encompass some major components of stratification and states:

It is evident that each of these groups represents not only a major segment of the Nation's labor force, but, also, a large population group with
a somewhat distinct standard of life, economically, and to a considerable
extent, intellectually and socially. In some measures, also, each group has
characteristic interests and convictions as to numerous public questions—
social, economic, and political. Each of them is thus a really distinct and
highly significant social-economic group.[9]

Most analysts would not go as far as Edwards in attributing such
clear distinctions to and between these occupational groupings. Nevertheless, the scale, if considered as a rather gross form of measurement,
is useful as an analytical and research device. The scale provides an
ordering of occupations without permitting the assumption to be made
that the intervals between the various positions on the scale are in any
way equal.

The census classification is designed to allow placement of occupations into relatively homogeneous categories in terms of socioeconomic
characteristics. Difficulties in placement of some occupations, lack of
real homogeneity, and the overlapping of socioeconomic characteristics
make such a scale less than perfect. It can, however, serve as a gross
indicator of the differential ranking of occupations. A quite different
approach has been taken by those interested in occupational prestige.
The prestige dimension of social stratification deals directly with the
status accorded occupations, since prestige is only something attributed
to something else. Occupations do not have prestige, rather they are
given it by the public. Since the public acts on the basis of its interpretation of an occupation, or any other social phenomenon for that matter,
prestige is an important component in the ranking of occupations.

Of the various attempts to measure occupational prestige, the best
known and most widely used approach is the North-Hatt or National
Opinion Research Center (NORC) survey, conducted in 1947 and since
expanded and refined. This study was designed to "secure a national
rating of the *relative prestige* of a wide range of occupations," to determine the standards of judgment people use in evaluating occupational
status, and to investigate the standards used in determining the relative
desirability of various occupations.[10] The study also was concerned with
attitudes about the appropriate amount of education needed to get along
in the world and with occupational mobility. In addition to being a
study of occupational prestige, the findings from the NORC survey become a major *scale* of occupational prestige. The original findings have
been extrapolated to include many more than the ninety occupations

[9]Alba M. Edwards, *Comparative Occupational Statistics for the United States, 1870–
1940* (Washington D.C.: U.S. Government Printing Office, 1943), p. 179.
[10]Reiss, *Occupations and Social Status*, p. 4.

analyzed in the original study, and the rankings obtained have been used to measure the prestige of occupations in a whole series of studies.

The data for the original study were obtained from a national sample of 2,920 respondents. A major problem encountered in the study was the varying amount of knowledge the respondents had about the occupations being rated. While over 99 percent of the respondents could rank occupations such as school teacher, garage mechanic, or truck driver, less than half were able to rank nuclear physicists. Other occupations were also difficult to rank. This presented a real problem in that the occupations included in the study were rather well known and did not include many with esoteric titles. The more education a respondent had, the more likely he was to know about the occupations being ranked. Differences in the ability to rank also were related to the type of community the respondent lived in and the respondent's own socioeconomic status. An additional problem encountered was that different criteria were used by respondents in their evaluations of the occupations.[11] The basic question asked was:

> For each job mentioned, please pick out the statement that best gives *your own personal opinion* of the *general standing* that such a job has.
>
> 1. *Excellent* standing
> 2. *Good* standing
> 3. *Average* standing
> 4. *Somewhat below average* standing
> 5. *Poor* standing
> X. I don't know where to place that one[12]

Each of the ninety occupations was then ranked by the respondent on the five point scale. The final rankings were obtained by a scoring system that gave an occupation that received 100 percent *excellent* a score of 100 and those that were unanimously rated as poor a score of 20. None achieved unanimity, of course. The occupations ranked, the final scores, and the proportion of the respondents giving each response are shown in Table 9-1.

The respondents were then asked to name "one main thing" about the jobs rated *excellent* that gave them this standing. The results of this question are shown in Table 9-2, with variations in the respondents' community type, age, education, general socioeconomic standing, and geographical region held constant. While the potential rewards from a job are the most frequently mentioned criteria, the expected variations by

[11]*Ibid.*, pp. 6–18.
[12]*Ibid.*, p. 19.

TABLE 9-1. Percent Distribution by Responding Rating, Average Score and Rank for 90 Rated Occupations: NORC, March 1947

Occupation	Excellent	Good	Average	Somewhat below average	Poor	Don't know	Score	Rank
U.S. Supreme Court justice	83%	15%	2%	%	% = 100	3%	96	1
Physician	67	30	3			1	93	2
State governor	71	25	4			1	93	2
Cabinet member in the federal government	66	28	5	1		6	92	4
Diplomat in the U.S. Foreign Service	70	24	4	1	1	9	92	4
Mayor of a large city	57	36	6	1		1	90	6
College professor	53	40	7			1	89	7
Scientist	53	38	8	1		7	89	7
United States representative in Congress	57	35	6	1	1	4	89	7
Banker	49	43	8			1	88	10
Government scientist	51	41	7	1		6	88	10
County judge	47	43	9	1		1	87	12
Head of a department in a state government	47	44	8		1	3	87	12
Minister	52	35	11	1	1	1	87	12
Architect	42	48	9	1		6	86	15
Chemist	42	48	9	1		7	86	15
Dentist	42	48	9	1			86	15
Lawyer	44	45	9	1	1	1	86	15
Member of board of directors of large corporation	42	47	10	1		5	86	15
Nuclear physicist	48	39	11	1	1	51	86	15
Priest	51	34	11	2	2	6	86	15
Psychologist	38	49	12	1		15	85	22
Civil engineer	33	55	11	1		5	84	23
Airline pilot	35	48	15	1	1	3	83	24
Artist who paints pictures that are exhibited in galleries	40	40	15	3	2	6	83	24
Owner of factory that employs about 100 people	30	51	17	1	1	2	82	26
Sociologist	31	51	16	1	1	23	82	26
Accountant for large business	25	57	17	1		3	81	28
Biologist	29	51	18	1	1	16	81	28
Musician in a symphony orchestra	31	46	19	3	1	5	81	28
Author of novels	32	44	19	3	2	9	80	31
Captain in the regular army	28	49	19	2	2	2	80	31
Building contractor	21	55	23	1		1	79	33
Economist	25	48	24	2	1	22	79	33

TABLE 9-1. (cont.)

Occupation	Excel-lent	Good	Aver-age	Some-what below aver-age	Poor	Don't know	Score	Rank
Instructor in public schools	28	45	24	2	1	1	79	33
Public-school teacher	26	45	24	3	2		78	36
County agricultural agent	17	53	28	2		5	77	37
Railroad engineer	22	45	30	3		1	77	37
Farm-owner and operator	19	46	31	3	1	1	76	39
Official of an interna-tional labor union	26	42	20	5	7	11	75	40
Radio announcer	17	45	35	3		2	75	40
Newspaper columnist	13	51	32	3	1	5	74	42
Owner-operator of a printing shop	13	48	36	3		2	74	42
Electrician	15	38	43	4		1	73	44
Trained machinist	14	43	38	5		2	73	44
Welfare worker for a city government	16	43	35	4	2	4	73	44
Undertaker	14	43	36	5	2	2	72	44
Reporter on daily newspaper	9	43	43	4	1	2	71	48
Manager of small store in a city	5	40	50	4	1	1	69	49
Bookkeeper	8	31	55	6		1	68	50
Insurance agent	7	34	53	4	2	2	68	50
Tenant farmer—one who owns livestock and machinery and manages the farm	10	37	40	11	2	1	68	50
Traveling salesman for a wholesale concern	6	35	53	5	1	2	68	50
Playground director	7	33	48	10	2	4	67	54
Policeman	11	30	46	11	2	1	67	54
Railroad conductor	8	30	52	9	1	1	67	54
Mail-carrier	8	26	54	10	2		66	57
Carpenter	5	28	56	10	1		65	58
Automobile repairman	5	21	58	14	2		63	59
Plumber	5	24	55	14	2	1	63	59
Garage mechanic	4	21	57	17	1		62	61
Local official of labor union	7	29	41	14	9	11	62	61
Owner-operator of lunch stand	4	24	55	14	3	1	62	61
Corporal in the regular army	5	21	48	20	6	3	60	64
Machine operator in factory	4	20	53	20	3	2	60	64
Barber	3	17	56	20	4	1	59	66

248

TABLE 9-1. (cont.)

Occupation	Excel- lent	Good	Aver- age	Some- what below aver- age	Poor	Don't know	Score	Rank
Clerk in a store	2	14	61	20	3		58	67
Fisherman who owns own boat	3	20	48	21	8	7	58	67
Streetcar motorman	3	16	55	21	5	2	58	67
Milk-route man	2	10	52	29	7	1	54	70
Restaurant cook	3	13	44	29	11	1	54	70
Truck-driver	2	11	49	29	9		54	70
Lumberjack	2	11	48	29	10	8	53	73
Filling-station attendant	1	9	48	34	8	1	52	74
Singer in a night club	3	13	43	23	18	6	52	74
Farm hand	3	12	35	31	19	1	50	76
Coal miner	4	11	33	31	21	2	49	77
Taxi-driver	2	8	38	35	17	1	49	77
Railroad section hand	2	9	35	33	21	3	48	79
Restaurant waiter	2	8	37	36	17	1	48	79
Dockworker	2	7	34	37	20	8	47	81
Night watchman	3	8	33	35	21	1	47	81
Clothes-presser in a laundry	2	6	35	36	21	2	46	83
Soda-fountain clerk	1	5	34	40	20	2	45	84
Bartender	1	6	32	32	29	4	44	85
Janitor	1	7	30	37	25	1	44	85
Share-cropper—one who owns no live-stock or equipment and does not manage farm	1	6	24	28	41	3	40	87
Garbage collector	1	4	16	26	53	2	35	88
Street-sweeper	1	3	14	29	53	1	34	89
Shoe-shiner	1	2	13	28	56	2	33	90
Average	21.6	30.9	29.5	11.4	6.6	4.0	69.8	

Source: Albert J. Reiss, *Occupational and Social Status* (New York: Free Press of Glencoe, 1961), pp. 54–57.

education and occupation stand out as a partial verification of the point that intrinsic rewards are more central to those higher in the occupational hierarchy. As Reiss points out, it is those lowest in financial status who are most likely to mention financial rewards as central to an occupation's standing. These responses also reflect the central values of Americans in regard to their work.[13]

[13]*Ibid.*, p. 35.

Table 9-2. Criterion Respondents Gave as the One Main Thing That Gives a Job Excellent Standing, by Selected Social Categories

Category	Pays well	Social prestige	Good future; field not crowded	Security, steady work, money	Education, hard work, money	Morality, honesty, responsibility	Intelligence, ability	Service to humanity, essential	Pleasant, safe, easy	Chance for initiative, freedom	Miscellaneous; don't know
All Respondents	18	14	3	5	14	9	9	16	2	*	10
Region											
Northeast	19	17	3	5	13	8	10	14	2	1	8
Midwest	15	15	4	5	14	11	8	16	2	*	10
South	21	12	4	3	14	8	8	15	1	*	13
West	14	11	2	4	17	9	11	22	1	1	8
Size of Place											
Metro. district											
1,000,000 and over	17	17	4	6	14	9	9	15	2	*	7
50,000–1,000,000	16	13	3	4	14	11	9	18	2	1	9
Urban places and towns	17	12	3	4	15	9	10	18	2	*	10
Rural farm	23	12	4	5	13	7	5	14	2	*	15
Age (years)											
14–20	21	15	4	3	13	5	8	17	3	*	11
21–39	16	16	4	6	15	6	9	15	2	1	9
40 and over	17	12	3	4	14	13	9	16	1	1	10
Sex											
Male	19	14	4	5	14	9	9	14	2	1	9
Female	16	14	3	4	14	9	9	18	2	1	10

Occupation Group											
Prof. and semiprof.	10	20	*	3	13	6	15	26	1	1	5
Mgrs., prop., and off.	14	16	3	4	19	9	10	16	1	1	7
Sales, clerical, and kindred	14	18	5	5	15	13	9	13	1	*	7
Crafts, fore., and kindred	16	13	5	5	14	10	8	19	2	†	8
Operatives and kind.	21	11	5	8	13	6	8	13	2	1	12
Pvt. household and service	22	14	*	4	13	9	7	12	3	†	16
All farm	24	11	4	4	12	8	6	14	2	*	15
Nonfarm labor	26	8	3	4	14	6	8	14	2	†	15
Yrs. of Schl. Comp.											
Some college	7	21	2	4	13	9	13	24	3	*	6
Some high school	17	14	4	5	13	9	9	16	*	1	88
8th grade or less	24	9	3	5	16	11	7	11	2	*	15
In school	18	19	4	3	13	5	8	19	3	*	8
Economic Level											
Prosperous	15	19	3	3	14	11	8	20	1	1	5
Middle class	15	15	3	5	15	9	10	16	2	1	9
Poor	23	10	4	5	13	9	6	13	2	*	15

*Less than one-half of 1 percent.
†No responses.
Source: Albert J. Reiss, *Occupations and Social Status* (New York: Free Press of Glencoe, 1961), pp. 32–33.

The NORC survey has become a benchmark in analyses of occupational status, despite the methodological and conceptual difficulties involved. The findings can only be considered as an ordering of occupations, since the intervals between the scores cannot be demonstrated to be equal. The original scores and extrapolations from them to occupations not included in the original study have been utilized as indicators of the relative status of occupations in a large number of studies and as indicators of the general social status of members of the occupations involved. There is some evidence that this is not an unwarranted procedure. Reiss, for example, reports that such "hard" indicators of socioeconomic status as income and educational level are highly associated with the NORC scores. Using the median income and educational levels of the civilian labor force of the occupations in the NORC study, he found rank order correlation coefficients (Kendall's *tau*) of +.85 between income and NORC score and +.83 for educational attainment and NORC score.[14] Prestige is thus rather strongly related to other indices of socioeconomic status.

While the NORC findings do show a general ordinal ranking of occupations, Reiss suggests that a unidimensional scale for all occupations cannot be derived from such an approach.[15] While income and education are strongly associated with occupational prestige, they do not always agree with each other. At the same time, since prestige scales rely upon the perception of the respondents and since such perception usually involves some distortion of reality, the prestige scales themselves cannot be taken as totally accurate appraisals of the stratification system. Distortions enter the picture from the tendency of people to underrate occupations lower than their own and overrate their own occupational positions. This problem is compounded when one remembers that the level of education affects an individual's ability to rank positions in the first place. High-status occupations are thus ranked high by people with greater knowledge, although those in lower status occupations, while ranking their own occupations rather high, lack the ability to rank much of the rest of the occupational system. Relying upon either high or low status occupations for ranking purposes introduces real distortions. Surveys such as the NORC study, which attempt to get a representative sample of the population, while minimizing the distortions introduced by reliance upon particular segments of the population, include in their composite scores the distortions from every population group. These distortions are apparently not eliminated by the inclusion of representative groups from the total population, since the kinds of distortions from

---

14*Ibid.*, p. 84.
15*Ibid.*, chap. 2, 3.

each group do not counterbalance each other. Despite these problems, the North-Hatt scale has been a widely used research device.

In an attempt to provide a more meaningful method for measuring and describing occupational status, Duncan combined measures of education and income. He correctly notes that occupation is "the intervening activity linking income to education."[16] Education prepares a person for an occupation from which he derives his income. While each can be taken separately as an indicator of social status, the combination of these two factors yields what is essentially a multidimensional scaling of occupations. Duncan calls this a "socioeconomic index," containing variables reflecting both the social and economic components of the stratification system.

Using sophisticated indicators of the education and income variables, Duncan's socioeconomic index can be used to predict scores on the NORC scale.[17] The socioeconomic index (SEI) is also systematically related to a more recent prestige scale developed by Paul M. Siegel.[18] Extremely high correlations of .86 to .91 are found between SEI scores and Siegel's prestige scale scores.[19] These scales have been developed to the point that "given the stable characteristics of the prestige structure in the U.S. and (apparently) throughout the world, scales based on these matrices can be used in time-series and comparative analyses as standardized, calibrated measures of the status which accrues to a person owing to his (her) incumbency of a particular occupation."[20] This, of course, is a level of measurement much above that usually achieved in the social sciences.

With the measurement of occupational status advanced this far, it is now possible to classify *all* of the occupations referenced by the U.S. Bureau of the Census. In its *Alphabetical Index of Occupations and Industries*, the Census Bureau lists some 20,000 jobs summarized by 296 detailed occupation titles and 18,000 industries summarized by 149 detailed industry titles. All a person has to do to determine occupational status is have information regarding a person's occupation, industry, and class of worker. Occupation here simply involves the kind of work the

---

[16]*Ibid.*, p. 117.

[17]*Ibid.* The details of the development of this scale are contained in chap. 6. The first edition of the present author's book [Richard D. Hall, *Occupations and the Social Structure* (Englewood Cliffs, N.J.: Prentice-Hall, 1969)] contained the full scale. Since the full scale is readily available elsewhere, it is not included in the present edition.

[18]"The American Occupational Prestige Structure" (Ph.D. diss., University of Chicago, 1970).

[19]Otis Dudley Duncan, David L. Featherman, and Beverly Duncan, *Socioeconomic Background and Achievement* (New York: Seminar Press, 1972).

[20]David L. Featherman and Robert M. Hauser, "On the Measurement of Occupation in Social Surveys" (Institute for Research on Poverty, University of Wisconsin, 1973).

person does, industry involves the kind of industry (this is part of the status picture), and class of worker involves whether a person's pay is in the form of salaries or wages, self-employment income, or if the person is working without pay.

While the relationship between occupation and social status is well established—the relationship is high, almost perfect—there is one area in which the research evidence is not clear. This is the case of women. Stated simply, the assumption is almost always made that women and other family members have the status of the husband. This is quite correct when the woman is not working and the woman is married. When exceptions occur, and they frequently do, the woman's place in the stratification system and her contribution to the status of her family becomes uncertain.[21] Marie R. Haug's research suggests that women in higher status positions than their husbands serve to raise the status of the family.[22] Acker concludes that if the wife is unemployed in the labor force but is a housewife, the status of the family is lowered because housewifing is a low status occupation.[23] This may not be the case, depending on one's values in regard to the family and housewifing, but the fact remains that this is an area that requires additional research. Certainly, a married woman's presence in the labor force has a status impact on the family, simply because of the dual incomes. If the dual incomes are low, the status impact is slight, but if they are high, the contribution to the status of the family can be high.

For the unmarried woman, there are also uncertainties. While all occupations can be given a status score, it would appear that a woman accountant, salesclerk, or waitress is accorded different status than her male counterpart. Whether or not this status is lower is not totally clear. In the past, the factor of being female tended to downgrade the status. With the growth of the women's movement and a sometimes more positive approach to women in occupations, it is possible that there is a status benefit for women or no effect at all.

We have established the relationship between occupations and social status. Before turning to the crucial question of *why* this relationship is so strong and why occupations have different statuses in the first place, we will briefly examine the concept of situs.

An occupational situs, or family, is a set of occupations whose status system may be viewed as a unit. The situs concept divides the occupational system into a series of relatively parallel status systems. Paul K. Hatt proposes eight such situses—political, professional, business, recrea-

[21]See Joan Acker, "Women and Social Stratification: A Case of Intellectual Sexism," *American Journal of Sociology* 78 (January 1973), 936–45.

[22]"Social Class Measurement and Women's Occupational Roles," *Social Forces* 52 (September 1973), 85–97.

[23]"Women and Social Stratification, p. 942.

tion and aesthetics, agriculture, manual work, military, and service. Each has its own status system, and mobility, when it occurs, is most likely to occur within a situs.[24] A later study by Richard T. Morris and Raymond J. Murphy utilizes a different set of situses based upon the functions performed in each situs for society.[25] These situses are represented in Fig. 9-1. The occupational titles in Fig. 9-1 were placed in the situses by a sample of undergraduate college students. The ambiguities in the placement of occupations on a prestige continuum can also be seen in this placement into situses. Another obvious problem posed by this approach is that some occupations perform functions in more than one situs. As Morris and Murphy suggest, the minister may be as concerned with teaching as with the alleviation of distress and the milk-route man is both a salesman and a truck driver. According to Morris and Murphy, this is symptomatic of a changing occupational structure that is on the way to greater specialization.

Although the occupations included in the Morris-Murphy study are not meant to be inclusive, those in the study suggest that the situs concept, if it is to be used, must include the realization that some situses may have shorter or longer hierarchies than others. By using the Duncan socioeconomic index, for example, we can see that the hospital attendant, the lowest ranked occupation in the health and welfare situs, is ranked higher than the lowest occupation in manufacturing. At the same time, the highest ranked occupations in the health and welfare situs are given higher scores than those in the manufacturing area. The situses themselves vary in terms of their outer status limits. Although Morris and Murphy state that situses should not be invidiously compared, there are obvious status differentials between situses.[26] The earlier discussion about the situational determinants of occupational status also supports the conclusion of differential status among situses. Reiss notes that there is a tendency for individuals to place occupations within the situs concept when occupations are being ranked, which suggests that the situses themselves are ranked.[27] The situs concept is thus a useful, but as yet undeveloped, addition to the understanding of occupational status.

EXPLANATIONS OF OCCUPATIONAL STATUS DIFFERENCES

An individual's occupation is a major determinant of his position within the stratification system. Reiss has suggested that characteristics

[24]Paul K. Hatt, "Occupations and Social Stratification," *American Journal of Sociology*, LV, 6 (May 1950), 533–43.
[25]"The Situs Dimension in Occupational Structure," *American Sociological Review*, XXIV, 3 (April 1959), 231–39.
[26]*Ibid.*, p. 233.
[27]*Occupations and Social Status*, p. 46.

SITUSES

Prestige rank quartiles (Student Ratings) / STRATA	1 Legal Authority	2 Finance & Records	3 Manufacturing	4 Transportation	5 Extraction	6 Building & Maintenance	7 Commerce	8 Aesthetics & Entertainment	9 Education & Research	10 Health & Welfare
1	Supreme Court Justice / Lawyer	City Manager	Owner of a large factory	President of a railroad				Conductor of a symphony orchestra	College president	Physician, Minister
2		Banker	Biologist for a pharmaceutical company	Airline pilot	Geologist in an oil company	Building contractor	Advertising executive, Commercial artist	Philosopher	County agricultural agent	Welfare worker
3	Policeman	Book-keeper	Machinist		Farmer, Forest ranger		Manager of a hardware store	Radio announcer, Singer in a night club	Music teacher	Fireman
4	Prison guard	Cashier in a restaurant	Restaurant cook	Mail carrier, Truck driver	Coal miner	Waiter in a restaurant, Garbage collector	Milk route man	Barber		

Figure 9-1 Theoretical Situs Location of Selected Occupations and Empirical Location Made by Sample of Student Raters. "Arrows indicate that 25 per cent of the students placed the occupation in a situs other than that theoretically expected on the basis of situs definitions supplied. ..." Source: Richard T. Morris and Raymond J. Murphy, "The Situs Dimension in Occupational Structure," *American Sociological Review*, XXIV, 2 (April 1959), 237.

of the work and the work situation contribute to the rankings assigned to occupations. Although prestige rankings are important indicators of the occupational status system, they represent only those characteristics of occupations as they are judged by some segment of the public involved in the prestige ranking process. The basic question to be considered is, Why do occupations occupy different positions within the stratification system? Why does a bank president, for example, have higher status than an airplane mechanic? In order to answer this basic question about the nature of the social order, two alternative explanations will be explored.

Perhaps the best known, and most often criticized, explanation for the differences in status is the "functional theory of stratification" as suggested by Talcott Parsons and fully articulated by Kingsley Davis and Wilbert Moore.[28] Davis and Moore approach stratification as a series of positions in society. Their concern is not with the specific individuals occupying those positions. A basic requirement for society is the placement and motivation of people in the social structure. The motivation must occur in two related ways. Individuals with appropriate skills must be motivated to fill the positions in which their skills can best be utilized. Once a person is in the position, the motivation to carry out the duties of the position must be maintained.[29] The argument thus far suggests that society needs to have a variety of tasks performed for the society to exist, that individuals must be motivated to fill the positions that perform these tasks, and that individuals must then be motivated to perform the tasks.

Any need for varying levels of reward would be eliminated if the duties associated with the various positions in society were all equally pleasant to perform, all equally important to societal maintenance, and all equally in need of the same ability and talent. Fortunately or unfortunately, this is not the case. Some positions are more pleasant than others. Some also are more important to the society as a whole. At the same time, the amount of ability, training, and skill required in the various positions varies widely. Since this is the case, a system of rewards must be established to act as inducements to fill positions that hold varying amounts of intrinsic appeal to the members of the society. A method for the differential distribution of these rewards according to the positions must also be developed.[30]

[28]See Talcott Parsons, "An Analytical Approach to the Theory of Social Stratification," *American Journal of Sociology*, XLV, 3 (November 1940), 841–62, and Kingsley Davis and Wilbert Moore, "Some Principles of Stratification," *American Sociological Review*, X, 2 (April 1945), 242–49.

[29]Davis and Moore, "Some Principles of Stratification," p. 242.

[30]*Ibid.*, p. 243.

According to Davis and Moore, the rewards can take a variety of forms. One type of reward is a contribution to the individual's "sustenance and comfort." This, of course, would be some form of material reward. A second form of reward is "contributions to humor and diversion." This would involve the intrinsic enjoyment of the work and satisfying social relationships. A final type of reward is "things that contribute to self-respect and ego expansion." These rewards are the feeling of accomplishment in a position and the sense that the position contributes to one's own and general societal welfare. All three types of rewards are differentially distributed according to position.[31]

The analysis thus far suggests that societal positions vary in their importance, their demands in terms of ability, and their ease of performance. The differences in their functional importance demand that society provide sufficient rewards to ensure that the positions are filled competently. The less essential positions should not compete with the more essential positions for personnel. If a position is easily filled, it does not have to be heavily rewarded. If a position is hard to fill, the reward structure must be such that people are attracted to the position despite its difficulties.

Another important consideration is that there is a "differential scarcity of personnel." The more scarce the personnel and the more difficult and important the position, the higher the rewards must be. The ability to fill a position can be acquired either through heredity or training or some combination thereof. From this perspective, it does not matter which source is operative, since it is the position itself that must be filled and the requirements can include hereditary considerations, as well as the more democratic training requirements. The Davis-Moore "theory" thus involves considerations of the differential importance of positions in society, variations in the requirements of the positions, and differences in the kinds of abilities necessary to fill the positions. The positions are thus differentially rewarded in order to ensure their occupancy by competent personnel. The differential rewards lead to a stratified society.[32]

The Davis-Moore formulation has led to a continuing dialogue and debate, principally with Melvin Tumin.[33] Tumin questions the explanatory power of the functional approach and suggests that the term "functional importance" is itself ambiguous and difficult to apply. It is difficult to establish if long-run or short-run functional importance determines the rewards structure. Tumin notes that unskilled workers in a factory are as important as its engineers, since the workers must be present to

[31]*Ibid.*
[32]*Ibid.*, pp. 242–43.
[33]See Melvin Tumin, "Some Principles of Stratification: A Critical Analysis," *American Sociological Review*, XVIII, 4 (August 1953), 387–94.

produce the product. Davis responds to this criticism by noting that while it is difficult to determine the exact functional importance of a position, the general process occurs whenever a totalitarian nation determines where its financial and social resources should be utilized or when organizations decide which positions are important and which are not. At the same time, Davis suggests that Tumin overlooked the differential scarcity of personnel component—engineers are more difficult to replace than are unskilled workers.[34]

Tumin criticizes the Davis-Moore formulation from the standpoint that the potential for locating the best possible talent for difficult positions is minimized in a stratified society. A stratified society does not give equal access to opportunities to develop and demonstrate one's talents. Access to education, for example, depends on parents' wealth, rather than on the potential of the person. Thus stratification in one generation limits the likelihood of discovering talent in the next. It also affects the motivational component of succeeding generations. In addition, according to Tumin, there is a noticeable tendency for elites to restrict access to their privileged positions.[35] To these criticisms Davis responds that it does not really matter how the valued positions are filled, so long as they are filled.[36] If a caste system decrees that positions are filled by inheritance and there is a belief in the appropriateness of the system, the fact that talent is not sought throughout all castes does not make any difference, because the higher position is valued as are the requirements for access to the position. At the same time, in another sense, it is unimportant if some potential talent is missed. If positions are filled adequately, the source does not matter. This is, of course, contrary to democratic principles, but in terms of explaining stratification patterns, such principles are on a moral rather than analytical level. These statements do not deny some of the negative consequences of stratification but rather place them in the context of undesirable, but not inevitable, consequences of an inevitable system.

A third criticism raised by Tumin regards the nature of the training for the more highly rewarded positions. This training, according to the functional theory, involves some sacrifice on the part of the individual, a sacrifice that is later compensated for by the higher rewards of the more valued positions in society. Tumin suggests that any financial sacrifice is not usually borne by the individual undergoing the training, but by his parents, who have accumulated wealth in their own lifetime. At the same time, income not earned during the training period can be

---

[34]Kingsley Davis, "Reply," *American Sociological Review*, XVIII, 4 (August 1953), 394.

[35]"Some Principles of Stratification: A Critical Analysis," pp. 388–89.

[36]"Reply," pp. 395–96.

rather quickly "made up" once the person is in the labor force. Tumin suggests that within a decade after professional school, for example, the professional will earn as much as he would have earned if he had been working during his training period and the succeeding decade. After his first decade, his earnings far outstrip those of his less well trained cohorts.

In addition to noting the trained person's relatively quick process of catching up financially with those who have not undergone advanced training, Tumin also points out that

> what tends to be completely overlooked, in addition, are the psychic and spiritual rewards which are available to the elite trainees by comparison with their age peers in the labor force. There is, first, the much higher prestige enjoyed by the college student and the professional-school student as compared with persons in shops and offices. There is, second, the extremely highly valued privilege of having greater opportunity for self-development. There is, third, all the psychic gain involved in being allowed to delay the assumption of adult responsibilities such as earning a living and supporting a family. There is, fourth, the access to leisure and freedom of a kind not likely to be experienced by the persons already in the labor force.[37]

To this criticism Davis responds that it in fact makes no difference who assumes the burden of the training period. The important point is that there is a burden. He also suggests that the criticism that the earning power of the well-trained person outstrips that of the person who has not undergone the training is itself a confirmation of the functional theory. Differential rewards must be available for the more functionally important positions. At the same time, the fact that such training does involve psychic rewards reflects the fact that these psychic rewards are largely a reflection of the anticipated rewards to be obtained after the training is completed. Davis also suggests that while the status and reward system surrounding the student role might be relatively high in comparison with systems for other roles, studying itself is burdensome. Many youths are unable or unwilling to undergo the difficulties of studying for the highly rewarded positions.[38]

An additional criticism of the functional theory is based on the motivation and reward system. Tumin suggests that additional motivational bases should be considered and that rewards available are often unequally utilized. Davis responds that this is true, but that it essentially makes no difference. Davis also notes that the original formulation includes the possibility of differing reward and motivational structures. A

[37]"Some Principles of Stratification: A Critical Analysis," p. 390.
[38]Davis, "Reply," p. 396.

final criticism of Tumin's regards the inevitability and dysfunctionality of stratification.[39] Davis replies that the theory is not concerned with the indefinite or utopian future in terms of inevitability but rather with societies as they are found in the historical and contemporary world. He also notes that dysfunctions can and do exist but that in the case of Tumin's criticisms, they revolve around the family rather than the differential positional rewards in terms of the inheritance of status.[40]

A later dialogue between Moore and Tumin reduces some of their areas of disagreement.[41] Tumin recognizes the general need for some differentiation of rewards; at the same time, he questions the extent of the differentiation necessary. Moore more explicitly recognizes some additional components of dysfunctionality in a stratified system. The basic issue regarding the moral rightness of differential rewards remains— Tumin arguing that the possession of talent, itself an inherited condition from either the biological or sociological perspective, should not necessarily be more highly rewarded. Moore maintains that the factor of individual motivation and effort must also be considered in any reward system. This functional approach to the nature of a stratified society and the closely related occupational system thus remains an explanation of why positions must be rewarded unequally if persons are to be motivated to fill the positions. From this perspective, the inheritance or learning of scarce talents becomes an irrelevant issue, since there is a differential distribution of such talent and those who possess greater amounts of some scarce talent must have some form of inducement to utilize the talent in ways societal values support. The form of inducement remains a point of contention. The contention on this point, however, exists far beyond the current debate.

The debate over the functionalist approach continues unabated. The functionalist perspective is viewed as a conservative one by those who adopt the more radical conflict perspective to be discussed below. While political positions and ideologies can keep a debate like this alive for decades, a more basic reason for the uncertainty over functionalist theory is the absence of solid empirical evidence that can confirm or disconfirm the basic ideas.

There has been little research in this area, despite the subject's importance. What research has been conducted comes to inconclusive answers. Part of the reason for this is the fact that functionalists think

[39]"Some Principles of Stratification: A Critical Analysis," pp. 391–93.

[40]Davis, "Reply," pp. 396–97.

[41]See Wilbert Moore, "But Some Are More Equal Than Others" and "Rejoinder," and Melvin Tumin, "On Equality," *American Sociological Review*, XXVIII, 1 (February 1963), 13–18, 26–28, and 19–26.

of society or a social system as dynamic and thus link stratification to the emergent situation. But, as Edgar Borgatta points out, we then must anticipate what the future is going to be like to know what the contribution of differentiated rewards will be.[42] This is clearly impossible to do. Since it is difficult to determine what is functional at the moment, some researchers have turned to historical data to help unravel the questions about the functional theory.

Mark Abrahamson, in an analysis of data on military pay in times of war and peace (one would expect that military pay would rise during times of war, given the greater importance of the military in those periods), essentially confirms the functionalist hypotheses, at least in terms of the rewards offered for these positions.[43] Abrahamson does not, however, come to the conclusion that these extra rewards are necessarily needed.

An opposite conclusion is reached by Randall Collins in his analysis of changing educational requirements.[44] Instead of arriving at conclusions in support of the functionalist approach, Collins's findings support the competing conflict approach. Collins suggests that as more and higher education became the socially approved thing for high status groups, the groups that were in charge of the employing organizations began to demand higher and more education on the part of entrants into the organization. The public began demanding more and higher education to gain access to more elite positions, and the spiral of increasing amounts of education began. Instead of advancing the functionalist argument that changed jobs require more education, Collins concludes that it was conflict between status groups that led to the demand for and achievement of more education, with job change not an important factor.

The *conflict* approach to stratification is probably evident by now. It basically posits that the stratification system takes the form that it does and that occupations are given certain statuses because of the control of elite individuals and groups over the social structure. This approach is of course identified with Karl Marx and has seen more recent expression in the works of Ralf Dahrendorf, who sees control of power as more central than Marx's notion of the control of economic conditions.[45] The conflict approach is based on the idea that large organizations control both the private and public sectors. These large organizations in turn are

[42]Edgar F. Borgatta, "Functionalism and Sociology," *American Sociological Review* 25 (April 1960), 267.

[43]"The Functional Theory of Stratification: An Assessment," *American Journal of Sociology* 78 (March 1973), 1236–46.

[44]"Functional and Conflict Theories of Educational Stratification," *American Sociological Review* 36 (December 1971), 1002–18.

[45]See Dahrendorf, *Class and Class Conflict in Industrial Societies* (Stanford, Calif.: Stanford University Press, 1959).

controlled by a small elite of people with common backgrounds.[46] The power of the elite, both in the past and at present, is such that the elite control the distribution of rewards and thus the stratification system. The motivation is to maintain in power those who are in power.

The clear differences between the conflict and functionalist explanations of stratification have not been resolved. Gerhard Lenski, while leaning toward the conflict perspective, has attempted to provide a perspective on stratification that is both historically accurate and theoretically reasonable.[47] His theoretical development will be used to contrast that of the functional school and at the same time will serve as the basis for an attempt to resolve the differences between the two approaches and to yield a more comprehensive view of the stratification process as it affects the occupational system.

After noting that men are obliged by nature to live with other people and that men almost always act on the basis of self-interest, Lenski notes that most desired objects are in short supply, which leads to competition for these objects. Like the functionalists, Lenski notes that men are unequally endowed with the attributes that lead to success in the competitive effort. Since men tend to follow habits and customs, the form of competition is likely to remain the same.[48] As societies develop, more or less coordinated efforts of the total society are directed toward common goals, even though this may harm individual members of the society. There is a general attempt to maintain political stability in more stratified societies or to maximize production in minimally stratified societies.[49]

A society will become more stratified as its survival needs are met more successfully and surpluses become available for distribution. According to this analysis, the distribution of the surplus valued items will be determined by the power structure of the society. A question not fully answered in this approach is the determination of the power structure in the first place. It would appear that power would be in the hands of those who perform valued functions for the society, such as the best hunter or fisherman or a religious leader. If this is the case, then at least a component of the functional theory would be operative at this level.

Since power determines the distribution of surpluses, it also then determines who has privileges in the society. According to Lenski, prestige is largely derived from privilege, privilege in this case being the

---

[46]See C. Wright Mills, *The Power Elite* (New York: Oxford University Press, 1956), and William Domhoff, *Who Rules America* (Englewood Cliffs, N.J.: Prentice-Hall, 1967).

[47]*Power and Privilege* (New York: McGraw-Hill, 1966).

[48]*Ibid.*, pp. 25–32.

[49]*Ibid.*, pp. 41–43.

differential opportunities available within the system. As technological advances occur, the power variable will grow in importance. In this formulation, the distribution of rewards in society (privilege and prestige) is a function of the distribution of power, not of *system* needs. While functional inequality existed in "primitive" societies, the basis of the inequality shifted to the power system.[50]

In order to support this thesis, Lenski amasses an impressive array of historical data. These data indicate that the amount of inequality within a system will continue to increase, based upon the power variable, until the onset of industrialization. At this point in a society's history the trend is reversed, and the degree of inequality lessens as the middle classes emerge. Related to the general shift toward industrialization is the movement toward more constitutionalism in government. This also facilitates the development of the middle class. As further industrialization and the development of constitutional forms of government occur, "for most members of industrial societies, *the occupational system* . . . is the chief determinant of power, privilege, and prestige."[51] This is essentially the same point noted at the outset of this chapter—the occupational system is the major determinant of status in industrialized societies. Lenski maintains that the occupational system is based upon power rather than functional importance in determining the stratification system in modern societies. In support of this position he notes the high level of many managerial salaries, which appears to be greater than that needed to ensure adequate motivation.

The Lenski approach attempts to bridge the gap between the functional and conflict approaches to stratification. In this attempt both approaches are utilized in a sequential model moving from functional inequality in primitive societies to a power-based system in preindustrial systems to essentially a combined system in the industrialized society. Lenski appears, however, to lean toward the power explanation rather than the functional approach in explaining societal stratification. Since the societal system is closely related to the occupational system, this approach can then be taken to indicate that the distribution of persons into occupations and the privileges and prestige derived therefrom are based largely upon the people's original (parents') power within the system. The various occupations have differing amounts of power themselves, leading to a maintenance of the system.

Walter Buckley's discussion of the functional theory lends credence to this interpretation. He states: "In other words, positions are determined on the whole by social inheritance, and only secondarily, *within*

50*Ibid.*, pp. 44–63.
51*Ibid.*, p. 346.

this pattern, by 'performance.' Although 'performance' by itself may be important, it is the *chance to perform* that is at stake here."[52] According to Buckley, the functional theory is not a theory of stratification, but a "theory of certain aspects of social differentiation and hierarchical organization. . . ."[53]

If Buckley's points are correct, a further *rapprochement* between the functional and conflict explanations is possible. Tumin and Lenski are undoubtedly correct in their assessment that parental position and power play a dominant role in educational and eventually occupational attainment. The data on intergenerational mobility, to be discussed, indicate that the majority of the labor force in modernized societies are at essentially the same level as their parents. At the same time, those who are mobile, in particular, and those who remain at the same general level are at the same time placed within the system according to the tenets of the functional theory. That is, once a person has gained entrance to an occupation, either by inheritance of the occupational level or further education than might have been expected according to his background, his movement or lack of movement within the system is based upon his performance, his contribution to the system, and the scarcity of his skills. In other words, once a person is in the labor force, many of the considerations of the functional theory are operative. This would appear to be particularly true for members of organizational hierarchies, where judgments about performance appear to be based on rational criteria. Thus the place of the individual within an organization depends upon the skills he possesses. The rewards of his position depend upon the importance of the position and the scarcity of personnel available to fill it. This assumes, of course, that he has the required amount and kind of training, a function of his original placement within the social system.

These various explanations of the presence of a stratification system and the differentiation among occupations serve to illustrate the central thesis of this volume. Occupations are vitally affected by the broader social system and at the same time affect it. Further evidence to support this thesis is available in the analysis of social mobility.

MOBILITY AND OCCUPATIONS

Mobility is an important consideration in the nature of social systems as a whole, as in comparisons of caste and open class systems, and an important consideration for the analysis of occupations. The

---

[52]Walter Buckley, "Social Stratification and Social Differentiation," *American Sociological Review,* XXIII, 4 (August 1958), 374.

[53]*Ibid.,* p. 370.

analysis of mobility in empirical research is increasingly and almost exclusively based on data about occupations. Mobility is usually approached from a number of dimensions.[54] One such dimension is the time phase of mobility. Here intergenerational mobility can be distinguished from intragenerational mobility, even though the two forms can exist simultaneously for individuals and collectivities. A second dimension of mobility involves its direction. Three separate but often related directional axes can be identified. The most commonly analyzed is vertical mobility, movement up or down within the stratification system. A second axis is a change in social function that does not involve a change in status, or horizontal mobility. The third axis is spatial mobility, change in the location of the occupation. While each of these axes is analytically distinct, they are frequently related in reality. Each also plays an important role in intergenerational and intragenerational mobility.

Caplow's discussion of the forms of mobility contains elements that should be considered in this analysis. A major point is that intragenerational vertical mobility can take a variety of forms. For example, a change in occupation has been a traditional means of moving up in the stratification system. At the same time, it is a relatively infrequent form inasmuch as there are limitations on the opportunities for such occupational shifts. Persons with professional or craft training are unlikely to change occupations and thus lose their educational investment. Seniority and tenure provisions also diminish the likelihood of occupational changes for many employees at all levels of large-scale organizations. For lower level white- and blue-collar workers, occupational changes may be fairly common, particularly at the outset of the work career. In most cases, however, such job changes do not involve much vertical mobility.

According to Caplow, there are occupational groups that engage in occupational change to a relatively high degree and at the same time experience vertical mobility. He states:

> The careers of agents and brokers (outside large business bureaucracies), small proprietors, artists and entertainers, politicians and salesmen are characterized by relatively frequent changes of employment and of specific occupational activity, accompanied by a tendency to move between related occupations. It is within this group that the sharpest short-run changes in income and prestige take place, and that the total range of social reward is greatest.[55]

Much of this sort of mobility involves occupations tied in one way or another to the communications system. Entertainers and athletes, for ex-

---

[54]These distinctions follow those suggested by Caplow, *The Sociology of Work*, pp. 59–99.
[55]*Ibid.*, p. 63.

ample, can demand extremely high incomes over short periods of time, after which they normally must change occupations at a financial loss to themselves. For most of the occupations subject to this form of status fluctuation, publicity and personal contacts appear to be a prime force. In general, however, occupational change does not appear to be a major contributor to vertical mobility. Blau and Duncan, in a major analysis of mobility within the United States, conclude that where occupational changes do occur, the move is likely to be a short-distance move rather than a long-distance one. In the light of the trends discussed throughout this chapter, the place of occupational change as a component of vertical mobility will probably decline in importance in the coming years.

A second form of intragenerational mobility is promotion or demotion within an organizational hierarchy. Given the importance of origanizational employment as a condition of contemporary occupations, this becomes a dominant component of the mobility process. While important, the promotional process is really meaningful only in terms of mobility within the executive-professional hierarchy of organizations. It has become extremely unlikely that a person will move from blue-collar or lower level white-collar positions into the executive-professional hierarchy, because of the educational prerequisites for the hierarchy. While the office boy to president or factory worker to plant manager image remains and many cases of this kind of promotion can still be found in the occupational system, today the system precludes such movement. Blau and Duncan note that there are two semipermeable lines that limit downward mobility between and within generations but permit upward mobility. These lines are between the blue- and white-collar occupations and between farm and manual occupations.[56] It would appear that the upward mobility in this case would almost exclusively come *between* generations. Given the rather universalistic standards of most organizations, the social origins of an individual should not be a hindrance to his mobility, if he has the prerequisites for such mobility. Within organizational hierarchies, the major such prerequisite is education. Once entrée to the hierarchy is gained at the outset of an individual's career, performance and other factors would be operative. The barrier between the organizational hierarchy and the rather undifferentiated lower level white- and blue-collar occupations is a real one within a generation. It can be crossed between generations, which opens up the possibility for mobility through promotions.

A final type of mobility within a generation that can be identified is that associated with a "normal" career. *Within* an occupation there is generally a normal progression that carries with it not only a higher

[56]Blau and Duncan, *The American Occupational Structure*, pp. 58–59.

income over a period of time but also some prestige, which accrues with the status of having seniority or tenure, being experienced, being an old-timer, and so on. Although there are limits to the extent to which advancing age is honored in Western societies, the normal career curve does carry with it some upward mobility.

The second major form of vertical mobility is that between generations. This form of mobility has been of particular interest because of the inferences that can be drawn from data on this form of mobility about the nature of the stratification system itself. High rates of intergenerational mobility are often taken as indicative of an open stratification system and a proper operation of the democratic system. In reality, the relationship between the amount of intergenerational mobility and the openness of the system is not that simple. In the first place, there are some occupations that exhibit a high degree of occupational inheritance and, hence, a low degree of mobility. Independent professionals, proprietors, and farmers "neither supply to other careers in the next generation or recruit from others in the last,"[57] according to Blau and Duncan. While this contributes to occupational solidarity, it also diminishes the gross mobility rate. At the same time, the data of Blau and Duncan suggest that the lower level blue-collar and white-collar occupations supply a disproportionate amount of manpower to the occupational system. The occupations at the top have expanded while those at the bottom have contracted. This in and of itself is a major factor in the continued presence of upward mobility between generations in the United States.

Blau and Duncan's data on intergenerational mobility indicate that mobility increased in the 1951–1962 decade. These data also indicate that the opportunity structure is greater for the United States than other Western countries. This is true for "distant moves," from working and manual classes into elite positions, and for the shorter move from other white-collar jobs into elite positions.[58] While these considerations are valuable in terms of the opportunity structure and its relationship to societal values, they are less relevant for an understanding of the relationships between intergenerational mobility and the occupational system.

Blau and Duncan's research points out an important characteristic of intergenerational mobility. One usual component of the measurement of intergenerational mobility is the father's occupation. The respondent is asked his own occupation and then that of his father. Differences between the socioeconomic standing of each are taken to be gross indicators of mobility. Among the problems in such an approach, the most severe is that the labor force itself changes in composition; some occupations

57 *Ibid.*, p. 76.
58 *Ibid.*, pp. 433–35.

decline and some grow. Farming, for example, turns out to be a dominant occupation among the fathers of adult males. As was discussed above, there has been an expansion of the labor force at the upper levels and a contraction at the lower levels, including farming. At the same time, farming undoubtedly was a higher status occupation in previous gen-erations. Thus comparisons across generations encounter difficulties that make exacting measurement of this form of mobility difficult. A further difficulty is that at any point in time, both the respondents (sons) and their fathers are at different periods in their careers. This problem can be partially overcome in the case of the fathers by asking for the father's major occupation, but even here lack of knowledge or the real possibility that the father is still in the labor force and has not reached his major occupation make such comparisons less than perfect.

Blau and Duncan recognize the methodological problems involved in this sort of analysis. The severity of the problem is lessened in their analysis by their important shift in the conceptualization of the impact of the father's occupation. They point out that the knowledge of fathers' occupations of a sample of 20,000 men in the labor force in 1962 does not yield distinctive socioeconomic groupings of fathers for the reasons noted above. This knowledge does, however, give good insights into the *social origins* of the sons.[59] This, after all, is really the important issue. What is important in terms of intergenerational mobility is the extent of movement from social origins on the part of the son. In this way, his-torical changes in the occupational structure have less impact on the measurement. Rather obviously, intergenerational and intragenerational mobility are interrelated. If a person moves up or down from his social origins, he is exhibiting both kinds of mobility. An important distinction, necessary here, is the idea of the first job. An individual, through educa-tion for example, may achieve a relatively high-level first job, after which he exhibits little upward movement. This would be an example of intergenerational mobility without intragenerational mobility. The son of an army officer who achieves the same rank in his own lifetime would exhibit intragenerational mobility without the intergenerational form. In most cases the interrelatedness of the two forms exists.

In summarizing their findings in regard to intergenerational mobility, Blau and Duncan conclude:

A man's social origins exert a considerable influence on his chances of occupational success, but his own training and early experience exert a more pronounced influence on his success chances. The zero-order corre-lations with occupational status are 0.32 for father's education, 0.40 for father's occupation, 0.60 for education, and 0.54 for first job. Inasmuch as

[59] *Ibid.*, p. 25.

social origins, education, and career origins are not independent, however, their influence on ultimate occupational achievements is not cumulative. Thus the entire influence of father's education on son's occupational status is mediated by father's occupation and son's education. Father's occupational status, on the other hand, not only influences son's career achievements by affecting his education and first job, but it also has a delayed effect on achievements that persists when differences in schooling and early career experience are statistically controlled. Although most of the influence of social origins on occupational achievements is mediated by education and early experience, social origins have continuing impact on careers that is independent of the two variables pertaining to career preparation. Education exerts the strongest direct effect on occupational achievements . . . with the level on which a man starts his career being second. . . .[60]

A major exception to the impact of education is the black; the better educated black does not achieve occupational status to the degree predicted from the model. In fact, the better educated black is less mobile than the poorly educated black. Blau and Duncan suggest that the effects of discrimination are more pronounced for the better educated black, since his movement would be up into occupations long dominated by whites.

Blau and Duncan's findings indicate that there is a high rate of occupational inheritance and that what movement there is tends to be into adjacent occupational status categories. Table 9-3 indicates the percentages of sons of each social origin supplied to the various occupations in 1962. Table 9-4 indicates the proportion of the men in each occupational category recruited from the various occupational origins. The categories of salaried professional and manager, for example, receive members disproportionately from the lower level white-collar groups. These occupations have expanded, with 18 percent of the sons in these occupations and only 6.5 percent of the fathers. In terms of recruitment, it is evident from Table 9-4 that farmers have supplied a disproportionate number of sons to the rest of the labor force and that sons of proprietors are also supplied to the more highly ranked occupations. The potential for mobility is strongly associated with changes in the overall occupational structure.

Horizontal and spatial mobility are generally closely related to vertical mobility. As has been discussed above, job changes are an important component of the vertical mobility process. At the same time, geographical mobility is also a component of this process. Blau and Duncan found that "immigration has in recent decades become increasingly effective as a selective mechanism by which the more able are channeled to places

[60]*Ibid.*, pp. 402–3.

TABLE 9-3. Mobility from First Job to Occupation in 1962, for Males 25-64 Years Old: Ratios of Observed Frequencies to Frequencies Expected on the Assumption of Independence

Respondent's Occupation in 1962

First Job	1	2	3	4	5	6	7	8	9	10	11	12	13	14	15	16	17
Professionals																	
1 Self-employed	37.3	2.5	0.2	1.5	0.4	0.2	0.0	0.2	0.1	0.0	0.1	0.0	0.0	0.0	0.6	0.0	0.4
2 Salaried	4.5	5.4	1.6	0.9	0.8	0.8	0.2	0.2	0.3	0.1	0.1	0.2	0.2	0.0	0.1	0.2	0.1
3 Managers	0.9	2.0	4.5	1.4	1.3	1.1	1.5	0.3	0.6	0.6	0.2	0.2	0.2	0.3	0.3	0.1	0.2
4 Salesmen, other	0.4	0.8	3.2	7.6	1.8	0.8	1.8	0.1	0.5	0.3	0.5	0.5	0.5	0.0	0.0	0.1	0.0
5 Proprietors	0.6	0.7	2.4	2.0	5.2	0.4	1.7	0.2	0.3	0.1	0.4	0.6	0.5	0.4	0.5	0.7	0.0
6 Clerical	1.1	1.3	2.2	2.3	0.8	2.9	1.2	0.6	0.6	0.5	0.6	0.6	0.8	0.5	0.4	0.2	0.1
7 Salesmen, retail	1.4	1.0	2.0	2.3	1.7	1.9	3.3	0.6	0.7	0.6	0.6	1.0	0.6	0.5	0.4	0.2	0.0
Crafts																	
8 Manufacturing	0.6	0.9	1.0	0.8	1.7	0.7	0.5	3.1	1.0[1]	0.9	0.9	0.5	0.7	0.4	0.9	0.4	0.0
9 Other	0.2	0.9	0.8	0.6	1.5	0.7	2.2	1.5	3.0	1.0	0.7	0.7	0.7	0.6	0.4	0.2	0.4
10 Construction	0.2	0.5	0.4	0.5	1.6	0.5	0.2	1.2	1.8	5.3	0.5	0.6	0.4	0.5	0.7	0.4	0.5
Operatives																	
11 Manufacturing	0.3	0.6	0.7	0.6	1.0	1.0[1]	1.1	1.9	0.9	0.9	1.9	1.0	0.9	1.5	0.8	0.4	0.3
12 Other	0.3	0.5	0.8	0.9	1.3	0.7	0.7	1.0[1]	1.5	1.4	1.0	2.0	1.1	0.7	1.0[1]	0.4	0.6
13 Service	0.3	0.7	0.6	0.4	0.9	0.8	0.8	0.5	0.9	1.3	1.3	1.0[1]	3.6	1.2	1.4	0.1	0.3
Laborers																	
14 Manufacturing	0.2	0.5	0.5	0.5	0.4	1.0[1]	0.8	1.5	0.7	0.8	1.8	1.2	1.3	3.8	1.5	0.3	1.0
15 Other	0.2	0.5	0.7	0.8	1.0	0.7	0.8	0.8	1.4	1.4	1.1	1.4	1.1	1.1	2.7	0.4	0.6
16 Farmers	0.2	0.2	0.3	0.6	0.5	0.5	0.8	0.6	0.8	1.1	0.8	0.7	0.9	0.7	0.8	7.0	3.0
17 Farm Laborers	0.1	0.2	0.3	0.2	0.7	0.4	0.7	0.7	0.9	1.1	1.0	1.2	1.1	1.3	1.6	3.7	4.1

[1]Rounds to unity from above (other indices shown as 1.0 round to unity from below).
Source: Peter M. Blau and Otis Dudley Duncan, *The American Occupational Structure* (New York: John Wiley & Sons, 1967), p. 34.

TABLE 9-4. Mobility from Father's Occupation to Occupation in 1962, for Males 25-64 Years Old: Inflow Percentages

	Father's Occupation	Respondent's Occupation in 1962																
		1	2	3	4	5	6	7	8	9	10	11	12	13	14	15	16	17
	Professionals																	
1	Self-Employed	14.5	3.9	1.5	3.8	0.8	0.8	1.1	0.3	0.3	0.6	0.3	0.3	0.4	0.2	0.6	0.5	0.6
2	Salaried	7.0	9.5	4.9	5.8	2.1	3.8	3.4	1.6	1.9	0.6	2.1	2.1	1.9	1.4	0.4	0.5	0.3
3	Managers	8.7	7.9	8.7	7.0	4.0	4.4	2.6	2.7	2.6	2.2	1.4	1.2	1.0	1.8	0.7	0.3	0.3
4	Salesmen, Other	5.6	3.4	5.2	8.1	2.6	1.7	4.4	0.8	1.5	0.8	0.5	1.0	0.6	0.0	0.4	0.4	0.3
5	Proprietors	18.5	9.6	16.5	13.2	16.3	7.1	15.2	3.5	5.2	5.7	3.7	3.4	3.7	1.6	2.0	1.5	1.6
6	Clerical	4.9	7.3	4.4	5.9	2.3	4.5	2.6	2.9	3.1	1.2	1.2	1.9	3.2	1.5	1.3	0.8	0.0
7	Salesmen, Retail	0.9	2.3	3.0	4.7	2.8	1.8	2.9	1.4	0.8	1.1	1.5	1.1	1.4	0.1	1.2	0.7	0.0
	Craftsmen																	
8	Manufacturing	3.8	8.3	6.1	4.3	5.1	5.7	6.3	12.0	5.1	5.1	6.2	4.7	4.8	4.5	3.2	0.5	0.4
9	Other	4.0	7.0	7.4	7.9	6.0	8.0	6.1	6.9	11.0	5.8	5.3	7.8	5.4	3.8	4.1	1.2	1.2
10	Construction	3.0	3.2	4.4	4.1	5.8	6.2	2.6	6.9	5.5	13.7	3.6	3.9	4.6	2.6	4.9	0.8	1.8
	Operatives																	
11	Manufacturing	5.2	6.4	5.1	6.4	6.1	7.5	7.1	12.9	7.7	4.9	13.7	6.9	7.1	14.5	6.3	1.2	2.8
12	Other	2.8	7.5	4.2	5.4	6.2	6.7	6.0	6.5	8.6	6.6	6.9	10.9	7.1	6.5	6.4	1.2	4.4
13	Service	2.3	3.7	4.0	4.8	3.7	6.3	5.3	4.8	3.9	4.7	5.1	4.6	8.2	5.4	3.3	0.8	0.6
	Laborers																	
14	Manufacturing	0.0	1.0	1.2	0.4	0.8	1.3	0.8	2.6	1.5	1.0	3.2	2.2	3.0	5.9	2.4	0.6	0.9
15	Other	1.0	2.0	1.9	3.3	2.1	6.0	4.7	4.5	4.8	4.8	5.3	5.9	6.2	6.7	9.6	0.7	2.8
16	Farmers	11.2	10.8	13.3	10.1	24.3	18.3	17.6	20.1	24.4	30.4	26.6	29.4	22.8	29.5	32.6	82.0	59.7
17	Farm Laborers	0.3	0.5	0.9	0.5	1.5	1.5	2.1	2.3	2.4	3.1	3.4	3.7	3.6	3.9	5.6	2.9	14.5
18	Total[1]	100.0	100.0	100.0	100.0	100.0	100.0	100.0	100.0	100.0	100.0	100.0	100.0	100.0	100.0	100.0	100.0	100.0

[1]Columns as shown do not total 100.0, since men not reporting father's occupation are not shown separately.
Source: Peter M. Blau and Otis Dudley Duncan, *The American Occupational Structure* (New York: John Wiley & Sons, 1967), p. 39.

where their potential can be realized."[61] Spatial mobility has in many ways become a prerequisite for vertical mobility. The obvious exception is the self-employed professional, proprietor, or farmer.[62] Another exception is the rural migrant to the large city who is likely to fare more poorly than the native of the large city or his rural counterparts who do not move.[63]

A replication and extension of the Blau and Duncan research is now (1974) being carried out at the University of Wisconsin. The findings basically substantiate the earlier work. There is a continuing shift out of lower status occupations into higher status occupations.[64] This is particularly true for blacks. The gap between blacks and whites remains large and is still based on persistent, life-long discrimination. The current research also indicates that while black men are experiencing advances in terms of mobility, there is an increasing absence of black men from the labor force. The factors related to mobility in the Blau and Duncan study are also operative in this replicative effort.

The data we have been discussing have been based on the mobility patterns of males. There is a small, but growing, body of research on female mobility.[65] The most interesting findings from this research is that female and male patterns of mobility are similar when "marital mobility" is considered. This type of mobility research involves a comparison of the status of a woman's father with that of her husband. When the status of working women is considered, the similarity with male patterns is much weaker. The comparison of women's fathers' occupations

[61]*Ibid.*, p. 274.

[62]See Jack Ladinsky, "Occupational Determinants of Geographic Mobility Among Professional Workers," *American Sociological Review* 32 (April 1967).

[63]Blau and Duncan, *The American Occupational Structure*, p. 272.

[64]See Robert M. Hauser and David L. Featherman, "Trends in the Occupational Mobility of U.S. Men, 1962–1970," *American Sociological Review* 38 (June 1973), 302–10; *idem*, "Socioeconomic Achievements of U.S. Men: 1962–1972" (Paper presented at the 1973 Meetings of the American Sociological Association, New York); and *idem*, "White-nonwhite Differentials in Occupational Mobility Among Men in the United States, 1962–1972" (Paper presented at the Population Association of America, New Orleans, 1973). The pattern of mobility for women is essentially like that for men so that a separate discussion is not necessary. The mobility patterns in Europe and the United States are also apparently quite similar. See Seymour Martin Lipset and Natalie Rogoff, "Class and Opportunity in Europe and the U.S.," *Commentary* 18 (1954), 562–63. See also Seymour Martin Lipset and R. Bendix, *Social Mobility in Industrial Society* (Berkeley: University of California Press, 1959).

[65]Andrea Tyree and Judith Treas, "The Occupational and Marital Mobility of Women," *American Sociological Review* 39 (June 1974), 293–302. See also Peter Y. DeJong, Milton J. Brawer, and Stanley S. Robin, "Patterns of Female Intergenerational Mobility: A Comparison with Male Patterns of Intergenerational Mobility," *American Sociological Review* 36 (December 1971), 1033–42; Elizabeth M. Havens and Judy Corder Tully, "Female Intergenerational Mobility: Comparisons of Patterns?" *American Sociological Review* 37 (December 1972), 774–77; and Natalie Rogoff Ramsøy, "Patterns of Female Intergenerational Mobility: A Comment," *American Sociological Review* 38 (December 1973), 806–7.

with the women's own occupations shows much less occupational inheritance among women than among men.[66] Several interpretations are possible. Lack of opportunities for women, the traditional socialization process, which trained women for only a limited range of jobs, the aspirations of the women involved and so on could be offered as explanations. At present, no explanation is definitive, but these findings certainly hint at the operation of factors different from those that are important for males.

Our discussion thus far has been focused primarily on elements in the social structure, such as point of origin of the individual and level of education achieved. We have ignored the motivation or aspiration level of the individual. Featherman maintains that "no support appears for the hypothesis that achievement orientations are highly relevant to the status attainment processes in our population."[67] Using the basic framework of the Blau and Duncan study, the addition of achievement motivation or aspiration factors does not add to the predictive equations based on the structural elements.

While the data that Featherman utilizes are powerful, some question remains in regard to the importance of the motivational factor. This is particularly true in regard to the motivation for education, itself one of the structural elements. The model developed by William Sewell, Archibald Haller, and Alejandro Portes is particularly instructive here.[68] They suggest that "socioeconomic status and mental ability affect the youth's academic performance and the influence significant others have on him; that the influence of significant others and possibly his own ability affect his levels of educational and occupational aspiration; and that the levels of aspiration affect educational and occupational status attainment."[69] What this approach is saying is that motivation or aspiration is an intervening variable that is added onto the social structural factors. While more psychologically oriented approaches would stress the motivational factors, the approach suggested by Featherman raises severe questions of whether or not motivational factors are strong enough to "overcome" the structural elements. Of course, there is also the strong likelihood that structural elements, such as the status of a school, have an impact on moti-

[66]Tyree and Treas, "The Occupational and Marital Mobility of Women," pp. 299–302.

[67]David L. Featherman, "Achievement Orientations and Socioeconomic Career Attainment," *American Sociological Review* 37 (April 1972), 139.

[68]"The Educational and Early Occupational Attainment Process," *American Sociological Review* 34 (February 1969), 82–92.

[69]William H. Sewell, Archibald O. Haller, and George W. Ohlendorf, "The Educational and Early Occupational Attainment Process: Replication and Revision," *American Sociological Review* 35 (December 1970), 1015.

vations.[70] While the evidence is not totally clear, students attending a higher status school (one in which the students come from high status families) probably have motivations for more or higher educational and occupational levels, regardless of the students' point of origin.

There is another element of the individual that should be touched upon. Sociologists have long been interested in the impact on the individual of being mobile.[71] The general suggestion is that as a person moves up in social status, this

> increases mental strain and the probability of mental disease; increases superficiality and impatience; favors skepticism, cyncism, and 'misoneism'; increases social isolation and loneliness; and facilitates the disintegration of morals. All of these consequences stem from the loss of investment in standards, values and social objects associated with the mobile person's class of origin.[72]

Simpson's research suggests that this is not necessarily the case in the United States, but does seem to occur in the more status ascriptive countries that he studied in Latin America. In the more ascriptive society, a person can be occupationally mobile, but not actually mobile in terms of social class. In societies such as the United States, with an emphasis on and belief in upward mobility, the negative effects of such mobility on the individual are undoubtedly minimized.

Not all mobility is up, of course. Some people move down the occupational status structure. Simpson's data suggest that downward mobility results in an intense feeling of powerlessness in both Latin America and the United States. Earlier research by Harold Wilensky and Hugh Edwards came to a rather different conclusion, however.[73] Their analysis suggests that managers who "skid" into blue-collar work retain their belief in the system. The difference in the findings is undoubtedly based on the differences in what they were studying—Simpson was looking specifically at powerlessness as found in samples of the total population, while Wilensky and Edwards studied managers who had skidded downward.

[70]See Ernest Campbell and C. Norman Alexander, "Structural Effects and Interpersonal Relationships," *American Journal of Sociology* 71 (September 1965), 284–89, and Joel I. Nelson, "High School Context and College Plans: The Impact of Social Structure on Aspirations," *American Sociological Review* 37 (April 1972), 143–48.

[71]See Emile Durkheim, *Suicide* (Glencoe, Ill.: Free Press, 1951); Charles Horton Cooley, *Social Organization* (New York: Charles Scribner's Sons, 1909); and Pitrim A. Sorokin, *Social and Cultural Mobility* (Glencoe, Ill.: Free Press, 1927).

[72]Miles E. Simpson, "Social Mobility, Normlessness and Powerlessness in Two Cultural Contexts," *American Sociological Review* 35 (December 1970), 1014–27 summarizes Sorokin's position in these terms.

[73]"The Skidder: Ideological Adjustments of the Downward Mobile Worker," *American Sociological Review* 24 (April 1959), 215–31.

We now turn our attention to another aspect of occupations and social stratification—career patterns.

CAREER PATTERNS

In order to understand more fully the components of intragenerational mobility, we will discuss approaches to the patterning of careers. This will provide additional insights into the factors that promote or impede mobility. Miller and Form provide a useful description of the phases of careers.[74] The first, or *preparatory*, phase is the period in school and family in which the individual begins to develop the behaviors and attitudes he takes into the occupational system. The second phase is the *initial* period of part- and full-time jobs during the educational process itself. These jobs are viewed as temporary but again have relevance for the development of behaviors and attitudes important in the full-time occupation. According to Miller and Form, this period provides the individual with important expectations and orientations relevant to his career.

The third phase of the career is the *trial* period, in which the person gets his first full-time job. The period continues, with rather frequent job changes, until the person secures a more or less permanent position (Miller and Form suggest that three or more years represents permanence). During this period, the individual develops distinctive career orientations, ranging from ambition to resignation and defeat. The factors that lead to these differing orientations are unfortunately not specified. The point that orientations are probably set in this period does seem to be correct, however. The fourth, or *stable*, period is characterized by real job permanence in which the individual develops strong ties to his position and the related social structure. The stable period continues until death, retirement, or a change in jobs. If job change occurs, a new trial period is entered. The final *retirement* period is affected by work experiences but is also a distinct period in that new adjustments must be made.

The Miller and Form framework allows categorizations of individuals within their careers and identifies career related factors contributing to the presence or absence of mobility. The framework does not allow the determination of the factors associated with differing mobility patterns, but it is somewhat useful as a means of ordering information about careers.

A more analytical approach to the nature of careers is taken by

[74]Delbert Miller and William Form, *Industrial Sociology* (New York: Harper & Row, 1964), pp. 539–604.

James D. Thompson, Robert W. Avery, and Richard Carlson.[75] They note that careers are actually unfolding sequences of jobs, usually related to one another. Most careers are orderly in that the various jobs utilize related skills, training, and experience. Disrupted careers occur when unrelated occupations are part of the individual's history. According to this formulation, careers have three bases. The first factor in a career is the competence of the individual. The second factor is the aspirational pattern of the individual. Aspirations are important in terms of both their direction, toward work or family for example, and their strength. The third factor in careers is the structure of opportunities as perceived by the individual. While the actual job market sets limits, the relevant factor is the belief of the individual in regard to his place within the market. The competence, aspiration level, and structure of the job market factors contribute to the patterns followed by the individual in the course of his career.[76]

These factors are modified by the orientation of the individual toward his career, according to this formulation. He can adopt one of four career strategies. The "heuristic" strategy is one oriented toward advancement, without regard to organizational or occupational boundaries. The individual is oriented toward personal attainment as he defines it. A second strategy is tied to the occupation. The individual is sensitive to opportunities within his occupation and does not consider organizational boundaries to be important. The "organizational" strategy is concerned with opportunities within the employing organization, without strong ties to a particular occupation. The "stability" strategy is one in which considerations of another job are irrelevant for the individual, representing resignation to or satisfaction with the present position. Thompson, Avery, and Carlson correctly note that these strategies may shift over the course of a career. The strategies may also be consciously or unconsciously adopted.[77]

Careers are vitally affected by the source of the occupational role definition. For many occupations, the role is defined by the employing organization or enterprise, which sets the job requirements and the duties and responsibilities of each position. For other occupations, of course, definition of the occupational role lies within the occupation itself, as in the case of the professions. Organizations generally adopt such occupations into their job structure, "rather than creating them."[78] Another basic consideration in a career is the progression within an occupation.

[75]See *Occupations, Personnel and Careers* (Pittsburgh: Administrative Science Center, University of Pittsburgh, 1962).
[76]*Ibid.*, pp. 5–6.
[77]*Ibid.*, pp. 12–14.
[78]*Ibid.*, p. 18.

Here Thompson, Avery, and Carlson identify two forms of progression. The "early-ceiling" occupation is one in which the pinnacle or ceiling in the career is reached at an early phase in the career. The machine operator or secretary can attain top skill and salary within a short time on the job and expect to stay at the same level. The "late-ceiling" occupation, on the other hand, contains possibilities for advancement in later stages of the career.[79]

On the basis of the source of the occupational role definition and the form of progression within a career, four basic career patterns can be identified. The *enterprise-defined–early-ceiling* career involves little advance preparation for the career and rather minimal skill and aptitude expectations. The individual going into this type of work adopts the heuristic strategy at the outset of his career as he shops around between jobs and organizations. As he attains seniority and responsibilities, he will shift to an organizational strategy and then to one of stability. The *enterprise-defined–late-ceiling* occupation is typified by the executive. Advanced education is generally a prerequisite. After finishing his formal education, he will generally develop the heuristic strategy as he looks for the best opportunities for his skills. After this he utilizes the organizational strategy and changes jobs within his organization until his personal ceiling is reached or his aspirations are satisfied, at which time the stability strategy is adopted.

The colleague-defined occupations are also late and early ceilinged. The *colleague-defined–early-ceiling* career is characterized by skills transferrable from organization to organization but also rather standardized in terms of the rewards offered. Nurses, teachers, and technicians exemplify this category in that merit is evaluated by the occupation itself and by the occupations that are given higher ranking (medical doctors or engineers, for example). Since the ceiling is achieved early in the career, any movement that does occur is usually based on an attempt to improve living conditions or other nonwork activities. The occupational strategy is followed at the outset of the career with a typically early shift to the stability strategy. As in the case of the early-ceiling enterprise defined group, further advancement is sought through collective action in the form of unions or professional associations once the stable strategy is employed. The final pattern is the *colleague-defined–late-ceiling* occupation, exemplified by the professions. Once the person has met the prerequisites for entrance to the occupation, the limits to his profession are few, assuming that aspirations and perceived opportunities remain high. Thompson, Avery, and Carlson note that there really is no assurance that skill levels will be maintained among this group but that once a person

[79]*Ibid.*, pp. 16–20.

is a member of the occupation, it is assumed that he has the required skills. This type will adopt the occupational strategy, which will continue until rather late in life, when the stability strategy will be adopted. An exception to this is in the case of professionals who are dependent upon clients, where the stability strategy is adopted rather early, even though the ceiling for the individual comes later in life.[80]

These orderly patterns are typical of most careers. Disrupted careers occur when these patterns are altered, as in the case of a person who moves from a colleague-defined occupation to an enterprise-defined position. The nurse or teacher who goes into administration exemplifies this. According to the authors, this sort of disruption is likely when the occupation has an early ceiling, when the individual lacks confidence in his ability to remain visible within his occupation, or when there is a demand for rewards that cannot be anticipated in the occupation. As might be expected, the individual can face problems in these cases if he has a strong attachment to his occupation. Another disrupted pattern is from enterprise to colleague definition. This is a rare pattern, but occupations in the process of professionalization may place their members in this situation. A final form of the disrupted career is the "late heuristic strategy." In this case the individual takes a position entirely different from preceding jobs, as in the case of retired generals or diplomats who become college presidents, or bankers or business executives who become members of presidential cabinets. This type of disruption is very dependent upon visibility within the social system and is again rare.[81]

The careers of individuals are carried out in organizations, even if they are colleague defined in most cases. In the study cited earlier by Tausky and Dubin,[82] the idea of career anchorage points was introduced. This is a useful concept for managers as they used it and also for all workers. As Silk comments, "How a person feels about his current position depends on how he measures himself. He can look backward; he can look around; he can look forward.[83] This implies that people anchor their assessments of their careers on their current position in relationship to where they have been, where their peers are, or where they would like to be. Pennings's research on white-collar workers emphasizes again that even the career orientations of the individual are anchored in the social structure.[84] Pennings found that the white-collar workers in a

[80]*Ibid.*, pp. 20–32,

[81]*Ibid.*, pp. 33–40.

[82]Curt Tausky and Robert Dubin, "Career Anchorage: Managerial Mobility Aspirations," *American Sociological Review* 30 (October 1965), 725–35.

[83]Leonard S. Silk, "Is There a Lower-Middle Class Problem?" in Sar A. Levitan, ed., *Blue-Collar Workers* (New York: McGraw-Hill Book Company, 1971), p. 35.

[84]Johannes M. Pennings, "Work Value Systems of White-Collar Workers," *Administrative Science Quarterly* 15 (December 1970), 397–408.

Dutch organization had different career orientations and reactions to their work depending on the actual prospects for promotion. For those with good promotion possibilities, the orientation was more like that of the positions into which they hoped to move—looking toward the intrinsic rewards from work and the career. For those with low advancement possibilities, the orientation was more toward the extrinsic factors of employment.

SUMMARY AND CONCLUSIONS

Two themes have provided the basis for this chapter. The first is the obvious one that the occupational structure is a major determinant of the social stratification system. It has been demonstrated that occupations have become more important as status determinants than other considerations and that occupational rank is closely associated with other means of ranking, such as education or income. Occupations are central, therefore, in conceptual and methodological approaches to stratification. The second major theme is that the stratification system itself vitally affects occupations. The social origins of an individual play a major role in the determination of his eventual occupational placement. The social system and the occupational system as part of the broader system are thus in a two-directional interaction process. An important consideration in this relationship is the linkage between the two systems. This linkage is largely provided by the family and educational systems, the next topics to be considered.

10

FAMILY AND EDUCATION

From the standpoint of the individual, the importance of family and educational socialization patterns for adult occupational life is probably already quite clear. The centrality of the family in the general socialization process has been documented to the point where the issue is one of detail rather than substance. Similarly, the importance of education as both preparation and prerequisite for occupational life is well established. The intent of this chapter is not to belabor these points but to discuss some aspects of the relationships not yet covered. The family will be treated from the perspective of change. The changing occupational system has brought about changes in the family. Pressures generated by the changing family may, in turn, lead to alterations in the occupational structure in the future. The emphasis in our discussion here will be on the *reciprocal* family-occupation relationship. We will first examine large-scale historical trends and then examine some contemporary patterns and changes in detail. The approach to education also will focus on reciprocity. We will examine the compatibility and incompatibility of both the familial and the educational systems with the occupational system.

The author thanks his colleague, Prof. Jeylan Mortimer, for her assistance with this chapter.

INDUSTRIALIZATION AND THE FAMILY

The closeness of the relationship between the occupational and familial systems can be seen from the perspective of historical change. The extended family was much more prevalent in past historical periods than it is today.[1] This form involves the presence of minors, their parents, and combinations of adult siblings, grandparents, aunts and uncles, and in-laws within the same effective family unit. The exact form such a family takes depends on the cultural context, which prescribes the line of descent and place of residence. The specific form is less important, however, than the fact that the extended family is well suited to societies in which agriculture or crafts dominate the occupational structure. In the agricultural setting, a relatively exacting division of labor can be established wherein each family member has specified tasks to perform. These tasks are learned through the process of family socialization and are thus only analytically separable from general family roles. As the individual passes through the life cycle, his specific duties change according to the ascribed tasks to be performed by his age cohort. Sexual ascription occurs in a similar fashion. For craft technologies the family is also an effective work group. Many crafts involve idiosyncratic methods and trade secrets effectively transmitted in the family context. The apprentice-master relationship lends itself to the family setting very easily. The same general factors are operative in the small family business or proprietorship.

This family form was almost totally compatible with nonindustrial occupations. In many cases the products of the farm or craft were consumed on the spot or in the local area. Little competition in the form of new techniques or ideas entered the picture. The advent of industrialization, either in the past during the industrial revolution or currently for areas in the process of modernization, has drastically affected the previous compatibility. As might be expected, it is typically the younger person who is at the forefront in experiencing and perhaps rebelling against the incompatibilities. He is usually the family member who is first to seek and find employment outside the home. When he does so, the opening wedge of change is brought into the family. As he earns money outside the home, has contacts with a wide range of individuals, and is exposed to differing behaviors and values, ties to the family are

---

[1] *Household and Family in Past Time*, ed. Peter Laslett with the assistance of Richard Wall (London: Cambridge University Press, 1972), suggests that the nuclear family was in fact the dominant form of domestic group in societies with historical records. The extended family, however, remains a dominant component of the United States family of the past.

weakened. He may not want to turn over all of his income to the family, as he did previously. He is also less dependent on the family. At the same time, new behaviors or values he learns at work may well conflict with those of his family, which adds another source of discontent.[2]

As this pattern is repeated throughout a society, the family form itself evolves into the nuclear family, in which the unit is simply the husband and wife and minor children. Other members of the extended family are expected to maintain their own residences and relatively independent affective units. Viewed from another perspective, this change appears to be inevitable, inasmuch as the extended family system contains a number of elements that are incompatible with the modern occupational system. For agricultural, craft, and some proprietary pursuits, large numbers of children are an economic asset, since more workers are provided. In the industrialized and urbanized setting, however, large numbers of children become an economic liability. Children contribute little or nothing from their own "occupation" as students. At the same time, they are an additional cost factor for the members of the occupational system. Large numbers of children also appear to limit the likelihood of spatial mobility for the parents, an important requirement for both locating employment and maintaining it if relocation is demanded.

Furthermore, in the extended family, workers are almost totally selected by chance rather than by rational personnel practices. As there is as yet no control over the genetic processes, the availability and quality of workers in such families (children), is beyond the control of the work unit. At the same time, the inclusion of the aged and infirm in the extended family means that incapable workers may be part of the work force, despite the fact that their inclusion might provide important emotional gratifications for both the individual and other family members. Thus in the extended family system, the workers are often those who are considered most marginal in the contemporary industrialized situation. Both the young and the old are important parts of the labor force.

In addition to personnel problems, the extended family as an occupational unit also contains some other elements that are incompatible with the contemporary occupational situation. Its highly traditional orientation and the span of generations within the household restrict acceptance of technological innovations. The family system would tend to limit the development of the skills required for new industrial occupations. In addition, the relatively small numbers of personnel involved make the family unsuited to a highly developed division of labor.[3]

---

[2]This discussion has generally followed the lines suggested by Theodore Caplow, *The Sociology of Work* (Minneapolis: University of Minnesota Press, 1954), pp. 248–52.
    [3]*Ibid.*, p. 251.

These incompatibilities were largely resolved by the nuclear family form that became much more dominant concomitant with the process of industrialization.[4] Although the extended family form has largely disappeared, some of its elements remain, in the face of industrialization and urbanization. Whereas there is a strong expectation that the adult will establish his own residence, he must still maintain social contacts and ties with other family members.[5] Recent studies have shown that financial assistance and visiting patterns are still strongly tied to the extended family.[6] These ties do not interfere with the occupational system in that they are compatible with occupational expectations. The effective family unit remains the small nuclear group.

The nuclear family is, in all probability, the optimal arrangement for the contemporary occupational system and about as small a family unit as can be developed.[7] The pattern is particularly pronounced among the urban middle classes. It should be noted, however, that while this type of family is beneficial for the occupational structure as a whole, persons outside nuclear families often experience strains and maladjustments. In the nuclear family system, the aged, widowed, divorced, or "never married" person is largely cut-off from ongoing family relationships. At the same time, these persons have more freedom of self-determination in their occupational lives, whether they want it or not.

Vestiges of the extended family are still visible in the United States, especially among the upper classes and among working class ethnic groups. Rural patterns also appear to be following the older norms, although the birth rate differential between urban and rural areas is declining. The well-documented female dominance of the lower-class black family is also an exception. Many analyses of the latter situation point to the incongruities between this family form and the demands of the urban occupational system. In the society at large, however, the nuclear unit is clearly the normatively dominant and most prevalent type.

While the small nuclear family is generally compatible with the modern occupational system, Talcott Parsons points out normative incompatibilities between the family—extended or nuclear in form—and the

[4]Morris Zelditch, Jr., has noted a number of exceptions to this pattern in "Family, Marriage, and Kinship," in *Handbook of Modern Sociology*, ed. Robert E. L. Faris (Chicago: Rand McNally & Company, 1964), pp. 724–25, but the basic relationship described appears to be the dominant pattern.

[5]The normative significance of residential independence is indicated by the 1970 census. Only 1.3 percent of all married couples (with and without children) were found to live in "subfamily" households—in which one spouse was related to the household head. Cf. U. S. Bureau of Census, Census of Population: 1970. *General Social and Economic Characteristics. Final Report PC(1)–C1 United States Summary* (Washington, D.C.: Government Printing Office, 1972), pp. 1–497, Table 159.

[6]Zelditch, "Family, Marriage, and Kinship," pp. 725–28.

[7]See Caplow, *The Sociology of Work*, p. 253.

modern occupational structure. Parsons notes that the occupational system is characterized by an emphasis on technical efficiency and acceptance of rational criteria. The family system, on the other hand, relies upon customary behavior and highly emotional relationships. Similarly, the occupational system utilizes objective and impersonal standards of performance as appropriate criteria for status placement, while in the family, status is ascribed on the basis of age and sex.[8] This analysis points out the problems that would be involved in attempting to carry out contemporary occupational functions within the family setting. An individual would be placed in the position of having to decide which set of norms to follow when contradictory normative pressures induced by the family and occupational requirements were operant.

Separation of work from the household and the tradition of having only one member of the family, the adult male, in the occupational system have served to insulate the conflicting norms and requirements of the family and occupational systems from each other. Analysis of the traditional role of housewife clearly demonstrates the reciprocity between the occupational structure and the family. This occupation is receiving increasing attention as more and more alternatives are available to women. Housewife is still, however, the dominant role and occupation for adult women in our society.

THE HOUSEWIFE

"A housewife is a woman responsible for running her home, whether she performs the tasks herself or hires people to do them."[9] It is an occupation that has the widest range of abilities and aptitudes of any occupation. Caplow states:

> This occupation is the only one which shows approximately the same distribution of intelligence and of all aptitudes as the general population. One of the reasons for the widespread maladjustment of housewives may be inferred from the circumstances that the same job requirements are imposed on morons and women of superior intelligence. There is no age requirement either. Girls of ten years and upwards may be able to keep house competently; and it is frequently done by women in their eighties.[10]

[8]See Talcott Parsons, "The Social Structure of the Family," in *The Family: Its Function and Destiny*, ed. R. N. Anshen (New York: Harper & Row, 1949), pp. 190–96, and Talcott Parsons and Robert F. Bales, *Family, Socialization and Interaction Processes* (New York: Free Press of Glencoe, 1955), pp. 12–13.

[9]Helena Znaniecki Lopata, *Occupation: Housewife* (New York: Oxford University Press, 1971), p. 3.

[10]*The Sociology of Work*, pp. 260–61.

Caplow's analysis focuses on the particular work performed by the housewife along the same lines used in this analysis. The important affective components in child rearing and husband satisfying are ignored. Qualitative differences in the nature of, and reactions to, these affective relationships are also ignored. These appear to be central to the role of the housewife but, at the same time, these affective components are present to varying degrees in all other occupations. Despite this intentional omission, Caplow's analysis is instructive as it pinpoints some major components of the housewife's role and dilemma.

Training for the role of housewife has changed little. The socialization process is still largely informal, as it is in the case of farming and some of the crafts. The vast majority of the training occurs in interaction with the mother. Since schooling takes a great amount of the time available, the learning takes place in evenings, on weekends, and over vacations. Caplow suggests that much of the training during adolescence is specifically oriented toward courtship.[11] The results of the courtship process determine the kind of house the woman will keep as a wife. Given the relative uncertainty of this period, the girl cannot be trained for a specific housewife role. In the educational system, little attention is paid to the occupation of housewife.

> High school curriculums and even college curriculums usually included a few courses on cooking and allied matters, but these are essentially meant as symbolic gestures, and are no more likely to train housewives than the shop courses offered to boys under similar conditions are likely to produce skilled carpenters. Full-scale training in home economics or household management is limited to correctional institutions, schools for the retarded, and a few colleges of agriculture.[12]

If this analysis is correct, then the rather harsh conclusion could be reached that the role itself perhaps does not require much training and, as Caplow suggests, anyone can do it.

The range of activities included in the housewives' role is enormous and runs from interior decorating to gardening, from diaper changing to gourmet cooking, and from mopping floors to arranging flowers. Caplow identifies three major components of the role under which the spectrum of activities can be arranged: *food preparation*, including activities from purchasing to eventual clearing of dishes; *cleaning*; and *child care*.[13] For the very young child, it is the mother who is the major socializer. This fact lends great importance to the housewife role, as early socialization sets the stage for what occurs throughout life. Although we do not know

[11]*Ibid.*, p. 261.
[12]*Ibid.*, p. 262.
[13]*Ibid.*

exactly how much of an individual's mental skills are "set" during early childhood, the indication seems to be that these years are crucial as the basis upon which later socialization takes place. Of the three activities, the one that varies the most is child care, since it usually is not present at the onset of the career and ends long before the career itself does.

In tracing a typical career, Caplow notes that at marriage the work load is usually quite light, since the living quarters are small and the duties involve only two people. The husband usually helps during this phase, and the wife typically is employed outside the home. This is generally the period in which the greatest amount of learning occurs. The arrival of a child drastically alters the role. There is little formal preparation for the work of child care, since the small family unit generally precludes much exposure to the processes involved and baby-sitting offers a limited experience for only some girls. Caplow states:

> Further, for reasons too complex to explore here, the entire pattern of middle-class child raising is marked by strong anxiety feelings centered on the child. This anxiety can only be held in check if the baby is raised by the most perfected technic available. The mainstay of the housewife's special literature is the provision of timely advice to mothers. The manufacture of clothing, furniture, and miscellaneous devices for babies is a major industry, and few medical specialties are more profitable than pediatrics. The presence of this elaborate apparatus to prevent or mitigate errors in child raising technic reassures the housewife, but at the same time strengthens the basis of her anxiety and strengthens the elements of compulsive ritual which are already present. Moreover, the whole complex —like any dynamic culture complex—tends to expand by continually accepting innovations, and each of the activities involved in child care has a tendency to grow increasingly complicated. It is not unusual for the feeding of a very small baby to require more time, effort, and equipment than the feeding of the rest of the household.[14]

This intense phase is, by definition, limited since the child will grow and enter the outside world through the educational system. As nursery and prenursery schools become more prevalent, the age for leaving the family for at least a portion of the day diminishes. There are undoubtedly limits on the extension of formal child care systems outside the home, but the intense period is lessening in its span. As the child gets into the regular school system and can begin self-discipline, with its related reduction of the work load for the family, the role requirements of child care are correspondingly lessened. The presence of more than one child will extend this period, but at most the intense child care period comprises only a small proportion of the overall career. Caplow notes that the intense period of child care usually alters the manner in which the

[14]*Ibid.*, p. 263.

other role requirements are met. The husband may help the wife with some of their activities during this period or provide assistance in the form of labor-saving devices or help from outside the home.[15] While the time spent in physical care of the child declines, the role of the mother actually expands as she interacts with other parents, takes the child to the doctor, and does the myriad of other things that bring her into contact with people who interact with her child or children.[16] The expectation remains that this is a *maternal* responsibility. One of the real ironies is the fact that if a male spends a lot of time with his family and children, he can be considered somewhat of a loafer.[17] For the female, the definition is the reverse—it is her "duty."

As the child or children approach adolescence, the work load is drastically reduced. It also appears to be a period of crisis for the woman. While her husband is typically at the period of greatest involvement in his own occupation, particularly in middle-class families, the wife is almost without an occupation. The range of alternatives open to the wife during this period include involvement in community activities, self-entertainment in clubs and social groups, self-improvement through varied forms of education, or returning to the labor force. The last alternative is difficult since the woman has been out of the labor force for some time and also faces the problems discussed above. Recognizing this dilemma, a number of colleges, universities, and other educational organizations are beginning to provide retraining facilities specifically oriented toward this group.[18] There appears to be a growing awareness of the problems involved by potential employers. Nevertheless, the period is one of crisis and potentially may leave the woman in partial idleness for over half of her life. Caplow states that the housewife at fifty comprises the "most conspicuously maladjusted segment of the population."[19]

Caplow's analysis is closely paralleled by Lopata's more recent research. She notes that the new housewife has an expanding social circle until the birth of the first child, at which time the woman puts more of her energies into the mother role. This is a satisfying period because it permits a good deal of autonomy and has intrinsic rewards. As more children come on the scene and the requirements of the role increase, dissatisfactions enter the picture. The "full house plateau" is reached fairly early in the marriage, with the full house emptying as children leave to go to school and engage in their own activities. The housewives

[15]*Ibid.*, p. 264.
[16]Cynthia Epstein, *Woman's Place: Options and Limits in Professional Careers* (Berkeley: University of California Press, 1970), 110.
[17]*Ibid.*, p. 99.
[18]See U.S. Department of Labor, Women's Bureau, Pamphlet 10, *Continuing Education Programs for Women* (Washington, D.C.: Government Printing Office, 1966).
[19]*The Sociology of Work*, p. 266.

participate in other activities at this time, of course, ranging from hobbies such as art or sewing to voluntary activities in the community. (An interesting facet of all of this, of course, is the extent to which the voluntary activities of women should be "counted" as an occupation. It would appear that many women actually do unpaid work that is not typically considered in terms of its economic and social consequences for the community.) After the full house plateau, the period of the "shrinking circle" is entered as the children leave home permanently. This situation is exacerbated by the common occurrence of widowhood, which puts financial, social, sexual, recreational, and housing strains on the woman.[20]

The housewife's role, then, can be analyzed in occupational terms. It contains intrinsic and extrinsic rewards and motivations. A major reward is the "vicarious achievement" that a woman may feel as her husband experiences success in the occupational system.[21] In many cases, the woman is a distinct help to the husband through her own social skills and relationships in the community. Papanek notes that many women almost become extensions of their husbands' employing organizations, whether the organizations are corporations, the government, the military, or universities. Papanek finds this situation to be particularly true among women who themselves are educated and have experienced life in a large organization. In these cases, the housewife is perhaps more than a vicarious participant in the occupational system.

This type of vicarious enjoyment is undoubtedly linked to husbands whose occupations permit the husband intrinsic satisfaction. John Scanzoni's survey of Indianapolis residents demonstrated a clear linkage between socioeconomic status and marital satisfaction for both men and women.[22] The higher the respondents' socioeconomic status (as indicated by education, income, or the husband's occupation) the more likely they were to describe their marriages as cohesive and happy. Wives whose husbands did not have rewarding careers felt less satisfied with their marriages and their spouses. This pattern is consistent with an assumption that vicarious satisfaction with the husband's job contributes to the wife's marital happiness. Scanzoni suggests that men of higher socioeconomic status are more apt to discuss their jobs with their wives, thus enabling vicarious participation to occur.[23] The pattern is also consistent with an exchange model of the family which Scanzoni posits. In short, the husband provides socioeconomic status and material comforts to the wife in exchange for her emotional and domestic support. When the

[20]Lopata, *Occupation: Housewife*, pp. 32–44.

[21]Hanna Papanek, "Men, Women, and Work: Reflections on the Two-Person Career," *American Journal of Sociology* 78 (January 1973), 852–72.

[22]John Scanzoni, *Opportunity and the Family* (New York: Free Press, 1970).

[23]*Ibid.*, pp. 19–21.

husband's status and income are high, he gives her more of what she feels is her "due," and, in gratitude and exchange, she is a more responsive and satisfactory companion and helpmate to him. The husband, in turn, is motivated to reciprocate in terms of emotional support, companionship, and affection.

The housewife role, like occupations that are considered within the labor force, reveals important strains and sources of dissatisfaction as well as vicarious, and more direct and tangible, rewards.[24] Dissatisfaction may result from inadequate preparation and socialization, isolation from adult contact and support in the nuclear family, and an absence of a sense of accomplishment resulting from the "open-ended" character of the work (as indicated by the expression "a woman's work is never done.") Much satisfaction in the role is of a vicarious nature or otherwise dependent on others. The housewife thus may be highly vulnerable to a sense of failure or dissatisfaction resulting from others' inability to succeed—the husband's low occupational achievement, the children's personality and social maladjustments, or their failure to succeed in school. This dependence on others, coupled with the generalized subservience of this traditional female role, may be particularly problematic when a culture places such emphases on the values of independence, individualism, activism, and personal achievement,[25] and when education, common to both sexes, tends to instill these values. The "shrinking circle" or "empty nest syndrome" described above, apparently leaves some women frustrated and desperate in their middle and old age.[26] Gove's finding that married women have consistently higher rates of mental illness than married men underscores the strains and problems inherent in women's traditional role.[27]

While in some sense wives may be said to "earn" both intrinsic and extrinsic rewards, never do they earn wages or salaries for being a housewife. John Kenneth Galbraith estimates that the wife should be paid $257 per week or $13,364 per year, at 1970 wage rates.[28] "Were the workers so employed subject to pecuniary compensation, they would be by far the largest single category in the labor force. The value of the services

[24]Gove discusses the numerous strains of the housewife role. See Walter R. Gove, "The Relationship between Sex Roles, Marital Status, and Mental Illness." *Social Forces* 51 (September 1972), 34–43.

[25]Robin M. Williams, Jr., *American Society: A Sociological Interpretation.* (New York: Alfred A. Knopf, 1970), pp. 452–502.

[26]Pauline B. Bart, "Depression in Middle-aged Women." In *Woman in Sexist Society*, ed. Vivian Gornick and Barbara K. Moran (New York: Basic Books, 1971).

[27]Walter R. Gove, "The Relationship between Sex Roles, Marital Status, and Mental Illness."

[28]John Kenneth Galbraith, "The Economics of the American Housewife," *The Atlantic Monthly*, 232 (August 1973), 78–83.

of housewives has been calculated, somewhat impressionistically, at roughly one-fourth of total Gross National Product."[29] Galbraith also points out that the housewife is the major administrator of consumption, enabling the ever-increasing accumulation, use, and maintenance of goods necessary in an economy dependent on continual expansion and "built-in" obsolescence. (Still, the male generally retains authority over the use of the family income, maintaining women's subordinate position.)[30] In spite of her economic contributions and the unmeasured, intangible, and, probably more important, expressive, supportive, and child-rearing functions, the housewife has low prestige in the eyes of many, and when asked what they do, many women will declare, "I'm just a housewife." Today many young women are questioning the value of this traditional status, questioning whether the rewards offered by our society are at all commensurate with the services and functions traditionally rendered by women.

FEMALE LABOR FORCE PARTICIPATION AND ITS IMPACT ON THE FAMILY

The traditional, and stereotyped, situation in which the father (of two or three normal and attractive children) goes off happily to work while the woman stays at home and is the happy housewife and mother is in reality becoming a myth. What the stereotype misses, of course, are those situations in which the woman is the only or major breadwinner or where both male and female work, with or without children present. These increasingly standard situations often present conflicts and dilemmas because of the incompatibilities of occupational and family norms and behavioral requirements.

"Families with more than one worker have increased to the point that [March 1972] they account for almost 55 percent of all families headed by married men in the labor force."[31] According to Hayge, this statistic is due to the large increase in young working wives. There has been "growing consensus on the desirability of controlling the number and timing of births; more women had college training and wanted to pursue careers; demand for women as white collar workers had been growing rapidly; and inflationary trends led some of these women, even with young children, to work."[32]

---

[29]*Ibid.*, p. 79.
[30]*Ibid.*, p. 80.
[31]Howard Hayge, "Labor Force Activity of Married Women," *Monthly Labor Review* 96 (April 1973), 31.
[32]*Ibid.*

What has happened is that the norm has shifted, and now both husband and wife are expected to pursue occupations simultaneously, at least for some period in their lives. The trends cited above appear to be continuing so that this pattern will become increasingly normative in future years. We will examine some of the results in later discussions.

For the moment, our interest will focus in more detail on *why* there is an increase in the participation of married women in the labor force. The major reason is economic. As a result of the changes in the economic and occupational structure discussed in the earlier part of this chapter, many women can make a greater contribution to their family's economic livelihood and standard of living by entering the labor force than by staying at home. No longer is the labor of several children needed to operate the family farm or business. Devoting one's life to the production and rearing of large numbers of children becomes a highly expensive proposition, in view of the cost of their care and education, when weighed against the alternative option to work and thereby increase the family's income. The process of industrialization separated the family from the workplace and precluded the woman's previous contributions to her family's agricultural, craft, or commercial activities.[33] Continuing inflation in modern industrial societies further exacerbates the costliness of the traditional wifely role. Women are not in the labor force for "pin money."[34]

> They work to secure additional income to provide their families with a car, home, or college educations that could not otherwise be afforded. The average woman worker is a secretary who increases family income by about 25 percent, and this permits many lower-middle-class families to achieve middle-class status, something the husband could not achieve for his family alone.[35]

As a result of these trends, it could be argued that the nuclear family would be even more compatible with the occupational structure if some of the woman's major family functions were carried out by nonfamily agencies, freeing her from the confines of the home and facilitating her occupational participation.

In addition to these broad economic needs and trends, there are

[33]Jessie Bernard discusses these changes in her book, *Women and the Public Interest* (Chicago: Aldine, 1971). Cf. chap. 4, "The Functions of Women," pp. 65–87.

[34]See Joan E. Crowley, Teresa E. Levitin, and Robert P. Quinn, "Facts and Fictions About the American Working Woman," Survey Research Center, University of Michigan, 1974.

[35]*Work in America: Report of a Special Task Force to the Secretary of Health, Education, and Welfare*, prepared under the auspices of the W. E. Upjohn Institute for Employment Research (Cambridge, Mass.: Massachusetts Institute of Technology Press, 1973), p. 63.

additional family-related factors that influence which wives will work. In a study of British married women workers, Viola Klein found that the attitude of the husband was an important consideration. Klein's findings, summarized in Table 10-1, indicate a strong relationship between the husband's approval of work and the fact of working. Essentially the same finding was reported by Mildred Weil, on the basis of a study of 200 suburban residents in New Jersey.[36] The family factor thus enters the occupational picture at the level of the dynamics of interaction between husband and wife. Existing evidence does not allow one to ascertain whether wives who wish to work are usually deterred by their husbands' negative attitudes or whether the husband's attitude is itself influenced by the wife's desires—her motivation to work or the benefits (especially the added income) of her actual employment. Klein's findings are inter-

TABLE 10-1. Men's Stated Views on Employment of Married Women (Classified by Marital Status and Type of Wives' Employment)

Attitude to Married Women Having Jobs	Percentage of Married Men Whose Wives Have				
	Full-Time Job	Part-Time Job	No Paid Job	Total	Single Men
	%	%	%	%	%
Unconditional disapproval	14	4	45	32	28
Unconditional approval	52	42	11	23	31
Approval conditional on:					
there being no young children	19	14	18	17	15
household being in financial difficulties	5	14	8	9	7
not working too long	1	2	1	1	2
its being a part-time job		6	1	2	1
miscellaneous circumstances		7	2	3	2
Neutral: neither approves nor disapproves	2	4	4	4	3
Neutral: but specifically says it is up to wife	3	3	3	3	3
Neutral: but disapproves if there are young children	3	2	5	4	2
Don't know	1	1	2	2	5
Not stated					1
Total	100	100	100	100	100
Total in Numbers	104	118	422	644	287

Source: Viola Klein, *Britain's Married Women Workers* (London: Routledge & Kegan Paul, Ltd., 1965), p. 66. (New York: Humanities Press, Inc.)

[36]Mildred Weil, "An Analysis of the Factors Influencing Married Women's Actual or Planned Work Participation." *American Sociological Review* 26 (February 1961), pp. 91–96.

esting in terms of the distribution of approval and disapproval along social class lines. She states:

> There is a distinct class differentiation in the answers. The higher the social class, the greater the percentage of married men approving, both conditionally and unreservedly, of married women being gainfully employed. The largest percentage of expressed disapproval is to be found among (the lower classes) and among men whose wives are not employed. The class distinction is, however, reversed among single men.[37]

The discrepancy between the responses of the married and single men, at least in the upper classes, is explained by Klein as probably resulting from the fact that the single men utilize their own mothers, who probably didn't work, as their models and have not had close contact with women who desire to work.

When the reasons reported by women for working outside the home are analyzed, several distinct patterns can be seen. The first is that financial considerations are the major factor regardless of their husbands' income or their own education. Tables 10-2 and 10-3 indicate these patterns. Table 10-2, based on the Klein study, shows that the importance of financial consideration increases as the women's socioeconomic status decreases. Table 10-3, based on a sample of 1957 college graduates who

TABLE 10-2. Main Reasons for Employment by Social Class of Respondent[1]

Main Reasons for Going Out to Work	Class			Total
	Upper	Middle	Low	
	%	%	%	%
Financial reasons	43	67	79	73
Need of mental stimulus (not enough to do at home, mind not occupied)	14	20	11	13
Enjoys it	21	10	4	7
Need of social stimulus (likes meeting people, company, not so lonely)	4	12	4	6
Works with husband, helps him	25	10	2	6
Independence (money of one's own)		4	2	2
Other answers (e.g., to make use of training, sense of achievement, "keeps me healthy," "keeps me young," absence of husband, own business, etc.)	18	6	9	9

[1]This table adds to more than 100 percent because some respondents gave more than one reason.
Derived from: Viola Klein, *Britain's Married Women Workers*, p. 37.

[37]Viola Klein, *Britain's Married Women Workers*, p. 37.

TABLE 10-3. Main Reason of Graduates for Working, by Marital Status, 1964

Main Reason for Working	Total Number	Total Percent	Single	Married (Husband Present) Total	Married (Husband Present) With Children Under 6 Years[1]	Married (Husband Present) 6-17 Years	With No Children	Widowed, Separated, Divorced
Graduates represented	42,845		12,685	27,175	13,654	2,192	11,329	2,985
Percent		100	100	100	100	100	100	100
To support self and/or others	14,881	35	78	8	5	10	12	92
To increase family income	13,509	32	([2])	49	51	55	46	2
To have a career	5,763	13	17	13	9	21	16	3
To get actual work experience	1,694	4	1	6	7	4	5	1
Like to work	1,402	3	1	5	4	3	6	1
To do something worthwhile	742	2	2	2	2	1	2	
To use talents and keep alert	330	1	([2])	1	2	2	([2])	
To help husband establish a career	1,929	5		7	8	1	7	
To escape house-hold routine	2,360	6		9	12	4	5	
Other reasons	235	1	([2])	1	1		1	

[1]Includes some graduates who had children 6 to17 years of age also.
[2]Less than 0.5 percent.
Source: U.S. Department of Labor, Women's Bureau, *College Women, Seven Years After Graduation, Resurvey of Women Graduates—Class of 1957* (Washington, D.C.: Government Printing Office, 1966), Bulletin 292, p. 41.

were surveyed in 1964, shows the obvious relationship between marital status and working patterns. These figures also suggest the relativity of financial considerations. In this study, over half of the 1957 graduates were working in 1964. For those who were married, the likelihood is that their husbands' incomes were reasonably high, since most would also be college graduates. The financial consideration in working for this group thus is not subsistence but the desire to obtain more comforts or luxuries or to develop savings programs.

These data also suggest that women work for the same configuration of reasons as do men. The configuration of reasons takes a somewhat different form, however. Crowley et. al.,[38] on the basis of their analysis

[38]Crowley, Levitin, and Quinn, "The American Working Woman."

of data from a large national sample in the United States, suggest that women are not more satisfied with undemanding jobs or less concerned with job challenge and opportunity to advance. If there is not a pressing economic need, however, women tend to be less inclined to work than men. Women are more concerned with matters of comfort and convenience and assign less importance to autonomy on the job than do men. These differences may in part result from earlier socialization, as different values for males and females are emphasized. Still, the basic finding from this study is that there are more similarities than differences between working men and women.

James A. Sweet has summarized the factors associated with wives' employment.[39] While his data come from an analysis of 1960 census materials and do not reflect many of the changes of the past decade and a half, the factors he cites remain relevant. The first factor is one we have already discussed—economic need. Sweet notes that where the economic need is the greatest, the income is the lowest, and that consequently the wives' contributions to the family income is not as great as where the need is less. This pattern is even more pronounced in black families than in white.[40]

The second important factor is employability and earnings potential —those women who are highly employable and have high earnings potential are more likely to be employed. The third factor is the family situation in regard to the presence or absence of young children. The fourth factor is employment opportunities. It would appear that there has been an increase in such opportunities in recent years, a situation that may become an increasingly significant factor when combined with employability.

The final factor considered by Sweet is what he calls psychological variables. They include the desire for upward mobility, the desire for a sense of competence, and other general work motivations.[41] Again, this set of variables is certainly of increased importance as women no longer are socialized into believing that the only role for a woman is that of the traditional wife. As more and more women enter and stay in the occupational world, we will undoubtedly see an increase in the number of dual-career families.

DUAL-CAREER FAMILIES

Dual-career families are particularly interesting because of the interplay of family and occupational norms and values. These are families

[39]James A. Sweet, *Women in the Labor Force* (New York: Seminar Press, 1973).
[40]*Ibid.*, p. 169.
[41]*Ibid.*, pp. 6–24.

in which both wife and husband are pursuing careers while maintaining a family together. They may or may not have children. An important attribute of the dual-career family is the fact that both family members are career oriented. It is more than just work for both. Most discussions of dual-career families thus have focused on situations in which both wife and husband are professionals or executives, such as when the wife is a dentist and the husband an engineer. This type of situation has to be distinguished from the extremely rare situation in which the wife and husband share a single job, as in the case where the two people hold a single professorship. In the dual-career situation, each marriage partner has her or his own career.

Analyses of dual-career families come to two basic conclusions. The first is that the traditional pattern of male dominance tends to continue. The man's career is typically viewed as more important than the woman's,[42] as can be seen when the husband is offered a better position in another location and the wife goes along despite her professional ties and interests. The reverse happens much less frequently. Holmstrom suggests that the wife is often expected to support the husband's career, much as in the traditional family situation, even at the expense of her own.[43] The wife also tends to remain the central figure in terms of child care.[44] Thus, the traditional sexual division of labor seems to remain even when both spouses work. Janice N. Hedges and Jeanne K. Barnett found that in professional families, when both partners work, the woman is more likely to shop, prepare dinner, and do the laundry, while the man does repairs, carries out the trash and garbage, and does other heavier chores. Both do the dishes and cook breakfast and share in child care.[45] Previous socialization and the normative expectations and sanctions that one receives in relations with parents, relatives, and friends tend to maintain the traditional and male-dominated patterns.

In an analysis of 53 couples in dual-career families, T. Neal Garland found four basic patterns or styles.[46] The first was the *traditional* situation in which the husband is the major breadwinner, and considerations of the home and children are the focus for the wife. In this case, the

[42]Lynda Lytle Holmstrom, *The Two-Career Family* (Cambridge, Mass.: Schenkman Publishing Company, 1973), pp. 29–85.

[43]*Ibid.*, pp. 157–160.

[44]Rhona Rapoport and Robert N. Rapoport, "The Dual-Career Family: A Variant Pattern and Social Change," *Human Relations* 22 (January 1969), 3–30. See also Rhona and Robert Rapoport, *Dual-Career Families* (Baltimore: Penguin Books, 1971).

[45]Janice N. Hedges and Jeanne K. Barnett, "Working Women and the Division of Household Tasks," *Monthly Labor Review* 95 (April 1972), 10–11. They also found that women who work spend less time per week on housework than their nonworking equivalents.

[46]"The Better Half? The Male in the Dual Professional Family," in Constantina Safilios-Rothschild (ed.), *Toward a Sociology of Women* (Lexington, Mass.: Xerox College Publishing, 1972), pp. 199–215.

wife's occupation often assumes the status of a "hobby," which she is expected to curtail or drop completely if it impinges on the needs of other members of the household. The *neo-traditional* situation is one in which both careers are taken into consideration in family decision making but the husband's career is still viewed as more important, and the wife has primary responsibility for child care. Eighty-nine percent of the families studied were in these first two categories, again suggesting the perpetuation of traditional patterns. The third situation is rather rare. It is the *matriarchal* one in which the woman, who has higher occupational status, is the major breadwinner and has the most power in the family. The final pattern is the *egalitarian* one, in which there is an equal division of labor. In this study, only one family was considered to be truly egalitarian.

The second basic conclusion in regard to dual-career families is that they are subject to severe strain. This strain results from multiple factors, many of which relate to the incompatibility of occupational and family demands—particularly the need to accomplish the domestic and child care functions of single career families while both spouses are pursuing demanding occupations. In short, neither spouse has a person working full time in the domestic arena, in effect supporting his or her career. This dilemma is certainly related to the fact that as the status level of occupations increases, the proportion of working women who are unmarried also increases.[47] There may be potential and real competition between spouses for work time and occupational achievement; both husbands' and wives' careers may require travel or working in the evenings and on weekends. As a result, there may be insufficient time to spend together in expressive, recreational activities with family and friends. The multiple social networks in which each person is engaged, as well as the need to rely upon external child care support, may produce additional strains. Frequently the "sheer physical overload of tasks and their apportionment is adumbrated by a social-psychological overload,"[48] resulting from the uncertainties and problems that occur when traditional expectations and norms are being breached. In short, the dual-career family is one in which both husband and wife experience a great deal of stress generated by both occupational and family demands.

The conclusion that dual-career families experience stress must be

[47]Elizabeth M. Havens, "Women, Work, and Wedlock: A Note on Female Marital Patterns in the United States," *American Journal of Sociology* 78 (January 1973), 975–81. This pattern is opposite to the one for men, where those in lower status are more unlikely to be unmarried.

[48]Rapoport and Rapoport, "The Dual-Career Family: A Variant Pattern and Social Change." This discussion is based on Rapoport and Rapoport and Holmstrom, *The Two-Career Family.*

balanced by the rewards and satisfactions experienced by women who pursue careers. The ability to cope with these stress-producing circumstances also will vary depending on the immediate objective circumstances of the family (financial resources, number and ages of children, the availability of relatives close by to aid in family emergencies, etc.) and the internal personality strengths, motivations, and values instilled through the process of childhood and adult socialization. The high work motivation and intrinsic occupational satisfactions experienced by career-oriented women might mitigate and offset strains that would be less tolerable if such rewards were not present. Susan R. Orden and Norman M. Bradburn found that marital happiness when both husband and wife work is related to whether or not the woman works by choice rather than necessity.[49] That is, if the woman chooses to enter the labor market, both husband and wife experience greater marital happiness than if the woman is forced into the labor market by necessity. This is not the case, however, if there are preschool children in the family. Here, entry into the labor market for either reason is related to less happiness as compared with women who choose to remain at home during this period. This latter finding is probably related to the increased family responsibilities and resultant time "overloads" associated with the presence of preschool children.

Furthermore, the extent to which the husband is supportive of his wife's working and is family-oriented in the sense of deriving major satisfactions from family activities and relationships is also related to the dual-career family's success and happiness. Lotte Bailyn's study of British dual-career couples found that marriages were notably unhappy when career-oriented women married men who considered their families relatively unimportant as a source of satisfaction.[50]

It should also be noted that considerable stress is experienced in many single-career families when the wife wants a career and cannot have one. This situation can occur because of the husband's resistance, the absence of opportunity, the inability to adequately reconcile conflicting demands of traditional female and occupational roles, or as a result of a combination of these factors.

The dual-career family is the exception, rather than the rule.[51] Whether or not the pattern will become more prevalent or not is con-

[49]"Working Wives and Marriage Happiness," *American Journal of Sociology* 74 (January 1969), 392–407.

[50]"Career and Family Orientations of Husbands and Wives in Relation to Marital Happiness," *Human Relations* 23 (April 1970), pp. 97–113.

[51]Much of this discussion is based on Janet Hunt's review of Rapoport and Rapoport's *Dual-Career Families*, in *Contemporary Sociology: A Journal of Reviews* 2 (November 1973), pp. 635–637.

tingent upon several changes—in the values, role structure, and life style of the family, in the structure of occupations, and in the society as a whole.[52] It is generally recognized that husbands must become more family oriented, sharing (not just helping their wives with) domestic and child care activities, and thus male-female roles must become less bifurcated, if more women are to pursue demanding occupations.[53] The requirements for home and child care have not been adequately resolved and institutionalized for dual-career families. Since female domestic help in the home is in many ways the antithesis of movements to upgrade the status of women, some have proposed new residential and communal living arrangements (involving the sharing of domestic and economic support roles by several families), or the establishment of routine house cleaning commercial enterprises, such as are now often used in commercial establishments.[54] Day and extended child care facilities outside the home are not always available or acceptable to traditionally high-middle-class standards. The occupational system must also be altered to permit part-time and discontinuous careers, to accommodate parents during the period of peak child care demands. Furthermore, it must become legitimate for husbands and wives equally to take time off from work for routine or emergency child care—e.g., paternity leaves, maternity leaves, or sick child leaves—to allow equal time for work and domestic functions on the part of both spouses.[55] It has also been suggested that the emphasis on high individualistic achievement must be altered significantly if men and women are to share work and family functions and thus forego the 70- to 80-hour work week often necessary to reach peak levels of professional and business careers.[56]

Despite the problems and uncertainties of the dual-career family, it is unlikely to disappear. Changes in the family because of urbanization, industrialization, and the separation of work from the household increased women's motivation to enter the labor force. Current societal affluence and the increasing education of women, coupled with changing values and the trends toward zero population growth, small family size, early child bearing, and close spacing of children, have increased women's

[52]Safilios-Rothschild details the many social changes that would enhance the feasibility of dual-career families. Cf. Constantina Safilios-Rothschild, *Women and Social Policy* (Englewood Cliffs, N.J.: Prentice-Hall, 1974). See also Alice S. Rossi, "Equality Between the Sexes: An Immodest Proposal," *Daedalus* 93 (Spring 1964) 607–52.

[53]See Alice S. Rossi, "Equality Between the Sexes"; Alice S. Rossi, "Sex Equality: The Beginning of Ideology," *The Humanist* 29 (September/October 1969); and Safilios-Rothschild, *Women and Social Policy*, chap. 3, "Social Policy to Liberate Men."

[54]See Safilios-Rothschild, *Women and Social Policy*, pp. 24–25.

[55]*Ibid.*, pp. 21–22.

[56]For further discussion of this issue, see S. M. Miller, "The Making of a Confused, Middle-aged Husband," *Social Policy* 2 (July/August 1971) 33–39.

desire and capacity to pursue careers.[57] These economic, demographic, and social trends make it likely that the dual-career family will become increasingly prevalent in future years.

ADDITIONAL FAMILY OCCUPATIONAL LINKAGES

There are additional influences of the family on the occupational structure above and beyond the point of women working. According to Lee Rainwater, the family serves as a basic source for the motivation to work for the stable working-class male.[58] The "central role" for the male is that of provider for his family. This pushes many men, particularly at younger ages when their families are just getting going, to moonlight or hold second or even third jobs.

> Wives sometimes recount incredibly demanding work schedules on the part of their young husbands—schedules that involve 10 to 14 hours of work a day at two different jobs. In this way, a young man who is able to command only two-thirds the median family income level on a single job may be able to lift the family's income above the median. Given the impermanence of some of these jobs, the family's income over a two- or three-year period may average around the median or somewhat less, but in any case the money provided by the second job can make the difference between a marginal working-class life and incremental approximation of a mainstream life.[59]

A study of affluent British workers by Goldthorpe et al. similarly noted that the men's work orientations were highly influenced by their families.[60] An unanswered question in this, of course, is how important would the family be if the work itself provided a great deal of intrinsic interest? The question is not one of choosing between work and family but rather whether or not a person would utilize the family as the sole source of intrinsic interest if the work itself provided such interest.

The occupational situation of the male likewise has important implications for the family. Research on unemployment suggests that when a man is unemployed, his power within the family diminishes. Joan

---

[57]Ridley discusses these trends and their implications for women. See Jeanne Clare Ridley, "The Effects of Population Change on the Roles and Status of Women: Perspective and Speculation," in *Toward a Sociology of Women* ed. Constantina Safilios-Rothschild (Lexington, Mass.: Xerox, 1972), pp. 372–86.

[58]Lee Rainwater, "Making the Good Life: Working Class Family and Life Style," in Sar A. Levitan, (ed.), *Blue Collar Workers*, (New York: McGraw-Hill Book Company, 1971).

[59]*Ibid.*, p. 215.

[60]John H. Goldthorpe et al., *The Affluent Worker: Industrial Attitudes and Behavior* (Cambridge: Cambridge University Press, 1970).

Aldous reports that among lower-class families the income of the husband is directly related to his participation in the family. The more he earns, the greater his power and involvement.[61] In Scanzoni's Indianapolis survey, while joint decision-making by the spouses was found to increase with the husband's occupational prestige, wives of higher status men assigned more legitimacy to their husbands as the decision-making heads of their families.[62] A consistent finding from another study is that college students from professional families report that their fathers are more central and unilateral decision makers than students of lower socioeconomic origin.[63] While there is thus a general relationship between occupational status and status within the family system, the relationship can become curvilinear in that very deep involvement in an occupation can lead to withdrawal from the family. Such involvement is particularly likely among persons in high status occupations, although it may also occur for those in lower status occupations.

The high-status occupation of the husband may also affect family relationships when he moves ahead of his wife in terms of educational or social accomplishments; the wife may perform her housewife and mother role very adequately but not keep up with her husband, who operates in a challenging intellectual and social milieu. Furthermore, occupations that demand a great deal of time away from home, such as truck or bus drivers or some salesmen, or that have hours incompatible with normal family relationships, have an additional impact on the family simply because the man is not available for participation.[64]

Occupations, as links to the wider social structure, thus have a significant impact on marital relationships. There are also occupationally-linked differences in parental values that may affect parental role performance. Melvin Kohn's nationwide survey has provided substantial evidence that autonomy-related dimensions of a man's work, such as its complexity, functional focus, and closeness of supervision, influence child-rearing values related to self-direction and conformity.[65] A recurrent theme in this and other socialization research is that fathers attempt to inculcate attitudes and values in their children, and particularly in their sons, that have proven useful in their own occupations. Joan Aldous has noted that professionals and executives have rather clear ideas of the kinds of sons they want to have. They attempt to instill in their sons

---

[61]Joan Aldous, "Parental and Marital Function as Related to Occupational Status," (University of Minnesota, 1967), pp. 3–4.

[62]John Scanzoni, *Opportunity and the Family*, chap. 6.

[63]Jeylan T. Mortimer, personal communication.

[64]Joan Aldous, "Parental and Marital Function as Related to Occupational Status," pp. 6–7.

[65]Melvin Kohn, *Class and Conformity: A Study in Values* (Homewood, Ill.: Dorsey, 1969).

the behaviors and mannerisms appropriate to their own status. Less concern about their daughters is expressed, under the assumption that their daughters will not be as involved in occupations outside the home.[66] The analysis of the work orientations of men and women by Crowley, Levitin, and Quinn points strongly at early socialization as the major influence in determining some of the differences by sex that they found.[67] While there is some question as to whether early socialization into sex roles must necessarily last into adulthood, the fact remains that young girls are taught to be different from young boys. Whether traditional sex role socialization will persist when mothers are increasingly entering the labor force is also an open question. Sandra Tangri's analysis of the vocational orientations of University of Michigan women indicated that the mother's occupation outside the home was a crucial factor influencing women's nontraditional career aspirations.[68]

The family's influence on occupational values and preferences persists as a person moves through the educational system into adulthood. In a study of men who graduated from the University of Michigan in 1966 and 1967, Jeylan Mortimer found that there was a strong tendency for occupational inheritance. Even when these graduates did not seek the exact occupations of their fathers, they tended to prepare themselves for occupations that offer the same kinds of rewards and experiences that their fathers possessed.[69] It was also found that fathers' occupations and sons' values became more congruent as the father-son relationship became more favorable, enhancing parental identification.[70]

The transmission of work values and preferences from generation to generation in the family reflects the fundamental reciprocity and interdependence of the two institutional sectors. The complexity and rapid change of the modern occupational structure, however, limit the extent to which the family can adequately prepare the child for his or her adult occupation.[71] Inheritance of family businesses or farms is becoming more

[66]Joan Aldous, "Parental and Marital Function as Related to Occupational Status," p. 12.

[67]Crowley, Levitin, and Quinn, "The American Working Woman." Research also indicates that young children learn quite accurate pictures of the occupational structure, including relative prestige of different occupations. See Roberta G. Simmons and Morris Rosenberg, "Functions of Children's Perceptions of the Stratification System," *American Sociological Review* 36 (April 1971), 235–49.

[68]Sandra Schwartz Tangri, "Determinants of Occupational Role Innovation among College Women," *Journal of Social Issues* 28 (spring 1972), pp. 177–99.

[69]Jeylan T. Mortimer, "Patterns of Intergenerational Occupational Movement: A Smallest Space Analysis," *American Journal of Sociology* 79 (January 1974).

[70]Jeylan T. Mortimer, "Occupational Value Socialization in Business and Professional Families," (University of Minnesota, 1974).

[71]For additional consideration of this change, see Robert F. Winch, *Identification and its Familial Determinants* (Indianapolis: Bobbs-Merrill, 1962), chap. 4, especially pp. 50–51.

and more rare. In the modern era, the educational institution largely takes over the vocational socialization and allocation functions that previously were performed in the family. Thus, during the process of industrialization, both occupation and education become increasingly differentiated from the traditional family structure.

OCCUPATIONS AND EDUCATION

The basic relationship between the modern educational and occupational systems is obvious. Particular amounts, and in many cases particular kinds, of education are prerequisites for entrance into the occupational system. In discussing this, Burton R. Clark states: "Men become part of the potential labor force by qualifying for the work required, and increasingly, capability is defined by formal schooling. Advanced education offers competence; little schooling defines occupational incompetence. Thus occupational achievement is prefigured by education."[72] Implicit, but vital, in this relationship is the fact that the educational system has become the basis for the distribution of individuals within the total social system. Since occupations are the link for the individual and his family to the stratification system and all that that implies and because occupations also take up a major portion of the life of the adult, the educational system can be viewed as a major factor in placement of people within the total social system.

The distributional aspect and the close relationship of education and occupations are very recent phenomena. The advent of industrialization was linked to a general growth of the educational system. Universal education became a fact and literacy became a general expectation. At the same time, however, formal educational requirements for most occupations were minimal until very recently. Most professions, for example, did not establish training schools until the nineteenth century. The practice of "reading" law or medicine at the feet of an established practitioner has only recently disappeared. Many major corporations were developed by real Horatio Alger types. While there are many executives at all levels who have not had a college education, almost no one today enters this organizational level without a college education. Within a generation the proportion of executives without such training will undoubtedly shrink to insignificance.

The same general trend is evident within all types of occupations. The untrained and unskilled individual has essentially lost his place in the labor market. There is a strong inverse relationship between unem-

[72]"Sociology of Education," in *Handbook of Modern Sociology*, ed. Robert E. L. Faris, p. 737.

ployment rates and level of education. Clark notes that the high-school dropout is in reality a problem because of his position in the labor force.[73] At one time he could sell his unskilled labor, but now he no longer can, since it is often less costly to mechanize work than utilize unskilled workers. Education in the form of retraining has become a major consideration for all occupational levels. Most professions engage in continuing educational programs for their members. "Engineers need to go back to the classroom to maintain competence; with the growth in new knowledge, the engineer of 10 years experience who has not engaged in substantial re-education may have less value than a new engineering graduate."[74] Retraining of workers displaced by automation has become a major societal concern. Most corporations have embraced the concept of "executive development" or continuing education.

The point made at the outset of this book that society is moving from the industrial era is related to the changing educational requirements. Research and development are dominant concerns of all sectors of the society. Clark states that "brain workers of an ever-higher calibre are *the* economic need of societies in advanced stages of industrialism."[75] As this trend continues, even more emphasis and pressure will be put on the educational system.

Before examining the contemporary situation in more detail, a brief look at the role of education in developing nations is instructive. These nations are attempting to industrialize as a means of economic development. Industrialization is viewed as being largely dependent upon educational development within the populace. Anderson has noted that "the importance of schooling for growth in the short run may be quite minor; yet, in the long run, schooling may be decisive by virtue of its role in sustaining the broader milieu that favors change."[76] This point is strengthened by Passin's examination of the Meiji and their emergence from a preindustrial stage. He concludes:

> At the very least, literacy made it possible for people to be aware of things outside of their own immediate experience. It also made it possible for them to conceive of arrangements that differed from those with which they were familiar. They were therefore much more accessible to new ideas and new techniques than they otherwise would have been.[77]

[73]*Ibid.*, p. 738
[74]*Ibid.*
[75]*Ibid.*
[76]C. Arnold Anderson, "The Impact of the Educational System on Technological Change and Modernization," in *Industrialization and Society*, eds. Bert F. Hoselitz and Wilbert E. Moore (Mouton: UNESCO, 1966), p. 261.
[77]Herbert Passin, "Portents of Modernity and the Meiji Emergence," in *Education and Economic Development*, eds. C. Arnold Anderson and Mary Jean Bowman (Chicago: Aldine Publishing Co., 1965), p. 419.

Education and the literacy resulting therefrom are thus viewed as necessary conditions for economic development and industrialization and technological change. From the perspective of this book, education is thus a prerequisite for occupations in the industrialized and technologically changing setting.

While education is clearly such a prerequisite, there is no one form of education that can be taken as optimal for economic development. In addition, the conditions that existed in a society before it embarked on the road to economic development have an impact on the nature of the educational process. Foster's excellent study of the educational system in Ghana illustrates both of these points.[78] During the colonial period, the education of the local population was oriented toward training clerical workers for governmental work. These workers were fed into the system in a rather automatic fashion, and the educational and occupational systems had a close and neat linkage. The education at this period was academically oriented, even though it was designed to fill specific vocations. At the same time, education was the only realistic means of upward mobility for the population. After independence and as the desire to industrialize developed, the traditional form of education remained. More important, the population maintained its belief that academic training was the route to the best occupations. This belief corresponds with reality in that the most prestigious positions are obtained through academic training.

At this point there is little difference between the developing nation and nations that have passed through the developmental stage. A major problem, however, arises from the fact that the occupational system in a developing society needs people with specific vocational training in both industrial and agricultural skills. Since such training is devalued by the population and since most people in the educational system seek the academic type of education, shortages of trained personnel exist in these important areas, thus inhibiting economic development. While education is an important prerequisite for development, perfect coordination between societal needs and the form of the system itself does not exist.

The case of the developing nation serves to illustrate the nature of the relationship between occupations and the educational system. Education is a prerequisite for development, even though in and of itself it does not ensure development.[79] At the same time, there is apparently no one best form that the educational system should take in such areas. Anderson has suggested that in developing countries a *loose* connection

[78]See Phillip Foster, *Education and Social Change in Ghana* (Chicago: University of Chicago Press, 1965).

[79]Anderson and Bowman, *Education and Economic Development*, p. 345.

between education and occupations is more valuable than a close one, since the latter builds in rigidities that would inhibit growth in the long run. He suggests that a diversity of types of schools is probably the optimal arrangement.[80]

Evidence from the developing countries indicates the importance of education at relatively low levels of industrial and technological development. For societies with rather fully developed technological systems, the importance of education is heightened. At the same time, there is not a perfect correspondence between the occupational system's needs and the educational system's output.

The relationship between the educational and occupational systems is one of mutual dependence. The occupational system essentially relies upon the educational system for its supply of personnel, while output of the educational system is consumed by the occupational system. This reciprocal relationship, which has grown in strength, contains a number of strains that prevent it from being viewed as one of total harmony. A major strain, which has existed over a period of time, involves the nature of those who attain the educational prerequisites for many positions in the occupational structure. Increasing proportions of the population are attaining high school and college educations, indicating the growing need for such education. At the same time, there are questions regarding whether those most qualified attain the educational level for which they are best suited.

Data from a number of sources suggest that the distribution of the population into the various educational levels is not closely related to potential educability. Intruding into the relationship between academic potential and academic attendance is the important factor of position in the stratification system. A. E. Halsey, in a summary of studies in this area, reports that social class still plays a role in determining who shall go to college. While the social class variable has perhaps diminished in importance in recent years, it still operates. The lower an individual's position in the stratification system, the less his chances for attaining college entrance or high school graduation. Since these two educational benchmarks are important criteria for the occupational system, this suggests that the occupational system is not receiving the potential that it might under a system of actual educational equality. The data Halsey reports hold the learning ability of the subjects, as measured by standard intelligence tests, constant so that even if learning ability is in any way differentially distributed across class lines, or less accurately measured by achievement tests in lower socioeconomic groups, the relationship between measured ability and its realization in the educational system is

[80]Anderson, "The Impact of the Educational System," p. 264.

vitally affected by the stratification factor.[81] Findings such as these, which have been repeated in a variety of social settings, raise important moral questions as well as those raised in regard to the occupational system.

A related study by William G. Spady suggests that while the general level of educational attainment has increased, the impact has not resulted in any real occupational upgrading.[82] Noting that today a son must obtain more schooling than his father to achieve the same level of occupation, Spady finds that the rate of college attendance for the sons of poorly educated fathers has actually decreased over time. The people in the bottom strata of society are more disadvantaged than in the past, according to this analysis. This pattern is particularly evident for the black. For those above the bottom level, the potential for educational attainment has increased. If this pattern for the lowest level persists, a perpetuation of poverty is most likely. For the occupational system this implies a continuation of unemployability for a segment of the population. The relative size of this segment will continue to shrink, but it is probable that the extremely poorly educated will soon be outside of the occupational system, except as recipients of the products and services of those in the system.

The exact contribution of education to eventual occupational attainment is unclear and the subject of a great deal of debate.[83] Jencks finds that the influence of education on a person's eventual socioeconomic status is negligible. The influence of what happens at home, and especially experiences associated with the social class of the family, the uncertainties in education itself, and the lack of persistence of educational influence after the school years are suggested as reasons for limited educational impact. Furthermore, the effectiveness of schools is affected by their own composition—schools that have bright students entering turn out bright students, and this fact is itself linked to socioeconomic factors.

Despite Jencks's conclusions, many other researchers emphasize the importance of education in occupational attainment. At the very least, education does provide credentials, and thus constitutes a necessary, if not sufficient, condition for achievement in many occupational areas.

[81]"The Sociology of Education" in *Sociology: An Introduction*, ed. Neil J. Smelser (New York: John Wiley & Sons, Inc., 1967), pp. 427–33.

[82]"Educational Mobility and Access: Growth and Paradoxes," *American Journal of Sociology*, LXXIII, 3 (November 1967), 273–86.

[83]A good deal of the debate has surrounded Christopher Jencks *et al.*, *Inequality: A Reassessment of the Effect of Family and Schooling in America* (New York: Basic Books, 1972). Reports in the mass media and some politicians have interpreted the findings to mean that schooling makes no difference. This was not the point of the book, but its findings provide excellent ammunition for those who are against the educational establishment and for those who seek to change it.

These credentials, be they simply an undifferentiated high school or college degree or a specific professional diploma, are used as a means of discriminating between who can and cannot enter an occupation. The approach of William Sewell and his colleagues exemplifies the argument that educational attainment is in fact an important variable in understanding occupational attainment.[84] The Sewell model is presented in Fig. 10-1. This model includes other important considerations, but the strength of the coefficient between educational and occupational attainment (0.522) is extremely high. Sewell's data deal with early occupational attainment but, as we saw from the Blau and Duncan study, early occu-

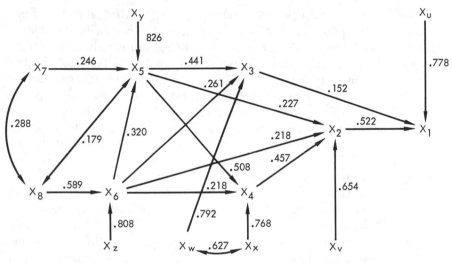

X_1 – Occupational Attainment

X_2 – Educational Attainment

X_3 – Level of Occupational Aspiration

X_4 – Level of Educational Aspiration

X_5 – Significant Others' Influence

X_6 – Academic Performance

X_7 – Socioeconomic Status

X_8 – Mental Ability

Figure 10-1. Path Coefficients for Antecedents of Educational and Occupational Attainment. From William H. Sewell, Archibald O. Haller, and George W. Ohlendorf, "The Educational and Early Occupational Status Attainment Process," *American Sociological Review* 35 (December 1970), 1023.

[84]See William H. Sewell, Archibald G. Haller, and Alejandre Portes, "The Educational and Early Occupational Attainment Process," *American Sociological Review* 34 (February 1969); William H. Sewell, Archibald G. Haller, and George W. Ohlendorf, "The Educational and Early Occupational Attainment Process: Replication and Revision," *American Sociological Review* 35 (December 1970); see the discussion in chapter 9 for additional detail on this model.

pational attainment is strongly associated with eventual placement in the socioeconomic system (early occupational attainment is roughly equivalent to the first job in the Blau and Duncan formulation).

The issue of the relative importance of education for socioeconomic status is still unresolved. In terms of occupations per se, the evidence is much clearer. The amount and type of education a person receives is directly related to occupational placement. The amount and type of education is highly varied. The well-known differences between inner city schools and suburban schools, regional variations, urban-rural differences, differing curricular emphasis, and variations in educational philosophies all play a role in the differentiated occupational outcomes that are evident.

Adding to this diversity of outcomes is the fact that educational programs may be quite different from what actually goes on in the schools. James S. Coleman's study of *The Adolescent Society* clearly demonstrates the impact of the social structure imposed by peers on fellow students.[85] The orientation and efforts of students are strongly affected by the prevailing student subcultures. Athletic and social prowess is typically stressed more than academic achievement in high schools. A study of medical students by Becker *et al.* also suggests that peers have an important influence in structuring behaviors and orientations at this level.[86] It would be difficult to make a strong case that the impact of peers is totally dysfunctional for the occupational system, for some of the influences may be very occupationally relevant. At the same time, however, these influences often deflect from the programs established by the schools. Any established educational program is the basis from which peer-based behaviors originate. At the same time, it appears that the occupational system is dependent upon the established, rather than the operating, program. This adds an additional discrepancy to the relationship.

The process through which an individual passes through the educational system en route to eventual occupational placement is not necessarily rational in terms of the individual's abilities and desires or in terms of the needs of the occupational system. The placement of individuals into the various curricula available at the elementary and secondary levels is often on the basis of original social class position. Teachers tend to push middle- and upper-class children into college preparatory curricula, while working-and lower-class youths either are not pushed in any direction or are encouraged to enter vocational or general programs.[87]

---

[85]See *The Adolescent Society* (New York: Free Press of Glencoe, 1961).

[86]See Howard S. Becker, *Boys in White: Student Culture in Medical School* (Chicago: University of Chicago Press, 1961).

[87]Such ascriptive bases of counseling in a high school are described by Aaron V. Cicourel and John I. Kitsuse, *The Educational Decision-makers* (Indianapolis: Bobbs-Merrill, 1963).

Vocational counseling itself is often restricted to those who receive more education. Many of those who leave high school before graduation receive no vocational counseling. For those in the system, occupationally relevant decisions often are made on nonoccupationally relevant grounds. The decisions in regard to courses taken, and even majors, are frequently made on the basis of the ease or difficulty of the courses, the hours at which they are given, dating patterns, the popularity of a particular teacher, and other factors of only limited relevance. Although the choice of curriculum can be made on rational or nonrational grounds, the choice itself both opens and closes opportunities. Once a choice is made, it tends to be irreversible. Continued education actually sets limits on the potential occupations for an individual. The range of occupational alternatives is probably greatest at the time of high school graduation. Before that period it is limited by the lack of education. Afterwords it is limited by specialization. The educational system thus serves as a channeling mechanism, wider at some points than at others.

The actual impact of education on occupational choice is difficult to determine given the wide range of variables that can enter such decisions. James A. Davis's findings and interpretations, based on a sample of 33,982 college seniors studied in 1961, are instructive. He states:

> The college freshman has already completed 12 years of education and has lived about one-fifth of his life span in a family and community environment that influences his plans; in many cases he goes to college precisely to implement a specific vocational choice rather than to choose a vocation. . . . The college years are not the sole determinant of vocational choice—nor is any span of 4 years—for vocational choice is the result of a continuous decision process over decades, but there is no evidence in our data that the college years do not contribute their fair share of influence. Although our guess is that the last 2 years of high school are the most strategic period of all for vocational choice, college is not without its effect. Half of the students appear to change their minds or reach a decision during college. . . .[88]

The patterns of change and choice during college, with some exceptions, indicate that people choosing, or changing into, an occupation tend to be like those who have already chosen it.[89] That is, there is a tendency toward homogamy during the college period in terms of the characteristics of those entering various occupations. For example, using the variables in the Davis study, the physical sciences were underchosen by those oriented toward working with people and by blacks, overchosen by those destined for high academic performance, by those opting for originality, and by students from larger cities, underchosen by Protestants, and over-

[88]*Undergraduate Career Decisions* (Chicago: Aldine Publishing Co., 1965), p. 33.
[89]*Ibid.*, p. 44.

chosen by Catholics. Education, on the other hand, was underchosen by men and by those wanting to make a lot of money, overchosen by those oriented toward working with people and by blacks, underchosen by students from larger cities and by those with high socioeconomic status families, and overchosen by Protestants.[90] The fact that in most cases the movement in college is towards homogamy suggests the complexity of the occupational choice process and the complexity of the sorting process performed by the educational system. While occupational choice is not a major concern here, it is clear that the choice is influenced by a whole series of factors. Some of these same factors appear to be operative within the educational system.

The role of education as preparation for and distribution into occupations is indisputable, even if not entirely harmonious in its implementation. An additional component, which adds some more confusion to the relationship, is that it is not clear what is exactly the optimum form the education should take for occupational preparation. The long-standing controversy between vocational and liberal arts forms of preparation has actually grown in intensity. At the high school level, much of the traditional vocational curriculum is clearly outdated. The rate of technological change is such that skills can quickly become outmoded. At this level there is some argument for a more liberal arts approach, since this might better prepare a person to adapt to changes. This is not a clearly demonstrable fact, however, and the exact form such training should take is also not clear. In higher education the same basic controversy continues. There is a tendency, as Clark notes, for specific vocational training to be put off until graduate school, as in the case of business or education.[91] The rapid expansion of knowledge would appear to make such a shift more necessary. At the same time, the contents of both the liberal arts and vocational programs may not be the best that could be developed in terms of the needs of the occupational system, which in its own right is not ideal.

SUMMARY AND CONCLUSIONS

The thrust of this chapter has been directed toward the interplay between the occupational system and the family and educational systems. Although it is correct to say that the systems are intimately intertwined, it is also clear that the series of incompatibilities discussed preclude any assumption of neat and harmonious reciprocity. Instead of

[90]*Ibid.*, pp. 12–13.
[91]"Sociology of Education," p. 739.

viewing the relationships either as harmonious or conflictual, a more appropriate perspective would be that of change. As each system changes, previously existing relationships are altered. These changes appear to induce additional changes in the related system, whether deliberately or not, leading to continued interplay between the systems but not, apparently, to a homeostatic condition.

The contemporary family with its nuclear form allows the division of labor whereby the man can participate in the occupational system with its different normative system and the woman can be in charge of most family functions. At the same time, the demands for trained individuals, the rising educational levels of women, and the availability of time for women are confronted by the historic discrimination against women, which has precluded women's full participation in the labor force. The changes that are occurring in regard to women's occupations are affecting the family and vice versa. New family forms are emerging, with husbands and wives both active in the labor force. There are growing demands in some quarters for more flexible work hours to accommodate this new family form.[92] The form and content of the contemporary nuclear family (in its stereotyped image) is unattractive to many people. This unattractiveness is at least in part a function of the occupations that people have. How much the family *or* occupations will change in light of some of these developments is not yet clear. The educational system serves as a distribution and preparation nexus between the family and occupational systems. Both the preparation and distribution aspects are generally compatible with the occupational system, but it is clear that the distributional function does not always permit the most qualified to pass through and that the preparation is less than perfect. Implicit in the discussion of both topics in this chapter was the idea of change. A major component of the change process is technology. Technological developments in the occupational system have an obvious impact on the family and on education. Technological developments in the last two systems similarly affect the occupational system. The next chapter will focus on technological developments as they affect occupations.

[92]John Scanzoni, *Sexual Bargaining: Power Politics in the American Marriage,* (Englewood Cliffs, N.J.: Prentice-Hall, 1972). This book contains an extensive discussion of the directions the family may take in the future.

11

TECHNOLOGY

Technology and technological change have been a pervasive theme of this whole book. We have discussed science and technology as they affect the total occupational structure in the move into the post-industrial era. Technological considerations were a major concern in our discussions of satisfactions and dissatisfactions of work. All of the occupational types that have been discussed are affected by technological change; from the professionals who are affected by the constant development of new knowledge, through managers and executives who require new knowledge, and on through other white- and blue-collar workers, technological variations decrease or increase the amount and type of discretion that occupations enjoy or suffer. Similarly, technological change is important in terms of stratification and mobility as new occupations are created and find their niche in the stratification system and as others become obsolete or decline in their market and social value. The family system is affected by labor saving devices. The educational system must keep up with the changes. Our topic here is thus not new.

In the present chapter, we will examine in detail the nature of technology and technological change. We will then consider some ways in which technological developments can be used to improve working conditions and work arrangements. Finally, we will examine the constraints imposed by the organizational world in which technological changes are implemented. Along the way, we will look at such developments as job redesign and worker participation as reactions to our rapidly changing technologies.

THE NATURE OF TECHNOLOGICAL CHANGE

Technology and technological change involve much more than simply tools and machinery. "By technology we mean knowledge and beliefs about manipulating and arranging materials and people to produce specific outputs or products."[1] Technological change refers to alterations in technological systems. The *impact* of technological change is a sometimes bitterly disputed issue. In discussing the impact of computers on society, for example, Joseph Weizenbaum comments:

> The structure of the typical essay on 'The impact of computers on society' is as follows: First there is an 'on the one hand' statement. It tells all the good things computers have already done for society and often even attempts to argue that the social order would already have collapsed were it not for the 'computer revolution.' This is usually followed by an 'on the other hand' caution which tells of certain problems the introduction of computers brings in its wake. The threat posed to individual privacy by large data banks and the danger of large-scale unemployment induced by industrialized automation are usually mentioned. Finally, the glorious present and prospective achievements of the computer are applauded, while the dangers alluded to in the second part are shown to be capable of being alleviated by sophisticated technological fixes. The closing paragraph consists of a plea for generous societal support for more, and more large scale, computer research and development.[2]

Weizenbaum goes on to note the power of advanced computer technology in terms of national and international decision making, which has the real and potential threat of removing decision making from people and turning it over to ongoing computer programs that are only minimally understood by the people who utilize the machinery or its outputs. The important point here for our purposes is the fact that there are at least two sides to the technological change issue. We will examine these sides and then consider some limitations to technology and its change.

The history of humanity is one of technological change. Nels Anderson states:

> Technological inventiveness is linked with man's work. It cannot cease unless man in his work ceases to be competitive and no longer tries to find

[1]Mayer N. Zald, *Occupations and Organizations in American Society* (Chicago: Markham Publishing Co., 1971), p. 5.

[2]Joseph Weizenbaum, "On the Impact of the Computer on Society," *Science* 176 (12 May 1972), p. 609.

easier and faster ways of performing his tasks. If he manages to take the heaviness out of work, he then feels the need to take the dullness out of it. The inventions that bring satisfaction in work are never sufficient to quench the thirst for still more invention to make work still lighter and more productive and the workday still shorter. Invention makes work increasingly a knowledgeable activity for man and makes the machine more an instrument for his handling.[3]

Anderson thus attributes change to the nature of man and implies that it is a continual and inevitable process. There have been periods and places in man's history where change has been opposed and postponed. Nevertheless, change does appear to be inevitable in that change has occurred. At the present time, change is really the normal state of affairs. Much of the general impact of change can be discerned from an analysis of the developing countries. These countries do not necessarily pass through the same stages as those that have already industrialized, but the impact of change on occupations in these societies is in general similar to what has occurred in all societies.

Neil J. Smelser points out that development leads to a differentiation of functions within the total society.[4] Tasks once performed by a single social unit, usually the family, are distributed among many units as occupational and other activities become separated from their traditional basis. Wilbert E. Moore elaborates on this point by noting that the change in the occupational structure during development actually involves five related processes. The first of these is that workers become involved in market participation.[5] Rather than existing on a simple subsistence level, both agricultural and industrial workers participate in the labor and financial markets. This is the same process identified in the discussion of the shift from the extended to the nuclear family, in that the occupation is carried on outside the home.

The second process is what Moore calls "sectoral relocation."[6] This refers to a shift of occupational situs away from subsistence agriculture toward economic production in industry or agriculture. As this occurs there may be heightened unemployment, since many traditional handcraft operations are no longer needed and the workers are not absorbed into the new industrial system. As was noted earlier, such unemployment would not exist during periods of subsistence farming. Moore also notes

[3]*Dimension of Work* (New York: David McKay Co., 1964), p. 125. See also the discussion by Robert Heilbroner, "Automation in the Perspective of Long-term Technological Change" (Paper presented at the Seminar on Manpower Policy and Program, U.S. Department of Labor, Washington, D.C., 1966).

[4]See "Mechanisms of Change and Adjustment to Change," in Hoselitz and Moore, *Industrialization and Society* (Paris: UNESCO-Mouton, 1963), pp. 35–40.

[5]*The Impact of Industry* (Englewood Cliffs, N.J.: Prentice-Hall, 1965), p. 62.

[6]*Ibid.*, pp. 63–64.

that this period is one in which marginal service occupations, such as being a car watcher or porter, flourish.

The additional processes during industrialization are the upgrading of skill requirements in the labor force, specialization of occupations, and greater status mobility, both within and between generations.[7] These processes in the industrializing societies are similar to those that have occurred in societies that have already passed through the period of industrialization. At the same time, some interesting differences do exist between current industrialization and that that took place in the now industrialized societies. The industrializing societies apparently are able to profit from some of the experiences of the past or are able to incorporate some of the features of modern societies in their own systems. Charles R. Walker has noted: "Even in the early stages of today's industrialization programs, social protection for the wage earner and his family in the form of health and welfare insurance, unemployment compensation, and other such measures must be provided."[8] Thus some of the problems associated with past industrialization are bypassed. This may, of course, decrease the amount of capital available for modernization, but important human values are supported.

In our analysis we will view technological change as the independent variable, with changes in the wider social structure taken as the dependent variable. This is simply a heuristic device, since the relationship is not unidirectional. A change in organizational structure, for example, could lead to alteration in the technological system through a number of devices, such as suggestions, emphasis on innovation, or accidental discovery. For the purposes of this analysis, however, technological change will be viewed as the starting point.

The nature of this change is almost totally unidirectional. That is, the alteration in the system is toward less physical labor on the part of humans. A simple example of this is the power shovel as a replacement for the hand shovel; a much more complex case is that of the computer as it performs complex mathematical manipulations. While the latter example does involve the use of ideas, the basis for the computer is actually physical manipulation of symbols as directed by the human mind. The direction of technological change is towards automation, defined by John R. Bright as any production process that is significantly more automatic than the one that previously existed in a given place of work.[9]

---

[7]Ibid., pp. 65–67.

[8]Modern Technology and Civilization (New York: McGraw-Hill Book Company, 1962), p. 338.

[9]Automation and Management (Cambridge, Mass.: Harvard University Graduate School of Business Administration, 1958), p. 6.

A number of forms of automation have been identified.[10] The first is simply the mechanization of conventional processes where transfer machines replace human labor in moving materials along a production process. The moving assembly line, which replaces the effort of lifting materials from work station to work station, is a simple example of this form. A second form of automation is the mechanization of processes in which machines are linked together for continuous production. These machines are supervised by mechanical control devices that are themselves controlled by feedback from the production process. The work of people in this setting is largely that of monitoring the system. The clearest example of this form is the oil refinery, where there is almost no direct contact with the product by humans. Another example would be the bread bakery in which ingredients are mixed, shaped, placed in cooking containers, baked, sliced, wrapped, and packaged for delivery without human contact. These two forms can be viewed as the extremes in automated production. The movement is consistently toward the second form.

An important consideration in the possible future applications of automation is whether or not a particular production process can be mechanized and regularized. If the technological system does not develop a mechanized system to begin with, no movement toward total automation is possible. For example, the mail service is only partially mechanized, and a great deal of the work is done by hand, such as the sorting process and deliveries made by individual workers. Further technological developments are required before any movement toward automation is possible. The product or service involved must be regularized in that a high degree of variance does not allow the ongoing process of automation. In the construction of office buildings, for example, variations in terrain, design, and composition preclude automated assembly beyond that involved in some of the components such as windows and floor materials. Private homes, on the other hand, can be produced in a more automated fashion if the design and location are kept constant. In general, it is easier to automate processes dealing with products than with services. Relatively simple services, such as food dispensing or shoe shines, can be provided through vending machines. In these cases the variation is reduced to a minimum.

The third form of automation is the application of computers to paper work. The preparation of payrolls, keeping inventories, maintenance of insurance policy records, and compilation of airline reservations are performed by computers. As in the other forms, the computers take over functions that have been performed by humans. At the same time,

[10]The following discussion is partially based on William Silverman's "The Economic and Social Effects of Automation in an Organization," *The American Behavioral Scientist*, IX, 10 (June 1966), 3–8. This article contains a comprehensive bibliography of empirical studies of automation.

the information fed into computers is highly regularized, whether it deals with inventory or human records. Much of the concern expressed about computers reflects the regularization of data about humans and is based on the belief that each human is a unique creature who is not amenable to categorization into regularized patterns. Evidence from history, psychology, sociology, and other behavioral and social sciences suggests, however, that regular patterns can be identified. The application of the computer to human data is based on such evidence. The computer is essentially like the second form of automation in that materials (data) are fed into a system, processed, and then come out as a finished product. The same principle of the substitution of mechanical or electronic processing for human effort is involved. The implications of the computer in terms of the speed with which information is handled and the greater amounts of information that can be encompassed are probably greater than those of automated production for the occupational and the wider social systems. As in the case of the second form of automation, the introduction of computers requires that the information be handled in a standardized and regularized form, which in turn implies that previously steps had been taken to put the information in such a form.

Computers can also be utilized in the decision-making process. This fourth form of automation has not been as fully implemented as the others and, therefore, its implications are quite unclear. A simple example of this form is inventories. The computer not only keeps inventory records but also decides when to reorder particular items. The decision is based on instructions included in the computer program. A more complex example is the utilization of computers in policy decisions. In this case, the probability of relevant future events, their interrelationships, and the probable consequences of the varying possible situations that would arise on the basis of a particular decision must be considered. As in the previous form, the quality of the decision made is only as good as the information fed into the computer. The quality of the input affects the quality of the output—"garbage in, garbage out." This is the crucial question with which Weizenbaum was dealing. If national and international policy decisions have incorrect economic, political, social, or military information or if for some reason the information or its interpretations become inoperative, there is the potential for disaster. If this is not the case, then there are obvious benefits.

THE IMPACT OF TECHNOLOGICAL CHANGE ON THE OCCUPATIONAL STRUCTURE

The discussion here must be regarded as tentative, since we are now experiencing technological change and can have neither the data nor the historical perspective for a comprehensive analysis. In terms of the impact of technological change on skill levels required, the impact varies with the form of automation. Bright, for example, found that the introduction of automated equipment affected the skill levels in factories that utilized the first form of automation.[11] At this level, skill requirements may actually be lessened as production work becomes more routinized. The second form also changes the skill requirements. Charles R. Walker, in a study of an automated pipe factory, found that some skills were no longer required, while new skills were introduced into the system.[12] At the same time, new skill requirements were introduced that involved different skills and a greater amount of judgment. A similar finding by Floyd C. Mann and L. Richard Hoffman was that jobs in an automated power plant required more knowledge than jobs in a traditional power plant.[13] The movement is generally from manual to mental skills in this situation. Since there has been the general upgrading of educational attainment in the social system, this shift will probably not be too disruptive over the long run. For the individuals involved, the shift could be quite threatening.

The introduction of computers to speed the processing of information has a dual effect. Routine jobs, such as filing, operation of tabulation machines, or posting and checking billings, are largely eliminated. At the same time, the equally routine job of key punching is introduced. There is also generally an increase in the proportion of professional and technical workers in the labor force. The overall skill requirements are generally higher, but the workers involved are different. Those who held the relatively low skill jobs in the past are seldom moved into the more skilled positions.

The occupational structure is affected by automation in more ways than the direct kinds of impacts just described. Management and administration deal with a changed situation and must themselves change. An important study by Joan Woodward illustrates the consequences of technological differentiation for the management level of organizations.[14] Woodward classified 100 English firms on the basis of their technology. At one end of a rough three-point scale of technological development were firms that produced goods in small batches or units, such as railroad locomotives or ships. At the midpoint were those firms that utilized

[11]"Does Automation Raise Skill Requirements?" *Harvard Business Review*, XXXVI, 4 (July–August 1958), 85–98.

[12]*Toward the Automatic Factory: A Case Study of Men and Machines* (New Haven, Conn.: Yale University Press, 1957), pp. 26–29.

[13]*Automation and the Worker: A Study of Social Change in Power Plants* (New York: Holt, Rinehart & Winston, 1960), pp. 65–73.

[14]*Industrial Organization: Theory and Practice* (London: Oxford University Press, 1965), pp. 51–53.

large-batch or mass production, such as the automobile assembly line or home appliance manufacturer. At the most technologically developed end of the scale was continuous-process production, as exemplified by the oil or chemical refinery.

The number of levels in the management hierarchy varied directly with the nature of the technology. Those firms with the most advanced technology had the most hierarchical levels. A study by Peter M. Blau corroborates this finding and offers some reasons for this relationship.[15] In this case the organizational sample was 254 finance departments of state and local governmental units in the United States. Despite the shift in functions from production to paper work, the same results were found. The major factor that leads to this relationship, aside from sheer growth in the size of the organization, which itself is strongly associated with the number of hierarchical levels, is the fact that automated processing of products or paper is a means of control over the workers involved. This impersonal form of control is based upon the fact that the worker does not control the pace of his work and also can be checked by performance records. Top management thus also does not have to be greatly concerned about worker performance. At the same time, in the agencies Blau studied, the organizations with the more automated processes also required higher level qualifications on the part of their workers. Blau states:

> Both the automation of the work process and the merit standards that the managerial and operating staff must meet contribute to the reliable performance of duties and help to make operations comparatively self-regulating within the framework of the organization's objectives and management's policies. These conditions reduce management's need to keep close direct control over operations and, consequently, often give rise to major changes in the hierarchy. To wit, vertical differentiation creates a multi-level hierarchy, which usually decreases the number of major divisions whose heads report to the agency director and increases the span of control of these division heads, and responsibilities become decentralized.[16]

Although the concern here is not with organizational change, the implications for the occupational structure within the organizations are quite clear. The positions at the various levels within the organization are given more autonomy in the sense that there is less direct supervision. The impact on the administrative structure is that responsibility is spread throughout the hierarchy, and the top levels have less direct responsibility while the lower levels have more. Much of the work of the lower levels

---

[15]"The Hierarchy of Authority in Organizations," *American Journal of Sociology*, LXXIII, 4 (January 1968), 453–67. See also Peter M. Blau and Richard A. Schoenherr, *The Structure of Organizations* (New York: Basic Books, 1971).

[16]"The Hierarchy of Authority in Organizations," 466.

in the hierarchy is involved in communications in that more information is generated and is processed upward in the organization. The management function thus shifts from supervision to communications and coordination, with an associated shift in skill requirements.

The Woodward study also found that the span of control (the number of persons controlled by each supervisor) varied according to the type of technology involved.[17] Both the unit and the process production systems had relatively low spans of control, while the mass-production firms had a higher span of control. Blau also found that the more automated offices had lower spans of control. This finding suggests that although the mass-production system can utilize fewer supervisors per worker, because of the impersonal control mechanism of the assembly line, in advanced technological systems the process-production system reduces the span of control because of the necessity for ensuring that errors do not occur. In this production system, errors are extremely costly, given the speed of the total process. Here again the emphasis is not on supervision per se but rather on the knowledge of the supervisor in error correction and detection. In the case of unit production, the employment of many craftsmen also reduced the need for direct supervision. Here the work units would tend to be organized around crafts and particular projects on each unit, accounting for the lower span of control.

Woodward's study also found that the ratio of managers and supervisors increased as the technological level increased, regardless of the size of the firm.[18] This is also related to the problem of error correction and detection with a concentration of personnel in inspection and control functions. Changing technology thus affects the specific functions performed by all levels of the hierarchy. It also affects the skills involved. Herbert Simon has suggested that managers will increasingly be freed from routine work and will have to be increasingly mathematically sophisticated in their analysis of organizational problems.[19] Whether the projection that mathematical expertise will become important is correct or not, it is probable that the greater amount of information available to managers will increase their communications and coordination activities, as the data discussed above suggest. It is also probable that this greater amount of information within an organizational system will require more training as a prerequisite for handling information. The increased educational requirements, discussed in the previous chapter, reflect this tendency.

Elmer H. Burack's review of studies of the impact of technological

---

[17]*Industrial Organization: Theory and Practice*, p. 62.

[18]*Ibid.*, p. 56.

[19]See *The New Science of Management Decision* (New York: Harper & Row, 1960), pp. 38–40.

developments on management supports these interpretations.[20] Burack found that there was a growing importance of technical staffs in automated operations. The requirement of greater amounts of education was also found, with an emphasis on technical education in many instances. An important finding was that experience became less important as technological expertise became more important. If this trend continues, personnel policies based upon seniority will increasingly come in conflict with organizational needs, as the well-trained young expert becomes more organizationally valuable than his more experienced superior. At the managerial level the possibility of a form of technological unemployment or underemployment is thus not remote. It is unlikely that the experienced, but technologically unsophisticated, manager or executive will be laid off as might be the case with lower level workers. At the same time, however, he may be bypassed in the promotion process and given work less organizationally and personally relevant than might have been the case if the technological system were not developing so rapidly. Many of these changes have been anticipated, of course. Herbert A. Simon has long suggested that the more routinized middle management tasks can give way to the computer; it is the ill- or non-structured situations—really the most critical ones—that are least amenable to computerized solutions.[21]

TECHNOLOGY AND THE WORKER

We have been examining the impact of technological change on the organizations in which work takes place. Clearly, organizations are the mediators between technological developments and individual workers. In previous chapters we saw how these technological variations impinge upon the individual, either through the automation of the office, working in process- as opposed to mass-production systems, or through increasing demands for knowledge updating on the part of professionals and executives. The purpose of this section is to summarize and extend our previous discussion.

In summary, automation of the office has been shown to make much of white-collar work more factorylike, while automation of the factory makes work there less oppressive and less like the traditional factory.

[20]Industrial Management in Advanced Production Systems: Some Theoretical Concepts and Preliminary Findings," *Administrative Science Quarterly*, XII, 3 (December 1967), 479–500.

[21]"The Corporation: Will it Be Managed by Machines?" in *Management and Corporations 1985*, Melvin Anshen and George L. Bach, eds. (New York: McGraw-Hill Book Company, 1960).

While technological change is the key variable in both cases, it occurs in different ways in each situation. For the office worker, technological change has meant a move away from close control over one's work to a situation in which the worker has only a small proportion of a total piece of work as his or her task. The key punch operator, the typist in a pool situation, or the person who processes incoming checks in a bank all work with machines in a mass-production context.

For those higher in the occupational system, the executive or the professional, technological change has an opposite effect. Since more and more emphasis is placed on the person's knowledge of some portion of specialized technology, the individual gains in power. The "knowledge worker," to use Peter Drucker's term, is depended upon by the organization.[22] Even though this person has perhaps a highly specialized job in which there is little opportunity to have a perspective on the total work process (this type of situation is one in which alienation in the form of meaninglessness is likely to occur), the integration of the individual into the work and organization through knowledge power appears to minimize the alienating potentialities of high specialization.

For blue-collar workers, technological change has an impact quite different from that on office workers. There are consistent research findings that suggest that work in an automated factory is less alienating and more integrating than in the assembly-line type of operation. There are several reasons for this.

In the first place, automation increases the interdependence of all work. The process itself requires integration.[23] Since any work stoppage due to errors or breakdowns is extremely costly, the workers are aware of their responsibility. There also is a strong tendency for the work to be carried out in small work teams. The second point is that given the higher ratio of managers and supervisors to workers, there is likely to be more interaction between hierarchical levels.[24] A third point is that in the automated factory, labor costs are a small proportion of the total production cost, so that wage increases are not as big an issue and wages are likely to be slightly higher than in nonautomated situations. Also, given the importance of integration, automated factories tend to pay more attention to industrial relations and personnel activities. Finally, promotional activities are present. "The typical production worker in an oil refinery enters the organization as a general laborer, and the

---

[22]Peter Drucker, *The Age of Discontinuity* (New York: Harper & Row, 1968).

[23]This discussion follows Michael Fullan, "Industrial Technology and Worker Integration in the Organization," *American Sociological Review* 35 (December 1970), 1028–39. See also, William Faunce, "Automation and the Division of Labor," *Social Problems* 13 (fall 1965), 149–60.

[24]See Floyd C. Mann and L. R. Hoffman, *Automation and the Worker* (New York: Holt, Rinehart & Winston, 1960).

expectation is that he will progressively move from third operator to second operator and then to head the production team as first operator. Elaborate on-the-job training, including formal courses, is a standard company-sponsored program for all workers in the oil industry."[25]

None of this is to suggest that automation is the panacea for production workers. There is some evidence to suggest that the severity of errors in automated situations leads the workers who must monitor the production process and detect such errors to suffer increased mental tensions.[26] At the same time, one major point is clear: *the state of technology utilized by an organization sets the physical and social parameters for each individual worker.*

Lest this last point be taken to mean that if we know the state of technology we know the state of the worker, we must return to an earlier theme. The technological situation interacts with worker expectations. These expectations are related to the social and cultural milieu from which the workers come. For example, in a study of automobile workers in four nations, William Form found that work satisfaction was a more salient expectation in countries that were already highly industrially developed.[27] Form's data also suggest that mass-production work in an auto factory is not the alienating, vicious situation that it is frequently portrayed as. He concludes:

This study casts serious doubts on the pronouncements of the machine haters. Even in the automobile industry, the *bête noire* of the antitechnicists, and in the United States, where technology is allegedly most dehumanizing, workers expect to find satisfaction in their work. The situation is not different in the less developed countries. The siren song of leisure is not deafening. Most auto workers would rather stay on the job not out of sense of duty (to satisfy the moralists) or to get their quota of sociability (to satisfy social scientists), but rather because working provides organizational cement to their lives. Factory work is not the nemesis pictured by the postindustrial romanticists. The noise and smell of the factory are much preferred to the dainty but dull routines of the office. Workers recently off the farm are not nostalgic and the urban-born rarely muse about the joys of farm life.

Auto workers everywhere seem to ignore the recommendations of social scientists that they should hate their jobs. However, by clever artifices, we can make a few more say that they dislike their jobs. Workers everywhere give similar reasons for liking their jobs; the rhetoric of the skilled resonates with job interest and that of the unskilled, money. Whatever their rhetorics, auto workers are not seeking jobs outside the industry.

[25]Fullan, "Industrial Technology and Worker Integration," p. 1030.
[26]See Ben R. Seligman, *Most Notorious Victory: Man in an Age of Automation* (New York: Macmillan Co., 1966).
[27]William H. Form, "Auto Workers and Their Machines: A Study of Work, Factory, and Job Satisfaction in Four Countries, *Social Forces* 52 (September 1973), 1–15.

They know that other jobs pay better and have more prestige, but this knowledge is not disturbing. Some feel that their children will escape the factory, but most workers have come to terms with their jobs.

Auto workers will not be the marionettes of intellectuals, striking poses of exhaustion from the monotony of the assembly line. Assemblers want only limited change in their work routines, as do other workers. The local technological situation is too complex for outsiders to describe panaceas. Social life in the automobile factory seems to be similar everywhere. While the skilled worker has considerable freedom to talk on the job, sociability is not responsible for his job satisfaction. For the unskilled worker, the opportunity to talk and move about makes the job more satisfactory, but he still would rather have more money than sociability.[28]

The same sort of conclusion is reached by Goldthorpe *et al.* in their study of British workers. The workers' expectations here were largely instrumental. As these were met, the technological situation of the job became of lesser importance.[29]

These last conclusions move us away from sheer technological determinism. Technology and the organization provide the parameters in which the worker interacts. It is the combination of the workers' expectations and the technology and the organization that yields satisfaction or dissatisfaction. One use to which technology has been put is altering work arrangements to provide a greater likelihood of worker interest and involvement on the job.

ALTERNATIVE TECHNOLOGIES

The occupational world does not suffer from a lack of suggestions on how to improve work content and work conditions. Indeed, the mass media, management, unions, and scholars alike use the terms job enlargement, job enrichment, participation in decision making, and so on as part of their everyday rhetoric. In this section we will examine some of these altered technologies. Later we will consider some limitations to large-scale alterations.

Most of the suggestions for alternative technologies are summarized in *Work in America*. The authors of this report suggest the following steps as solutions to boring, monotonous, dead-end types of work:

1. Autonomous work groups—teams of eight to twelve members who decide on their own division of labor and who have responsibility for some fairly large segment of the production process.

[28]*Ibid.*, pp. 13–14.
[29]Goldthorpe *et al.*, *The Affluent Worker: Industrial Attitudes and Behavior* (Cambridge: Cambridge University Press, 1970), pp. 181–86.

2. Integrated support functions—quality control, maintenance, custodial work, personnel functions, and industrial engineering are built into the operating team's responsibility.

3. Challenging job assignments—this involves designing tasks so that each team member can do things that require his or her best abilities. The more tedious and boring tasks that still must be performed are shared, so that no one is stuck with the more menial housekeeping chores.

4. Job mobility and rewards for learning—all workers are given the same job classification. Pay raises occur when the individual learns more tasks and can perform more duties. Theoretically, all workers in a work team can continue to learn new tasks and earn higher wages, contributing to upward mobility.

5. Facilitative leadership—team leaders are selected whose task is to improve decision making and team development rather than continuing supervision in the traditional foreman's role.

6. Managerial decision information for operators—managerial decision-making rules and economic data are supplied to the workers. This permits decisions to be made at the team level.

7. Self-government for the plant community—rules come from the work team in terms of hours, behavior, dress, and the like.

8. Congruent physical and social context—status symbols such as privileged parking spots for executives and executive sections in cafeterias are eliminated. The physical plant is to be designed to encourage informal meetings.[30]

These suggestions are meant to improve the quality of work *and* to be profitable or efficient for the employing organization. In many situations, such alterations have been found to be related to increased productivity and greater work satisfaction. Participation in management decision making and profit sharing in private industry are additional ways in which the motivations and performance of workers can be enhanced. Table 11-1 summarizes some of the efforts at altered technologies and indicates the direction of the results.

While these results are at first glance impressive, there are several cautions that must be raised. The results in Table 11-1 have some strange characteristics. Almost all of the examples come from rather small work units, particularly those in the United States. This leads to the question of whether or not such applications are possible in large organizations, which are the major employers. In addition, many of the examples cited are in branches or divisions of larger organizations. One wonders why such changes are not instituted throughout the total organization if they are in fact so beneficial.

The point of these last comments is to temper the idea that the sug-

[30]*Work in America: Report of a Special Task Force to the Secretary of Health, Education, and Welfare,* prepared under the auspices of the W. E. Upjohn Institute for Employment Research (Cambridge, Mass.: Massachusetts Institute of Technology Press, 1973), pp. 96–98.

TABLE 11-1. Variations in Technology

	General Foods	AT&T	AT&T	Bell System	Polaroid Corp.
1. Establishment(s) or Employee Groups	Pet Food Plant Topeka, Kans. All plant employees.	Long Lines Plant, N.Y. Private Line Telephone District. Framemen.	Shareholder Correspondents, Treasury Department.	17 groups of workers in diverse occupations, including toll operators, installers, clerks, equipment engineers.	Production-line employees.
2. Year Initiated	1971	1966	1965	1967	1959
3. No. Employees Affected	70	35–40	95–120	about 1,200	2,000 +
4. Problem	In designing this new plant management sought to solve problems of frequent shut downs, costly recycling and low morale that plagued an existing plant making the same product.	There was low productivity, high errors, schedule slippage and no worker's pride.	High turnover, absenteeism, low morale, low productivity.	Are the methods and results of the AT&T Shareholder Correspondents Study transferable to other employee groups?	Top management wanted to increase the meaningfulness of work.
5. Technique used	Workers were organized into relatively autonomous work groups with each group responsible for a production process. Pay is based on the total number of jobs	The framemen's work was expanded to include taking full responsibility for the job and negotiating with the "customer."	Workers were given less supervision and more job freedom. The authors of letters to complainants were allowed to sign without review by supervisors.	Same as AT&T Shareholder Correspondents Study.	Factory operators were rotated between their factory jobs and more desirable nonfactory jobs.

328

6. Human Results	Job attitudes a few months after the plant opened indicated "positive assessments" by both team members and leaders. Increased democracy in the plant may have led to more civic activity.	Grievances were practically eliminated (from rate of one per week). Morale was higher in the year's experiment.	There was more pride in group achievement. Higher job satisfaction was measured.	After a year's experience, where measured, attitudes improved and grievances dropped.	For some there was challenge and reward while learning, then frustration until they were permanently transferred.
7. Economic Results	The plant is operated by 70 workers, rather than the 110 originally estimated by industrial engineers. Also, there were "improved yields, minimized waste and avoidance of shut downs."	There was no significant change in absenteeism or tardiness. However, at the end there was a slight increase in productivity with fewer workers and less overtime.	After a year's trial, absenteeism decreased from 2% to 1.4%. Turnover practically eliminated.	Turnover decreased by 9.3% in the experimental group and increased 13.1% in the control group. Overtime hours decreased about 50%.	Turnover and absenteeism decreased. Recruitment was easier for factory jobs, since they were no longer dead-end.

TABLE 11-1. (cont.)

	Texas Instruments, Inc.	Hunsfos Pulp & Paper Mill Kristiansand, Norway	Nobø Fabrikker A/S Trandheim, Norway	H. P. Hood & Sons Boston, Mass.	Rade Koncar Zagreb, Yugoslavia
1. Establishment(s) or Employee Groups	Small group of women —electronic instrument assemblers.	Chemical pulp department of papermill.	New unit making electrical panels for metal manufacturing plant.	Unspecified number of company plants and occupations.	Plant manufacturing heavy electrical equipment. All employees.
2. Year Initiated	1967	1964	1965	Over 20 years ago.	1945
3. No. Employees Affected	600	32	10 to 40	Not specified.	1946—890; 1966—7,946
4. Problem	Top management wanted better utilization of human resources.	Segregation of jobs, lack of overlapping skills and permanent shifts increasingly hindered work as the process became more complex.	Management wished to improve simple repetitive jobs.	There was no specific problem. The goal was to improve operations and to involve employees more in the affairs of the company.	National need for rapid industrialization and a desire to transfer management to the worker-producer.

330

5. Technique Used	The group was asked to set its own production goal and given more information concerning costs and terms of the government contract on which it was working.	The group of 32 workers was given greater responsibility for the operation of the department as a whole and was encouraged to increase its control of the process.	Production groups and subgroups were established and put on group bonus rates. A "contact person" (with department head) was substituted for the supervisor and was chosen by election.	On numerous occasions workers teamed with supervisors to simplify work, often using films of actual operations. Workers with two or more years of seniority are secure against layoff.	Under worker's self-management, all workers are members of working units, have the right and obligation to manage their units, make decisions, establish economic policy, and to submit suggestions, criticisms, questions, etc. "to authoritative management," who is obligated to consider them.
6. Human Results	A survey revealed that employees were deriving more satisfaction from their work and had fewer complaints about so-called maintenance items.	Workers showed greater job interest through their suggestions.	... general satisfaction among the workers ... and absenteeism ... much lower than for the factory as a whole.	The program manager reported, "The employees do not resist the approach, an attitude which may have been fostered by a cash award system for suggestions."	Not explicitly stated.
7. Economic Results	During the experiment, assembly time per unit decreased from 138 to 32 hours. Absenteeism, turnover, leaving time, complaints and trips to health center decreased.	In the four-year experiment, the average quality bonus increased about 24%.	In the one-year experiment, production rates increased 22% and hourly earnings increased 11%.	Not explicitly stated.	From a small company in 1945, Rade Koncar has taken a leading role in equipment for power plants, including nuclear, and transformer plants.

TABLE 11-1. (cont.)

	Sisak Ironworks Yugoslavia	I. C. I.	P. P. G. Industries	Monsanto	Monsanto Chemical
1. Establishment(s) or Employee Groups	Iron and Steel Industry in Sisak, Caprag	Imperial Chemical Industries—Gloucester, Great Britain Factory floor workers.	P. P. G. Industries Lexington, N.C. Twist frame operators.	Electronics Divis on West Caldwell, N.J. Foremen.	Textile Division Pensacola, Fla. Chemical operators.
2. Year Initiated	1961	1968	1969	Not specified.	1968
3. No. Employees Affected	About 6,000	19,500	675	Not specified.	50
4. Problem	Low productivity of labor.	Low morale. "Five walkouts in a week."	Loss of efficiency in twist frame machines because frame cleaning was dirty work; repetitive and routine.	High employee turnover among new hires.	Rising production costs beset the automated control room for chemical reaction and conversion.
5. Technique Used	Self-management bodies were established in each department in which the workers decided on production norms and pay rates (including incentives).	Weekly staff assignments provide job rotation. Small groups (8) input "own ideas" into work process.	The frame cleaner job was eliminated. Since cleaning takes 15% of the time on each job, the machine operators took over the cleaning function.	The foremen were given responsibility for interviewing, indoctrinating, and giving skills training to new hires.	Four employee "task forces" (one from each shift) restructured certain jobs and eliminated some dirty jobs through automation. Operators now manage their own restructured jobs.
6. Human Results	Not specified.	"... it's their (the workers') factory, not just a place where they come to work," a supervisor reported.	Personnel and production managers report that "morale is high."	Not specified.	Employee suggestions increased 300%.

332

| 7. Economic Results | In eight years, product quality improved. Production was expanded and modernized. | Since the experiment there has been a 20% reduction in labor, 20% increase in production, 25% increase in pay, and a 30% cut in supervision. | Productivity increased by 12% over the previous two years. | Turnover, which had been high among unskilled jobs averaged 6% annually in the five years of the program. | Waste loss dropped to zero, operators monitor 50% more instruments and half of the old supervisors not needed. |

TABLE 11-1. (cont.)

	Weyerhauser	Araphoe	Syntex	American Velvet Co.	Monsanto
1. Establishment(s) or Employee Groups	Weyerhauser Co. Tacoma, Wash. Paper production employees.	Araphoe Chemical Boulder, Colo. Chemists.	Syntex Corporation Mexico City, Mexico; Research Center Palo Alto, Calif. Salesmen.	All employees of manufacturer of velvet. Stonington, Conn.	Agriculture Division Muscatine, Iowa Machine operators.
2. Year Initiated	1968	1968	1966	Not specified	1967
3. No. Employees Affected	300 (pilot project)	125	Not specified	400	150
4. Problem	Low productivity.	Low productivity and morale.	The innovativeness of scientists was not being utilized.	None specified.	There was a production "bottleneck" in the bagging section.
5. Technique Used	An "I Am" plan (short for "I Am Manager of My Job") was implemented, based on the assumption that all people want to be responsible, to succeed, and can best manage their own jobs.	Each chemist was made directly responsible for an entire project.	Team work groups were formed "where employee set own standards and quotas."	Workers plan and organize own work and have profit sharing plan.	Seminars were held with employees who analyzed their own jobs and made changes. Production goals were set by baggers.

334

6. Human Results	The project manager said, "they became a fraternity . . . and were enthusiastic about the challenge of their new jobs."	Not specified.	A vice president reports, "less skepticism, more volunteering, more introspection and instantaneous feedback, managers more concerned with career paths—career planning of employees, rank-and-file employees appear more committed and involved."	"Consultation, participation, and involvement are a way of life at the top of the company and at the production level as well."	Not specified.
7. Economic Results	"Increased productivity" according to an executive.	Productivity increased and deadlines on customer orders were met promptly.	Volume sales in the two experimental groups increased by 116% and 20% over the control groups.	Not specified.	Production increased 75% in the four months after the change.

TABLE 11-1. (cont.)

	Oldsmobile	Norsk	Texas Instruments	Corning Glass Works Medfield, Mass.	Donnelly Mirrors, Inc. Holland, Mich.
1. Establishment(s) or Employee Groups	Oldsmobile Division, GM Lansing, Mich. Engineering and assembly employees.	Norsk Hydro Oslo, Norway Production workers.	Texas Instruments, Inc. Dallas, Tex. Maintenance personnel.	Instrument assembly workers.	Auto mirror mfg. All employees.
2. Year Initiated	1970	1966	1967	1965	Long-term project
3. No. Employees Affected	Two plants	About 50	120	6	460
4. Problem	High absenteeism and turnover.	Competition was becoming tougher and profits were declining.	100% quarterly turnover and failure to get buildings clean.	Not specified.	To "come to grips with the problems of productivity."
5. Technique Used	A volunteer hourly employee task force held meetings with foremen and other employees, conducted surveys, and made broad recommendations to improve employee relations.	Autonomous work groups were established without first hands (supervisors). A group bonus plan was installed based on productivity.	Workers were organized into 19 member cleaning teams. Each member voice in planning, problem-solving, goal-setting, and scheduling.	Assembly line techniques were abandoned. Workers were allowed to assemble entire electrical hot plates with the freedom to schedule their work as a group so as to meet weekly objectives.	Workers determine their annual salaries. They receive productivity bonuses and must find ways to assure that the bonuses are paid through higher production, elimination of needless jobs, etc.

336

6. Human Results	"The results included more positive employee relations."	Not specified.	"I feel like a human being. You know what you have to do and you push to do it," says an employee.	Not specified.
7. Economic Results	Absenteeism decreased 6% in engineering and 6.5% in assembly—while rising 11% in the rest of Oldsmobile. There were "improved product quality . . . . and reduced costs."	Production costs per ton decreased 30% over the first six months of the project, but other factors were also involved. Absenteeism was 4% in the experimental factory vs. 7% for the control factory.	Quarterly turnover dropped from 100% to 9.8%. Personnel requirements dropped from 120 to 71. Cost savings averaged $103,000 annually between 1967–1969. Building cleanliness ratings increased from 65% to 85%.	In the six months after the change, rejects dropped from 23% to 1% and absenteeism from 8% to 1%.	Wages, costs, and profits all have increased during the past few years, even as the company has lowered its prices.

TABLE 11-1. (cont.)

	Monsanto-Textiles Co. Pensacola, Fla.	Alcan Aluminum Corp. Oswego, N.Y.	Micro-Wax Dept.— Shell Stanlow Refinery, Ellesmere Port; Cheshire, England	Philips Electrical Industries— Holland	Ferado Company United Kingdom
1. Establishment(s) or Employee Groups	Production workers of nylon tire yarn.	Rolling mill operators.	Chemical operators.	Assembly workers.	Production workers making brake linings.
2. Year Initiated	1971	1965	1963	1960	Not specified.
3. No. Employees Affected	6,000	Not specified.	Not specified.	240–300	Not specified.
4. Problem	Not specified.	High rates of absenteeism and tardiness.	Low productivity, low morale, and possibility of "shutdown."	Not specified.	Not specified.
5. Technique Used	Four-day classroom sessions were held to involve production workers in problem-solving. Also, employees set production goals and rotated jobs.	Time clocks were removed and production jobs designed to give workers unusual freedom and decision-making responsibilities. Salaries were guaranteed during absences or layoffs.	Operators formed group teams that provided both more flexibility within shift teams and rotation in jobs. Time clocks were also removed.	Independent work groups were formed and made responsible for job allocations, material and quality control, and providing delegates for management talks.	Groups of six men were trained to use all machines involved in the process and allowed to move from one machine to the other. Each group sees the batch of marketable products they have made.

6. Human Results	"For the employee the program means 'humanized' working conditions," the plant manager reported.	"Monotony is relieved," says the plant manager.	"It is well known that absence and sickness may be symptomatic of alienation . . . from the work situation. Thus . . . [these] statistics are partly an indication of morale," said that plant manager.	The members of semi-autonomous groups derived more satisfaction from their work compared with workers in the old situation.	Job satisfaction in the plant has been found to increase.
7. Economic Results	"The cost of the program more than pays for itself in higher productivity through fewer idle machines and lower repair costs —a possible gain of 100,000 pounds of yarn a year," says the plant manager.	Absenteeism decreased to about 2.5% compared to an industry average of about 10%. Productivity increased.	"Output" in three sections increased by 35%, 40%, and 100% over 1965. Absence and sickness decreased from 4.3% in 1963 to 3.3% in 1969.	By 1967 waste and repairs decreased by 4% and there was an unspecified savings of lower managerial personnel.	There is less turnover, and original delivery times have been cut by seven-eighths.

TABLE 11-1. (cont.)

	Netherlands PTT	Kaiser Aluminum Corporation Ravenswood, W.Va.	Bankers Trust Company New York	Operations Division, Bureau of Traffic— Ohio Dept. of Highways
1. Establishment(s) or Employee Groups	Clerical workers— data collection.	Maintenance workers in reduction plant.	Production typists in stock transfer operations.	Six field construction crews.
2. Year Initiated	Not specified.	1971	1969	Not specified.
3. No. Employees Affected	100	60	200	Not specified.
4. Problem	Jobs were routine. Workers and supervisors were both "notably uninterested" in their work.	Productivity was low. There were walkouts and slowdowns.	Production was low and quality poor. Absenteeism and turnover were high and employee attitudes were poor . . . Jobs were routine, repetitive and devoid of intrinsic interest . . . Too much overseeing.	Low productivity and poor quality of performance.

340

5. Technique Used	Jobs were enlarged to comprise a whole collaborative process (e.g., listing, punching, control punching, corrections, etc.) instead of a single stage of this process.	Time clocks were removed and supervision virtually eliminated. Workers now decide what maintenance jobs are to be done and in what priority and keep their own time cards.	Typists were given the opportunity (1) to change their own computer output tapes, (2) to handle typing for specific group of customers, (3) to check their own work, and (4) to schedule their own work. Training was given in these areas.	Three experimental groups were established, each with a different degree of self-determination of work schedules. Crews were unaware that they were participating in an experiment.
6. Human Results	88% of the workers in the experimental group said the work had become more interesting.	"Morale has improved along with pride in workmanship," says the maintenance chief.	A quantitative survey disclosed improved attitudes and greater satisfaction.	Data showed that as participation increased, so did morale.
7. Economic Results	There was a 15% increase in output per man-hour.	Tardiness is "non-existent." Maintenance costs are down 5.5%. Maintenance work is done with more "quality."	Absenteeism and tardiness were reduced while production and quality increased. Job enrichment programs were extended.	There was no significant change in productivity.

gestions for altered technology are universally acceptable and applicable. There are many barriers to the adoption of such altered technologies, which will be discussed in a later section. The point here is that while these altered technologies appear seductive, there are many factors that have precluded their widespread utilization. Before discussing these factors, it will be of interest to examine an area in which a truly revolutionary alteration in work arrangements has been instituted—Yugoslavia.

THE YUGOSLAVIAN APPROACH

Yugoslavia has attempted to develop a totally different approach to the organization of work and work organizations. The basic component is *worker control* of the enterprise (organization). Since the 1950s, the official policy of the Yugoslav government has been that the workers are to control the internal and (since 1965) the external affairs of the enterprise. What this means is that the workers elect a "workers' council." The workers' council is composed of representatives elected by all of the workers in the enterprise. The workers' council in turn elects a managing board for the organization. The managing board includes the director of the enterprise and other top executives. Department heads and supervisors are elected who oversee the work of the workers themselves. These organizations thus have a hierarchy like that in other parts of the world, but the hierarchy is elected by the workers' representatives on the council. Influential in the election process are the Communist party and the trade unions. What is particularly unique here is the fact that the workers' council decides on such critical issues as the distribution of profits, capital investments, and new ventures. Profits can be distributed to the workers, reinvested, or put into social causes such as housing.

The results of this worker participation program are mixed. On the one hand, several researchers report that the oligarchic patterns found in American organizations are also present in Yugoslavian enterprises.[31] Hierarchical patterns are strong but in altered form, with the workers' council, managing board, workers, managers, and supervisors being the hierarchy.[32] General organizational matters and technical decisions are

[31]Mitja Kamušic, "Efficiency and Self-management," in M. J. Broekmeyer, ed., *Yugoslav Workers' Self-management* (Dordrecht, Holland: R. Reidel Co., 1970), and Josip Županov and Arnold Tannenbaum, "The Distribution of Control in Some Yugoslav Industrial Organizations as Perceived by Members," in Arnold S. Tannenbaum, ed., *Control in Organizations* (New York: McGraw-Hill Book Company, 1968).

[32]Eugen Pusic' and Rudi Supek, "Introduction" (Presented at the First International Conference on Worker Participation and Self-Management, Dubrovnik, Yugoslavia, 1972).

dominated by executives and technical experts, while workers are more concerned with social and job-related issues.[33] As the technology of these organizations becomes more complex, the technical decisions apparently move increasingly into the hands of experts. Thus, technological change has its impact even under conditions of worker control.

While the Yugoslav enterprise is subject to the same technological pressures as its counterparts in other nations, the point of worker participation should not be overlooked. While there is no direct evidence that compares workers' satisfactions and reactions to their work, the rise of the Yugoslav economy has been more rapid than in other developing countries. This cannot be attributed just to worker participation, of course. The program in Yugoslavia has served political and cultural goals in addition to being a technique whereby work is drastically rearranged.

The conditions of work in Yugoslavia are not that much different from conditions elsewhere. Factories remain factories and offices, offices. There are still important technological limitations on how specific types of work can be organized. Worker participation alters the power arrangements within the enterprise and the relationship of the worker to the means of production. This, and similar alterations in Europe and Israel, can only be compared with the American or Canadian experiences when specific technological conditions with equivalent economic conditions and workers with comparable orientations toward work are included. This sort of comparison would provide more conclusive evidence regarding the extent to which productivity, worker behavior, and worker satisfaction are affected by full worker participation.

LIMITATIONS ON JOB REDESIGN

We have discussed approaches to job redesign in the United States and elsewhere. The gist of the arguments in favor of such redesign is that such redesign is relatively inexpensive and is applicable across a wide variety of occupational settings. The argument also contains the implication that if organizational management were just more enlightened and worker oriented, many of the problems surrounding the technological

---

[33]Rudi Supek, "Two Types of Self-managing Organizations and Technical Progress" (Paper prepared for the First International Conference on Worker Participation and Self-Management, Dubrovnik, Yugoslavia, 1972); Josip Obradovic; "The Structure of Participation in the Process of Deciding the Business Policies of the Firm on the Workers' Council Meetings," *Sociology Review*, Zagreb 1 (1972); and Josip Županov, "Employees' Participation and Social Power in Industry" (Paper prepared for the First International Conference on Worker Participation and Self-Management, Dubrovnik, Yugoslavia, 1972).

shaping of jobs could be eliminated. In this section we are going to argue the reverse—job redesign is unlikely, if not impossible, in many situations. This is perhaps pessimistic, but it is also realistic.

The first limitation on job restructuring is the organizational setting of the occupation. The major influence, somewhat paradoxically, on an organization's capabilities to redesign work is the technological system in which the organization operates.

People familiar with the literature on organizations are well aware of the interest that the technological variable has received in recent years. The gist of this literature is that the technology (ies) employed by an organization is (are) critical for the structure of the organization. Mohr has pointed out that the link between technology and structure is probably not as close as some writers have suggested, but there is a good deal of evidence that suggests that the technology-organizational structure link is of crucial, although perhaps not causal, importance.[34] The position to be taken here is that technology and organizational size are the major explanatory variables in terms of the structure of organizations.

The importance of organizational structure for the worker is obvious. It is through the organizationally defined routinization of tasks, formalization and standardization of rules and procedures, centralization or decentralization of power, and emphasis on hierarchical distinctions that the work is presented to the worker. It is of little importance here that work groups and worker behavior develop that are at variance with the organizational structure. It is the organization that defines for the worker what is to be done and how it is to be done. The worker responds to the organization.

Technological effects or organizations can best be understood if a distinction is made regarding types of technology. Hickson, Pugh, and Pheysey have provided a classification that will be useful in this discussion.[35] They note that the operations technology involves the techniques used in workflow activities (equipping and sequencing of activities in the workflow). These are the organizationally defined mechanisms by which the organization's work is accomplished. Components of operations technology include the degree of automation, workflow rigidity, specificity of evaluation, and the continuity of units of throughput, such as single-unit, batch-, mass-, and continuous-flow production systems. It should be noted that nonproduction organizations also have an operations tech-

[34]Lawrence W. Mohr, "Organizational Technology and Organizational Structure," *Administrative Science Quarterly* 16 (December 1971), 449–59.

[35]David Hickson, Derek Pugh, and Diane Pheysey, "Operations Technology and Organizational Structure," *Administrative Science Quarterly* 14 (September 1969), 378–97.

nology in the form of definitions of how and when information or people are to be processed.

A second class of technology is *materials* technology. This is centered around the characteristics of the materials used in the workflow. Rushing has indicated that a seemingly mundane factor such as the "hardness" of the materials has an impact on the organization.[36] It is obvious that working on steel requires different organizational arrangements than working on petroleum or people. (Rushing does not suggest the possible organizational consequences of working on hard or soft people.) It is important to note that the same material is not in and of itself a constant factor across organizations. As Perrow has pointed out, the organization has a conception about the materials being worked on and structures itself accordingly. Nonetheless, we cannot ignore the quality of the materials if we are to understand organizational structure.[37]

The final type of technology is *knowledge* technology. This is the knowledge used in the workflow. Although this aspect of technology is only minimally developed in the Hickson, Pugh, and Pheysey formulation, it appears that knowledge technology is a key in understanding the other forms of technology. An organization brings knowledge into itself through staff experts and the general management structure as it is exposed to new and old ideas. This would seem to have a clear impact on the definition of the situation in regard to materials and the operations to be performed thereupon.

In discussing the relationship between operations technology and organizational structure, Hickson, Pugh, and Pheysey state:

> Structural variables will be associated with operations only when they are centered on the workflow. The smaller the organization, the more its structure will be pervaded by such technological effects; the larger the organization, the more these effects will be confined to variables such as job-counts of employees or activities linked with the workflow itself, and will not be detectable in variables of the more remote administrative and hierarchical structure.[38]

The authors here are trying to resolve some of the issues regarding the relative importance of organizational size and technology. What is missed in this conclusion is the fact that the "more remote administrative and

---

[36]William A. Rushing, "Hardness of Materials as Related to Division of Labor in Manufacturing Organizations," *Administrative Science Quarterly* 13 (September 1968), 229–45.

[37]Charles Perrow, "A Framework for the Comparative Analysis of Organizations," *American Sociological Review* 32 (April 1967), 194–208.

[38]Hickson, Pugh, and Pheysey, *Operations Technology and Organizational Structure*, pp. 394–95.

hierarchical structure" has its own operations technology. The administrative operations technology is unfortunately largely overlooked in the methodology that these researchers employ. The point remains, of course, that in the production process, the operations technology is shown to have a dominant impact on the manner in which the work is structured.

James Thompson has suggested that in organizations with "long-linked" technologies and in some parts of organizations with "mediating" technologies, individual discretion is an "unwelcome influence."[39] The work tasks are designed to be highly standardized and repetitive, so that the individual does not intrude with this unwelcome discretion. Thompson also notes that there are organizational positions, such as those at the boundary of the organization, that do require discretion. At the same time, organizations attempt to standardize even these positions by gaining control over the environment. If Thompson is correct, then there is a form of organizational imperative toward standardization and routinization based on the form of technology employed by the organization.

In another set of related studies, Woodward, and later Zwerman, examined the impact of different productions systems of organizational structure.[40] Both found that in large-batch and mass-production systems, there is a strong tendency for "mechanical" organizational systems. This involves a rigid and precise division of labor, clear power lines, and an emphasis on the organizational hierarchy. Among unit, small-batch, and continuous-process production organizations, there is a stronger tendency for "organic" systems, which emphasize less rigidity and power and hierarchical differences. If technology is seen as rather unidirectional in the sense that there is a consistent attempt to replace human labor with mechanical or electronic counterparts, then these findings lead to both optimism and pessimism in terms of the outlook for the worker. If it is possible for production and some administrative tasks to move through a progression from unit to small-batch to large-batch to mass to continuous process, then, depending upon the starting point, a shift from organic to mechanical *or* mechanical to organic can be predicted. Putting conjecture aside, however, the point remains that the nature of the operations technology in these studies has a crucial impact on the organizational structures involved.

Woodward presents another finding that is important for the present discussion. The span of control of first-line supervisors has been of consistent interest to organizational researchers. The span of control has important implications for the organizational control system and, as later

[39]Thompson, *Organizations in Action* (New York: McGraw-Hill Book Company), p. 103.
[40]Woodward, *Industrial Organization: Theory and Practice*, and William Zwerman, *New Perspectives on Organizational Theory* (Westport, Conn.: Greenwood Publishing Co., 1970).

research suggests, reflects the kinds of tasks being performed. Woodward found that in continuous-process and unit production systems there is a low span of control for first-line supervisors, while for the other production systems, the span of control tends to be higher. The reason for this is apparently as suggested by Bell.[41] Bell found a similar relationship to that reported by Woodward. With complex jobs (the study here was based on hospitals and not production organizations), there was a lower span of control. The jobs in unit and continuous-process organizations were similarly complex. Bell suggests that impersonal mechanisms of control are operative in less complex jobs and implies that control is actually tighter when the span of control is wider. Blau and Schoenherr's work confirms this finding in administrative organizations.[42] If the technology available to an organization permits it to routinize and standardize its work, the organization can rely on wider spans of control, reducing supervisory costs. This is obviously desirable for the organization, other things being equal.

Additional fuel for this line of reasoning can be found in Meyer's work.[43] Meyer also dealt with administrative organizations. In his analysis of automation (use of the computer) in such organizations, Meyer found that the computing departments studied had wide spans of control at the first-line level, when compared with other departments of the same organization. He suggests that this is a consequence of the low skill level needed at this level. He also found that these same departments had a deeper hierarchy above the first-line supervisor. He explains this on the basis of the need for consultation with other departments and the requirement that these higher levels require more expertise.

Another, more intensive, analysis of the expertise issue is provided by Meyer.[44] The evidence from this study (also based on an administrative organization) is that the span of control of first-line supervisors decreases as the level of expertise increases. Meyer explains this phenomenon by the need for consultation and two-way communications between superior and subordinate. The narrow span of control in the case of more expert subordinates is not based on close supervision. This finding suggests that as organizations utilize more expert employees in order to keep up with changes and advances in the knowledge technology, the outlook for these workers in terms of less rigid, standardized, and routinized work is good. The literature on professionals in organizations, of course,

---

[41]Gerald D. Bell, "The Determinants of Span of Control," *American Journal of Sociology* 73 (July 1967), 100–9.

[42]Blau and Schoenherr, *The Structure of Organizations*.

[43]Marshall W. Meyer, "Automation and Bureaucratic Structure," *American Journal of Sociology* 74 (November 1968), 256–64, and *idem*, "Expertness and Span of Control," *American Sociological Review* 33 (December 1968), 944–51.

[44]Meyer, "Expertness and Span of Control."

suggests that this type of organizational structure is exactly what the more expert employees want. For the nonexpert, of course, the outlook is not nearly so bright.

The role of technology in the determination of organizational structure has been stressed thus far. Before returning to other ways in which this affects the worker, some other factors that affect organizational structure should be mentioned. Size is clearly important here, as the work of Hickson, Pugh, and Pheysey has suggested. Most research has found an increase in formalization, routinization, standardization, and so on with increased size. While there is an active debate now raging regarding the primacy of technology versus size in terms of organizational structure, few would argue that size is of no importance. Thus a large organization utilizing an operations technology that is amenable to standardization and routinization would be more standardized and routinized than a smaller organization with the same technology or a comparable sized organization with a less routinizable technology.

The broader environment also presents the organization with factors that affect its structure. Khandwalla, for example, suggests that when an organization must deal with an environment that is uncertain, heterogeneous, and nonhostile, the organization will be more structurally differentiated, with greater differentiation of personnel, will use a variety of tools and techniques for communications and coordination, and will make greater use of integrative devices than organizations with more certain and homogeneous environments.[45] If, in the former case, the environment becomes hostile, more centralization of power and less internal differentiation will be evident. If Khandwalla is correct, the workers in any organization are affected by the environment, in terms of the structuring of their own work.

As yet, research in the field of organizations has been unable to sort out the relative importance of the various factors that have been discussed. There is certainty that the environment, technology, and size are all critical for the nature of organization structure, but the causal ordering and the weights to assign each factor have not yet been determined. For the purposes of the present discussion, this does not really matter, since all of the factors have been shown to have an effect on the organization. What does matter is that these factors are out of the control of the worker. They are also not totally controlled by the organization, even though there is some organizational determination of organization size, and there are attempts to control the environment and influence technology.

[45]P. N. Khandwalla, "Environment and Its Impact on Organizations," *International Studies of Management and Organization* 2 (fall 1972), 297–313.

It is at this point that the organization's knowledge technology again becomes important. Organizations make decisions in regard to their environment. They also make decisions on how to develop their own operations technology. If an organization's knowledge technology includes the notion of worker participation, for example, this can be part of the set of alternatives that are considered in the decision-making process. If organizational decision makers are unaware of this phenomenon or have received information that it is organizationally damaging—a Communist plot, or whatever—then worker participation is unlikely to become part of the operations technology. Similarly, if an organization is engaged in working on materials that are rather routinely handled and about which there is little likelihood of technological innovation, and if the organization exists in a highly competitive (hostile) environment, then the organization is most likely to remain centralized, routinized, and standardized.

Organizations in heterogeneous and rapidly changing environments engage in extensive search processes through research and development. Such organizations are rather likely to be innovative in terms of their operations technology. The search process in such organizations is likely to become aware of different ways of organizing the work in the organization. Such an organization is probably most likely to engage in alternative means of organizing the work, including some of the techniques proposed for improving the lot of the worker. On the other hand, organizations that are not so active would tend to be less aware and to deal with their employees in more traditional ways.

There is still another aspect to all of this that sociologists all too often tend to ignore. Even if an organization is aware of alternative ways of organizing the work being performed and sees some benefits in making some changes that might benefit the workers, it may not be able to make any changes because of the costs involved. These can be costs of equipment that would have to be replaced or of people who are wedded to the traditional practices and who would have to be replaced. Unless the organization has some discretionary funds available, a changed structuring of work would seem unlikely.

In addition to the obstacles posed by organizational technology, there are additional organizational factors that must be taken into consideration. Many employers are reluctant to move to programs of job redesign because of their perception that the schemes don't work, because of the presence of alternative personnel strategies in the "knowledge technology" of the organization, or because of the absence of information from organizations exactly like theirs.[46] In addition, of course, management can be threatened by job redesign. First-line supervisors

---

[46]See *Work in America*, pp. 111–12.

are particularly vulnerable in such situations, and the total management structure would be potentially threatened by movements toward self-management.[47] The resistance of management, for whatever reason, is important for the simple reason that the power in the organization lies in the management.

A final source of limitation on job redesign comes from the workers themselves. Collectively, labor unions have been important sources of opposition to redesign programs.[48] Unions have traditionally been concerned with the more extrinsic characteristics of their members' jobs and have not adjusted to concerns about job design as rapidly as some would have liked. Of course, the union response might be a reflection of their workers' and members' own perceptions and interests. As was noted earlier, the evidence that workers want enlarged jobs and more participation is just not all that impressive.[49] While many workers do express dissatisfaction with boring and meaningless work, there is hardly what might be called a workers' movement on this issue.

In this section we have attempted to indicate some of the barriers to the adoption of programs designed to alter the content and conditions of work that have been affected by technological change. This attempt has not meant to downplay the benefits or the possibility of making work and life more meaningful for the white- and blue-collar worker. The author has tried to suggest that what may appear to be easy solutions are not really very easy. Such changes take place in the organizational setting where technology itself is a limitation. When the managerial and worker resistance is added on, the prospects for immediate change are dim.

TECHNOLOGICAL CHANGE AND EMPLOYMENT VERSUS UNEMPLOYMENT

The impact of automation and general technological change on employment patterns can be analyzed from three perspectives. Gross employment rate changes, case studies of the introduction of automated operations, and analyses of the impact of unemployment on the individual have all been utilized in assessing the consequences of automation. In this section we will focus on the first two types of analyses.

[47]See Harold L. Sheppard and Neal Q. Herrick, *Where Have All the Robots Gone?* (New York: Free Press of Glencoe, 1972), p. 178.

[48]*Work in America*, pp. 112–14.

[49]See William H. Form, *Auto Workers and Their Machines*; also, *idem*, "Technology and Social Behavior of Workers in Four Countries: A Sociotechnical Perspective," *American Sociological Review* 37 (December 1972), 727–38, and Milton R. Blood and Charles L. Hulin, "Alienation, Environmental Characteristics, and Worker Responses," *Journal of Applied Psychology* 51 (March 1967), 284–90.

It is difficult to determine exactly what the impact of automation has been from the data on the total employment patterns within the society. The relatively constant low rate of unemployment suggests that the forecasts of optimists regarding automation have been correct—the long-run effect of automation will be to *increase* employment. Employment rates have remained relatively constant over the past decades with the exception of recessions that appear to be unrelated to automation. At present it is thus extremely difficult to determine the impact of automation on gross employment rates.

When a more detailed analysis of employment patterns is employed, some significant patterns are apparent. The decline in the proportion of unskilled and semiskilled workers in the labor force indicates the diminished demand for this level of worker. At the same time, the rising educational level of the total population allows many who would have gone into this type of work to go into other occupations, which have expanded. For those who do not attain the education necessary for such mobility, the outlook is bleak in the sense that these lower level manual occupations will continue to contract. It is at this point that the possibility or probability of a population segment that is unemployable becomes apparent. In both urban and rural areas the likelihood of such continuing unemployment patterns has already established itself.

It is difficult to determine what the employment patterns among office workers affected by automation have been or will be. Since there is a high rate of turnover among the young females, the backbone of this segment of the labor force, and since there is no definitive pattern of attempts to reenter the labor force, the rate of unemployment is difficult to assess. Unless the individuals involved are actively seeking work, they will not show up in the statistics on unemployment. At the same time, of course, the fact that they are not actively seeking work implies they do not feel great need to find employment, and it is thus difficult to make a case for a severe problem in this area. The automation of the office does reduce the occupational possibilities for the unskilled high school graduate or dropout girl. If this segment of the population does want to be employed, the problems facing them are evident.

When the focus of the analysis is shifted to particular instances of the introduction of automation, more definitive patterns can be seen. In a summary of the general principles operative in these situations, Silverman notes that the introduction of automated equipment into a plant or office reduces costs.[50] If the price of the product or service involved is responsive to cost reduction, the price will decline. When this occurs, the demand for the product or service may increase. If the demand increases, employment is likely to increase or at least stay at the same level.

---

[50]"The Economic and Social Effects of Automation in an Organization," p. 4.

On the other hand, when the price of the product or service is not responsive to reduced costs, workers are likely to be laid off in an attempt to further reduce costs. When the demand stays constant, regardless of pricing patterns, workers are likely to be laid off.

Another important consideration is that even if employment stays constant and output is increased, as a result of the automated situation, jobs that normally would have been created as a result of pressures for more output are not created. In this sense automation reduces the potential number of jobs. If this aspect of technological change continues, it is conceivable that the overall rate of employment will decline *if* additional forms of employment are not developed through demands for new products and, more particularly, services not previously in demand. This latter point assumes that those persons not hired because of the lowered demand for workers due to automation can transfer their skills to the new situation. If the potential office clerk, for example, can perform adequately in some new service organization, such as a travel agency, the possibility of reduced employment rates is minimized. This assumes, of course, that such new service organizations are in demand. If, on the other hand, the new service organizations are developed but the skills of those workers not hired due to the introduction of automation are not compatible with the demands of the situation, the potential for higher rates of unemployment increases.

Shifting the analysis from these hypothetical situations to actual case studies, we find that employment is generally reduced. In the case of the first form of automation, some of the changes are dramatic. For example, in a factory producing automobile engine blocks, an automated line can produce an engine block in twenty minutes with forty-eight workers. Previously, 400 men working forty minutes were required for the same output.[51] Another case from the automobile industry shows the same trend. Before automation, 18,000 men were required to turn out stampings for some 755,000 cars. The introduction of automated equipment into this process reduced the required labor force to 13,000 men and also raised the output to 2,241,000 cars.[52] In this sort of automation the major reduction in the labor force is accomplished through reduced need for materials handling. According to Bright, some additional personnel are often hired for the maintenance function, but the numbers involved here are generally insignificant.[53]

Studies by Mann and Hoffman of power plants and Walker of an

[51]Gerald G. Sommers, Edward L. Cushman, and Nat Weinberg, *Adjusting to Technological Change* (New York: Harper & Row, 1963), p. 13.

[52]Harold L. Sheppard and James L. Stern, "The Impact of Automation on Workers in Supplier Plants," *Labor Law Journal*, VIII, 10 (October 1957), 714–18.

[53]Bright, *Automation and Management*, p. 202.

automated pipe mill suggest that the same pattern is evident in the second form of automation.[54] In these cases rather complete automation allowed the organizations to have much more output with substantially less human input. In these cases the automated plants supplemented pre-existing operations and did not result in layoffs, but the pattern of jobs not created remained.

Automation of the office generally occurs in an ongoing situation rather than in the form of a new plant, as in the previous cases. The result is the aforementioned displacement of bookkeepers and clerks. Here the work force is typically reduced through normal attrition. In some cases of this form of automation, the work force can actually be increased. Jack Stieber found that an insurance company added person-nel after the introduction of computers to the system.[55] Field agents were relieved of much of their paper work by the computerized system, which itself required personnel. In this sense the field agents could concentrate more heavily on their basic tasks leading to a more rational system.

TECHNOLOGICAL CHANGE AND THE FUTURE OF OCCUPATIONS

No discussion of technological change would be complete with-out a consideration of the future. As was noted in chapter 2 on the con-text of contemporary occupations and in chapter 4 on the professions, creating knowledge and technology is an activity that contains the seeds of continued knowledge and technology generation.

For occupations, two trends are frequently noted. One is the devel-opment of a meritocracy based on knowledge. Daniel Bell openly favors such a meritocracy in his discussion of the postindustrial society.[56] In Bell's conceptualization, this will be a "just" meritocracy in which achieve-ment is earned by the individual and confirmed by one's peers. This, of course, is the ideal in the professional model.

But what of those who because of birth, bad living, or bad associates somehow are below the top levels of the meritocracy? Here the second trend enters the picture. Writers such as Jacques Ellul[57] suggest that the rest of the society will become increasingly manipulated by the tech-

---

[54] See Mann and Hoffman, *Automation and the Worker: A Study of Social Change in Power Plants*, pp. 104–9, and Walker, *Toward the Automatic Factory: A Case Study of Men and Machines*, pp. 26–29.

[55] "Automation and the White Collar Worker," *Personnel*, XXXIV, 3 (November-December 1957), 8–17.

[56] Bell, *The Coming of the Post-Industrial Society*, pp. 446–55.

[57] Jacques Ellul, *The Technological Society*, trans. John Wilkinson (New York: Alfred A. Knopf, 1964).

nological elite, who will not only control the creation of knowledge but also its production and distribution. Social technologies are already available that can manage the amount and type of information available to the non-elites, as events in the Soviet Union in regard to authors and in the United States regarding presidential elections suggest.

In the meritocracy system, people's occupations will be linked into the knowledge system and rewards and status will be accorded to those who are proficient in this system. Occupations will be increasingly knowledge based. The second perspective suggests that occupations will be about the same, but the control will increasingly be in the hands of those with material and social technological knowledge, and thus the occupations without such controls will be powerless.[58]

Both of these arguments and forecasts are probably correct in part. Certainly, if past history is any indicator, we will move toward more and more emphasis on knowledge with continued technological change, and we will have increasing potentialities for social control through technology. Whether or not a meritocracy *or* subjugation of the individual to the technical system is achieved has to do with factors other than sheer technology, however. Economic, social, and political factors must be considered in conjunction with technology. The trends we have been discussing, like all social movements, occur in the context of the total social system and not in isolation. It is possible, due to economic, social, and political considerations, that the investment in technological developments could slow. It is possible, for the same reasons, that the individual could be given more control of the parameters of his own life. Technology is a powerful force, but it is not the only social force.

SUMMARY AND CONCLUSIONS

In this chapter we have considered the impact of technology and technological change on occupations, having basically dealt with the impact of the occupational structure on technology in the chapter on the professions. We have seen the nature of technological change and how it has differential consequences for different types of occupations. Technological change increases the demands for knowledge on the part of professionals and executives and managers. It can make blue-collar work more enjoyable and white-collar work less so. The various suggestions regarding job redesign in the face of this technological change were

[58]For a discussion of some of the alternatives of work and technology in the future, see: Fred Best, ed., *The Future of Work*, (Englewood Cliffs, N.J.: Prentice-Hall, 1973).

then considered and evaluated. Throughout this chapter we have emphasized the fact that technological change does not occur in a vacuum. The organization, while critically affected by technology itself, is also the "gatekeeper" in terms of implementing technological change or job redesign for occupations. The wider social structure will influence the rate and direction of technological change in the future.

We are now ready to examine the intersection of occupations with an important aspect of this wider social structure—the political system.

12

OCCUPATIONS AND
THE POLITICAL
SYSTEM

The link between occupations and the political system is at once obvious and obscure. It is obvious in the sense that certain occupations seem to dominate the political sphere; yet it is obscure when the occupation of politician is considered. The exact role of political considerations without the occupational structure is not clear. In this chapter, members of various occupational groups will be examined as participants in politics—both as active political office seekers and as members of political movements—in an effort to analyze the relationships between occupations and the political system. The occupation of politician will also be examined to determine if it can actually be considered an occupation and, if so, where it fits within the total occupational system. A final consideration will be the nature of the political process within the occupational system. Here the concern will be the exercise of power as a component of the nature of occupations.

OCCUPATIONS AND POLITICAL PARTICIPATION

There are two basic kinds of political participation—running for elected office and participating through campaign work, contributions, and voting. Both types of participation are unevenly distributed in the occupational structure.

In terms of elected officials, there is a startling preponderance of

356

lawyers in public office. Table 12-1 summarizes a series of studies in this regard. Even though the proportion of lawyers declines at the state level, law is still the highest single occupation in political office. We can probably safely assume that the losers in the political contests in which these people were elected also equally heavily represented the legal profession (there are few analyses of losers in any field).

Michael Cohen offers several explanations for this pattern.[1] In the first place, law and politics share a common subculture. Since so many office holders are lawyers and there is movement back and forth between the practice of law and politics, the new lawyer can learn the political system rather easily and quickly. Secondly, law is a profession in which

TABLE 12–1. Comparison of Percentages of Lawyers Holding Various Public Offices

Public Office	Percentage of Lawyers
Presidents, Vice-Presidents, Cabinet members, Supreme Court Justices, Speakers of the House, 1789–1952	75
Southern Governors, 1938–1948	72
Presidents, Vice-Presidents, Cabinet members, 1877–1934	70
U.S. Senate, 71st–75th Congresses, averaged	68
All Presidents	66
U.S. Senate, 77th Congress	61
U.S. House of Representatives, 71st–75th Congresses, average	61
U.S. House of Representatives, 77th Congress	58
U.S. Senate, 81st Congress	57
U.S. House of Representatives, 81st Congress	56
All U.S. Senators, 1947–1957	54
Governors, 1930–1940	52
Missouri Senate, 1937–1957	49
New York Senate, 1904–1964, average	48
New York Assembly, 1904–1964, average	47
Illinois Senate, 1937–1957	42
18 State Senates, c. 1963, average	39
28 State Senates, 1899, average	35
Governors, 1870–1949, minimum	32
13 State legislatures, both houses, 1925–1935	28
Illinois House, 1937–1957	27
18 State lower houses, c. 1963, average	24
Missouri House, 1937–1957	23
28 State lower houses, 1899, average	19

Source: Michael Cohen, "Lawyers and Political Careers," *Law and Society Review* 3 (May 1969), 569.

[1]"Lawyers and Political Careers," *Law and Society Review* 3 (May 1969), 563–74. For an early discussion of this phenomenon see H. H. Gerth and C. W. Mills, trans. and ed., From *Max Weber: Essays in Sociology* (New York: Oxford University Press, Inc., 1946), pp. 94–95.

the individual can control his own work arrangements more than in many other occupations. Finally, there are many role models of successful lawyer-politicians. For lawyers who have been in politics, even a losing campaign can at times be parlayed into a judgeship or public attorney-ship. Knowledge and practice of law also may shape political views and provide an understanding of governmental processes. There is thus a nice fit between law and politics. Indeed, politics can be viewed as a legiti-mate and legitimated career pattern for a lawyer.

At the more general level, Seymour M. Lipset and Robert E. Lane have noted that occupations vary in the degree to which they allow members to be politically active.[2] Time must be available for participa-tion. Intellectual stimulation of the ideas necessary for entrance into politics also varies by occupation. This is particularly evident in the case of political scientists, another occupation that is overrepresented in active political life.

As a general rule, according to Scott Greer and Peter Orleans, "per-sons more educated, higher paid, and with more highly regarded jobs are more likely to be better informed and interested in politics."[3] Lipset suggests that a potential politician must have *psychic* leisure time to de-vote to the development of ideas.[4] The extremely poor and those with physically and mentally exhausting jobs are unlikely to have the desire or energy to engage in reading, listening, or thinking about things politi-cal.[5] This is reflected in the simple act of voting, as well as participation at higher levels.

Indirect support for the idea of the importance of intellectual stimu-lation and the availability of leisure time can be developed by con-sidering the role of families and individuals of established wealth in contemporary American politics. The Roosevelts, Rockefellers, and Ken-nedys all exemplify education at elite schools and probably had freedom to develop political ideas through unencumbered periods of leisure. Lip-set concludes that the political position of these men, typically some type of noneconomic liberalism (in the areas of foreign relations, civil rights and liberties, and urban affairs) stems largely from their education, general sophistication and, perhaps, psychic security.[6]

To the idea of training and availability of time for the pursuit of political office must be added the idea of visibility. The importance of

---

[2]See Lipset, *Political Man* (New York: Doubleday & Co., 1959), pp. 197–98, and Lane, *Political Life* (New York: Free Press of Glencoe, 1959), pp. 331–32.

[3]Political Sociology," in *Handbook of Modern Sociology*, ed. Robert E. L. Faris (Chicago: Rand McNally & Company, 1964), p. 824.

[4]*Political Man*, p. 198.

[5]*Ibid.*

[6]*Ibid.*, p. 298.

the mass media at the national and local levels in political campaigns has apparently allowed those who receive a good deal of exposure to the public to become more likely to be active and successful candidates than those who lack such exposure. The most obvious case of this is movie actors who enter the political arena. Cases of football coaches and other sports figures who go into politics illustrate the same point as does the historical tie between military prominence and political office seeking. While such exposure to the public does not in itself guarantee a successful candidacy, it is an asset not possessed by the majority of potential candidates.

Entrance into active political involvement as an office seeker is thus linked to the nonpolitical occupations of the participants. Occupations vary in the degree to which they provide the knowledge background and allow participation. Occupations that demand a heavy and regular time involvement, such as medicine, executive positions, or the whole array of hourly paid work, almost preclude participation unless the individual is willing to forego his occupation and the derivative income during his office seeking campaign. Since occupations are a major basis for the individual's frame of reference, those occupations that do not provide the intellectual stimulation or basic ideas necessary for political activity are unlikely to be sources of political candidates. The exact patterns of recruitment into political activity are not clear, either from the perspective of the motivations of the individual or an individual's place in the social structure.

While the exact motivations for entrance into active political participation are not clear, there is some evidence that occupationally linked factors affect the direction of political beliefs for the politically active. Lipset reports that Republican office seekers and party officials at the local level tend to come from the professional and business-managerial occupations, while the Democrats have a heavier representation of manual and lower level white-collar occupations.[7] Despite this evidence, our knowledge about the processes of entering the political arena is quite fragmentary. Much of what has been discussed in this chapter has been a common-sense appraisal of the existing situation, rather than a theory grounded on sound research findings. The aspect of political activity discussed above remains quite unexplored.

Part of the reason for the absence of extensive research on politics as an occupation is undoubtedly that politics is usually only part-time work. At the local and state level, most legislators and many administrators have full-time occupations in addition to their political work. A state legislator, for example, is only committed to his political occupation dur-

[7] *Ibid.*, p. 288.

ing that period in which the legislature is in session. This can be a very brief period of time. While legislative committees and the important task of campaigning for office use up a great deal more time, the legislator typically maintains an "outside" occupation. In addition, at least half of the politicians at any point in time are not employed in political office. They have been defeated in their bids for office and thus must be engaged in some other form of activity.

The small amount of research available in regard to politics as an occupation probably also reflects the fact that a great variety of behavior can be observed among office holders. Heinz Eulau *et al.* have pointed out that "in politics, the skills presumably necessary for professional success are much less specific [than for other professions]."[8] While the question might be raised as to whether politics can be considered a profession, the authors' point is appropriate. This fact and the rather transitory nature of most political careers make analysis difficult, which is reflected in the scarcity of available information.

Some components of the political occupation have, however, been identified. In their analysis of state legislators, Eulau *et al.* noted that the level of competition between parties was a major variable in ordering the career patterns of the legislators. In states in which there is active and close competition between the major parties and the parties themselves are well organized, the following tendencies have been found:

1. state legislators will have had some prior governmental experience, on the local level and in a legislative or quasi-legislative capacity;

2. state legislators will have held party office or done party work at the local level;

3. state legislators will view the political party as a sponsor of their legislative careers;

4. state legislators will appreciate the opportunity given them by the political party in promoting their candidacies;

5. state legislators will not perceive interest groups and/or friends as agents sponsoring their careers;

6. state legislators will value the possession of particular skills thought relevant to a political career;

7. state legislators will have legal training and skills;

8. state legislators will not see opportunities to combine their private and political careers;

9. state .legislators will not stress "opportunity" in general as a factor facilitating their careers;

10. state legislators will not look upon their political careers as a means for achieving personal—selfish and/or altruistic—goals;

11. state legislators will be committed to their legislative careers insofar as they plan to run for their seat again;

---

[8]"Career Perspectives of State Legislatures" in *Political Decision Makers*, ed. Dwaine Marvick (New York: Free Press of Glencoe, Inc., 1961), p. 229.

12. state legislators will attribute their continued commitment to their legislative careers to their "personal involvement" in the legislative job.[9]

Despite the small sample involved, this study does suggest that, under the circumstances of political competition and party organization, the idea of a political career has some meaning. In other cases, however, involvement in the state legislature is likely to be opportunistic, with little thought given to a continued level of activity in political office. However, it is difficult to generalize from this study of state legislators to other political office holders at higher and lower levels. Our knowledge of the occupation of politician and the occupational backgrounds of politicians is basically limited to the fact that political office holders tend to come from the more advantaged occupations.

The findings discussed above and an analysis by Peter H. Rossi suggest that part-time office holders are most likely to take non-official considerations into account.[10] The part-time mayor, councilman, or legislator is more likely to respond to pressures from his regular occupation and other outside interests than is the full-time office holder.

If office holding and office seeking have a distinct relationship to occupations, so do other forms of political activity. There is a general socioeconomic status linkage to voting patterns. That is, the higher a person's status, the more frequently he or she will vote.[11] Lipset found higher rates of voting among businessmen, white-collar employees, government employees, commercial-crop farmers, and some skilled blue-collar-level workers. Lower voting turnouts were evident among unskilled workers, servants, service workers, and subsistence farmers.

Several factors are at work here. John McCarthy and Mayer Zald have focused on some factors that are associated with political participation.[12] In the first place, they discount the idea that those with more affluence and leisure time will be politically active. While there has been a general increase in affluence for most of the population, this has not been accompanied by an overall increase in political participation; neither have the increased leisure and affluence of the middle of the occupational structure resulted in more political activity. This is coupled with the fact that people in upper level occupations, while also more affluent, spend more time at their occupations than the middle class. Clearly, it is not just availability of time that determines political participation.

McCarthy and Zald conclude that "discretionary time" is a major

[9]*Ibid.*, pp. 259–60.

[10]See Rossi, "Power and Community Structure" in *Political Sociology*, ed. Lewis A. Coser (New York: Harper & Row, 1966), p. 138.

[11]Lipset, *Political Man*, p. 184.

[12]*The Trend of Social Movements in America: Professionalization and Resource Mobilization* (Morristown, N.J.: General Learning Press, 1973).

factor in political participation. By this they mean that the individual can arrange work or other activities so that blocks of time are available for political involvement. Thus

> the growth of mass higher education creates a large pool of students whose discretionary time can be allocated to social movement activities; as the relative size of the social service, administrative, and academic professions increases, more and more professionals can arrange their time schedules to allow participation in social movement-related activities; and a relative increase in discretion over work-time allocation permits the emergence of transitory teams to engage in socio-political activities.[13]

In addition to this, political participation has become something of a full-time occupation in and of itself, with community organizers, street ministers, and poverty lawyers exemplifying new political occupational forms. These occupational forms depend upon support not only from private donations, but also from the "establishment" in the form of organized religion, business, and government support.

There has to be economic support for full-scale political participation and political movements, but there also has to be awareness and concern, especially for general political participation. Here the role of education is critical. In a study of scientists, L. Vaughn Blankenship found a strikingly high rate of participation in the form of attending rallies, writing letters to congressmen, contributing money to political causes, etc.[14] While these findings are colored by the fact that the data were collected during the height of the Vietnam war and other war-related issues, the fact remains that the general high level of education in scientific specialties is related to a general high level of reading and other information-gathering activity. In general, those engaged in intellectual pursuits are oriented to the left, while professionals in more entrepreneurial roles, such as in medicine, dentistry, or law, oriented to the right.[15] Alford attributes these political differences to the occupations' linkages with the dominant economic interests. Business executives and the entrepreneurial professions are linked into the dominant economic interests, while the intellectual professions and government civil servants, who are in an equivalent position in regard to the economic interests, are not.

Political movements have additional occupational linkages. Groups drawn to such movements have much in common. In his analysis of political extremism to either the right or the left, Lipset has noted that

---

[13]*Ibid.*, p. 10.

[14]"The Scientist as 'Apolitical' Man," *The British Journal of Sociology* 24 (September 1973), 269–87.

[15]Robert R. Alford, *Party and Society* (Chicago: Rand McNally & Company, 1963), p. 36.

"extremist movements have much in common. They appeal to the disgruntled and psychologically homeless, to the personal failures, the socially isolated, the economically insecure, the uneducated, unsophisticated, and authoritarian persons at every level of society."[16]

In viewing the same phenomenon, Kornhauser is more occupationally specific. He suggests that the small businessman and the marginal farmer tend to join movements of the radical right. Also likely to go in this direction are newly wealthy individuals, usually from the business sphere of society, who are not accepted by the established upper class. Turning to the left are workers in isolated industries, such as miners, farm laborers, and maritime workers and longshoremen. Intellectuals who do not have ties to any corporate body, such as universities or colleges, are also likely to move toward the radical left. Cases of this would be writers or artists who work on their own.[17]

Participation in such mass movements is based on much more than simple occupational membership. The occupation does, however, set the conditions under which a person lives and it thus contributes to his political orientation. Norbert Wiley's insightful analysis provides some indications of the reasons for this form of political participation.[18] As discussed in chapter 5, Wiley notes that there are three dimensions of the class system: "(1) the labor market, which is the source of the conflict among occupational and property-owning groups, (2) the credit or money market, which is the basis for the conflict between debtors and creditors, and (3) the commodity market, which is the basis for the conflict between buyers and sellers, and landlords and tenants."[19] There are thus three axes of potential conflict and three bases upon which identification with others can occur.

Wiley suggests that part of the reason that the United States has not had political activity divided along simple class lines is the fact that most people occupy positions (occupations) inconsistent in terms of these bases of conflict. The majority of urban industrial workers, for example, have been concerned about wages and working conditions and less concerned about the credit or commodity market. During the nineteenth century, the workers did not unite with farmers in a socialist movement, despite the fact that both were evidently disadvantaged. From the perspective of this analysis, while both were disadvantaged, the disadvantage was along

[16]*Political Man*, p. 174.

[17]Kornhauser, *The Politics of Mass Society* (New York: Free Press of Glencoe, Inc., 1959), pp. 185–219.

[18]See Norbert Wiley, "America's Unique Class Politics: The Interplay of the Labor, Credit, and Commodity Markets," *American Sociological Review* 32 (August 1967), 529–41.

[19]*Ibid.*, p. 531.

different axes, and each group would desire a different form of political action. In the case of the isolated worker in mining or farm labor, the inconsistency between axes is minimized. Both the credit and commodity markets are out of his control, and there is often a clear and common enemy who can be identified, the company and its store or the farm owner and his housing and low wages.

Wiley uses a different, but persuasive, interpretation of persons attracted to the radical right. He suggests that people with inconsistent class attributes are especially prone to support right-wing groups. The small businessman and marginal farmer both fit this category in that

> while both make their living by selling, they also do capital buying from powerful sellers, and their incomes are often affected as much by buying as by selling. In addition, they are often heavily in debt and may be employers of labor, at least sporadically. Both groups, consequently, are afflicted with economic cross pressures and cannot identify with either big business or labor unions.[20]

The same general explanation is used for the emerging orientation toward the extreme right among some manual workers. Here the growing amount of capital investment in real estate and the possibility of holding two jobs put the worker in the property-owning group, while on the other axes he is among the disadvantaged. The inconsistency that follows thus leads to the right-wing involvement, according to this interpretation. From the perspective of this analysis, members of occupational groups that do not show this inconsistency should take a more moderate political stance. This is consistent with the available evidence.

A great deal of political activity does not take the form of extreme social movements, of course. Several analyses suggest that among blue-collar workers, "bread and butter" issues are still the dominant determinant of voting patterns. Howard L. Reiter notes that in times of economic stress, as in recessions and periods of inflation, blue-collar workers tend to vote Democratic, the party that has traditionally promised more for the "working man." When the economy is not a major issue, factors such as law and order or other social issues come into the fore, and the blue-collar worker may vote Republican or for an independent candidate.[21]

The same type of conclusion is reached by William Form in his study of automobile workers in four countries—the United States, Italy, Argentina, and India. Form concludes that the average auto worker is job conscious, with his orientation toward his union in terms of wages

[20]Ibid., p. 536.
[21]Howard L. Reiter, "Blue-Collar Workers and the Future of American Politics," in Sar A. Levitan, ed., Blue-Collar Workers (New York: McGraw-Hill Book Company, 1971).

and working conditions, rather than political goals in the wider society.[22] This is despite the fact that union leaders can be highly politicized. Form also found that the skilled workers in the four countries tended to be more active in community politics, which is consistent with our earlier discussion of the impact of status differences on political participation.

Occupation is not the sole determinant of political activity, of course. Factors such as race, ethnicity, age, and sex are important. The total socialization of the individual throughout life is critical. At the same time, the occupational factors noted intersect with these factors and the general social, economic, and political situations to yield rates and directions of political participation.

Political activity or involvement in the power system at the local or national level is not, of course, limited to the types of activity discussed above. A whole series of studies has suggested that a great deal of power is held by individuals not in public office. Robert S. and Helen Lynds's *Middletown* and C. Wright Mills's *The Power Elite* stand as major contributions to the knowledge of the realities of power at the local and national level.[23] The Lynds identify a family that, without holding public office, controls much of the activities of the community in which it owns the principal industry. Mills's work, although severely criticized on methodological grounds, nonetheless has gone relatively unchallenged in its insistence that leaders of government, industry, and the military exercise a tremendous amount of influence in decisions that affect the total society. This influence is far above and beyond that contained in their official positions. Although a wide range of motivations, from conspiratorial to extreme altruism, have been and can be attributed to the holders of such unofficial power, the fact remains that such power is part of the political system.

In order to obtain a more systematic perspective on such power systems, a large number of investigations of local communities have studied the power system as it operates at the local level. The literature that has developed from these studies is confusing in the sense that there is no consensus whether there is *a* power structure at this level. Despite this confusion, there is consensus that the power factor does operate outside of the official governmental channels.

Much of the lack of consensus over the nature of the power system is attributable to the methodological and conceptual approaches taken

[22]William H. Form, "Job vs. Political Unionism: A Cross-National Comparison," *Industrial Relations* 12 (May 1973), 224–38, and *idem*, "The Internal Stratification of the Working Class: System Involvements of Auto Workers in Four Countries," *American Sociological Review* 38 (December 1973), 697–711.

[23]See R. S. Lynd and H. Lynd, *Middletown in Transition* (New York: Harcourt, Brace & World, Inc., 1937) and C. Wright Mills, *The Power Elite* (New York: Oxford University Press, Inc., 1956).

in the analyses. Sociologists have generally utilized a model of communities that involves a monolithic stratification system, leading them to conclude that the power system takes the form of a unified system.[24] This is coupled with a reliance upon the use of informants asked to identify influential community members. Since the informants are given lists of supposedly influential people, it is inevitable that the same names will be mentioned time after time, leading to the identification of a monolithic power structure.

The alternative perspective is largely taken by political scientists who do not begin with the same assumption about the nature of the stratification system. They also focus on decisions made in regard to specific issues rather than trying to identify a single elite system.[25] The methodology involved is to determine the leadership in the decision-making process in regard to a series of community issues. The findings from these investigations generally identify a pluralistic power structure in which more than one set of individuals emerges as important holders of power.

While much of the literature on power within the local community is taken up with the debate between advocates of these alternative approaches, the important point for this analysis is that there *is* such a structure. In a sense it does not matter whether this unofficial power structure is monolithic or polylithic, since holders of such unofficial power have been identified as important in the decision-making process. Their influence is felt through their support of or opposition to issues such as zoning ordinances, school bond issues, and the creation of civilian review boards for police. While their influence over official office holders undoubtedly varies widely by community or state, they do wield power.

When the occupational characteristics of the members of community power structures are examined, the same conclusion is reached as was the case for those active directly in politics. People who have power in the community are better educated and have higher status occupations than those uninvolved in the power structure. In general, the specific occupations appear to be somewhat different. Lawyers do not dominate the system. Instead, the power structure is made up of leaders from the central interests of the community. In an industrial community, for example, power is held by executives from the major industries, whereas

[24]See, for example, the works of Floyd Hunter, *Community Power Structure* (Chapel Hill: University of North Carolina Press, 1953) and the discussion by Delbert C. Miller in *Power and Democracy in America*, eds. William D'Antonio and Howard Ehrlich (Notre Dame, Ind.: Notre Dame University Press, 1961).

[25]See, for example, Robert Dahl, *Who Governs?* (New Haven: Yale University Press, 1961); Raymond E. Wolfinger, *Readings in Political Behavior* (Englewood Cliffs, N.J.: Prentice-Hall, 1966); and Nelson W. Polsby *Politics and Social Life* (Boston: Houghton Mifflin Company, 1963).

in a diversified community more segments of the community are part of the structure. The major factor in the composition of the community power structure appears to be the position of the individual in the general social structure. Occupation thus again becomes a major determinant of the involvement in the power system.

The relationship between occupations and social power is more complex than simply being a one to one relationship between position in the stratification system and position in the political system. Certainly stratification and power are related, and those at the bottom of the stratification system also have the least power and vice versa. At the same time, particular occupations emerge as important in the political process, while others at the same level do not. The position of lawyers can be contrasted with that of medical doctors. The latter occupation is essentially apolitical in terms of either official or unofficial political power. At the same time, other occupations, such as labor union official, can emerge as important in the community power structure, while the local sports hero can be elected sheriff. The nature of the occupation appears to be a critical variable in determining official or unofficial political participation. While occupations are intimately related to the stratification system, occupational considerations appear to outweigh stratification factors in determining political involvement.

POWER AND POLITICS
IN THE OCCUPATIONAL SETTING

This final section deals with a topic that has already been touched upon in a number of places. The power variable is central in the relationships between professionals and other members of the organizations of which they are a part. Staff-line conflict can similarly be approached from the power perspective, as can the attempts on the part of skilled workers to maintain their monopoly over their market. The emergence of new occupations in the services-human resources era raises power issues for the occupations and organizations involved. The establishment of professional licensing and professional schools is often accomplished through legislative acts. This in itself requires the exercise of political skills on the part of the professions involved.

While aspects of the political are found throughout the occupational system and must therefore be included in any analysis of the system, the most direct impact of political considerations on occupations is found within the organizational setting. Since contemporary occupations are organizationally based, the power systems within organizations vitally affect the occupations themselves. The concept of power is central to most organizational analyses. Some form of power hierarchy is inescapable in organizations, even in the most democratic or collegially based system.

The most occupationally relevant consequence of the power system within organizations is the simple fact that the members of occupations behave in ways prescribed by the organization. Whether or not the control system is tight or loose, the behavior generally conforms to organizational expectations. Similarly, the power contained in a position is itself determined by the organization. The power of the executive is essentially given to the position and the incumbent utilizes that that is available. He may extend or diminish that power by his own actions, but the basic parameters are preset. In the conflict situations, which have been discussed previously (professional-organizational or labor-management), the positions of the participants have been set by the organization. Alterations in the organization that are a result of the conflict restructure the power positions of the participants, but even this restructuring is within the organizational context. The power position of one occupation *vis à vis* another is thus largely determined by the organization.

In addition to organizationally determined or formal power, the relationships between occupations can also be affected by the power-granted expertise. Richard L. Peabody has pointed out that acknowledging professional competence, experience, or ability in dealing with other people gives the person recognized power over the acknowledger.[26] This type of power, which Peabody labels functional authority, generally supports formal or organizationally derived power in the organizational setting. Outside of the organizational setting, as in the case of the private practitioner in the professions or the skilled worker, this form of power dominates. The important consideration here is that the power factor operates from either or both of these bases, ordering the relationships between occupational incumbents.

There are two major exceptions to these generalizations that should be noted. The first is the fact that at times persons in relatively low positions in an organization can hold more power than their position would indicate. David Mechanic has pointed out that the secretary, for example, can gain quite a bit of power through her control of information, work flow, and individuals.[27] She may permit some people to see her boss and not others and may do the work of some people before that of others. While this form of power could be reduced by rigorous application of the formal rules, the fact is that this type of situation is

[26]"Perceptions of Organizational Authority: A Comparative Analysis," *Administrative Science Quarterly*, VI, 4 (March 1962), 463–82.

[27]"Sources of Power of Lower Participants in Complex Organizations," *Administrative Science Quarterly*, VII, 3 (December 1962), 349–64.

quite common. A secretary can exert much more power than her position in the organization would predict. In most cases, however, such power can only be exerted until the formal rules are strongly enforced.

The second exception is when the formal or functional authority system is questioned and threatened. Student power movements among university students have affected the power relationships between students and university officials. Labor-management confrontations can alter the prerogatives of either party. The power system is thus not immutable. The dynamics of interaction between occupational groups in and out of organizations alters the power relationships both formally, in the case of organizationally derived power, and informally, in the case of relationships between occupations outside of the organizational setting. Each new power relationship does, however, structure future interaction.

SUMMARY AND CONCLUSIONS

This final chapter has been in many ways a capsule version of the theme of the entire book. Occupations serve as a major link between the individual and the society. Knowledge of the occupational system provides a basis for prediction about the participation of individuals and groups in the wider social structure. It is thus not surprising to find that certain occupations are more likely than others to be found active in the political system, both in terms of official office seeking and involvement in the regular political processes and through mass movements of one sort or another. Similarly, the nature of the occupation allows prediction of the distribution of power in the occupational system.

The rather tentative conclusions reached in regard to the political system and its relationships with the occupational system also illustrate another important point. There is a great deal that is not known about the relationships that have been the focus of the entire discussion. While many of the conclusions have a solid empirical base, many others were hypotheses, which must be examined in the light of evidence as it becomes available.

In this chapter on political power and its relationships with occupations, there has been little indication of the shift to the postindustrial era, which probably reflects two related considerations. First, the shift in emphasis away from industrialization is not yet complete and has not permeated the total society. The increasing reliance upon experts at all levels of government does indicate some shift toward the postindustrial emphasis, but the shift is not complete in most areas of political life. A conspicuous exception is the growing power of professionals and specialists of all sorts in the occupational setting. Here the movement seems to have been accomplished. The second consideration is linked to the subject at hand. The political scene is one of power. The power system is perhaps one of the most conservative in society in terms of its rate of change. Since power holders by definition have the power to maintain their position, it is less likely that change will occur as rapidly in this sphere as in many other segments of society. If the general discussion has been correct, however, this change should be increasingly evident in political life.

This chapter has illustrated a point implicit throughout the entire book; the occupational system is a major structuring element for the total social system. From the discussion in this chapter, it is evident that occupations form a better basis for prediction of the involvement of individuals in political life than does knowledge of the stratification system. While the stratification system can serve as a general predictor of behavior, the occupational system is probably a stronger basis for prediction. As was discussed above, occupations are the major source of placement in the stratification system. At the same time, occupations do more than make this simple, but vital, placement. They provide the individual with skills, knowledge, values, opportunities, and limitations reflected in his total involvement in social life. Specific occupations have characteristics that reflect more than their simple placement in the stratification system.

Our discussion of the occupational system began with the idea that changes in the total social system are reflected in the condition of contemporary occupations. The shift of occupations to the organizational environment and the growth of services-human resources oriented occupations with the related decline in importance of strictly production occupations has profoundly affected the manner in which an individual relates to his occupation. Motivations, training, and reactions to occupational life are influenced by these changes. The type of work that once might have been very satisfying may no longer be so, because of the different type of motivations people bring to their work. The same occupation may no longer receive the kind of rewards it did in the past. New organizational requirements, restrictions, and opportunities confront many previously "free" professions. For the individual, therefore, the occupational system is one of change.

The discussion of types of occupations is indicative of the changing social structure. The proportion of the labor force in the various categories ebbs and flows as societal demands and occupationally generated factors shift over time. The lines between the types of occupations blur as more occupations professionalize and white-collar and blue-collar work becomes less differentiated. The requirements for entrance and success in the various occupational types have changed as the general educational level demanded is continually upgraded. Social skills, in the broadest meaning of the term, are becoming increasingly important throughout the occupational system.

The chapters in this last section have dealt with the relationships between the occupational system and the total social system and have illustrated the close relationships and points of disharmony that exist. They have also illustrated the dynamic nature of the relationships. The changes in the occupational system mean that the stratification system also is changing. The kinds of work that are regarded with high or low prestige shift over time. The manner in which an individual can be socially mobile has been drastically affected by the organizational and services-human resources emphases. At the same time, the central fact remains that it is through the occupational system, in terms of where a person is born and where he enters the system, that mobility is possible in the contemporary situation.

The relationships between occupations and the family, education, technology, and the political environment all reflect the level of overall societal integration. As we have seen, there is not total integration. In every area discrepancies exist. Rather clearly, the adjustment of one discrepancy, by whatever means, leads to new arrangements that further affect the level of integration. As the educational system might change to prepare students to deal more adequately with occupations in a period of technological change, resistance to such change might emerge from the family and political sectors. The fact that resistance to change does exist is itself indicative of the interlocked nature of the components of the social system.

The occupational system is a major basis for order and change within the total social structure. While the place of occupations within the social order has been the main theme of this book, the idea that the social order likewise affects the occupational system is equally important. The dynamic interaction between the total system and its occupational component exists in a number of directions and at a series of points within the system and leads to conditions and changes within both systems.

INDEX

A

Abegglen, James, 141, 160
Abrahamson, Mark, 262
Achievement orientation, 15
Acker, Joan, 254
Aiken, Michael, 61
Aldous, Joan, 302–3
Aldrich, Howard, 163
Alexander, C. Norman, 275n
Alford, Robert L., 362
Alienation, 54–61
Alienation and organizational character-
   istics, 56–57
Alienation and social status, 60–61
Alienation and technology, 56
Anastasi, Anne, 33
Anderson, C. Arnold, 305–7
Anderson, Nels, 3, 12, 15, 315–16
Anshen, Melvin, 323n
Anshen, R. N., 285n
Argyris, Chris, 68, 138n
Aronowitz, Stanley, 167n, 185, 213n
Ascription orientation, 15
Aubert, Vilhelm, 231
Auto worker, 37, 42–46, 57–58, 215–17
Automation and white-collar work, 170

Aveling, Edward, 11n
Avery, Robert W., 277–79

B

Babchuk, Nicholas, 173
Bach, George L., 323n
Bailyn, Lotte, 299
Baldi de Mandilovitch, Martha S., 51n
Bales, Robert F., 205
Barber, Bernard, 78n
Barker, Gordon H., 173
Barnard, Chester I., 139
Barnett, Jeanne K., 297
Bart, Pauline B., 290
Baum, Samuel, 19n
Beattie, Christopher, 162–63
Becker, Howard S., 76, 310
Belitsky, A. Harvey, 194
Bell, Daniel, 20–21, 23, 353
Bell, Gerald D., 347
Bendix Reinhard, 13, 273
Bensman, Joseph, 221–23
Berkanovic, Emil, 129–30
Berlew, David E., 141
Bernard, Jessie, 292

Best, Fred, 354
Blankenship, L. Vaughn, 362
Blau, Peter M., 99–100, 111, 240, 267–73, 274, 321, 347
Blauner, Robert, 54–60, 191–92, 215, 217–18
Blood, Milton R., 33, 350
Blum, Albert A., 170n, 185
Bolaria, Bhopinder S., 35
Bonjean, Charles M., 149, 153, 154–55
Borgatta, Edgar, 262
Bowman, Mary Jean, 305–6
Bradburn, Norman M., 299
Brawer, Milton J., 273n
Braybrooke, David, 144–45
Bright, John R., 317, 320, 352
Broekmeyer, M. J., 342n
Broom, Leonard, 5n, 161n
Bruner, Dick, 185
Bucher, Rue, 81n
Buckley, Walter, 264–65
Burack, Elmer, 322–23
Bureaucracy, 109–15

C

Cabdrivers, 218–19
Campbell, Ernest, 275n
Campbell, John P., 136, 138, 141, 147n
Cantor, Muriel, 116n
Cantril, Hadley, 43n
Caplow, Theodore R., 12n, 154, 156–57, 181, 188–91, 195–97, 202, 214, 226–27, 231n, 240–42, 266, 283–88
Career patterns, 6, 276–80
Carlin, Jerome E., 85–88, 108, 127
Carlson, Richard, 277–79
Carr-Saunders, A. M., 72
Case, Clifford, 91
Cavanagh, Ferald F., 200n
Centers, Richard, 43n
Chaplin, David, 320
Chemical operator, 59, 217–18
Chinoy, Ely, 42–44, 152, 156, 208–9, 216
Cicourel, Aaron V., 310
Clark, Burton R., 304–5, 312
Clarke, Alfred C., 30
Clergymen, 31
Clerical workers, 169–70, 178–80

Clients and professionals (see Profession and clients)
Cohen, Michael, 357
Coleman, James S., 191, 310
Collins, Randall, 262
Cooley, Charles H., 275n
Corwin, Ronald C., 100–101
Coser, Lewis A., 84
Cottrell, Leonard S., Jr., 5n, 161n
Craft production, 12–14
Craftsmen, 188–201
    characteristics, 188–200
    labor market, 194–96
    occupational identification, 191–94
    socialization, 197
Craftsmen and professionals, 196–200
Crowley, Joan E., 172n, 292, 295, 303
Crozier, Michael, 169n, 178–79, 181
Cummings, Milton C., 158–59
Cushman, Edward L., 352

D

Dahl, Robert, 366n
Dahrendorf, Ralf, 262
Dalton, Melville, 149, 211
Daniels, Arlene K., 67n, 71n
D'Antonio, William, 366n
Davis, Fred, 218–19
Davis, James A., 311–12
Davis, Kingsley, 257–61
Dean, Dwight, 54n
DeJong, Peter Y., 273n
Deviant occupations, 233–34
Dewey, Lucretia M., 185
Dewey, Thomas E., 91
Dissatisfaction, job (see Job dissatisfactions)
Domhoff, William, 21n, 263
Donnell, John D., 105–8
Drucker, Peter, 324
Dual-career families, 296–301
Dubin, Robert, 150, 225, 279
Dulles, John Foster, 91
Duncan, Beverly, 253
Duncan, Otis Dudley, 240, 252, 267–74
Duncan, Robert, 143n
Durkheim, Emile, 275

E

Economy and occupations, 237–38
Educational requirements, 14
Education and modernization, 305–7
Education and occupations, 304–12
Edwards, Alba, 244–45
Edwards, Hugh, 275–76
Ehrlich, Howard, 366
Elliott, Phillip, 78n
Elliott, Rodney D., 173
Ellul, Jacques, 353–54
Employment, government, 20
Engel, Gloria, 116, 132n
Engels, Frederick, 11n
Engineers, 117–18
Epstein, Cynthia Fuchs, 121–22, 288
Etzioni, Amitai, 14–15, 102n, 118n, 137n,
    205–8
Eulau, Heinz, 360–61
Executives, 45–47, 138–47
    careers, 141–43
    characteristics, 140–41
    conformity, 145–46
    constraints on, 146–47
    decision making, 143–45
    functions, 139–40
    job dissatisfactions, 61–64

F

Factory workers, 53–60
Family and occupations, 282–304
    historical changes, 282–85
    occupational socialization, 302–4
    work motivation, 301–2
Faris, Robert E. L., 18n, 284n, 304n, 358n
Farming, 13, 153–54, 156
Faunce, William, 324
Featherman, David L., 253, 273–74
Football player, 37
Foremen, 201–11
    changes in role, 204–5, 210–11
    desirability of role, 208–9
    orientations, 205–6
    role conflicts, 202–4
Form, William H., 6, 12n, 30, 148–49,
    201, 203, 205, 221, 225n, 276, 325–
    26, 350, 364–65

Fortune Magazine, 140
Foster, Phillip, 306
Freidson, Eliot, 71, 81, 96–97, 106n, 116,
    124, 132n, 133n
Friedman, Georges, 53
Fromm, Erich, 53n
Fullan, Michael, 324–25

G

Galbraith, John Kenneth, 290–91
Garbage men, 4
Garland, T. Neal, 297–98
Geer, Blanche, 76
Gerth, H. H., 357n
Gerver, Israel, 221–23
Giovaelli, F., III, 53n
Gittelsohn, Alan, 123
Glaser, Barney C., 104n
Glassworkers, 192–93
Gold, Ray, 231–32
Goldberg, Joseph, 185
Goldner, Fred, 150–52
Goldthorpe, John H., 200, 208, 224n, 301,
    326
Gomberg, William, 198n, 230
Goode, William J., 70n, 76, 173
Goodwin, Leonard, 29, 232–33
Gornick, Vivian, 290n
Goss, Mary, E. W., 123, 124
Gouldner, Alvin, 160n
Gove, Walter, 290
Government officials (*see* Officials)
Greenlick, Merwyn R., 133n
Greenwood, Ernest, 73–74
Greer, Scott, 358
Gross, Edward, 74–76, 181, 190, 193
Gross, Neal, 161n
Grossman, Joel B., 81n
Guest, Robert H., 44–46, 53–54, 201–2,
    209–10, 220, 223n
Guzzardi, Walter, Jr., 142–43

H

Hage, Jerald, 61
Hall, Douglas T., 141
Hall, Oswald, 125, 127

Hall, Richard H., 24–25, 79, 81, 84, 109–
    14, 116, 161n, 253n
Haller, Archibald O., 274, 309
Halsey, A. E., 307–8
Hamilton, Richard F., 198
Hatt, Paul K., 254–55
Haug, Marie, 80, 129, 132n, 254
Hauser, Phillip, 17–18, 26
Hauser, Robert M., 253, 273n
Havens, Elizabeth, 273n, 298
Hayge, Howard, 291
Hedges, Janice N., 297
Heilbroner, Robert, 316n
Henderson, A. M., 14n
Herrick, Neal Q., 171, 224n, 350
Herzberg, Frederick, 34–35
Heydebrand, Wolf V., 111
Hickson, David, 344–45, 348
Hoffman, L. Richard, 320, 324, 352–53
Holbek, Jonny, 143n
Holmstrom, Lynda L., 297
Homans, George C., 179–80
Hoos, Ida R., 182–83
Hopson, Dan, Jr., 108–9, 112, 125
Hoselitz, Bert F., 305, 316
House, Robert J., 34–36
Housemaid, 231
Housewife, 4–6, 285–91
Howard, David, 133n
Howton, F. William, 175
Hughes, Everett C., 5, 67, 77, 100, 127,
    128
Hulin, Charles L., 33, 350
Hunt, Janet, 299
Hunter, Floyd, 366

I

Industrialization, 13–14, 15–16
Inkeles, Alex, 41–44
ISR Newsletter, 232n

J

Jackson, J. A., 78n
Janitors, 231–32
Jencks, Christopher, 308
Jennings, M. Kent, 158–59
Job dissatisfaction, 46–64

Job dissatisfaction (cont.)
    executives, 61–64
    extent, 48–49
    sources, 49–51
Job dissatisfaction and mental health, 59
Job dissatisfaction and social status, 49–53
Job satisfaction, 41–47
Job satisfaction and social status, 41–44
Johnston, William B., 169n, 183
Johnstone, Quintin, 108–9, 112, 125

K

Kahn, Robert, 61–64, 161n, 224n
Kammerer, Gladys M., 161
Kamŭsic, Mitja, 342
Kaplan, H. Roy, 35, 48
Kassalow, Everett M., 165–66
Khandwalla, P. N., 348
Kilpatrick, Franklin P., 158–59
Kitsuse, John I., 310
Klein, Viola, 293–94
Knowledge, role of, 10, 20–21
Kohn, Melvin L., 41, 146, 159, 302
Kornhauser, Arthur, 59–60, 232
Kornhauser, William, 102–5, 363
Krauss, Elliott A., 141, 172n, 225n
Krauss, Irving, 38

L

Labor force, 18–19
    projections, 20–21
    world, 18–19
Ladd, Everett C., Jr., 131
Ladinsky, Jack, 81n, 87–88, 108, 128,
    273n
Lane, Robert E., 358
La Porte, Todd R., 105
Laslett, Peter, 282
Lawyers, 31, 37, 85–96, 105–9, 356–58
    ethics, 88, 107–8
Lebeaux, Charles N., 100
Lenski, Gerhard, 31, 238, 263–65
Lefton, Mark, 126
Leisure, 30–31
Levitan, Sar A., 169n, 183, 232n, 234n,
    279, 301n, 364n
Levitin, Theresa E., 172n, 292, 295, 303
Lieberson, Stanley, 146–47

Likert, Rensis, 137
Lipset, Seymour Martin, 43n, 131, 191n, 273, 358–59, 361–63
Litwak, Eugene, 24n
Lopata, Helena Znaniecki, 285, 289
Lynd, Helen, 365
Lynd, Robert S., 365

M

Mackenzie, Gavin, 201n
Managers, 136–37, 147–52
    conflicts, 148–49
    demotion, 150–52
    orientations, 149–50
Manzione, Thomas W., 51n
Mann, Floyd C., 182, 320, 324, 352–53
Manasse, Henri, Jr., 79
March, James G., 143–44
Marcson, Simon, 103
Marvick, Dwaine, 360n
Marx, Karl, 11n, 53, 67, 262
Maslow, Abraham, 32–33
Mason, Ward, 161n
Mausner, B., 34n
McCarthy, John, 361–62
McCeachern, Alexander, 161n
McClelland, D. C., 33n
McGregor, 137
Mechanic, David, 184–85, 368
Meltzer, Leo, 60
Merton, Robert K., 5n, 61, 160n
Meyer, Marshall W., 347
Miller, Delbert C., 6, 30, 148–49, 201–3, 205, 221, 276, 366n
Miller, George A., 115–16
Miller, S. M., 227–29, 300
Miller, Stephen J., 174–75
Mills, C. Wright, 21n, 149, 157–58, 167–69, 175–76, 263, 357n, 365
Mills, Donald, 77
Miner, John B., 33n, 145
Minorities, 4
    in crafts, 200–201
    in management, 162–63
    in professions, 132–33
Mohr, Lawrence W., 344
Monthly Labor Review, 214
Moore, Samuel, 11n
Moore, Wilbert E., 78n, 113, 126–27,

Moore, Wilbert E. (*cont.*)
    257–61, 305, 316–17
Moran, Barbara K., 290n
Morris, Richard T., 255–56
Morse, Nancy, 17, 169
Mortimer, Jeylan, 281, 302–3
Motivations for work, 28–39
    components, 29–35
    energy expenditure, 30–31
    expectancy theory, 35–39
    financial, 29–30
    hierarchy of needs, 32–33, 35
    intrinsic satisfaction, 31
    organizational environment, 39–41
    social interaction, 33
    social status, 32, 39
    two-factor theory, 34–35
    variations in, 36–39
Murphy, Raymond J., 255–56
Myers, Richard M., 193–94

N

Neal, Arthur G., 60
Nelson, Joel I., 275n
Nosow, Sigmund, 12n

O

Obradovic, Josip, 343
O'Connor, James F., 146–47
Occupational choice, 311–12
Occupational situs, 254–55
Occupations and organizations, 24–25
Occupations, contemporary context, 17–24
Occupations, definition, 3–7
Occupations, history, 10–17
Occupations, typology, 67–68
Officials, 157–63
    characteristics, 158–60
    role conflicts, 160–61
Ohlendorf, George W., 274, 309
Orden, Susan R., 299
Organizational employment, 12
Organizational environment, 24–25
Organizations, 10, 23
    coercive, 14
    normative, 14–15
    utilitarian, 15

Orleans, Peter, 358
Orzack, Louis, 225n
Ouichi, William, 183–84

P

Padfield, Harland, 229, 232–33
Papanek, Hanna, 289
Paraprofessionals, 133–34
Parsons, Talcott, 11n, 14n, 24n, 72, 205,
    238n, 257, 285
Passin, Herbert, 305
Peabody, Richard L., 368
Pearson, Judson B., 173
Pennings, Johannes M., 279–80
Perrow, Charles, 345
Perrucci, Robert, 117–18
Pheysey, Diane, 344–45, 348
Physicians, 4, 96–97, 116, 124–26
Political participation, 356–67
Polsby, Nelson W., 366n
Porter, Lyman, 46–47
Portes, Alejandro, 274, 309
Postindustrial society, 20–24
Power in occupational settings, 367–69
Presthus, Robert, 12n, 39–41, 59, 61,
    142–43
Printers, 57, 191–92
Professional autonomy, 115–17
Professional model, 72–78
    an alternative, 115–17
    criticisms, 78–81
    and managers, 137
Professional-organizational conflict, 83–84,
    102–5, 111–15
Professional-organizational relationship,
    109–15
Professional Standard Review Organiza-
    tions, 123–24
Professions, 69–135
    autonomous organizations, 82, 90–98
    discrimination, 92–93
    external regulations, 122–24
    heteronomous organizations, 82, 98–102
    individual practice, 81–82, 84–90
    knowledge, 116–18
    knowledge obsolescence, 116–18
    power, 70–71
    professional departments, 82–83, 102–
    15

Professions (*cont.*)
    reasons for prominence, 69–71
    self-regulation, 96–98, 124–26
    sex-typing, 120
    sources of variation, 81–132
    women, 98–99, 118–22
Professions and clients, 90, 126–30
    client movement, 128–30
    conflict, 129–30
Professions and pay, 69
Professions and professionalization, 77
Professions and unionization, 130–32
Professors, 131
Proprietors, 152–57
Pugh, Derek, 344–45, 348
Purcell, Theodore V., 200n
Pusic, Eugen, 342

Q

Quinn, Robert P., 51n, 172n, 292, 295, 303

R

Rainwater, Lee, 301
Ramsoy, Natalie Rogoff, 273n
Rapoport, Rhona, 297–99
Rapoport, Robert, 297–99
Record, Jane Cassels, 133n
Reiss, Albert J., Jr., 163, 187n, 240, 242–
    43, 245–52, 255
Reiter, Howard L., 364
Religion and occupations, 237–38
Retirement, 2
Rettig, Salomon, 60
Rhea, Buford, 96–97
Richard, Michael, 133n
Ridley, Jeanne Clare, 301
Ritzer, George, 72n, 81n, 133, 148, 161n,
    184, 199–200, 234
Robin, Stanley S., 273n
Roe, Anne, 5–6
Roethlisberger, Fritz J., 204
Role ambiguity, 105–8
Role conflict, 61–64
Rosenberg, Bernard, 175
Rosenberg, Morris, 303n
Rosengren, William, 126
Rosenthal, Neal H., 21n
Rosow, Jerome M., 213n, 234

Rossi, Alice S., 300
Rossi, Peter H., 361
Roth, Julius A., 67n, 71n, 78–80
Rothman, Robert A., 117–18
Roy, Donald F., 223n
Rushing, William A., 166, 345
Ruzek, Sheryl K., 67n, 71n

S

Safilios-Rothschild, Constantina, 297,
    300–301
Salespersons, 173–77
Salter, James, 60
Salz, Arthur, 5
Sanders, Dero A., 39, 61
Satisfactions (see Job satisfaction)
Scanzoni, John, 289, 302, 313
Schoenherr, Richard, 321n, 347
Schooler, Carmi, 41
Schulman, Marion L., 132n
Scientists, 31, 102–5
Scott, W. Richard, 82–83, 98–100
Secretaries, 37
Seeman, Melvin, 54n
Seidman, Joel, 180
Seligman, Ben R., 325
Semiskilled workers, 214–25
    characteristics, 215–20
    reactions to work, 223–25
    social interactions, 220–23
Service occupations, 19–20
Sewell, William H., 274, 309
Sex role differences, 33
Sex typing, 178
Shepard, Jon M., 169–70, 183–84
Sheppard, Harold, L., 171, 194, 224n,
    350, 352
Shostak, Arthur B., 198n, 230
Siegel, Paul M., 253
Sikula, Andrew, 159
Silk, Leonard S., 232n, 279
Silverman, William, 318, 351
Simmons, Roberta G., 303n
Simon, Herbert A., 143–44, 322–23
Simpson, Ida Harper, 118–20
Simpson, Miles E., 275
Simpson, Richard L., 118–20
Skilled workers (see Craftsmen)
Slocum, Walter L., 153–54, 156

Smelser, Neil J., 154, 308n, 316
Smigel, Erwin O., 12n, 91–96, 108, 128
Snyderman, B., 34n
Social control, 20–22
Social mobility, 265–76
    aspirations, 274–76
    minority groups, 270
    women, 273–74
Social status (see Social stratification)
Social stratification, 33, 239–65
    determinants of occupational status,
        242–44
    measurement, 245–55
    reasons for, 255–65
    reasons for link to occupations, 240–41
    women, 254
Social workers, 99–100
Sofer, Cyril, 149–50
Sommers, Gerald G., 352
Sorokin, Pitrim, 275n
Spady, William G., 308
Spencer, Byron G., 162–63
Stauffer, Robert E., 111
Stern, James L., 352
Stevenson, Adlai, 91
Stewart, Jesse N., 79
Stewart, Phyllis L., 116n
Stieber, Jack, 353
Stinchcombe, Arthur, 199–200
Strauss, Anselm, 81n
Strauss, George, 210–11
Students, 6–7
Supek, Rudi, 342–43
Survey of Working Conditions, 225
Sussman, Marvin, 80, 129, 132n
Sweet, James A., 296
Sweezy, Paul M., 21n

T

Taguiri, Renato, 145
Tangri, Sandra S., 303
Tannenbaum, Arnold, 342
Tausky, Curt, 35, 150, 279
Taylor, Frederick W., 137
Teachers, 31, 99–101
Technological alternatives, 326–42
    limitations, 343–50
Technological change, 315–19
    and employment patterns, 350–53

Technological change (*cont.*)
and the future, 353–54
and occupations, 319–23
Technology, 23
Technology and alienation (*see* Alienation and technology)
Technology and the worker, 323–26
Textile worker, 57–58
Theodore, Athena, 119 21
Thompson, James D., 144n, 161n, 277–79, 346
Tilgher, Adriano, 16–17
Touraine, Alain, 22n
Treas, Judith, 273–74
Trice, Harrison M., 148
Trow, Martin A., 131n, 155
Tryce, Andrea, 273–74
Tully, Judy C., 273n
Tumin, Melvin, 258–61, 265
Turkel, Studs, 213n
Turner, Arthur N., 201–2, 209–10

U

Unemployed workers, 29
Unemployment, 25–26
U. S. Bureau of the Census, 284
U. S. Bureau of Labor Statistics, 188
U. S. Department of Health, Education, and Welfare, 4
U. S. Department of Labor, 288, 295
Unskilled workers, 226–32

V

Veblen, Thorstein, 13–14
Venn, Grant, 197n
Vollmer, Howard, 77
Vroom, Victor, 29–31, 32, 36

W

Wager, L. Wesley, 115–16
Waitresses, 177
Walker, Charles R., 44–46, 53–54, 201–2, 209–10, 220, 223n, 317, 320, 352–53
Wall, Richard, 284
Warner, W. Lloyd, 141, 158, 160
Weber, Max, 11n, 14n, 31, 155, 238
Weil, Mildred, 293
Weil, Simone, 53

Weinberg, Nat, 352
Weiss, R. S., 17
Weizenbaum, Joseph, 315
Wennberg, John, 123
Whaba, Mahmoud A., 35–36
White-collar workers, 165–86
automation, 170
changes, 171–72
growth, 165–67
history, 167–69
organizational controls, 183–84
power, 184–85
social interaction, 181–82
unionization, 185–86
Whyte, William F., 177, 192–93, 217
Wigdor, Lawrence A., 34–35
Wikstrom, Walter S., 210–11
Wilensky, Harold L., 100, 275–76
Wiley, Norbert, 155–56, 363–64
Williams, Lawrence K., 182
Williams, Robin M., 290
Williams, Roy, 229, 232
Wilson, P. A., 72
Winch, Robert F., 303n
Wolfinger, Raymond E., 366n
Women, in crafts, 200–201
Women, in labor force, 291–301
Women, in management, 162–63
Women, reasons for working, 292–96
Women and unions, 185–86
Women and professional dilemmas, 120–22
Women professionals (*see* Professions, women)
Woodward, Joan, 201, 320, 322, 346
Work, definition, 3–5
Work, meanings, 17
Work in America, 4, 47, 48–53, 153, 171, 181, 184, 211, 224, 292, 327–42, 349–50

Y

Yugoslavian program, 342–43

Z

Zald, Mayer N., 315, 361–62
Zaltman, Gerald, 143n
Zelditch, Morris, Jr., 284
Županov, Josip, 342, 343
Zwerman, William, 346